D0301646

THE
**PAUL HAMLYN
LIBRARY**

DONATED BY
THE PAUL HAMLYN
FOUNDATION
TO THE
BRITISH MUSEUM

opened December 2000

2675p.

The Creation of
the Roman Frontier

The Creation of
the Roman
Frontier

STEPHEN L. DYSON

Princeton University Press

937

Copyright © 1985 by Princeton University Press

Published by Princeton University Press, 41 William Street,
Princeton, New Jersey 08540

In the United Kingdom: Princeton University Press, Guildford, Surrey

All Rights Reserved

Library of Congress Cataloging in Publication Data will be
found on the last printed page of this book

ISBN 0-691-03577-6

Publication of this book was made possible (in part) by a grant from
the Publications Program of the National Endowment for the Humanities,
an independent Federal agency

This book has been composed in Linotron Janson

Clothbound editions of Princeton University Press books are printed on acid-free
paper, and binding materials are chosen for strength and durability

Printed in the United States of America by Princeton University Press
Princeton, New Jersey

BEXLEY LIBRARY SERVICE		
CARD CC	CL No. 987.02 DYS	
PRICE 26.75	- 9 JUN 1986	BK JL
MSTAT 2	MAT. TYPE	
BYER	TRACE	LANG	CH

0710696

TO THE MEMORY OF

James Louis Giddings

AND

Charles Alexander Robinson

V . S . L . M .

CONTENTS

LIST OF MAPS

PREFACE

This book has been a long time in the making. While an undergraduate at Brown University, I began thinking about the nature of frontiers, the relation between classical and prehistoric archaeology, and the need to use anthropological models to interpret certain aspects of the classical past. My real introduction to the archaeology of the Roman provinces came during graduate work at Oxford University, where I studied Roman Britain under the late Sir Ian Richmond.

I began serious research on a book dealing with the Roman frontier and the interaction of the peoples on both sides during a sabbatical leave in Rome in 1967–68. This initial research was supported by a fellowship from the National Endowment for the Humanities. Over the years the focus shifted from the Empire to what I saw as the roots of Roman frontier policy in the Republic.

I have been privileged to discuss the topic with many people and to present preliminary ideas in the form of lectures and articles. Thanks are due to several people. Much is owed to the bibliographical assistance of the librarians of the American Academy in Rome and Wesleyan University, especially the Wesleyan interlibrary loan librarians William Dillon and Steven Lebergott. Preliminary drafts of sections were read by Professor R.E.A. Palmer of the University of Pennsylvania, Professor Robert Rowland of the University of Missouri, Professor J. David Konstan of Wesleyan, and Professor Robert Knapp of the University of California at Berkeley. My father, George W. Dyson, has supplied me over the years with useful bibliographical references in comparative frontier studies. To them is extended my gratitude for many ideas and corrections of errors.

Preparing this long and complicated manuscript was not an easy task. Mrs. Carol Kelley prepared the final version, while Mrs. Phyllis Vinci, Carol Foell, and Susan Potter prepared preliminary ones. Natalie Diffloth did much of the preliminary work on the index. Professor Andrew Szegedy-Maszak prepared the Greek translations used in the text, and Professor J. David Konstan checked the Latin translations. The abbreviations of ancient authors and works are from *The Oxford Classical Dictionary*, 2d ed. (Oxford, 1970), pp. ix–xxii.

I am also very grateful for the care and patience shown by the staff of Princeton University Press for seeing this manuscript from initial submission to final publication. Special thanks are owed to my editors Joanna Hitchcock and Rita Gentry for their overall supervision and many helpful suggestions, and to my manuscript editor Barbara Stump, who caught many errors and removed many infelicities of style.

The final thanks must go to the two scholars to whom this book is dedicated. Professor J. Louis Giddings in Antropology and Professor Charles Alexander Robinson in Ancient History introduced me to those disciplines during my years at Brown and made me aware of the excitement of work in those fields. Unfortunately, their careers were cut short. I hope that this book is a worthy result of the interest and effort they showed on my behalf.

*The Creation of
the Roman Frontier*

INTRODUCTION

Hadrian's Wall symbolizes the Roman frontier. Massive and permanent, it separates the world of Rome from that of the barbarian. This wall in the north of England and the remains of the *limes* along the Rhine and Danube have created the image of the Roman frontier as basically a fortified barrier. Yet walls and forts were only part of a larger diplomatic, military, political, social, and economic system that embraced both sides of the frontier and created a gradual transition from Roman to non-Roman society. While fortifications are explicit, even blunt reminders of imperial policy, the other aspects of the system are more subtle and less easy to reconstruct. Formal treaties, informal agreements, and the complex daily interactions have left little trace in the frightfully small historical record that survives from antiquity. Ancient historians are, however, becoming increasingly aware of the need to reconstruct as completely as possible this frontier world, and to use every relevant methodology to extract scraps of information and insight from the preserved record.

This book began as a study of the western Roman frontier that was created by Augustus and his successors. The focus was to have been the use of anthropology and comparative frontier studies to interpret the Roman imperial system. But as research progressed I became increasingly aware that the roots of Roman frontier thinking and the development of methods of border control lay in the rich experience of the Republic. By the time Augustus came to power, the Romans had been dealing with frontier problems in Italy and the west for nearly four hundred years.

If the Roman frontier is considered from this perspective, the Republican experience assumes enormous importance. The time span is in itself impressive. The period covered in this book stretches from the early fourth century B.C. to the mid-first century B.C. It parallels the growth of the Roman state itself. Early in the period, border control had an urgency and immediacy not known again until the days of the late Empire. Citizen soldiers were forced to defend their farms and the city itself against Gallic attacks. Then the frontier gradually moved farther away, and the problems of border control, like so many other issues of the late Republic, became too remote and complex for the average citizen to grasp. Nevertheless, the experience of those early trials and disasters remained in the national consciousness. Even in the cynical days of the late Republic, the defeat of the Cimbri and

Teutones by Marius and Caesar's conquest of interior Gaul stimulated
great interest and enthusiasm in all sectors of Roman society.

Another important aspect of the frontier experience during the Republic was the intensity and diversity of Roman involvement. Roman
troops were fighting almost every year on some frontier in Italy, Sardinia, Gaul, or Spain. The areas differed widely in their geographical,
political, and social setting, and each frontier required innovative
thinking and sensitive policy application. The experience gained and
the forms of intervention developed were the foundations of the imperial frontier system. The post-Augustan frontier represented more
a refinement of Republican techniques than something newly created.

A third important result of the Republican frontier was the creation
of the most permanently Romanized sections of the Empire. Northern
Italy, Provence, Spain, and Portugal still show vividly their debt to
the Republican frontier policies. A premise of this book is that the
creation of true frontiers involved the development of new societies
within the frontier zone, a process that permanently separated those
peoples under Roman control from those outside it. The lack of formal, visible institutional structures under the Republic has led historians to underrate the degree of social engineering that took place during that period.

In considering the Republican frontier I have concentrated on the
northwestern section, specifically northern Italy, southern France,
Sardinia, Corsica, Spain, and Portugal. As any reader of Fernand
Braudel's *The Mediterranean* will know, it is difficult to separate devel-
opments in one section of the Mediterranean from those in another.
Republican frontiers in Macedonia, Thrace, Anatolia, Syria, and North
Africa all interacted with one another, as well as with the northwest-
ern frontiers. Moreover, many shared a long-term historical experi-
ence that included not only Romans but also Greeks, Phoenicians, and
Celts.

The frontier in the northwestern Mediterranean does, however, seem
to have a certain coherence. It was the principal area where under the
Republic the Romans created their own frontier system and their own
provincial society; in most other areas, the Romans maintained and
refined systems created by predecessors. In addition, the intensity of
the involvement in the northwest and the relatively abundant sources
favor its consideration as a unit.

The Roman frontier experience in each area will be considered as
part of a larger process that combined Mediterraneanization and growing native social complexity. In all areas, the Romans found complex,
changing societies and became involved in political, social, and economic processes whose roots often lay deep in the past. Too often

Roman frontier historians, like American frontier historians, have tended to see frontier areas as tabulae rasae where the imperial power could exercise its will freely. The previous inhabitants were seen either as obstacles to progress or as ephemeral entities who rapidly disappeared with the advance of the conqueror.

This approach is misleading. Rome was often drawn to a frontier because the local cultural and political dynamics affected their interests. We cannot understand why the Romans acted as they did if we do not know what cultural developments and events in a specific area led the Romans to intervene. Moreover, once the decision to intervene had been made, Roman success depended on a shrewd analysis of the nature of local conditions and of those forces that might favor Rome, as well as those that would oppose it. Again, this presupposes that both the Romans and historians reconstructing the actions of the Romans understand the local situation. It should also be remembered that one of the most impressive qualities of the Romans was their ability to build on existing social structure and to stress continuity in the creation of their own system. In most of the frontier areas under consideration, the Romans tried more to turn the natives into Romans than to bring their own people into deserted lands.

Because Celtic chieftains or Punic urban traders formed part of the leadership group in the new Roman provinces, it is important to understand their place in pre-Roman society. For this reason, each chapter will open with the pre-Roman history of the area as it can be reconstructed from literary and archaeological sources. In most cases I have begun with Iron Age developments, since it was generally during that period that processes that were to continue into the Roman period began. The part of the information deriving from archaeological research I have tried to simplify and synthesize as much as possible. Given the pace of such research, this will obviously be the aspect of the book most rapidly outdated.

The second point of concentration will be the development of Roman attitudes toward the frontier and its peoples, and how these attitudes affected the creation of institutions and policies. Modern historians interested in frontiers have given increasing attention to the way the values of an imperial society affected its approach to the frontier experience. This is also relevant for Rome. From the rhetoric of a Cicero to the response of the senate to a Gallic embassy, from the selection of statuary for a temple to the solemn religious rite involving the burial of Greeks and Gauls in the Forum Boarium, the frontier interacted with Roman values and historical experience. These values and attitudes were more complex than generally believed and for comparative frontier historians provide another case study in imperialism.

Growing out of events, attitudes, and accumulated experience were policy and institutions. The Roman Republic provides a fascinating study of a highly complex but basically prebureaucratic society. Modern historians of Rome have tended to stress the individual power politics and elite group dynamics of Republican society. But no system functions without a policy and the means for instituting it. This is especially true for frontier situations where the convergence of two societies requires clear policy and flexible application. The apparent informality of policy-making during the Republic and the stress on personal and familial control have obscured continuities in both policy and action. One advantage of considering the frontier in larger perspective is that isolated events in a particular area can be seen as part of a larger policy.

This western Republican frontier experience has been relatively neglected. The reasons are easy to understand. It is a world of relatively few spectacular events. Its subtle frontier processes are often strange to scholars trained in traditional ancient diplomatic and political history. Perhaps most important is that the sources are limited and filled with problems. The epigraphical record is slight. Most of the archaeological material in the Roman west dates to the Empire, and in few areas has the interpretation reached a level of sophistication sufficient to allow effective use of it. Too often one is forced back on the literary sources and the problems they pose.

As the author, I am aware of the limitations of this work. The modern literature on the subject is immense, with much of it buried in local journals and antiquarian histories. In doing the research I have tried to focus on the complex and changing nature of the forest but certainly many important trees have been missed. I have avoided embracing any overarching theory since I do not believe any is relevant to this subject. I have tried to avoid overloading the text with numerous references to comparative frontier studies or to the anthropological research on acculturation, although my reading in those areas has obviously shaped my interpretations. I view this as a preliminary study, with all the limitations a work of that kind has. It is hoped that this will serve as a stimulus for further thought and research.

CHAPTER I
THE GALLIC FRONTIER
IN NORTHERN ITALY

From the beginning, Rome was a society of frontiers. For the first Palatine communities, political boundaries were close at hand. The shrines of Janus preserved the folk memories of their existence.[1] Nor was the experience of Rome exceptional for the communities of the Italian peninsula during the first millenium b.c. The whole area was a crazy quilt of political units varying in ethnic background and level of social development. Etruscans, Greeks, Italians, and Gauls all met along complex and changing frontiers.

For this study, the meeting between Rome and the Gauls seems the most appropriate place to begin. Starting with the traumatic events of the defeat on the Allia and the sacking of the city by the Celts, the Romano-Gallic wars developed into some of the longest, most brutal conflicts in the history of the Republic. The Gauls seared themselves into the Roman national consciousness in a way that no other group did. Art, rhetoric, and even religious ritual reflected this. *Gallorum autem nomen quod semper Romanos terruit.*[2]

The initial involvement with the Gallic folk was almost accidental and largely the result of forces shaped well outside central Italy. It was the Etruscans who first brought the Gauls into contact with Rome, and it was Rome's concern with Etruria that led to her first Celtic confrontation. Some background is necessary in order to understand the events at Clusium, the Allia, and Rome that were to open the frontier experience for the Tiber state.[3]

During the last third of the sixth century b.c., the Etruscans extended their trade and colonizing networks over the Apennines into northeastern Italy. The expansion resulted in new contacts with local tribes and Greek traders along the east coast of Italy. It also allowed Etruscans to tap trade routes extending into and beyond the Alps.[4]

---

[1] L. Holland (1961).

[2] Just. *Epit.* 38.4.9. Julius *Obseq* 21 speaks of the Sibylline books requiring special sacrifice in Gallic territory when Rome began a Gallic war. On the Gauls in Roman art cf. P. R. von Bienkowski (1908); A. Levi (1952).

[3] Livy 5.32.6–5.35.6; Polyb. 2.17–2.18.3; H. H. Scullard (1967) pp. 198–220.

[4] H. H. Scullard (1967) pp. 198–220; L. Barfield (1972) pp. 113–16; P. S. Wells and L. Bonfante (1979).

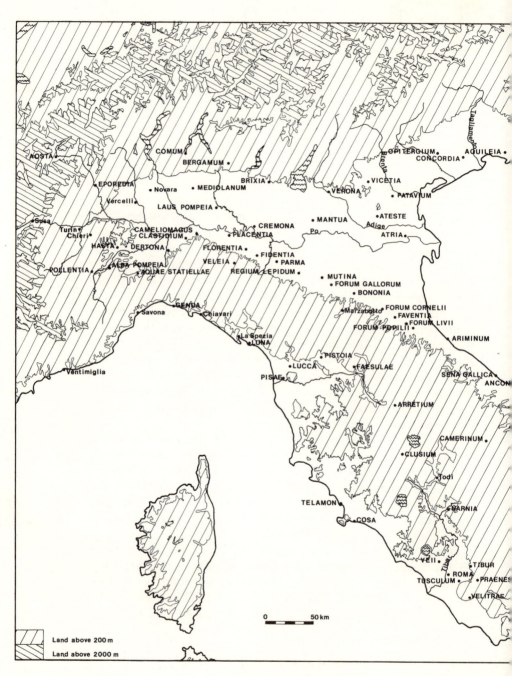

1. Northern Italy

This new expansion was undoubtedly related to the political changes taking place north of the Alps. By the fifth century B.C. the Hallstatt culture in west-central Europe was being replaced by the new group known as La Tène. The main La Tène power centers lay more to the east.[5] This meant that the trade routes linking continental Europe to the Mediterranean were shifting eastward, increasing the importance of the Alpine passes and the Po drainage. Northeastern Italy and transalpine Europe were drawn more closely together. Trade networks developed and along these routes were soon to move peoples from central Europe.[6]

By the time these ultramontane invaders had arrived, the Etruscans had produced considerable changes in the region. Later tradition spoke of the foundation of twelve cities; some important centers such as Felsina and Marzabotto were established.[7] The number of Etruscan settlers was probably smaller than later tradition implied. It is often difficult to distinguish in the archaeological records between the Etruscans and the natives whose culture had rapidly acquired an Etruscoid veneer. Students of Etruria have increasingly realized the distinctive quality of this transapennine Padane culture and its blend of Etruscan and native elements.[8]

Quite early, transalpine migrants moved into the area, thus starting the sequence of events that led to Rome's intervention. Traders spread news of fertile lands south of the mountains that were sparsely populated and dotted with rich centers. This appealed to the Celts in the north, who lived in a poor and overpopulated country. More migrants began moving through the mountain passes. At first they were tolerated or perhaps even welcomed, but they slowly became a menace to the people of Italy. Archaeologists and ancient historians continue to disagree about when this movement began. The classical authors offer radically different versions, and the fragmentary evidence of archaeology has not yet helped to resolve the dispute. Yet the issue calls for some discussion, since it is fundamental to an understanding of the kind of Gallic society the Romans met when they crossed the Apennines.

The ancient writers provide us with two traditions. The first placed the initial Celtic migration in the period of Tarquinius Priscus, during the sixth century B.C. Livy is our main source for this. Whatever faults

[5] W. Kimmig (1958); S. Piggott (1965) pp. 215, 260.

[6] O. H. Frey (1966); S. Milisauskas (1978) pp. 270–73.

[7] A. Grenier (1912) esp. pp. 62ff. For the tradition of twelve Etruscan cities cf. Livy 5.33.7–11; Diod. 14.113.1–2.

[8] *Mostra dell'Etruria Padana* (1961); M. Pallottino (1962); H. H. Scullard (1967) pp. 198–220.

the Patavian historian might have had, he was a child of the Padane region and undoubtedly knew its Celtic traditions.[9] In this version the motives for migration were basically economic. The Celts went through the western Alpine passes to the area of Milan, where the first Celtic center south of the mountains was founded. Livy makes it clear that there were several Celtic migrations and that the process of domination of northeastern Italy was only completed in the early years of the fourth century B.C.

The second tradition, which ultimately rests on the authority of the second-century Greek Polybius, places the arrival of the Celts during the late fifth century B.C., shortly before the attack on Rome.[10] Historians have tended to favor this second version, partly because of the generally greater respect accorded Polybius over Livy. The arrival of the Celts has been seen as a sudden folk migration in the pattern so beloved of prehistorians. This acceptance of the Polybian version may be rash. Before this problem is addressed, however, the archaeological evidence should be briefly reviewed.

In the field of Celto-Italian archaeology, both the quantity of evidence and its interpretation are rapidly changing. Until recently it had been a somewhat neglected subject.[11] This was in part a result of a certain lingering prejudice against the barbarian invaders, but it was also related to the paucity and ambiguity of the physical remains. Except for a few cemeteries such as Filottrano and Ornavasso, the traces left by the Celts are unimpressive. Nothing like the great oppida sites of France and Germany survive, although a few centers, such as Mediolanum, must have once rivaled their counterparts north of the Alps. Settlement sites are still almost unknown, and nearly all cultural reconstruction is based on cemetery finds. A further complication for the cultural historian is that Celtic society was undergoing rapid change during this period, partly because of contacts with the Italic and Greek world. Thus it is often difficult to tell whether one is dealing with a Celtic site that has undergone some degree of Mediterranean acculturation, or a site of a local Italic group that shared many cultural characteristics with the Celtic invaders and was even slightly influenced by them.[12] Moreover, the Celts appear to have arrived in different areas at different times and thus possessed diverse blends of cisalpine and transalpine traits. New excavations and the renewed study of ma-

[9] J. Bayet (1964) pp. 156–62; R. Ogilvie (1965) pp. 706–15; G. A. Mansuelli (1978); P. Santoro (1978). Diod. 7.3.1 has Gauls in Italy by 524 B.C.

[10] Polyb. 2.18; F. Walbank (1957) pp. 184–87.

[11] R. Chevallier (1959) p. 139. The volume *I Galli e l'Italia* (1978) shows how much our knowledge has advanced in recent years.

[12] G. Colonna (1974a); C. M. Govi (1978); D. Vitali (1978); M. Zuffa (1978).

terial from older excavations have helped clarify our picture of Celto-Italian culture, but much needs to be done. We are still far from such basic reconstructions as the Celtic settlement pattern and forms of sustenance, especially for the early period before the invaders were heavily influenced by Greco-Etruscan ways.[13]

The current state of the archaeological evidence suggests that a compromise needs to be made between the two ancient literary traditions. Some Celtic influence is evident in Italy relatively early in the fifth century B.C. Undoubtedly these movements through the Alps were similar to the migrations of the early second century B.C. that were to cause so much concern to the Roman senate. Mercenary service and the prospect of good land probably drew the Celts into Italy.[14]

What seems clear from both the literary and the archaeological record is that the pace of invasion accelerated during the late fifth and early fourth centuries B.C. During this period the new arrivals became sufficiently numerous to challenge the Etruscan hegemony in the north. For the ancients, the critical turning point came with the fall of the Etruscan city of Melpum in 396 B.C. The exact location of Melpum is disputed, but it lay north of the Po and represented an Etruscan outpost in the part of Italy that was first to become Celticized.[15]

As new arrivals crossed the Alps and pressed farther into the peninsula, the Etruscanized communities south of the Po felt the impact of the invasions. The most vivid testimony that we have of this conflict is the series of tombstones found at Felsina, the Etruscan Bologna.[16] During the late fifth and early fourth centuries, scenes of combat between Etruscan warrior and nude Gaul appeared on these grave monuments. The Etruscans of the north helped create the artistic motif of the Celtomachy that was to have its greatest expression in the school of Pergamon.[17]

The growing dominance of the Celts affected the urban communities that the Etruscans had established in the Aemilia area. Most dramatic was the decline of the Etruscan center at Marzabotto.[18] Some of the Etruscans may have been driven out. Tradition had one group under King Rhaetus pushing north toward the Alps to form the Rhae-

---

[13] G. A. Mansuelli (1962) pp. 1068–80; L. Mercando (1978); F. Facchini (1968).

[14] V. Kruta (1978) pp. 150–55; G. Bermond Montanari (1969a); G. Bermond Montanari (1969b) pp. 227–28.

[15] Pliny *HN* 3.125; *RE* 15.1.590.

[16] P. Ducati (1910); A. Grenier (1912) pp. 191–92; H. H. Scullard (1967) p. 202 fig 93.

[17] P. R. von Bienkowski (1908).

[18] F. Tamborini (1950) pp. 69–70; G. A. Mansuelli (1962) p. 1084; H. H. Scullard (1967) p. 219.

tian nation.[19] But the Etruscan decline may not have been quite as sudden and dramatic as is sometimes supposed. Vergil recalls a continuity of Etruscan tradition in his native Mantua. At Adria on the coast, graffiti of the third and second centuries B.C. have a number of Etruscan names.[20]

One reason why certain Etruscan groups could survive was that the Gauls were politically fragmented and often led a partly mobile existence. The Roman historians described the Gauls as being scattered in *castella sua vicosque*. Pliny mentions 112 distinct groups as having lived in the territory of the Boii.[21] Evidence both literary and archaeological suggests a pastoral element in the society of the Gauls, and it is possible that their agriculture was based on something resembling slash and burn. Even their cemetery sites are generally small and scattered. There is no evidence for the development of oppida like those that apparently emerged north of the Po.[22]

The richest concentrations of Celtic material come from graves around Bologna.[23] In general the Gallic tombs were modest inhumation burials. Only 60 of 203 burials from Bologna contained grave goods. In addition to weapons, these included personal ornaments, imported bronzes, and ceramics. A few tombs of the third century B.C. were more opulent, including one that had a diadem of gold. This suggests the emergence of social and economic differentiation. The literary sources mention *reges* and *reguli* well established before the Romans appeared on the scene. It is significant that the names of more Celtic chieftains have survived than those of any other native ethnic group the Romans faced in these early Italian tribal wars.[24]

Without sufficient data on settlements, it is difficult to discuss the level of economic development among the Gauls. The finds in the burials suggest, however, that certain individuals had access to Med-

[19] Just. *Epit.* 20.5.9–10.

[20] Verg. *Aen.* 10.201–3; P. E. Arias (1948) p. 41. For the graffiti at Adria cf. G. Fogolari and G. B. Pellegrini (1958).

[21] Livy 33.36.4–5, 34.22.1–4; Pliny *HN* 3.15.116; G. A. Mansuelli and R. Scarini (1961) pp. 278–79; G. A. Mansuelli (1962) p. 1083. L. Barfield (1972) pp. 152–53 notes a wide scattering of Gallic sites in the Aemilia and the generally small size of cemeteries, suggesting a diffused agricultural population. P. E. Arias (1953) argues for a reasonable concentration of population.

[22] Just. *Epit.* 20.5.8–9 credits the Gauls north of the Po with the foundation of such centers as Mediolanum, Comum, Brixia, Verona, Bergomum, Tridentia, and Vicentia. On this Celtic community development cf. G. A. Mansuelli (1962) pp. 1083–84. Polyb. 2.17.10–11 stresses the importance of cattle. Varro *Rust.* 2.10.4 praises the ability of Gauls as herdsmen.

[23] E. Brizio (1899); G. Sassatelli and D. Vitali (1978).

[24] Livy 34.46.4, 34.48.1. G. Bermond Montanari (1969b) p. 226 notes the difference in grave goods at S. Martino in Gattara.

iterranean luxury goods.[25] The presence of items such as strigils shows the adaptation of Hellenic customs.[26] Some of these items may have been booty, but others were certainly trade goods acquired either from Etruria or from trading centers along the Adriatic.[27] Polybius mentions the importance of gold as an indication of wealth among the Gauls. The Romans at one point issued a prohibition against anyone giving gold or silver to a Gaul.[28] The prohibition was probably intended to prevent certain persons from acquiring excessive wealth and upsetting the delicate social and political balance in Gallic society. A final indication of the growth of wealth among the Gallic elite is the list of items, including finely worked objects in precious metal, carried to Rome for Gallic triumphs.[29]

The impression of Gallic society given by literary and archaeological sources contrasts with the accounts provided by Polybius.[30] He describes the Celts as sleeping in crude abodes and constantly on the move, preoccupied only with war and agriculture and uninterested in art and science. References to the unstable, shiftless, and even drunken nature of the Gauls are commonplace in the ancient literature.[31] In part, this stereotype reflected the subconscious or conscious need of the Greeks and Romans to denigrate the group they were trying to expel or exterminate. Like the settlers on the American frontier, they stressed the cultural inferiority of the natives in an attempt to justify their elimination.[32] Nevertheless, the great majority of the Gallic burials do suggest relative poverty.

Much of the material that has been discovered in Gallic burials dates to the late fourth and third centuries B.C., and reflects Gallic society on the eve of the final Roman conquest rather than in the first migration period.[33] During the early fourth century it was the unacculturated natives whom the Romans met in the series of encounters lead-

[25] E. Brizio (1899); E. Baumgartel (1937); F. Tamborini (1950).

[26] E. Brizio (1899) pp. 673, 680–82, 742–43; R. De Marinis (1978) pp. 98–99. E. Baumgartel (1937) p. 278 notes that the lack of fibulae suggests non-Etruscan-style dress.

[27] Here the presence of Gauls at Adria is significant as noted by G. Fogolari and G. B. Pellegrini (1958). On mercenary service see Xenophon *Hell.* 7.1.20; Polyb. 1.77; Just. *Epit.* 20.5.4–7; L. Braccesi (1971) pp. 101–6.

[28] Zonaras 8.19.2.

[29] Livy 36.40.

[30] Polyb. 2.17.8–12. F. Walbank (1957) p. 184 notes that Polybius underestimated the artistic interests of the Gauls.

[31] Polyb. 2.19.1; Dion. Hal. 14.8; Amm. Marc. 15.12.4.

[32] A. J. Toynbee (1965) vol. 2 p. 256; J. Muldoon (1975).

[33] C. M. Govi (1978) pp. 133–37; G. Sassatelli and D. Vitali (1978) pp. 119–21, 123–25, 129.

ing up to the sack of the city. This traumatic period in Roman history, which began at Chiusi and ended on the slopes of the Capitoline, must now be considered. Many variants of the story have survived in the Roman historiographical tradition.[34] They reflect both the obscurities of the early Roman historical sources and the need the Romans felt to alter these traditions in the light of later historical experiences. Yet certain key elements are common and probably reflect a basic reality. They can be briefly stated.[35]

The sequence of events started when a group of Gauls searching for land crossed the Apennines and invaded the territory of the Etruscan city of Clusium, the modern Chiusi. One legend claimed that they had been invited by a certain Arruns of Clusium who was seeking revenge for the seduction of his wife by the *lucumon*, or ruling magistrate of the city. Behind this romance may lie the reality of factional fighting in an Etruscan city and the use of the Celts as mercenaries.[36]

Chiusi stands on the western slope of the Apennines and controls not only the mountain passes but also access to the headwaters of the Tiber. If the stories surrounding Lars Porsenna are to be accepted, the city had an early link with Rome. Chiusi supposedly played a key role in isolating Veii from the rest of the Etruscans when that city came under attack from Rome.[37] When the Gauls appeared in Clusian territory, the Etruscans turned to Rome for assistance. Concerned about the spread of the Celts to the western slope of the Apennines, the Senate sent an embassy led by members of the Fabii family, a clan traditionally interested in advancing Rome's frontier up the Tiber.[38] The mission of the embassy was supposed to be peaceful and the ambassadors neutral. Fighting erupted while the envoys were at Clusium, however, and members of the Fabian clan joined in the fray against the Gauls. One of the Fabii slew a Gallic chieftain. The Gauls then demanded satisfaction from the Roman senate for this violation of the rules of international conduct.[39]

Our surviving account of the Roman reaction to the Gallic demand was undoubtedly shaped by similar episodes in Republican history in which the demands of international justice clashed with the power of individual factions.[40] The mood may be anachronistic and many details distorted, but even the reworked account says much about how

[34] G. Thouret (1880); J. Wolski (1956); M. Sordi (1960) pp. 1–6.

[35] Livy 5.35.4–5.43.5; Diod. 14.113–16; Plut. *Cam.* 18.

[36] Livy 5.33.1–6; Dion. Hal. 13.10; A. Alföldi (1963) pp. 157–59.

[37] H. H. Scullard (1967) pp. 151–56; W. V. Harris (1971) pp. 125, 210–12; M. Pallottino (1978) pp. 118–19.

[38] Dion. Hal. 13.12; R. Ogilvie (1965) pp. 716–17.

[39] Livy 5.36; Dion. Hal. 13.12; Diod. 14.113.4–7.

[40] Livy 5.36.8–10; Diod. 14.113.4–7.

the Romans allocated blame for one of their most important national disasters. The Gauls are portrayed as moderate in the face of this clear violation of the norms of diplomacy and the senate as initially willing to reach an accommodation. But the power and prestige of the Fabian *gens* prevented the Roman government from taking any disciplinary action. The Gauls, insulted by the rebuff, marched toward Rome, and the Roman army sent to intercept them was defeated at the river Allia. The unprotected city lay open to sack by the Gauls.

The many variations of this narrative reflect not only historiographical confusion but also the need of the Romans to doctor the account to suit later, specific needs. One controversy centers on the ethnic identity of the Gauls who attacked Rome. Later accounts blamed the tribe of the Senones.[41] Their territory, located in the area between Rimini and Ancona, was among the least desirable pieces of land taken by the Gauls. The Senones appear to have been among the groups that arrived last in Italy and would thus have been most tempted to cross the nearby mountains to seize western Etruscan lands. As evidence of their culpability Roman historians mentioned that gold, taken at the sack of Rome, was recovered from the Senones during the Roman wars of conquest in the third century.[42] It should be remembered, though, that the Senones were among the first Gallic tribes conquered by the Romans and that the subjugation was effected with a thoroughness and brutality close to genocide. The Romans coveted Senonian land, and they may well have been tempted to justify their actions by blaming them for the sack. Other Gallic groups may have been involved. Polybius stated that the Gallic withdrawal from Rome was in part caused by Venetian attacks on their territory. The Senones who lived well south of the Veneti would have been little affected by this action.[43]

Also disputed has been the role of the Fabii, since Polybius omits the whole episode. The historian Fabius Pictor, whose involvement in the Gallic Wars of 225–222 B.C. made him an important source for Romano-Gallic relations, has been accused of inventing the story to improve the historical image of his own family. The interest of the Fabian family in Rome's development up the Tiber is clear. Their possible role in precipitating a confrontation seems most plausible.[44]

Great national historical myths are not usually known for their sense

---

[41] Livy 5.35.3; Diod. 14.113.3; Dion. Hal. 19.13; Strabo 5.1.6; App. *Celtica* 11; J. Wolski (1956) pp. 30–35; R. Ogilvie (1965) p. 715.

[42] Suet. *Tib.* 23.2. J. Gagé (1954) pp. 174–75 associates the tradition blaming the Senones for the sack of Rome with the wars of the third century B.C.

[43] Polyb. 2.18.3–4; J. Wolski (1956) p. 35.

[44] Dion. Hal. 13.12; Oros. 4.13.6; A. Alföldi (1963) pp. 355–56; R. Ogilvie (1965) p. 716.

of moral ambiguity. Nevertheless, a sense of ethical uncertainty pervades the account of the events leading up to the sack of Rome by the Gauls. While some descriptions of the Gauls reflect ethnic stereotypes, these are balanced by instances of restraint. The general level of Gallic behavior compares favorably with that of the representatives of Rome. Nowhere is it claimed that the Gauls as barbarians were unworthy of decent consideration. As a result, the history of Romano-barbarian relations not only began with a catastrophe but one in which the Romans acknowledged their own ethical faults. This ambivalence toward the moral mission of Roman imperialism was to be a recurring theme in later Roman historiography. Not accidentally, the debate concerning the embassy of the Fabii became a *topos* in the rhetorical schools where each generation of future Roman administrators would have had the opportunity to explore its ethical implications.[45] The ethical questions raised by these events would have their ultimate expression in the musings of Tacitus in such works as the *Germania* and the *Agricola*.[46]

There is no need to discuss the detailed archaeological and historical controversies surrounding the sack of Rome.[47] Whatever the physical destruction may have been, the defeat and sack was a political and psychic blow of great proportions. Less clear cut are the immediate consequences for the Gauls, or even many of their motives. Land hunger has been cited as a prime reason for their invading Clusian territory, but it is doubtful that they could have found much free territory to settle and cultivate in the thickly inhabited area around the Etruscan city. The prospects in Rome and Latium would not have been better. Moreover, the descriptions of the sack of Rome make no reference to Celtic women and children, thus suggesting the work of a war band rather than a migrating tribe. Mercenary service and the prospect of loot may have led the Gauls initially to Clusium. After the sack of Rome, some of the Gauls appear to have entered the service of Dionysius I of Syracuse in his various wars in Italy. Others may have been employed by the Latin states in their conflicts with the newly weakened Rome.[48]

[45] Quintilian 3.8.19.

[46] Relevant here is the speech of Calgacus in *Agricola* 30–33. Parallels are to be found in Sall. *Iug.* 10.14 and Caesar *BGall.* 7.77.

[47] F. Castagnoli (1974) pp. 425–27 stresses the difficulty of assigning any Republican destruction level to a Gallic sack. M. Torelli (1978) pp. 226–30 rejects the association of any burnt level in the forum to a Gallic sack. J. Gagé (1962); A. Alföldi (1963) pp. 325–28, 355–59; J. Bayet (1964) p. 156; R. Ogilvie (1965) pp. 719–40.

[48] Polyb. 2.22.5 has the Gauls staying in the area seven months. Just. *Epit.* 20.5.1–6; J. Wolski (1956) p. 32; M. Sordi (1960) pp. 30–31, 34–35, 62ff.; A. Alföldi (1963) p. 357. L. Braccesi (1971) p. 102 n. 46 dates the Gallo-Dionysius alliance to 386–385 B.C.

The principal result of the defeat on the Allia and the sack of the city was the weakening of Rome's position in Latium. In the fifth century Rome gradually built its power base in central Italy, culminating in the destruction of the Etruscan city of Veii in 396 B.C.[49] Now the vulnerability of Rome had been exposed, and its neighbors felt able to challenge its hegemony. The middle years of the century saw much intercity strife within Latium, as the Gauls reappeared as allies of the cities opposed to Rome.[50] This second phase of Romano-Gallic frontier relations is as important as the sack in reconstructing early Roman policies toward the Celts. Unfortunately, our understanding of the period is hampered by the confusion and contradictions of the sources.

Two historians provide the bulk of the information we have on the wars between Rome and the Gauls in Italy. They are the Greek Polybius writing in the late second century B.C and the Roman Livy of the late first century B.C. Other authors such as Dionysius of Halicarnassus, Diodorus, Dio, and Orosius appear to follow the Livian tradition but with some significant deviations.[51] Most modern historians have favored the account of Polybius. This judgment is based in part on his greater proximity to the events described, on his access to the Roman ruling class, and on the belief that he was a more skilled and objective historian.[52] Greeks, after all, invented the discipline of history. Livy, writing after the Latin annalistic historians of the early first century B.C., is considered to have been more swayed by rhetorical traditions and the need to glorify Rome and its history.

This is not the place to debate the whole of the Polybius versus Livy issue. In regard to the Gallic wars in Italy, however, I feel that the clear preference given Polybius is unfair and requires serious modification. In many instances it is Livy and authors using his work who provide a clearer and more reasonable picture of these events.[53] It is true that Polybius lived a century closer to the events he described. He had visited the contested lands of northern Italy and observed the surviving remnants of the native population.[54] But most of these visits

---

A. J. Toynbee (1965) vol. 1 p. 25 and R. Ogilvie (1976) p. 164 think Dionysius may actually have encouraged the attack on Rome. For attacks of Caeretans on Gauls see Diod. 14.117.7; Strabo 5.2.3.

[49] H. H. Scullard (1967) pp. 267–72.

[50] Livy 6.23; M. Sordi (1960) p. 58; A. Alföldi (1963) pp. 377–419.

[51] M. Sordi (1960) pp. 143–82.

[52] H. Homeyer (1960); A. Alföldi (1963) pp. 360–65; A. J. Toynbee (1965) vol. 1 p. 26.

[53] M. Sordi (1960) pp. 154–58 feels that the Livian version fits in better with the politics of the period.

[54] Polyb. 2.35; F. Walbank (1957) pp. 172–73.

were relatively brief passages. Historians tend to exaggerate the ability
of Greek observers on these excursions to absorb the complex history,
anthropology, and geography of a region. In contrast, Livy was a
proud native of the Po area.[55] Patavium, his native city, had from the
fourth century B.C. been in close contact with the Celts.[56] Livy grew
up absorbing local tradition and legends both Roman and native, and
in contact with the surviving Celtic population of northern Italy. He
had perhaps better access to source materials. As a professional scholar
he had more time for investigation and probably more opportunity for
independent reflection and judgment than the politician, hostage,
courtier, and part-time historian Polybius.

More disturbing to the argument that favors the objectivity of Polybius is the Greek's self-proclaimed viewpoint on the subject of the
Gauls. This may well have been formed before he left Greece.[57] He
was writing for a Hellenistic audience whose members had recently
experienced the Gallic attacks on Asia Minor and recalled the Celtic
incursions into Greece during the third century B.C. Polybius stresses
this when he says:

ὁ δ᾿ ἀπὸ Γαλατῶν φόβος οὐ μόνον τὸ παλαιόν, ἀλλὰ καὶ καθ᾿
ἡμᾶς ἤδη πλεονάκις ἐξέπληξε τοὺς Ἕλληνας.[58]

Fear of the Gauls is not only something from long ago, but even
in our day it has often struck the Greeks.

For the Hellenes the Gallo-Italian wars had a lesson, and the nature
of that lesson is made clear:

ὑπολαμβάνοντες οἰκεῖον ἱστορίας ὑπάρχειν τὰ τοιαῦτ᾿
ἐπεισόδια τῆς τύχης εἰς μνήμην ἄγειν καὶ παράδοσιν τοῖς
ἐπιγινομένοις, ἵνα μὴ τελέως οἱ μεθ᾿ ἡμᾶς ἀνεννόητοι
τούτων ὑπάρχοντες ἐκπλήττωνται τὰς αἰφνιδίους καὶ παρ-
αλόγους τῶν βαρβάρων ἐφόδους, ἀλλ᾿ ἐπὶ ποσὸν ἐν νῷ
λαμβάνοντες ὡς ὀλιγοχρόνιόν ἐστι καὶ λίαν εὔφθαρτον ⟨τὸ
τοιοῦτον⟩, τὴν ἔφοδον αὐτῶν ὑπομένωσι καὶ πάσας ἐξελέγ-
χωσι τὰς σφετέρας ἐλπίδας πρότερον ἢ παραχωρῆσαί τι-
νος τῶν ἀναγκαίων.[59]

believing that it is suitable for history to memorialize such chance
events and bequeath them to posterity so that those after us might

[55] M.L.W. Laistner (1947) pp. 66–67.
[56] G. A. Mansuelli (1964) p. 69 mentions an Etruscan stela from Padua showing a
Celtomachy.
[57] F. Walbank (1957) pp. 213–14.
[58] Polyb. 2.35.9–10.
[59] Polyb. 2.35.4–6.

not—in unfamiliarity with such things—panic at the sudden, unexpected barbarian incursions; instead, they can understand how brief and very easily reversible such things are, and they can await the attack and try out all their hopes before surrendering anything important.

Even the most conservative estimation of the impact of the Gauls on Italy makes the statement of Polybius seem very strange. The Gauls had arrived in Italy at least by the fifth century B.C. They were not finally subdued until the second century B.C. This subjugation involved some of the most brutal fighting and serious losses in Roman military history. It was hardly a short-lived and perishable phenomenon. With a historian who used such clearly stated and distorted preconceptions, one must ask to what degree he has altered the facts and whether his narrative should be given precedent over that of a local historian removed from the passion of nearly contemporary events.

After the sack of Rome the Gauls disappeared for twenty years from the Roman historical record; they reappeared in 367 B.C.[60] The Romans were besieging Velitrae some forty kilometers southeast of Rome. Just as victory was assured, the menace of a Gallic attack forced a change of plans. The Gauls were apparently routed and retreated in the direction of Apulia. Even Livy admitted the historiographical confusion surrounding these events. The ancient sources did not connect the siege of Velitrae and the arrival of the Gauls. From a consideration of the geography of the area, however, it is clear that an attack down the Alban hills would cut off and endanger any Roman force besieging Velitrae. It raises the possibility that the Velitraeans or other Latins had recruited the Gauls as mercenaries to aid their cause.

From that moment on, the Gallic attacks increased. In 361–360 B.C. the Gauls advanced down the Via Salaria and camped at the third milestone beyond the Anio bridge.[61] Checked by the Romans, they pulled back into the territory of the city of Tibur and formed an alliance with the Tiburtines. Since their services were apparently not needed, they set off in the direction of Campania.[62] The Romans, however, attacked Tibur. Rather than assisting Tibur directly, the Gauls attacked the Alban area and the Latin cities of Labici and Tusculum, and then advanced on Rome. Their intention must have been

[60] Livy 6.42.4–8; Dion. Hal. 14.8–9; Plut. *Cam.* 40–42; T.R.S. Broughton (1951) p. 113.
[61] Livy 7.9–10; Oros. 3.6.2–3 (listed for 366, but similarity of details suggests that it should be associated with 361 B.C.); T.R.S. Broughton (1951) p. 119; A. Alföldi (1963) pp. 362–63.
[62] Livy 7.1.3, 7.11.1–3; A. Alföldi (1963) p. 361; A. J. Toynbee (1965) vol. 1 p. 26. Both in 367 B.C. and after the sack of Rome, Gauls went south to find mercenary opportunities among the Greeks.

to divert the Roman forces from Tibur. The Romans met the challenge. The Gauls were defeated first near Rome and then near Tibur.

In the Fasti Triumphales, the victory of 361–360 B.C. is described as *de Galleis et Tiburtibus*.[63] Moreover, in the final settlement between Rome and the Latins that came in 338 B.C. Tibur received especially harsh treatment, *quod taedio imperii Romani cum Gallis gente efferata arma quondam consociassent*.[64]

It is interesting to contrast this reconstruction of events based on Livy with the same episodes as described by Polybius. The Greek merely states that the Gauls invaded the Alban hills and that the Romans, not being able to gather their allies in time, did not oppose them.[65] The Gauls then mysteriously disappeared for twelve years. The raid is pictured as a transitory event with no strategic sense. The narrative is designed to calm Greek nerves and not to explain strategy. The picture of relative unity in the face of the Gallic menace is better suited to the *tota Italia* image in Fabius Pictor's description of the Gallic wars of the late third century than to the bitterly divided world of fourth-century B.C. Latium.[66]

The Romans had not faced their last Latino-Gallic army. Two years later the Gauls again moved on Rome, this time by way of Praeneste. Nothing is said about an alliance between the Praenestines and the Gauls. But in 338 B.C. Praeneste, like Tibur, was singled out for special punishment for its cooperation with the Gauls. This time the Gauls were defeated by C. Sulpicius Peticus, who was awarded a triumph for his accomplishments.[67]

Between 357 and 351 B.C. Gauls are not mentioned in connection with the Roman wars in Latium. The hiatus may not be accidental. In 356 the Syracusan ruler Dionysius II had been deposed. Mercenary connections between the Gauls and the tyrants of Syracuse had been strong. It seems reasonable to assume that the Syracusan tribes would have looked with concern at the new rising power in central Italy and would have been interested in preserving a buffer of independent Latin states. Gallic mercenaries would have been an excellent way of accomplishing this. The fall of the tyrants and the subsequent unrest in southern Italy and Sicily probably disrupted this indirect diplomatic and political effort.[68]

[63] A. Degrassi (1947) p. 540.

[64] Livy 8.14.9–10.

[65] Polyb. 2.18.6–7; F. Walbank (1957) pp. 185–87.

[66] J. Wolski (1956) pp. 28–30, 46–52.

[67] Livy 8.14.9–10; A. Degrassi (1947) p. 540; T.R.S. Broughton (1951) p. 121.

[68] M. Sordi (1960) pp. 62–72; A. J. Toynbee (1965) vol. 1 p. 26.

Around 350 B.C. the Gauls returned to the Latin scene. Our two sources provide different accounts of the events. Livy says that the troubles began in 350 with the arrival of the Gauls in Latium. M. Popillius Laenas defeated them and drove their forces into the Alban Hills. His triumph *de Galleis* is recorded in the Fasti Trium-phales.[69] The victory was not decisive, though, since in the following year the Gauls came down from the Alban Hills to raid. The problems of the Romans were compounded by the refusal of the Latins to sup-ply soldiers. In spite of the absence of their allies, the Romans rallied and drove the Gauls out of Latium. The Celts retreated to the terri-tory of the Volsci. Some made their way to Apulia, while others fled to the sea coast where they were picked up by ships. This naval force would presumably be Syracusan and implies the revival of Sicilian interest in the events of Latium.[70]

The account of Polybius is very different.[71] He places the invasion in 348 B.C. and has the Gauls met by a strong force of Romans and allies. Faced with this united opposition, the Gauls retreated and did not return for thirteen years. The solution of the crisis was simple and soothing. Barbarian menaces were easily overcome when faced by the united forces of Mediterranean high culture.

Modern historians have tended to follow Polybius, arguing that the Livian narrative has the reduplications, confusions, and corruptions so characteristic of the historian from Patavium. Yet Livy better reflects the confusion and unrest of Latium and of Italy in general during the mid-fourth century B.C.[72] The period 347–346 saw Roman victory over Antium, Satricum, and the Volsci.[73] Latin unrest continued and cul-minated in the wars of 340–338, which ended with the defeat of La-tium and the dissolution of the Latin League.[74] It is significant to note that the Gauls did not become involved in these last struggles of Rome's immediate neighbors.

The second phase of Romano-Gallic relations had come to an end. Polybius records a peace treaty between the Romans and Gauls in 334 B.C. that was supposed to last for thirty years. One of the reasons for

[69] Livy 7.23–24, 7.24.10, 7.25.1–2; App. *Celtica* 1.4; A. Degrassi (1947) p. 541.

[70] Livy 7.25, 7.26, 7.32.9–10, 9.14–15; A. Alföldi (1963) pp. 364–65.

[71] Polyb. 2.18.7–9; F. Walbank (1957) p. 187.

[72] A. Alföldi (1963) pp. 363–364: "But here again emerges the curious fact that though the original chronological framework of event is the one found in the summary of the great Greek historian, the Roman annalist preserved nevertheless the authentic infor-mation with regard to the attitude of the Latins."

[73] Livy 7.27; A. Degrassi (1947) p. 541.

[74] A. Degrassi (1947) p. 541; A. Alföldi (1963) pp. 391–414.

the conclusion of this peace agreement was the growing respect of the
Gauls for the power of Rome, which was probably related to Rome's
defeat of the Latins.[75] The agreement, like that of 295 B.C., may have
included stipulations that prohibited Gallic mercenary service with
any enemy of Rome.[76] Even with this treaty, fear of the Gauls kept
Romans on edge. Both 332 and 329 B.C. produced false alarms of a
Gallic *tumultus*.[77] No great Romano-Gallic conflict is recorded, however, until the next century.

This first period of Romano-Gallic contact had two distinct phases.
The first and most traumatic had been the defeat at the Allia and the
sack of the city. It created an intense collective fear of the Gauls that
was to carry over into later Roman history. Yet it was itself a single
event from which Rome recovered, and it could be regarded as a transitory incident in the Polybian sense. The emergence of the Gauls as
an element in Rome's periodic war with the Latins and other neighboring groups created another, more permanent source of ethnic tension. To the sudden terror of the single attack was added the repeated
devastation of frontier raiding. The combination of the two experiences developed in the Romans a fierce hatred and fear of the Gauls
that was to fuel the wars of conquest and extermination of the next
century.

For a generation, the Gallic frontier was superficially quiet. Then
the last years of the century saw changes in the direction of Rome's
advance. The year 311 B.C. brought the first triumph over the Etruscans, and this was followed by others in 309 and 301.[78] In 310 B.C.
Rome established an alliance with Camerinum in Umbria.[79] Located
on the eastern side of the Apennines and just south of the Gauls, the
city could provide Rome with an important listening post and a base
for future conquests. With the advent of the third century, a new
phase in Romano-Gallic relations began. By then, another century had
passed since the arrival of most of the Gauls in Aemilia. Trade had
developed not only with Etruscans and the Italic peoples but also with
the Greeks along the Adriatic coast. Mediterranean objects increasingly appeared in Celtic burials, especially among the Senones.[80]
Demographic pressure was also intensifying, especially as the Celtic
population expanded. There is no indication of real change in the

[75] Polyb. 2.18.8–9; F. Walbank (1957) p. 187. Livy does not mention the treaty.
[76] App. *Celtica* 11.
[77] Livy 8.17.6, 8.20.2–5.
[78] Livy 9.32.1–10, 9.40.2, 10.5.13; A. Degrassi (1947) pp. 542–43; T.R.S. Broughton
(1951) pp. 161–64, 172–73; W. V. Harris (1971) pp. 49–66.
[79] W. V. Harris (1971) p. 56 supports the validity of the tradition about this treaty.
[80] G. A. Mansuelli (1962) pp. 1078–79; V. Kruta (1978) pp. 163–66.

pastoral-agricultural life or more intensive use of the land.[81] The Romans' increasing power limited Gallic access to mercenary markets. An escape valve had to be found, and again, as in the early fourth century, the Gauls looked toward Etruria. The year 299 B.C. saw a new attack on Etruria by the Gauls. The Etruscans bought them off and even attempted to turn them against Rome. The Gauls were only willing to follow that risky course if the Etruscans promised them land on which to settle. Fearing such barbarian neighbors, the Etruscans paid off the Gauls and sent them home.[82]

Livy mentions the false rumor of a Gallic *tumultus* at Rome in 299 B.C., while Polybius describes a full-fledged Gallic raid, sparked by the arrival of new tribesmen from over the Alps.[83] The stereotypical accounts of Gallic drinking and internecine strife suggest that the details of Polybius' account should be viewed with caution. The fears of the Romans were real, however, and they reacted vigorously. Ties with Picenum were strengthened. At Narnia, some seventy kilometers up the Tiber valley, a settlement was founded to guard the Apennine approaches to Rome.[84] Unrest continued in both Etruria and in the Samnium. Finally, in 296 B.C. Etruscans and Samnites coalesced into a threat to Rome. The uprising ended only with the great Roman victory at Sentinum in 295 B.C.[85]

There seems no doubt that the Etruscans and the Samnites were the instigators of the war. The emphasis placed on Sentinum as a victory over Gauls tends to obscure that. The actual course of events that led up to the battle is uncertain. The Romans did suffer a stinging defeat at the hands of the Gauls near either Clusium or Camerinum. The disaster became known when the Romans saw the heads of their slain comrades dangling from the horses of Gallic scouts.[86] The main Roman army continued to advance over the Apennines, no doubt to split the Gauls and Umbri and support wavering Umbrian allies in the area. Raids were conducted in Etruria that drew off the Etruscan forces. At Sentinum, Gaul and Samnite faced Roman in an epic battle filled with historic and religious significance. In the end the Romans were victorious.[87] A triumph was celebrated over the Etruscans, Sam-

---

[81] G. A. Mansuelli (1962) pp. 1083–86.

[82] Livy 10.10.6–12.

[83] Polyb. 2.19.1.

[84] Livy 10.10.5; E. T. Salmon (1970) pp. 59–60; W. V. Harris (1971) p. 155.

[85] Livy 10.11.1–6, 10.12.3–8, 10.14.2–4, 10.16.3–8.

[86] Livy 10.26.11–12.

[87] Polyb. 2.19.6–7; Livy 10.27–30; Frontin. *Str.* 1.8.3; J. Bayet (1962); W. V. Harris (1971) pp. 70–72.

nites, and Gauls. This was followed in 294 B.C. by more campaigns in Etruria and Samnium, and additional triumphs.[88]

The battle of Sentinum, a hard-won victory on the very doorstep of the *ager Gallicus*, left a strong memory in the Roman historical consciousness. The events were given a religious tone by the omens before the battle and the *devotio* of P. Decius Mus during the action. During the first half of the second century B.C., a temple was erected at Civita Alba, less than five miles from Sentinum. The theme of the terra cotta relief on the pediment was the repulse of the Gauls from the temple of Delphi. The role of Apollo was emphasized.[89] The connection with Sentinum seems obvious. In the century after the battle, new wars must have hardened the attitude of local Italian peoples toward the Gauls and made them identify even more with the struggle of Mediterranean civilization against barbarism.[90]

The campaign of Sentinum had acquainted large numbers of Romans with the fertile lands beyond the Apennines. They too were experiencing the pressure of an expanding population. The Celtic territory must have seemed open and underused to the peasants of central Italy, much as to the American colonists of the seventeenth and eighteenth centuries Indian land-use practices seemed intolerably wasteful.[91]

A decade was to pass before Gauls and Romans fought again. Rome continued to strengthen its hold in central Italy. The wars against the Samnites ground on. In Etruria internal strife increased. The population in the Celtic homeland was again growing. In 284 B.C Gauls invaded the territory of Arretium and started a sequence of events that ended with the near extermination of the Senones.

Once again, the sources make it difficult to reconstruct the events. The problem is compounded by the loss of the full text of Livy. According to Polybius, the sequence of events was relatively straightforward.[92] The troubles began when the Gauls attacked Arretium. The Romans came to the aid of that city, but were attacked and defeated

[88] A. Degrassi (1947) p. 544; T.R.S. Broughton (1951) p. 179; W. V. Harris (1971) pp. 4–76.

[89] A. Andrén (1940) pp. 307–8; M. Zuffa (1956) pp. 269–88; S. Mazzarino (1966) pp. 284–85. G. C. Susini (1965) pp. 148, 162–63 stresses the role of Apollo at Rimini and in northern Italy in general as an anti-Celtic deity. M. Verzar and F. H. Pairault-Massa (1978).

[90] G. C. Susini (1965) pp. 161–63.

[91] W. Jacobs (1971) pp. 299–300; R. H. Pearce (1965) pp. 20–21, 65–75.

[92] Polyb. 2.19.7–2.20.10 associates the victory at Vadimon with the defeat of the Gauls at Delphi and regards it as a preparation for the wars with Pyrrhus. E. T. Salmon (1935); G. Forni (1953) pp. 204–14, 235–37; F. Walbank (1957) pp. 188–91; G. De-Sanctis (1967) vol. 2 pp. 357–58; W. V. Harris (1971) pp. 79–83.

with the loss of their leader, L. Caecilius. His successor, M' Curius Dentatus, dispatched ambassadors to the Gauls to negotiate for the recovery of prisoners, but these ambassadors were slain by the Gauls. The Romans then marched on the territory of the offending tribe, the Senones, drove them from their land, captured the area, and founded the city of Sena Gallica. The larger Gallic tribe of the Boii, seeing the fate of their neighbors and kinsmen, solicited the aid of the Etruscans for a joint war against Rome. The combined forces were defeated by the Romans in a battle at Lake Vadimon on the upper Tiber.

The other tradition, which goes back to Livy, is noticeably different.[93] The Senones became involved in a much wider uprising against Rome that included Etruscans, Samnites, Bruttians, Lucanians, and even southern Italian Greeks. The Romans had sent their ambassadors to warn the Gauls that mercenary service with any of those groups would be a violation of their agreements with Rome. The ambassadors were slain by the Gallic chieftain Britomarus to avenge the death of his father, killed by the Romans in Etruria.[94] In retaliation for the outrage, the Romans sent P. Cornelius Dolabella to ravage the territory of the Senones, where they slew the men and carried the women and children off into slavery. References in Orosius, Augustine, and the Perioechia of Livy all connect the defeat of Caecilius with that event.

The pattern of the Polybian narrative is clear and rather trite. The Gauls attack suddenly without apparent motivation. After some Roman reverses, the Gauls are defeated and the menace removed. The Gallic attack is consciously related to the Celtic assault on Delphi in the same way it was used by the terra cotta sculptor at Civita Alba. The main result for the Romans was a sharpening of war skills for the conflict with the Hellenic adventurer Pyrrhus.

The non-Polybian tradition shows a much more subtle grasp of the complex political situation in Italy during the late 280s. Although overt war may have been limited, resentment was simmering. There were triumphs over Etruscans in 281 and 280, and over Samnites in 282, 280, 278, 276, 275, 273, and 272 B.C.[95] In 273 a colony was founded at Cosa to watch over the restless Etruscans at Vulci. Pyrrhus had been drawn actively into the resistance against Rome. It is not

[93] Livy *Per.* 12; Florus 1.8.21; Eutropius 2.10; Dion. Hal. 19.13.1–3; App. *Celtica* 11, *Sam.* 6; Dio Cass. 8 fr. 38; Oros. 3.22; Augustine *De Civ. D.* 3.17.2. S. Mazzarino (1966) pp. 284–87 derives Appian's account from Cornelian tradition and prefers it to that of Polybius.

[94] S. Mazzarino (1966) pp. 286–87 regards this whole episode as an invention.

[95] A. Degrassi (1947) pp. 545–46; T.R.S. Broughton (1951) pp. 189, 194–95, 197.

surprising that one of these groups would revert to the tradition of using the Gauls as semimercenary forces.

Factors other than simple hostility to Rome may have led to the use of the Gauls as mercenaries in Etruria. Arretium had been the scene of fierce factional strife among the leading families. The Cilnii had been restored as the dominant family only by armed Roman intervention.[96] As at Clusium a century before, it seems reasonable that opponents of the Cilnii might have called in Gauls to help expel their rivals and that this action would have provoked the intervention of Rome. Other Etruscans may have been using Gauls, since the father of Britomarus had been slain fighting on the side of the Etruscans against Rome.

The question of which Gallic tribes were involved now arises. Polybius held the Boii responsible for the organization of the war. Several factors cast a doubt on this assertion. First of all, the territory of the Boii was well removed from the scene of action and from extensive contacts with Etruscan states. It was a long march from their territory to the battlefield of Lake Vadimon on the Tiber. Moreover, the Fasti Triumphales mention only victories over Senones. A Boian conflict is not recorded until the outbreak of war following the land reforms of Flaminius in 232 B.C. Although certain Boian mercenaries may have been involved in the fighting, there seems no reason to assume a massive tribal intervention.[97]

What is clear is that the Senones were subjected to a level of devastation that approached genocide. The slaying of the ambassadors served as a convenient excuse. All adult males were to be slain, and the women and children sold into slavery. Britomarus was held for special execution.[98] The Roman aim was to eliminate the Senones as an ethnic unit. Not every tribesman was slain, though, for there were natives living in the area when the Romans undertook *ad viritim* divisions of Senonian territory.[99] But they were no longer a menace to Rome.

During this period, the Romans founded the city of Sena Gallica on the eastern coast of Italy. Polybius placed the foundation after the victory at Vadimon. Livy apparently dated it to the consulship of M'Curius Dentatus five years after the victory at Sentinum.[100] Here the logic of events would favor the Polybian version. After Sentinum,

---

[96] Polyb. 2.19.7; Livy 10.3–5; W. V. Harris (1971) pp. 115, 130.

[97] A. Degrassi (1947) p. 545.

[98] App. *Celtica* 11.

[99] Polyb. 2.21.7–9; F. Walbank (1957) pp. 192–93. G. C. Susini (1975) p. 111 on the basis of cult evidence sees more Senones surviving than Boii.

[100] Polyb. 2.19.12; Livy *Per.* 11; E. T. Salmon (1970) pp. 62, 78, 81.

the settlement would have been in a perilously exposed position. Although the Gauls had been defeated at Sentinum, they had not been eliminated. On the other hand, a colony founded after Vadimon and the destruction of the Senones could easily keep watch over the Celtic remnants. One thinks of the similar position of Cosa among the Etruscans.[101]

In the wake of the annihilation of the Senones, peace with the Gauls lasted for nearly fifty years. The Romans, however, were laying the groundwork on their northeastern frontier for the conquest of the *ager Gallicus* in the late third century. The first step was the foundation of the Latin colony at Ariminum in 268 B.C. It was located between the old land of the Senones and that of the Boii.[102] As a Latin colony, it had a population of several thousand families apparently drawn from several parts of central Italy. In many ways the foundation was a turning point in Romano-Gallic relations. Previously Rome and the largest Gallic tribes had only indirect frontier contacts. Now the Romans had moved several thousand settlers into territory that the Gauls had considered their own for a century. In addition, these settlers, like the veterans returning from Sentinum and Vadimon, must have passed the word to compatriots at home that there were rich lands between the borders of Ariminum and the Po that were poorly farmed by semisavages.

The foundation of the colony did not provoke an immediate reaction from the Boii, and the outbreak of the First Punic War turned Rome's attention elsewhere. The Carthaginians did not exploit Rome's tense relations with its neighbors to the north.[103] Moreover, the Roman and Italian losses during the war must have relieved the pressure for colonization. Within Ariminum itself, the reductions in manpower would have removed the need to advance the territorial boundaries of the colony and take over Gallic land. Colonies as self-disciplining units had means of controlling unruly border populations and of cultivating expedient relationships with the neighboring Celts.

Tensions mounted over the following years—probably as a result of trade abuses, land poaching, and the mistreatment of settlers on both

[101] F. E. Brown (1980).

[102] Livy *Per.* 15; Vell. Pat. 1.14; U. Ewins (1952) p. 54; V. Righini (1970) pp. 75–81. G. C. Susini (1965) pp. 146–55 on the basis of cult evidence traces settlers of Ariminum to Sabine, Umbrian, Marsian, and Pelignian areas. S. B. De Caro (1978) pp. 259–60 notes bronze coins with Gallic heads on them that seem to originate at Ariminum; the date is uncertain but relates to the general atmosphere of victory over Gauls. See G. Uggeri (1977) pp. 133–35 on a sherd from Spina with the words *Galicos colonos* inscribed in it, which he relates to the Ariminum colony.

[103] G. DeSanctis (1967) p. 278.

sides of the border—and in 238 B.C. the Boii took to the warpath. They demanded the land of Ariminum and the removal of the Romans from the thirty-year-old colony. Attacks were apparently made on Ariminum itself, and the Boii called in fellow tribesmen from across the Alps. The arrival of these newcomers, however, soon caused internal friction between ethnically related but now culturally different groups. Fighting broke out, and the weakened Boii were forced to sue for peace. As part of their peace arrangement, they were obliged to cede more land.[104]

At this point the fate of the *ager Gallicus* became intertwined with the domestic politics of Rome. Land was becoming a hot political issue in Rome, and politicians were exploiting the agrarian discontent. An important potential area of settlement was the *ager Gallicus*. In 232 B.C. the tribune C. Flaminius proposed its division in a land bill.[105] This legislation marked a radical change in Roman frontier policy. The tribune wished to assign confiscated land in the *ager Gallicus* to the settlers on an individual plot (*ad viritim*) basis. The result would be a dispersed settler frontier. Flaminius was using the frontier as an escape valve in the classic sense defined by the American historian Frederick Jackson Turner. Like Turner, the Romans forgot that there were natives on these borders with claims on the land and fears of the new settlers.[106]

Of concern to the natives was not only the increase in number of settlers but also the form of settlement itself. It required more native expulsions and confiscations, and the neighboring tribes looked on this with apprehension.[107] More important, it placed poorly controlled groups in tense border areas. Both sides saw the action as provocative, and this the opponents of Flaminius argued.[108] Their arguments failed, however; the bill passed and the stage was set for new wars. Although hostility did not break out immediately and it took time to implement the legislation of Flaminius, the frictions of the frontier experience had a cumulative effect. These Gauls were not naïve, and they knew how

[104] Polyb. 2.21.2–6; Livy *Per.* 20; Zonaras 8.18; F. Walbank (1957) pp. 191–92; W. V. Harris (1979) pp. 197–200.

[105] See Varro *Rust.* 1.2.7 on the fertility of the *ager Gallicus*. On Flaminius in general cf. P. Fraccaro (1919); Z. Yavetz (1962); G. C. Susini (1965) pp. 150–51; G. Radke (1969).

[106] Cic. *Brut.* 14.57; Polyb. 2.21.7–9. On F. G. Turner and the escape valve see R. A. Billington (1966) pp. 36–38; M. Lombardi (1975) pp. 440, 447; F. Shannon (1945).

[107] Polyb. 2.21.7–9 has the Boii convinced that now "the Romans no longer fought them for the sake of domination and sovereignty but with a view to their complete expulsion and extermination."

[108] Val. Max. 5.4.5; P. Fraccaro (1919) pp. 202–3.

far the military balance had tilted in Rome's favor. After seven years, they were ready for war.

The fragmentary sources hint at the growing border anxiety. In 230 B.C. the senate passed a decree that prohibited trade in gold with the Gauls.[109] The Gauls' love for gold was proverbial, as was the effectiveness of its clever use in influencing internal Gallic politics. The Roman officials undoubtedly had their own factions and individuals whom they supported in the interest of stability. Ambitious traders or irresponsible border magnates could upset delicate political and social balances. Whatever the truth of the story of Arruns of Clusium, the Romans knew the legend and did not want a similar episode repeated on their own Gallic frontier. Moreover, the flow of too much gold, even through responsible channels, would provide the means of recruiting transalpine mercenaries and increase the ability of the Celts to wage war.[110]

In 228 B.C. a thunderbolt fell on the Capitoline near the temple of Apollo, a deity associated with defense against the Gauls. The oracle of the sibyl warned that the Romans should beware of a Gallic attack. Soon after that, the Romans attempted to exorcise the Gallic danger by burying two Gauls and two Greeks in the Forum Boarium. Such sacrifices were rare but indicate the level of tension in the city.[111]

By 225 B.C. the Romans felt that war with the Gauls was imminent. Rumors about the recruitment of transalpine Gauls by the Celts in Italy had certainly reached them.[112] They stepped up their own precautions, making peace with Hasdrubal in Spain in order to free themselves from concerns over that area, and recruiting strong armies and gathering stores.[113] To outflank the Boii, Rome established alliances with the Veneti and even with the northern Italian Gallic tribe of the Cenomani. One of the consular armies was dispatched to Ariminum.[114]

The Gauls surprised the Romans by crossing the Apennine passes and attacking a lightly defended Etruria. At Fiesole a Roman army was ambushed.[115] A substantial portion of the Gallic army was naturally the Boii, but the forces also included Insubres, Taurisci, and the

[109] Zonaras 8.19.2. On the importance of gold in Gallic society in general see Diod. 5.27.
[110] Polyb. 2.22.2
[111] Dio. Cass. 12 fr. 50; Zonaras 8.19; K. Latte (1960) pp. 256–57. This is the first attested use of this rite.
[112] Polyb. 2.22.
[113] Polyb. 2.22.10–11.
[114] Polyb. 2.23.5–7, 2.24.7–8.
[115] Polyb. 2.25.5–10.

Gaesutae, apparently mercenary troops from over the Alps.[116] Polybius mentions a certain Aneroestes who was a dominant influence in
the Gallic war council as war chief, although references to other kings
imply generally fragmented tribal leadership.[117]

The exact course of Gallic movements in Etruria is difficult to reconstruct. This may reflect confusion and lack of purpose on the part
of the Gauls themselves. Initially, they probably hoped for support in
socially tense Etruria. When this did not materialize, they turned to
looting the rich Etruscan countryside. Their forces marched as far
south as Clusium but did not feel strong enough to attack Rome. The
Romans hastily summoned to Etruria the army in Aemilia and a consular army in Sardinia, and these forces met with the Gauls at Telamon on the northern border of the colony of Cosa.[118] The battle was
bloody but decisive. The cisalpine Gauls bore the brunt of the fighting
and presumably the bulk of the casualties. Aneroestes escaped the
fighting but soon committed suicide together with his band of closest
followers.[119] The loot taken by the Gauls in Etruria was returned to
its owners, while rich Gallic spoils and Gallic prisoners were dispatched to Rome. L. Aemilius Papus celebrated the first of a new
series of Gallic triumphs.[120]

The defeat at Telamon was a multiple disaster for the Gauls. It
demonstrated their lack of sustained offensive capability in the face of
the sophisticated Roman military machine, as well as their loss of any
real support in Etruria. The casualties must have been massive. Moreover, the offensive into Etruria had provided the Romans with a justification for new attacks and new land seizures. Both Boii and Insubres had been guilty of bringing war upon Rome. In the words of
Polybius:

ἀπὸ δὲ τοῦ κατορθώματος τούτου κατελπίσαντες Ῥωμαῖοι
δυνήσεσθαι τοὺς Κελτοὺς ἐκ τῶν τόπων τῶν περὶ τὸν Πάδον
ὁλοσχερῶς ἐκβαλεῖν.[121]

On the basis of this success, the Romans were confident that they
would be able to drive the Celts completely out of the area around
the Po.

[116] Polyb. 2.28.2–8; Oros. 4.13; R. Heuberger (1938); F. Walbank (1957) pp. 194–95.
[117] Polyb. 2.26.4–7, 2.31.2
[118] Polyb. 2.26.31, 2.27.1; F. Walbank (1957) pp. 204–7.
[119] Polyb. 2.30.5–2.31.2.
[120] Polyb. 2.31.3–6; A. Degrassi (1947) pp. 549–50. On the problem of associating
archaeological finds with battles cf. F. H. Pairault-Massa (1978) pp. 207–20.
[121] Polyb. 2.31.8.

The opportunity was exploited by a succession of consular generals eager to advance Roman interests in the Po area. The consul elected for 223 B.C. was C. Flaminius, whose actions as tribune had started the chain of events that led to Telamon.[122] Roman imperialism was on the advance, and the Gauls were to be its victims. In taking on the Boii and the Insubres, however, the Romans were attacking groups that were populous, well settled in Italy, and developed in their political and military organization. The many Gallic cemeteries around Bologna provide a sense of the Boian population. The Insubres across the Po had full-fledged oppida and the type of protourban culture that the Romans were later to meet in transalpine Gaul.[123] The strength and resiliency of these tribes, especially the Boii, are demonstrated by the long and bitter wars the Romans had to wage against them.

This new Roman offensive was divided into two main phases by the Second Punic War. Immediately after Telamon, the Roman armies crossed the Apennines and ravaged the territory of the Boii. The Roman advance did not stop there, for the two consuls of 224 B.C., T. Manlius Torquatus and Q. Fulvius Flaccus, became the first Roman commanders to cross the Po.[124] In the following year, the consuls C. Flaminius and P. Furius Philus renewed the attack into the transpadane area. Further attempts were made to surround the enemy with tribes friendly to Rome: relations had already been established with the Cenomani, and the Romans won the friendship of the Anamares who lived south of the Insubres. In 223 B.C. the Romans attempted to use the territory of the Anamares to mount a direct assault on the Insubres. Their advance was checked, and the legions swung north to gain support from the Cenomani. Aided by these allied Gauls, the Romans invaded the territory of the Insubres, assailing it until the Gauls were forced into battle and defeated.[125] Flaminius celebrated his triumph *de Galleis*, while his colleague, P. Furius Philus, recorded a triumph over Gauls and Ligurians.[126]

The Insubres at this point were ready to settle for peace at any price. The war party was in control at Rome, however, and the two consuls of 222 B.C., M. Claudius Marcellus and Cn. Cornelius Scipio, smelled the opportunity for further victories. With their overtures for peace rejected, the Insubres summoned aid from the Gaesutae of the

---

[122] T.R.S. Broughton (1951) p. 232.
[123] G. A. Mansuelli (1964) p. 45.
[124] Livy *Per*. 20; Polyb. 2.31.8–10; Oros. 4.13; Zonaras 8.20.
[125] Polyb. 2.32–33; G. DeSanctis (1967) pp. 305–7; F. Walbank (1957) pp. 207–10.
[126] A. Degrassi (1947) p. 550.

Rhone area and awaited the final confrontation.[127] The Romans advanced across the Po and besieged the center of Acerrae, a frontier oppidum dependent on the Insubres. The Insubres countered by attacking Clastidium in the territory of the Anamares. This new emphasis on sieges in the transpadane wars reflects the different settlement and social organization of these more sophisticated tribes.

The Romans raised the siege of Clastidium and took Acerrae. The battles saw heroic actions on both sides. The Roman commander, Marcellus, won the *spolia opima* for slaying the Gallic chieftain Virdumarus at Clastidium, for which the Roman poet Naevius wrote a play celebrating the events.[128] With these frontier centers firmly under control, the Romans moved into the heartland of the Insubres, besieging and capturing their main oppidum at Mediolanum. Marcellus advanced as far as Como, probably with the intention of winning the support of the non-Gallic groups that controlled the foothills of the Alps.[129] The Insubres made a total submission, and the war appeared to be over.

These campaigns marked a spectacular shift in Roman policy. From a cautious, defensive policy the Romans had moved to the undertaking of massive offensives that had carried their armies to the Alps. The submission or friendship of each of the main tribes had been obtained. Now important decisions of political organization had to be made. The primary question was what balance was to be maintained between buffer lands inhabited by cowed or friendly tribes and territory that was cleared of Gauls and resettled by the Romans and their Italian allies. The decision was to determine the future history of the land south of the Alps.

The first indications of the new Roman policy came in 218 B.C., four years after the capture of Mediolanum. The two principal Latin colonies were founded at Placentia and Cremona. Both were substantial settlements with six thousand families apiece and extensive *territoria*.[130] Their positioning was significant. Placed on opposite sides of the Po, they controlled the river at its juncture with the Adda. Their location allowed them to control communications between the In-

---

[127] Plut. *Marc.* 6.12; Polyb. 2.34.1–3.

[128] Polyb. 2.34–2.35.1; Plut. *Marc.* 7; F. Walbank (1957) pp. 210–11.

[129] Plut. *Marc.* 7; A. Degrassi (1947) p. 550. The Fasti Triumphales mention that Marcellus also triumphed *de Germanis*. The Alpine group of the Germani were later located well to the west beyond the Taurini. It is doubtful that Marcellus extended his campaigns that far west. It is, however, not impossible that he wanted to explore the headwaters of the Po.

[130] Polyb. 3.40.3–9; Asc. *Pis.* p. 3 (Clark); Livy 31.47.6; Livy *Per.* 20; Tac. *Hist.* 3.34; A. J. Toynbee (1965) vol. 2 pp. 265–68; E. T. Salmon (1970) pp. 67–69.

subres and the Boii while providing access to the allied tribes, the Cenomani and Anamares.[131] In addition, Placentia was able to keep a watch over the hills of Liguria, whose peoples had already assisted the Gauls against Rome. The land for the colonies was presumably seized from the Boii and the Cenomani respectively.

These colonies were not the first Roman settlements in the lands bordering the Boii. When the Boii rose against the Roman commissioners engaged in land division, the officials fled to Mutina. That community was described by Polybius as a Roman colony.[132] Mutina had a key location. It controlled the routes from Fiesole over the Apennines. From there the Romans could keep an eye on both the Boii around Bologna and the Ligurian hill tribes. Other less formal settlements developed. Polybius says that Romans fleeing the Gauls also took refuge at Vicus Tannetis, the site of Tannetum just southeast of Parma.[133] Livy mentions a Victumulae (perhaps a corruption of the Vicus Tannetis), which he describes as *id emporium Romanis Gallico bello fuerat, munitum inde locum frequentaverant adcolae mixti undique ex finitimis populis, et tum terror populationum eo plerosque ex agris compulerat.*[134] This was the beginning of the line of colonies and smaller settlements that would eventually flank the southwestern border of the Boii and separate them from their Ligurian allies in the Apennine mountains.

The Boii realized the significance of these settlements. Encouraged by the news of the impending arrival of Hannibal, they revolted against the land commissioners and settlers around Cremona and Placentia. Livy summarizes the motives well:

> Boii sollicitatis Insubribus defecerunt nec tam ob veteres in populum Romanum iras quam quod nuper circa Padum Placentiam Cremonamque colonias in agrum Gallicum deductas aegre patiebantur.[135]

> The Boii having sought the help of the Insubres defected, not so much on account of their old animosities toward the Roman people but because they had difficulty tolerating the colonies near the Po at Placentia and Cremona in the Gallic lands.

Settlers and land commissioners were pursued as far as Mutina, where they were captured by the Gauls. A relief army under the praetor L. Manlius was ambushed and decimated. It took the arrival of an-

[131] G. A. Mansuelli (1962) p. 41; G. Pontiroli (1967–68) p. 165.
[132] Polyb. 3.40.8–9. The description of Mutina at this time as a formal colony may be premature. E. T. Salmon (1970) pp. 105–6; P. Tozzi (1975) p. 48.
[133] Polyb. 3.40.13–14; K. Miller (1916) cols. 206–7.
[134] Livy 21.57.9–11.
[135] Livy 21.25.2–3.

other praetor, C. Atilius Serranus, followed shortly by the consul
P. Cornelius Scipio, to cow the Boii.[136]

The arrival of Hannibal in northern Italy could not have come at a
more critical time for the Romans. Native resistance had been crushed,
but the victories had not been so overwhelming that peace was ensured. The delicate stage of securing frontier control by new settlements had just begun. Native hostility had been aroused, and the
colonies and smaller settlements still needed protection. Traders drawn
to frontier emporia such as Victumulae probably added to frontier
tensions. The long process of informal Romanization had just begun.
The situation was fluid and ripe for exploitation by a man possessed
of Hannibal's genius in uniting diverse ethnic groups.

What is surprising is the limited use that Hannibal, and the Carthaginians in general, made of this opportunity. He made an early
attempt to win the support of the Insubres by defeating the mountain
Taurini who had been raiding their land.[137] Some Celts in Roman
military service, especially Boii, did desert to Hannibal. The Cenomani, however, remained loyal to Rome, and other Celts attempted
to be neutral.[138] Hannibal, angered by this lack of support, began
plundering Gallic territory, driving the Gauls into the arms of Rome.[139]
Soon the Carthaginian army marched south leaving the Romans an
uneasy peace in the *ager Gallicus*.

This shaky truce was shattered by the Roman defeat at Cannae. In
215 B.C. the consul designate, L. Postumius Albinus, was ambushed
and slain near Mutina, and his army was largely destroyed. The head
of the consul, suitably adorned with gold, was placed in the sacred
sanctuary of the Boii, an honor the Gauls bestowed upon the heads of
important people they had killed. The Romans, their resources strained
by recent disasters, were unable to respond to this defeat.[140]

The level of Roman control in the area during this crucial phase of
the Second Punic War must have been minimal. There are passing
references to Roman officials, but little is said of their accomplish-

[136] Polyb. 3.40.7–14; Livy 21.26.2, 21.39; H. H. Scullard (1973) pp. 42–43.

[137] Livy 21.39; App. *Hann.* 5–6.

[138] Polyb. 3.60.8–13 notes that Hannibal massacred the defeated Taurini. Polyb. 3.67.1–
7 has two thousand infantry and two hundred cavalry of the Keltoi desert after beheading some Romans. In Polyb. 3.68.8 the Celts provision Hannibal, while in Polyb.
3.69.5 the Celts between Po and Trebia are allied with Hannibal but negotiate with
Rome after Hannibal's raids.

[139] Livy 21.52.3–7.

[140] Livy 23.24.11–13, 23.25–26. On the importance of severed heads cf. Diod. 5.29.5;
G. A. Mansuelli and R. Scarini (1961) p. 284.

ments.[141] Placentia and Cremona did hold out, and in 206 B.C. the Romans managed to reinforce the colonies. Fortunately the Carthaginians, too, remained inactive. When in 205 B.C they began pursuing an imaginative strategy in northern Italy, the balance had already shifted toward Rome.

In 205 B.C. Mago, the brother of Hannibal, was sent to Savona on the Ligurian coast in an attempt to establish a Carthaginian beachhead.[142] His initial actions were directed toward winning support among the natives around Savona and destroying the important Roman base at Genoa.[143] Control of that stretch of Ligurian coast, however, provided access to important passes through the Apennines that had long been exploited by the Massilians and other traders.[144] Moving toward the interior, Mago summoned a massive durbar of Gauls and Ligurians and began to form a new tribal alliance against Rome with the Insubres as the central group. The Romans counterattacked with a powerful four-legion army. Mago was defeated and mortally wounded. He died while trying to remove the vestiges of his army to Carthage.[145]

The death of Mago ended the Carthaginian threat on the Tyrrhenian coast. But Mago had left Hamilcar—an officer who must be ranked with Sertorius as one of the great organizers of native forces—in the interior. Cut off from the coast and any effective Carthaginian aid, Hamilcar sustained for four years Gallic and Ligurian resistance to Rome. The core of his support came from the still unbroken Boii and Insubres. He also managed to win over other tribes including the Cenomani, who had remained loyal to Rome even during the darkest days of the Second Punic War.[146] The high point of his successes came in 200 B.C., when he managed to capture briefly the colony at Placentia. From there he went on to besiege Cremona.[147] Placentia was quickly retaken by the Romans, but in 199 B.C. the Insubres destroyed a major Roman army.[148]

Now the tide began to turn against Hamilcar and his Gallic allies.

[141] Livy 24.10.4 has M. Pomponius continue as propraetor in Gaul in 214 B.C. Livy 28.11.10–11 notes that Q. Mamilius Turrinus is sent in 206 B.C. to protect the repopulated colonies of Cremona and Placentia.
[142] Livy 28.46.7–14, 30.10; A. J. Toynbee (1965) vol. 2 pp. 267–68.
[143] Livy 28.46.8, 30.1.10.
[144] This Massilian influence in northern Italy is best reflected by the adoption of Massilian types on third-century B.C. Celtic coins. Cf. H. Rolland (1949).
[145] Livy 30.18–19.
[146] A. J. Toynbee (1965) vol. 2 pp. 268–69.
[147] Livy 31.10.1–2.
[148] Livy 31.10.2–7, 32.7.5–7.

The elders of the Cenomani were able to reassert their control over the restless younger warriors and return the tribe to its Roman allegiance. Two powerful consular armies were dispatched against the Gauls. In 197 B.C. Hamilcar was defeated in battle by C. Cornelius Cethegus, a Roman commander who had already proved his ability in frontier warfare by important victories in Spain. Hamilcar was captured along with several Gallic leaders and taken to Rome to participate in the triumph of Cethegus. The success was considered of sufficient importance in later Roman history to be included among the *elogia* in the forum of Augustus.[149]

The defeat of Hamilcar, combined with the collapse of Carthaginian resistance in Africa, removed the last danger of outside interference in cisalpina. It did not solve the Gallic problem immediately or restore frontier stability. In many ways the work of the 220s had been undone. The Boii were again fully aroused. They drew support from other Gallic tribes, such as the Insubres and the inland Ligurians. Placentia and Cremona remained isolated outposts, weakened physically and spiritually.[150] Most of the individual settlers and small pockets of Romanization in the Gallic border areas must have disappeared. It would take Rome six more years to reverse this situation and once more make its hold on the Po secure.

The new offensive started out with high hopes of rapid success. Both consuls of 196 B.C. were sent to Gaul.[151] L. Furius Purpurio had already fought with success in the area as praetor, while M. Claudius Marcellus was following in the footsteps of his famous father.[152] It was a team that combined experience with personal and family connections in a tribal area where such loyalties were important. The campaign was designed to follow up the victories of the previous year and further decimate the Insubres and the Boii. Marcellus, after an initial check at the hands of the Boii, managed to slip through their territory to the Po. There he used the newly recovered loyalty of the Cenomani to outflank the Insubres and attack the Como area, defeating a combined army of Insubres and Comenses.[153] Purpurio concentrated on distracting the forces of the Insubres and Boii until the initial mission of Marcellus had been completed. Then the two armies combined to attack *urbs ceteraque circa castella*. The oppidum at Felsina was cap-

---

[149] Livy 32.30.1–3, 32.29.6–32.30.13; A. Degrassi (1939) pp. 5–10; A. Degrassi (1947) p. 551; A. J. Toynbee (1965).

[150] Livy 37.46.9–10.

[151] Livy 33.36–37; Oros. 4.20.11.

[152] Livy 31.10–31.11.3, 31.21–31.22.3.

[153] Livy 33.37. Livy 33.36.4–5 identifies a Boian *regulus* who attacked Marcellus as Corolamus. In Livy 33.36.8–9 the Boii disperse *in castella sua vicosque*.

tured, and Livy could state optimistically that all the Gauls had surrendered except the *iuventutem* who had taken up arms for the purpose
of spoil and had fled into the recesses of the woods. The war was far
from over, but in seizing the center at Felsina and its dependent hill
forts, the Romans had broken up a concentration of Boian resistance.
Marcellus triumphed and the loot was considerable.[154]

The events of the next three years proved that the Romans' hopes
of a final pacification of the Gauls had been overly optimistic. In part,
unrest in places like Spain drew attention and resources elsewhere. In
addition, the Boii seem to have shifted their tactics to take advantage
of their often rough and wooded terrain and their dispersed settlement
pattern. In 195 B.C., while Cato was attempting to restore the Roman
frontier in Spain, L. Valerius Flaccus was ambushed in the *silva Litana*
near Mutina.[155] Although the Romans claimed a victory and the Boii
scattered to their villages, Flaccus was able to do little more than withdraw to the protection of Cremona and Placentia, where he spent time
repairing the damage of past wars. In the meantime, a Boian leader
named Dorulatus was stirring up resistance among the Insubres.[156]
Flaccus was forced to march north to Mediolanum to suppress this
new uprising. In 194 B.C. the consul Ti. Sempronius Longus was
drawn into battle with another Boian force led by the *regulus* Boio-
rix.[157] Again the combat was indecisive. The Romans fell back on
Placentia, and the Gauls retired to the interior of their own country.

By 193 B.C. the situation in northern Italy had deteriorated enough
for the senate to declare a state of *tumultus*. The Gallic problem was
compounded by the increasingly bold actions of the Ligurians, who
in cooperation with the Celts looted and burned their way to the very
walls of Placentia itself.[158] The seriousness of the problem required
that both consuls for 193 B.C. be assigned to the Gallo-Ligurian front.
Additionally, one of the consuls, L. Cornelius Merula, had assigned
as legates in his army two men of consular rank with Gallic combat
experience: M. Claudius Marcellus and Ti. Sempronius Longus.[159]
The pattern of the previous year was repeated. Merula attacked the
Boian territory. The Gauls withdrew before the advancing army, then

[154] Livy 33.36–37, quoting Valerius Antias and Claudius Quadrigarius. According to
Livy 33.37.9–12 Marcellus was awarded a triumph, although the details of the campaign
were unclear in the historical tradition. A. Degrassi (1947) p. 552; A. H. MacDonald
(1974) p. 49.

[155] Livy 33.43.4, 34.22, 34.56.10–11. Valerius received only two legions, since the
spirit of the Boii and Insubres had been broken.

[156] Livy 34.46.1; Oros. 4.20.15.

[157] Livy 34.46.4–34.48.1.

[158] Livy 34.56.10–11.

[159] Livy 35.5.1–2; T.R.S. Broughton (1951) p. 349.

regrouped and counterattacked near Mutina. The Romans claimed victory after a bloody battle, but no triumph was awarded to Merula.[160]

This battle proved to be more of a turning point than many initially thought. The Boii, especially, had sustained heavy losses in the battles of 195, 194, and 193 B.C. Livy claims that 14,000 warriors, 721 *equites*, and 3 *duces* fell in the clash at Mutina. In 194 B.C. eleven thousand Gauls were supposedly slain, and in 195 B.C. eight thousand.[161] While certainly exaggerated, these figures still show heavy loss in manpower. In addition, the losses in crops, cattle, and the portable wealth a Gallic aristocracy used to cement its position were considerable. We can presume that at no time was the Boian aristocracy united in its desire to resist Rome. The anti-Roman faction had dominated tribal politics during recent years. Now many of its leaders lay dead at Mutina, and the facade of unified resistance to Rome began to crumble.

In 192 B.C. the Romans launched both consular armies in a two-pronged attack against the Boii.[162] In the face of this new display of Roman power, defections to Rome among the ruling class of the Boii mounted. Livy describes the phenomenon in this manner:

> Primo equites eorum pauci cum praefectis, deinde universus senatus, postremo in quibus aut fortuna aut dignitas erat ad mille quingenti ad consules transfugerunt.[163]

> First of all, a few of the cavalryment with their commanders deserted to the consuls, then the whole senate and finally all those who had any fortune or social standing to the number of one thousand five hundred.

A class cleavage had appeared among the Boii, with those of higher wealth and status preferring to seek their fortune with Rome. These men brought only themselves and their retainers over to the enemy, however. The anti-Roman factions, weakened by losses and defections, still commanded widespread support among the ordinary Boian warriors. Only the wars of the following year would crush that.

191 B.C. saw the last great battles, and the defeat of the Boian resistance at the hand of P. Cornelius Scipio Nasica. The Boii made a formal *deditio* giving hostages and agreeing to surrender half of their territory.[164] This was presumably the best cleared land in the plain.

---

[160] Livy 35.4–5.
[161] Livy 34.22.1, 34.47.8, 35.5.13–14.
[162] Livy 35.22.3–4.
[163] Livy 35.22.4.
[164] Livy 36.38.5–7, 36.39.3–6, 40.11–14.

The centuriation lines along the route of the Via Aemilia stop at the hills.[165] The remaining Boii, whose male population consisted mainly of old men and young boys, were left the poorer, wooded terrain.[166] Appropriately, Scipio received a triumph that was celebrated with splendor. Even after years of warfare, the Gallic spoil was considerable.[167]

A long and bitter war had come to an end. In terms of losses, triumphs, and consular armies involved, it was one of the most important in Roman history.[168] Years of raids and ambushes had left a legacy of bitterness and revenge that only frontier conflicts can generate. Burned farms and ruined fortunes, atrocity and counteratrocity, created an atmosphere that boded ill for the conquered. The sense of relief and triumph that came after the final victory of Scipio is reflected in the temple at Civita Alba, mentioned above, which was probably erected at this time.[169] The mood of vengeance is illustrated by an episode of 192 B.C. One of the Boian nobles who had surrendered voluntarily to the Romans was murdered by the consul L. Quinctius Flamininus under especially sordid circumstances. The act was morally indefensible, politically senseless, and provocative. The anti-Boian feeling was so strong, however, and the power of the family of Flamininus so great that effective action was impossible. Justice had to wait until 184 B.C. and the censorship of Cato, when the Roman name was partly cleared by the expulsion of Flamininus from the senate.[170]

Their long resistance and the richness of the land they held sealed the fate of the Boii as a political entity. The Romans renewed their aim of turning most of the land up to the Po into an extension of Roman Italy. One half of the Boian tribal land had been confiscated after the final victory, and in 190 B.C. the native population was removed. The displaced Gauls were numerous enough for the Romans to summon strong reinforcements to the area.[171] The colonies of Placentia and Cremona, much devastated by the frontier warfare of the preceding three decades, were reinforced. Colonists who had left out

---

[165] R. Chevallier (1962).

[166] G. C. Susini (1965) pp. 155–63.

[167] Livy 36.40.6–7, 36.40.11–14; A. Degrassi (1947) p. 553. F. Tamborini (1950) p. 74 notes the absence of Gallic tombs dating after 250 B.C.

[168] A. J. Toynbee (1965) vol. 2 pp. 268–71.

[169] On the theme of Gallic struggle in sarcophagi from Chiusi and Volterra of the second century B.C. see F. H. Pairault-Massa (1978) pp. 197–98, 217–19.

[170] Livy 39.42.5–39.43.5; Cic. Cato 42; F. Münzer (1905) pp. 73–74; A. E. Astin (1978) pp. 78–80.

[171] Livy 37.2.5–6. A. J. Toynbee (1965) vol. 2 p. 272 suggests Brixellum as a new center for surviving Boii. G. DeSanctis (1967) p. 415.

of fear of living with Gallic neighbors could return.[172] New colonies
were founded at Bononia in 189 B.C. near the Etruscan and Gallic
centers of Felsina, and at Parma and Mutina in 183.[173] In 187 B.C. the
consul regularized the developing route between Ariminum and Placentia with the building of the road that bore his name,[174] and in 173
more *ager publicus* consisting of confiscated native land was divided *ad
viritim* among new settlers.[175]

These principal foundations were supported by a well-spaced in-
frastructure of smaller settlements, especially along the line of the Via
Aemilia. On the line of this road from Ariminum to Placentia were a
Forum Popili, a Forum Livii, a Faventia, a Forum Cornelii, a Lepidum Regium, a Fidentia, and a Florentia.[176] In other parts of the cispadane zone, Pliny lists a Forum Clodii, a Forum Licinii, and a Forum
Druentiorum.[177] Although lacking official colonial status, these smaller
settlements, often founded with the blessing of Roman commanders,
were important foci of social and economic activity in the area. One
of their roles was linking local market areas with the great trunk roads.
They also brought the Roman settlers into contact with the remnants

[172] Livy 37.46.9–37.47.2.

[173] Livy 37.57.7–9 (Bononia), 39.55.6–8 (Mutina and Parma); P. Tozzi (1975). D. C.
Scagliarini (1975) p. 159 notes the divergence of Via Aemilia at Bononia, suggesting
that the town came before the road. See R. Scarini (1970) pp. 38–39 for La Tène II
material found near Parma. On centuriation around Bologna see R. Chevallier (1962)
pp. 404–13.

[174] Livy 39.2.6–7, 39.2.10–11; D. C. Scagliarini (1975) p. 153.

[175] Livy 42.4.3–4.

[176] Pliny *HN* 3.115–16. *Forum Livii*: A. J. Toynbee (1965) vol. 2 pp. 662–63 dates
this to 191–183 B.C. and C. Livius Salinator. G. C. Susini (1965) p. 151 has it founded
next to the native center as part of a policy of accommodation and Romanization of
Gauls. P. A. Brunt (1971) pp. 571–72 considers the 188 B.C. date to be too early, and
suggests that the settlers were Umbri moving into vacated Boian land. *Forum Cornelii*:
A. J. Toynbee (1965) vol. 2 p. 667 dates this to 181 B.C. G. C. Susini (1965) p. 160
notes a Bona Dea dedication that has a Celtic association. *Not. Scav.* (1926) p. 40.
D. C. Scagliarini (1975) p. 151 sees a possible Sullan foundation in an effort to break
the power of major centers. P. A. Brunt (1971) pp. 572–73 also favors a later date.
Forum Novum: G. C. Susini (1965) p. 161 notes the presence of a Celtic-type oracular
shrine. The Vicarello Itinerary has between Placentia and Ariminum a Florentia, Lepidum Regium, Forum Cornelium, Faventia, and Forum Livii: J. Heurgon (1952). This
pattern of large primary urban frontier cities with smaller service centers has parallels
with the southern Russian frontier of the seventeenth and eighteenth centuries: D.J.B.
Shaw (1977).

[177] Pliny *HN* 3.115–16. *Forum Licinii*: A. J. Toynbee (1965) vol. 2 p. 669. It is perhaps
to be equated with Forum Gallorum. *Forum Clodii*: A. J. Toynbee (1965) vol. 2 p. 669,
who equates it with Fornovo di Taro, dates its foundation to 155 B.C. and relates it
more to the needs of Ligurian frontier.

of the native population and encouraged interaction among the diverse ecological zones of the Po plain and Ligurian foothills.[178]

Cato had listed 112 subgroups in the Boii tribe, but by the time of Pliny, they had all disappeared as political entities.[179] Symbolic of their disintegration was that the Boii, unlike the other main northern Italian Gallic tribes under Roman hegemony, never issued their own coinage. The nobles who had surrendered early to Rome presumably retained some of their land and wealth. Among the others, some may have fled over the Alps,[180] but those who remained probably led a marginal existence. Although the impoverishment of Celtic graves in the second century B.C. may be a general cultural phenomenon not limited to Italy, those in Italy do suggest a declining access to material wealth.[181] Yet some Celts remained. Evidence of their cults survived in the landscape, suggesting an ongoing native population, and traces of the Celtic language survived down to the Civil Wars.[182] The presence of a center like Forum Gallorum near the former Boian center at Felsina shows that a native population remained and the Romans were taking positive steps to provide them with a local focus of social and economic activity.[183]

The most optimistic reconstruction of Celtic survival suggests a marginal existence. Settlement of a formal and informal nature turned the Aemilia into an Italian land. This pattern ended on the banks of the Po. Beyond that river, the change in Roman policy and practice was striking. The tribal organization of the Insubres and Cenomani as well as that of the Veneti remained intact. There was almost no Roman colonization and little of the secondary settlement so common south of the river. This difference is important for understanding the development of later Italy. The origin and evolution of this policy will be followed in the next chapter.

---

[178] G.E.F. Chilver (1941) pp. 71–80.

[179] Pliny *HN* 3.116; P. A. Brunt (1971) pp. 191–92.

[180] Strabo 5.1.6; G. A. Mansuelli (1962) p. 193.

[181] F. Tamborini (1950) p. 74; V. Kruta (1978).

[182] App. *BCiv.* 3.47 speaks of the survival of the Celtic dialect in Aemilia. G. A. Mansuelli and R. Scarini (1961) p. 273; G. A. Mansuelli (1965) pp. 45–46; G. C. Susini (1965) pp. 153, 156 feels that the Roman policy of extermination has been exaggerated.

[183] A. J. Toynbee (1965) vol. 2 pp. 663–64.

CHAPTER 2

THE TRANSPADANE FRONTIER

By 191 B.C. the Boii had been subjugated, and the process of final Romanization of the Aemilia could begin. The Roman senate in 183 B.C. declared that the Alps were the *prope inexsuperabilem finem* of Italy.[1] The future form of Italy had been defined, and the frontier advanced to the natural border of the peninsula. The northern mountains were to serve partly as barrier and partly as filter, controlling the movement of new groups into Italy while at the same time allowing the continuation of the transmontane trade that had existed for centuries, if not for millennia. The tribes located between the Po and the mountains were to be left socially and politically intact to merge slowly into the Romanized peninsula. They formed the first line of defense for Italy. This frontier system of mountain barrier and buffer tribes that took shape during the first years of the second century B.C. remained basically operative until Caesar conquered Gaul and transformed the frontier geography of the Western Roman Empire.

The social, political, and economic situation in the transpadane zone differed radically from that found in the other two Italian frontier zones of cispadane Gaul and Liguria. In both Liguria and the Aemilia the Romans found an unstable and generally unsatisfactory frontier arrangement. Within the cispadane area the Romans demographically decimated and politically destroyed the recently arrived and still expanding Gallic groups. The region was then largely resettled and made into an extension of Roman Italy. The Ligurians of the mountains were contained, eliminated, or transported. The potential for stable political development among both peoples was limited, and the chance for real integration into the Roman system was slight.

Stability and a solid symbiotic relationship with the bordering mountain groups characterized the peoples across the Po. Some of the tribes had deep ethnic roots in the area and had developed contacts within and beyond the mountains, providing trade opportunities and effective lines of communication. More recent arrivals such as the Insubrian and Cenomanic Gauls had been in the area for several centuries, and had well-developed centers of population and subtle links with the mountain peoples. In general, the level of political and cul-

---

[1] Polyb. 3.54.2; Livy 39.54.12. Servius *ad Aen.* 10.13: "Alpes quae secundum Catonem et Livium muri vice tuebantur Italiam." A. Degrassi (1954) pp. 11–13; G. Barruol (1969) p. 86.

tural development was far superior to that of other northern frontier groups. This meant not only a stable population but also a leadership class on which Rome could depend and that could be integrated into the aristocratic Roman ruling system. With this solid base the Romans, with a minimum of military action and almost no demographic change, were able to create a stable frontier at the Alps and, by the first century B.C., turn the transpadane region into one of the most acculturated areas of Italy.

Unfortunately, the evidence for the Republican development of the transpadane area is scarce. The conquest and control of the area did not involve the continuous military activity that attracted the attention of the annalistic historians. Republican inscriptions are almost nonexistent. The archaeology of the area is rich in earlier, Iron Age sites associated with such cultures as the Golasecca around Como and Este in the Veneto and in imperial remains. But the crucial period of the Republic is the least represented archaeologically, or at least the least adequately studied. Some sites are probably buried under the alluvium of the Po and its tributaries. More significant, many of the important pre- and early Roman centers such as Mantua, Verona, Padua, and Milan were so successful that the early remains have been obliterated by imperial, medieval, and modern development.[2] Yet the situation is not totally bleak. In recent years a far clearer picture of pre-Roman cultural development has emerged, a picture essential for understanding Roman policy and action. More attention has been given to the Republican archaeological evidence, and the imperial remains have been scanned with increasing skill to extract information on preceding Republican developments.

One cannot understand the development of the transpadane frontier without a sense of its complex geography, which embraces a wide range of features from the Pannonian mountains on the east to the Maritime Alps on the west. On the south the region is defined by the Po River, which traverses most of the territory and has shaped much of the history of the area.[3] Its eastward flow links the whole valley more with the Adriatic than with the western coast of Italy. With

[2] G. A. Mansuelli (1963) p. 16. A. Radmilli (1963) p. 60 discusses alluviation in the Po valley. P. A. Brunt (1971) p. 178 notes that most of the Roman inscriptions from the area have been found in the hillside areas that flank the Po. L. B. Brizio (1967–68) p. 55 n.15 stresses the lack of Greek interest in the transpadane zone before the Romans.

[3] P. A. Brunt (1971) pp. 178–84; D. C. Scagliarini (1975) pp. 154–55. Polyb. 2.16.10-1 has the river navigable for two thousand stades up to Tanaro. By the time of Pliny (HN 3.123) it was navigable to Turin. S. Panciera (1972) p. 89 shows that Greek wine was being imported up the Po as far as Cremona by the first half of the second century B.C. G. A. Mansuelli (1971) p. 59 and Vitr. De Arch. 2.9.16 discuss lumber coming down the Po from the Alps. R. Chevallier (1980) provides a geographical overview of the area.

tributaries such as the Tanarus, Dora, and Ticino, which have their origins in the mountain valleys, the Po system has served as a link between mountain and transmontane peoples and those of the plain, funneling trade and population movements over long periods of time. Yet it is not the only river system. In the northeast smaller but still important rivers such as the Piave, the Tagliamento, and the Frigidus also connect the coast with the interior mountain passes.

Traditionally, the main population centers of the area have not been located down in the river plain, but in the more hilly country leading up to the mountains and their passes. These areas were more healthy, and they allowed the exploitation of a greater variety of local ecological zones, ranging from the plains through lower hills to the mountain pastures. They also provided easier access to the Alpine passes and the trade connections beyond. Important native centers such as Comum, Bergomum, Brescia, Verona, and Vicetia grew up in such locations. Even Padua with the Eugeneian hills immediately behind enjoys some of these advantages of a geographically mixed environment.[4]

Exceptions to this pattern of settlement development existed but are often explained by special circumstances. Cremona as a colony was really an artificial creation. Mantua apparently grew with the Etruscan trade and linked the Mincio valley with the Etruscan centers around Bologna. Trade also accounted for the development of such coastal settlements as Adria and, later, the Roman colony at Aquileia. Mediolanum, dominating the Lombard plain and having easy access to key mountain passes, is also something of an exception.

Mountain passes formed another geographical determinant in the region, linking the transpadana with a bewildering variety of areas. On the southwest the river valleys and mountain passes connected with the Tyrrhenian Sea and such important coastal centers as Savona and Genoa. Farther to the northwest the twin valleys of the Dora Riparia through Turin and Susa and the Dora Baltea through the Valle d'Aosta joined the Po to eastern France and the Rhone. The routes beyond Como and Verona tied the area to central Europe. On the eastern edge routes up the valley of the Tagliamento connected the Veneto with Noricum, while those up the Frigidus linked the same area with Slovenia. Each of these routes had been the focus of population movements and trade connections long before the arrival of the Romans. Their control was a key element in the development of a Roman frontier policy.

[4] Pastoralism was a major factor linking the different ecological zones. P. Agostinetti (1972) notes the large number of implements associated with sheep-raising found in the Ornavasso tombs. Strabo 5.1.12 comments on the importance of weaving at Patavium.

The geographical diversity of this territory was matched by its ethnic complexity. Mountain tribesmen, Gallic invaders, Greek and
Etruscan traders, and sophisticated indigenous groups were all part of
the mix. Few groups in Italy were more loyal to Rome than the Veneti, who inhabited the northeastern section of the transpadana. Through
the crisis of Telamon, the Second Punic War, and the Gallic rising of
the late third and early second centuries, this people did not waver in
its support and formed a keystone for local Romanization. Ethnic pride
and cohesion ran deep. Archaeologically, the origins of the Veneti lie
in the Este culture, which formed during the tenth century B.C. and
reached its most prosperous period from the sixth to the mid-fourth
century B.C.[5]

The most striking remains of the Este culture are the bronzes, especially the bucket-shaped situlae. These show connections with the
Bologna-area Villanovans to the southwest and with groups in Slovenia and Noricum east and north of the mountains.[6] The scenes embossed on these situlae, most of which date to the sixth and fifth centuries B.C., provide insight into the life of the Venetian aristocracy of
this period. Featured are military processions, banquets with musical
contests, and scenes of farming and the hunt. Pride in horsemanship,
both for cavalry and for chariots, is obvious. The Veneti remained
famous for horses, and horse cults played an important role in the
religion of the area.[7] Pride in family is evident in the long lineages
available from Este, some of which link the Venetian to the Roman
period.[8]

Centers that were later to become important Roman cities played
an important part in the life of the Veneti. At Padua there is continuity of settlement going back to the Bronze Age. By the fourth century B.C. it had a considerable concentration of population and urban
characteristics.[9] Livy records with the pride of a native son the fact
that the Venetians of Padua had thwarted the attempt by Cleonymus
of Sparta to conquer the area in 302 B.C. He portrays the Padua of
the period as the center of a well-armed and organized people, with a
series of dependent villages surrounding the main settlement and a

[5] D. Randall-MacIver (1927) p. 5; L. Barfield (1972) pp. 116–26.

[6] J. Kastelic (1965); G. A. Mansuelli (1967); L. Bonfante (1979).

[7] G. A. Mansuelli (1964) pp. 93–95; L. Braccesi (1971) pp. 4–6. G. Colonna (1979)
p. 495 notes that horse burials of the Este period have been discovered. The Greek poet
Alcman (1.51) writing in the sixth century B.C. already spoke of the horses of the
Veneto. Strabo 5.1.9 mentions the custom of sacrificing a white horse to Diomedes,
which was still being practiced in his own time.

[8] *Padova preromana* (1976) p. 35.

[9] *Padova preromana* (1976) pp. 6–9, 12–14. See also G. Ghirandini (1901) on palaeo-
venetic inscription at Padua.

land rich in grain and cattle. Long after the event, dedications and
festivals celebrated that victory over Cleonymus. Sculptured stelae from
Padua show aristocratic funerary processions and scenes of combat
against the Celts.[10] Este was a similar community. Its large cemeteries
and evidence of noble families indicate a flourishing civic aristocracy.[11]

One of the most striking qualities of the Veneti, and a trait that
made them especially useful and appealing to Rome, was their sense
of cultural independence and self-confidence. Although they adopted
an Etruscan-derived alphabet, they continued speaking their Italic language into the Roman period.[12] The Veneti had some trading contacts
with the Greek emporium of Spina and with Etruscan Bologna, but
they imported relatively few Etruscan and Greek goods and continued
to develop their own distinct culture.[13] By the fourth century B.C.,
however, the Gauls were having a strong influence on the Venetian
culture of the Este IV period.[14] Polybius in the second century B.C.
described the Veneti as indistinguishable from the Gauls in all but
language. Nevertheless, images of warriors and scenes of Celtomachy,
as well as scattered historical references, show a tradition of resistance
to the Gauls, and archaeological evidence suggests Venetian cultural
continuity.[15]

One source of this cohesion was obviously the native religion. Important cult centers have been found at the shrine of Reiteia at Este
and at other sanctuaries at Montebelluna, Lagole, and Magre. They
attest to the vital role that religion played in Venetian life.[16] Female
deities and the healing properties of water were among the important
elements in the religion. Many of these shrines continued to be in use
into the Roman period.[17]

Also making the Veneti valuable to the Romans was their tradition
of trade contacts across the mountains. The world of the situlae is one

---

[10] Livy 10.2; Strabo 5.1.7. On the growing evidence for the Veneti at Padua see
Padova preromana (1976) pp. 16, 25–36, 303.

[11] M. S. Beeler (1956); F. R. Ridgeway (1979) pp. 424–53.

[12] C. B. Pascal (1964) pp. 103ff. notes inscriptions in the language found as far west
as Vicenza.

[13] This resistance to Greek acculturation can be seen in items such as the red-figure
vase illustrated in a Venetian style: G. Riccioni (1962). For Venetic objects at Spina see
P. E. Arias (1962).

[14] G. A. Mansuelli (1964) p. 160; C. B. Pascal (1964) p. 87. M. Lejeune (1954) pp.
136–37 discusses the large number of Celtic names attested at Lagole.

[15] Polyb. 2.18.3, 2.24.7–8; R. Cessi (1957) pp. 185–86 fig. 57; G. A. Mansuelli (1964)
p. 69.

[16] M. Lejeune (1954); R. Battaglia (1957) pp. 140–50; C. B. Pascal (1964) pp. 113,
189; G. A. Mansuelli (1964) p. 94.

[17] Suet. *Tib.* 14; M. Lejeune (1954) p. 121; G. A. Mansuelli (1965) pp. 43–45; C. B.
Pascal (1964).

that embraces Noricum and Slovenia as well as the Venetia. Venetian shrines at such places as Lagole on the Piave show their penetration well into the mountains, and their influence is apparent among mountain peoples such as those of the Santa Lucia culture.[18] These groups were ideal potential collaborators with the Romans in establishing a sensible frontier policy in the northeast of Italy.

While the high period of situla production had passed by the early fourth century, there is no reason to assume that the Venetians had lost their basic cultural and military vigor. The repulse of Cleonymus came at the end of the fourth century, and the Venetians evidently brought significant aid to Rome during the campaign of Telamon. Embossed plaques and votive finds of the late fourth and third centuries from Venetian sanctuaries have a strong military iconography.[19] It was the kind of friendly local strength that was most pleasing to the Romans.

The second strong cisalpine cultural tradition north of the Po was that of the Golasecca. In a period from the late thirteenth to the eighth century B.C., this culture evolved in the subalpine lake area above Milan.[20] Linguistically, the Golasecca culture is probably to be identified with the later Lepontic language group.[21] A series of rich wagon graves found in the Golasecca area dates from the late eighth to the early fifth century B.C.[22] They recall the Hallstatt burials on the other side of the Alps, and it is tempting to regard them as belonging to local chieftains who accumulated wealth by controlling the transalpine trade.[23] It should be noted, however, that these graves generally predate the Etruscan use of the Alpine trade routes. Any trade would relate to more northern Italian needs.[24]

The phase of the Golasecca culture that most interests the student of Romanization is that from the early fourth century B.C. onward. Unfortunately, it is also the phase least documented and least studied. The custom of rich burials had long since ceased. Nevertheless, the Golasecca culture of the fifth and early fourth centuries B.C. was a dynamic one.[25] Finds indicate that these people were increasingly influenced by the Gallic groups that were coming over the Alps to settle

[18] L. Barfield (1972) p. 125.

[19] Livy 10.2.9–15; A. Callegari (1938); G. Fogolari (1956).

[20] L. Pauli (1971) pp. 48–52; L. Barfield (1972) pp. 127–36; F. R. Ridgeway (1979) pp. 453–85.

[21] J. Whatmough (1933) pp. 65–73.

[22] D. Randall-MacIver (1927) pp. 69ff.; L. Barfield (1972) pp. 129–34; L. Pauli (1971) pp. 98–116.

[23] L. Barfield (1972) pp. 133–34; N. Negroni Catacchio (1975–76) pp. 459–60.

[24] N. Negroni Catacchio (1975–76) pp. 450–58.

[25] F. R. Ridgeway (1979) pp. 473–82.

in the Lombard plain.[26] When the Romans first entered the area during their assault on Mediolanum in 221 B.C., they found the people of the Como area allied with the Insubres, but ethnically and politically distinct.[27] This independence is corroborated by the local artifact tradition, which includes native pottery with Latin graffiti on it, and by the persistence of the Lepontic language in the area. Again the Romans realized the importance of this strong ethnic tradition. They encouraged local client rulers and paid special attention to the settlement around Como.[28]

The people of the Veneto and Como areas had strong roots in the transpadane zone. The main intrusive element in the centuries preceding the arrival of the Romans was the Celts. Their infiltration probably began slowly during the late sixth century. Certainly by the early fourth century the Gauls were well established in the territory between Milan and Brescia.[29] The archaeological evidence, though gradually progressing in quality and quantity, is still sorely inadequate. Especially unfortunate is the lack of Gallic remains from the great Celtic oppidum at Milan. Nevertheless, the fragmentary information we do have from the literary and archaeological record suggests that by the time the Romans crossed the Po during the third century B.C., the transpadane Gauls had reached a much higher level of political, social, and economic organization than their kinsmen to the south.[30]

First in importance among the Celtic tribes were the Insubres, and the most important Celtic center north of the Po was their oppidum at Milan. Strabo described it as having been only a village during the period when the Insubres were independent. But Milan had been the

[26] N. Negroni Catacchio (1975–76) pp. 461–66 sees Celtic influence from the sixth century B.C. in northern Italy but no actual Gallic presence before the fourth century B.C.

[27] At Como they had developed an oppidum, with the Ca' Morta cemetery located below. There was a heavy concentration of Golasecca II–III period material. Ca' Morta was used until the first century B.C. The inscription found at Prestino near Como of second-century B.C. date is probably Gallic: F. Rittatore Vonwiller (1962). F. Rittatore Vonwiller (1975–76) pp. 548–52 notes Attic pottery recently found in the Como area. M. C. Tibiletti Bruno (1966) pp. 279ff.

[28] J. Whatmough (1933). A. Pautasso (1975–76) p. 474 notes that three Lepontic coin types with legends Anarekartos, Toutiopouos, and Rikoi all have been found within a fifty kilometer radius of Lugano. Anarekartos appears to be early. The Rikoi coin types date to the first century B.C. *Popoli e Civilta* (1980) vol. 4 p. 267 describes native pottery with Latin graffiti.

[29] Just *Epit.* 20.5.8 identifies Mediolanum, Comum, Brixia, Verona, Bergamum, Tridentum, and Vicentia as Gallic foundations. Ptol. 1.27; G. A. Mansuelli (1965) pp. 11–12; L. Barfield (1972) pp. 149–50.

[30] Polybius notes that the Gauls north of the Po had gained sufficient prosperity for the Alpine tribes to consider it worthwhile to raid them.

central focus of Roman campaigns to subdue the Insubres and it grew rapidly under Roman domination into a great city, suggesting that the Gauls had developed an important oppidum there.[31] Celtic Mediolanum was quite possibly similar to such transalpine oppida as the Heuneberg. According to legend, it was founded by the Celtic chieftain Bellovesus during the first period of Gallic settlement in northern Italy. The location allowed it to dominate the surrounding Lombard plain and to tap trade routes over the Alps. Mediolanum prospered under the Republic and, by the time of Vergil, was the chief educational center north of the Po.[32] The limited sources allow us to say little about the social, economic, and political organization of the Insubres, but they do mention specific chieftains who were probably much like the warrior chief whom Marcellus defeated in single combat.[33]

The other principal transpadane Gallic tribe was the Cenomani. Their center was at Brescia, and they were the neighbors of the Veneti. Cultural influences passed between the two groups.[34] This close connection with the Veneti is reflected in their political loyalties. Unlike the Insubres, the Cenomani willingly joined the Roman cause, no doubt in part out of fear of the growing power of the Insubres to the west and of the Boii south of the Po.[35]

The base on which the Romans built their power and their frontier structure in the transpadane zone was the indigenous Veneti on the east, the well-settled Gallic groups of Cenomani and Insubres on the west, and some friendly Alpine and subalpine groups such as the Lepontii around the Lombard lakes. But two more groups—the Etruscans and the Greeks—must be considered in order to understand the development of this area before the Romans.

Etruscan influence began to affect the peoples across the Po during the fifth century B.C., as the Tuscan traders expanded their connections with the newly emerging La Tène groups across the Alps. The mechanisms of this trade are uncertain, as are its exact routes.[36] Only two transpadane Etruscan centers are mentioned in the literature.[37]

---

[31] Livy 5.34; Strabo 5.1.6; Plut. *Marc.* 7.5. A. Calderini (1938) pp. 13–25 notes Bronze Age as well as Iron Age finds. J. Collis (1976); D. Nash (1976).

[32] Polyb. 2.34.10; Livy 5.34.9; Strabo 5.1.6; Plut. *Marc.* 7; Just. *Epit.* 20.5.7; Amm. Marc. 15.9.2; Isid. *Etym.* 15.1.57; C. Jullian (1908) vol. 1 pp. 286ff.; A. Calderini (1938) pp. 13–34; P. Vallette (1944). On Vergil studying at Mediolanum see T. Frank (1922) pp.15–17.

[33] Plut. *Marc.* 7.1–3.

[34] G. A. Mansuelli (1965) pp. 11–12, 18.

[35] Strabo 5.1.9 on loyalty of Cenomani; P. Tozzi (1972) pp. 102–3.

[36] P. S. Wells and L. Bonfante (1979); P. Wells (1980a), (1980b).

[37] Dion. Hal. *Ant. Rom.* 13.11; Strabo 5.1.10; Plut. *Vit. Cam.* 15.

The first was Mantua, which is just north of the river. This city was proud of its Etruscan origins. Historical references and archaeological finds suggest lingering Etruscan elements among an increasingly Gallic-influenced population down to the Roman conquest.[38] The second center was the mysterious Melpum, possibly located near Milan or Como and destroyed by the Gauls in the early fourth century B.C[39] Another Etruscan center was recently located at Forcello, southeast of Mantua, and scattered Etruscan finds elsewhere include an Etruscan-style tomb near Bergamo.[40] The Etruscan-derived alphabet that was widely used in the transpadane area is an even stronger indicator of this influence. Still, the Veneti seem to have resisted to some extent the Etruscan and Greek influences. The arrival of the Gauls, a movement that ironically may have been stimulated by the growing Etruscan transalpine trade, marked the end of any real Tuscan hope of penetrating the area. Melpum fell and even the Etruscans at Mantua increasingly merged with the local Gallic population.[41]

Greek cultural influence on the northern Padane area before the Romans was funneled mainly through the trading emporia of Spina and Adria.[42] The ancients attributed the foundation of Spina to a variety of people. It began receiving Greek goods by the last quarter of the sixth century B.C., and flourished as a trading center during the fifth century B.C.[43] The identity Spina felt with the mainland Greek world is expressed by its building a treasury at Delphi. The massive finds of Greek vases around Spina show the volume of the exchange that connected the city with both the north and the transapennine Etruscan zone around Felsina.[44]

[38] Verg. *Aen.* 10.198–203; Pliny *HN* 3.19.130; Ptol. 3.1.27; Servius *ad Aen.* 10.201. A. M. Tamassia (1970) pp. 15–17 notes the presence of Attic red-figure pottery at Mantua. Pottery of the fourth to the second centuries shows connections with Spina and Adria. A. M. Tamassia (1970) pp. 33ff. notes Etruscan names at Mantua in the third and second centuries B.C. P. Tozzi (1972) pp. 64–66 comments on the limited number of Etruscan finds around Mantua and notes several Gallic finds. C. B. Pascal (1964) p. 131 and *CIL* 1.2 pp. 253, 337 discuss the festival of the Gallic deity Epona at Mantua. M. Gordon (1934) p. 4 notes Etruscan associations of the family of Vergil. G. A. Mansuelli (1965) pp. 9–10; A. M. Tamassia (1967) pp. 366–78.

[39] Pliny *HN* 3.125.

[40] L. B. Brizio (1967–68) pp. 53–54; M. Hummler et al. (1983).

[41] G. Colonna (1974a) pp. 9–11 stresses that the survival of Mantua may have led to the exaggeration of the Etruscan position north of the Po in later legend. R. De Marinis (1978) pp. 91–94 discusses the large third-century B.C. Gallic cemetery at Carzeghetto between Mantua and Cremona.

[42] L. Braccesi (1971).

[43] Strabo 5.1.7, 9.3.8; Pliny *HN* 3.16.120; N. Alfieri and P. E. Arias (1958); G. A. Mansuelli (1965) pp. 12–13, 19–20.

[44] N. Alfieri and P. E. Arias (1958). S. Panciera (1972) pp. 83–84 dates main trade at Spina to 480–400 B.C.

The origins of Adria are also uncertain. Its location, just north of the mouth of the Po, suggests a Venetian foundation. And yet Greek imports were frequent by the early fifth century B.C. By the mid-fifth century there was a decline in Greek contacts, but these revived again in the early fourth century with the growing interest of the Syracusan Dionysius I in the northern Adriatic area.[45] By the third century B.C. the town had a mixed population, with Etruscans, Gauls, and Veneti all living and trading there.[46] The third-century horse and chariot burial discovered at Adria illustrates the problem of identifying ethnic groups. The burial custom is archaic. It may represent the survival of old-fashioned aristocratic practices among the Etruscans or Veneti, or a fresh barbarian element coming in with the Gauls.[47] The presence of the mixed population shows the continuing importance of Adria as a trading center. The spread of black-glaze pottery from Adria up the Po to places such as Bergamo and the centers around the subalpine lakes demonstrates that this role continued into the early Roman period.[48]

When the Romans first penetrated this area during the 220s, they quickly grasped the potential of the diverse native groups for forming buffers within the emerging frontier system. Contacts with the Veneti must have existed well before the campaign of Telamon, when they rendered significant aid to the Romans. It is likely that the Veneti were thought of similar to the way the Greeks were at Massilia; as non-Gauls in Celtic territory, they could serve as intermediaries and sources of information.[49] Like the Massiliotes, the Veneti felt themselves under increasing pressure from a dynamic and expanding Gallic population and welcomed the intervention of Rome.

The Romans first crossed the Po in 224 B.C. These campaigns have already been discussed, but the basic facts should now be situated in a transpadane context. The Romans gained access to the Po through an alliance with the Anamares near Clastidium.[50] This association not only allowed them to threaten the southern flank of the Insubres but helped protect the route over the Ligurian mountains from Genoa to

---

[45] L. Braccesi (1971) pp. 57–60. On Dionysius and the Adriatic coast see G. A. Mansuelli (1965) pp. 20, 23 and L. Braccesi (1971) pp. 100–1.

[46] G. Fogolari and G. B. Pellegrini (1958) p. 158 note the number of Venetic inscriptions at Adria. They date to the third century B.C. or later. The authors see Veneti at Adria from its foundation.

[47] G. Fogolari (1940) pp. 440–42; M. Zuffa (1978) p. 150.

[48] G. Fiorentini (1963).

[49] Polyb. 2.18.3, 2.24; F. Cassola (1972b) pp. 48–53. G. A. Mansuelli (1965) pp. 20–21 relates the rise of the Antenor cult in Venetian territory to Roman connections and notes possible similarities in the strategic position of Massilia and Venetia.

[50] Polyb. 2.32.1–3; A. J. Toynbee (1965) vol. 2 pp. 264–65. U. Ewins (1952) p. 56 notes the geographical importance of Clastidium.

the Po. Perhaps not coincidental is the involvement of a consul of the
Furius family in these wars and the foundation of a center named
Camillomagus among the Anares.[51] The Romans, unable to force the
river at this point, had to move northeast and attack the Insubres from
the territory of the Cenomani.[52] These campaigns culminated in 221
B.C., with the capture of Mediolanum and the advance to Comum.[53]
The Insubres made their submission.[54] In 220 B.C. the consuls gain
campaigned as far as the Alps. The sources also mention that Roman
sovereignty was peacefully established over many peoples. This suggests that the Romans were beginning to establish friendly relations
with the smaller subalpine groups, with the aim of developing a deep
buffer zone on the mountain frontier.[55]

In 219 B.C. a colony was founded at Cremona, just across the Po in
the territory of the Cenomani.[56] At least six thousand families were
involved. Although the initial years of the colony were stormy and
the Romans had to send massive reinforcements in 190 B.C., the inhabitants over time developed good relations with the Gauls.[57] It was
not by accident that the cardo of the town was aligned with the Via
Brixia, which led to the Cenomanic center at Brescia thirty-four kilometers away. The colonists mingled with the Gallic natives, and Tacitus, in discussing the city, could remark that *adnexu conubiisque gentium
adolevit floruitque*.[58]

This initial program of pacification was disrupted by the invasion
of Hannibal. The relative failure of Hannibal to exploit the insecure
situation in the north has already been discussed. Local legend claimed
that the Veneti provided Rome with military assistance during the
crisis.[59] But the arrival of the Carthaginian agent Hamilcar led to a
general revolt north as well as south of the Po, drawing in the local
Cenomani along with the restless Insubres. In 199 B.C. the Insubres

[51] K. Miller (1916) col. 232.

[52] Polyb. 2.32.4.

[53] Polyb. 2.34; Plut. *Marc.* 6–8; Frontin. *Str.* 4.5.4. F. Coarelli (1978) p. 108 mentions
the find of a helmet possibly associated with this combat.

[54] Livy 33.36.9–15; A. Degrassi (1947) pp. 551–52.

[55] Zonaras 8.20.

[56] Polyb. 3.40.4–6; G. Pontiroli (1967–68); P. Tozzi (1972) pp. 9–22. Tac. *Hist.* 3.34.1
describes the colony as a *propugnaculum adversus Gallos trans Padum*, using language similar to that which Cicero employed in the *Pro Fonteio* (13) in describing the Roman
colony at Narbo. P. Tozzi (1972) p. 9 argues for a settlement of twelve thousand families.

[57] Livy 37.46.10–11; P. A. Brunt (1971) p. 196; P. Tozzi (1972) pp. 19, 36, 40.

[58] Tac. *Hist.* 3.34. On the alignment of the cardo with Via Brixia see G. Pontiroli
(1967–68) pp. 183, 193–94, 198.

[59] Sil. *Pun.* 8.604 has Veneti fighting with the Romans at Cannae.

destroyed the army of the praetor Cn. Baebius Tamphilus.[60] The Romans, deeply involved with Philip of Macedon, had to wait until 197 B.C. before mounting an effective counterattack. This was entrusted to the consul C. Cornelius Cethegus, a hardened veteran of the wars in Spain.[61] He played effectively on political and generational differences among the Cenomani and won back their loyalty to Rome. Hamilcar and his allied Gauls were defeated, and the military threat ended. The gratitude felt by the colonists of Placentia and Cremona for their rescue from captivity and the general restoration of order is shown by their participation in the triumph of Cethegus.[62]

The Cenomani apparently surrendered under reasonably favorable terms and received light punishment. They are represented as still being armed in 187 B.C. and on good terms with Rome.[63] C. Cornelius Cethegus may have attempted to secure the Pax Romana as well as extend the sphere of influence of his family by establishing familial ties with the *principes* of the Cenomani. Name distribution in the transpadane area shows a concentration of Cornelii appearing on the inscriptions from the Brescia-Verona area, the land of the Cenomani.[64]

The victories of Cethegus did not completely restore the frontier zone. In 196 B.C. M. Claudius Marcellus attacked the Como area, defeating a combined Gallic and Coman army. Como was captured, and twenty-eight castella in the foothills of the Alps surrendered. Listed among the booty were 732 wagons, an item which recalls the wagon burials of earlier Celtic and Golaseccan days.[65] In 194 B.C. the proconsul L. Valerius Flaccus had to fight the Insubres.[66] This campaign apparently resulted in the final subjugation of the Insubres, for they do not appear again as antagonists in the continuing war with the Boii.

By this time, the Romans had made the fundamental decision that the transpadane area was to be treated very differently from the *ager Gallicus* to the south. First of all, much of the land was held by allies of Rome or peoples whose relations with Rome had been on the whole friendly. The only tribe that might have received the treatment accorded the Senones and the Boii was the Insubres. But their resistance to Rome had not been nearly as prolonged as the Boii, and their level of cultural development was higher. Moreover, they could be an important element in the new frontier system that the Romans were

---

[60] Livy 32.1.2–6, 32.7.5–8.
[61] Livy 32.28.9, 32.29.5, 32.30.4–13, 33.22.4–33.23.3
[62] Livy 33.23.1–2; A. Degrassi (1947) p. 551.
[63] Livy 39.3.1–3.
[64] *CIL* 5.1 for Brixia (pp. 440–507) and for Verona (pp. 328–90).
[65] Livy 33.36.9–15.
[66] Livy 34.46.1.

creating. The decision reported by Cato that the Alps were to be the boundary of Italy had presumably already been made. The Romans certainly realized the complexities of controlling the Alpine area itself and preventing movement through the mountains by transalpine peoples. Conquest of the Alps would have been difficult. Even if it had been accomplished, the Romans would have been left with the task of policing the mountains themselves and controlling groups located on their northern slopes. Instead, the friendship or at least the relative passivity of the mountain tribes left the Romans with an acceptable first line of defense. The main tribes of northern Italy, such as the Insubres, had developed long-standing symbiotic relations with the Alpine groups. They also had contacts beyond the Alps. These could not only provide intelligence but help to develop trade, an important consideration in the increasingly commerce-oriented Italy of the second century B.C. The best course was to leave the tribal groups intact.

The first significant decision seems to have been not to colonize the transpadane zone. Cremona near the Po and Aquileia in the far east were the only colonies founded there. This contrasts sharply with the large number of new or reinforced colonies located south of the Po during this same time. Nor were systems of *ad viritim* land settlements like those Flaminius had encouraged in the Aemilia attempted. The evidence for informal Romanized Italian emigration and settlement in the transpadana is ambiguous. Italian names are present, but many of them may represent settlers who went there during the colonizing of the Civil War period.[67] Some land must have been seized from rebellious tribes such as the Insubres and Cenomani. And yet there is no tradition of social unrest arising from land confiscation and displacement like that found in cispadane and transalpine Gaul.[68] Many of the Italians and Romans who did come must have been merchants and traders who served the needs and stimulated the tastes and appetites of the rapidly Romanizing ruling groups of northern Italy.

Little is known about the peace treaties with the natives. Presumably provisions were established for tribute. The Insubres were apparently prohibited from obtaining the Roman citizenship, and the Cenomani were allowed to keep their arms, a necessary provision if they were to serve as an effective frontier defense. Weapons found in graves of the second and first centuries B.C. demonstrate this ongoing military tradition among the Gauls.[69] Rebellious leaders and perhaps even some clan and subtribal units that appeared to have the potential

[67] E. Rotti (1967–68); P. A. Brunt (1971) pp. 196–97.

[68] P. A. Brunt (1971) pp. 196–98.

[69] Cic. *Balb.* 14.32; N. Degrassi (1945); L. B. Brizio (1967–68) pp. 57–58. E. A. Arslan (1978) pp. 82–84 mentions weapons in local graves.

for rebellion were undoubtedly removed. Pliny mentions a group called the Caturiges who are described as *Insubrum exules*, suggesting that the Romans applied a policy of selective forced migration similar to that used later in Liguria.[70]

Efforts were made to draw the natives into the Roman system. These involved not only the formal agreements between the tribes and Rome but also the informal links between Roman and native aristocrats that were the basis of control in this prebureaucratic Roman world. These attachments would then serve as the means of encouraging Romanization on the economic, social, and cultural level. The evidence we have for the transpadana suggests that these efforts were successful. Since our sources are so fragmentary, however, the task of tracing the process proves difficult. Still, the effort must be made. The two primary sources of information we have for this purpose are the inscriptions and the coins.

Most of the Latin inscriptions found in the transpadana date to the Empire.[71] But certain items in them, especially the family names, reflect traditions going back to the Republic and in some cases even the pre-Roman period. With caution they may be used to reconstruct some aspects of Roman policy in the years immediately following the conquest. One feature that is especially striking is the frequency with which the names of great Republican families occur. The most popular are the Valerii (by far the most common), Cornelii, Cassii, Claudii, and Vibii, with Caecilii and Domitii not far behind. It is known that leading natives in different parts of the Empire began taking the names of important Roman families during the second and first centuries B.C.[72] It is also known that one must approach the study of these names with caution, since factors other than the presence of a consular Republican official could account for the appearance of a particular name. Nevertheless, as I have argued elsewhere for Spain, I believe that the distribution of names can be used to trace the development of Roman influence in a particular area.[73]

Certain general observations should be made at the outset. Some centers are particularly rich in inscriptions with Republican high-status names, while others lack them altogether. The cities best repre-

[70] Pliny *HN* 3.125; J. Prieur (1968) pp. 53–54; J. Heurgon (1974) pp. 246–47.

[71] The earliest datable Latin inscription from Milan is A.D. 29: P. G. Ucelli (1967–68) p. 109; E. Ratti (1967–68).

[72] G. A. Mansuelli (1961) p. 117 sees the attested Cornelii, Valerii, and others as Romanized natives of the second and first centuries B.C. L. B. Brizio (1967–68) pp. 85–89 discusses the families of Bergamo.

[73] On the use of this method in general see S. Dardaine (1969–70); R. C. Knapp (1978); S. L. Dyson (1980–81).

sented by these names are those of what might be called the central
frontier, especially Verona and Brixia, and to a lesser extent Mediolanum.[74] Aquileia must be excluded from a study of this kind, since
its commercial activity and colonial origin meant it attracted people
from many sections of Italy. Far fewer names come from the old centers south of the Alpine frontier, such as Mantua, Cremona, Ateste,
and even Patavium. Of the Augustan settlements, only Turin yields
a large number. Some of these differences may be attributable to collecting in the various centers. Yet it is striking that older cities like
Mantua and Ateste with strong local family traditions produce fewer
names than the emerging centers that had strong associations with the
tribal Gallic populations and their tradition of war leaders and personal loyalty.

A few of the principal families may be examined in greater detail.
Three *gentes* strongly associated with the early conquests across the Po
were the Claudii Marcelli, the Cornelii, and the Valerii. Claudius is,
of course, a difficult name to use for this purpose since it also has
imperial connections and was taken by many imperial freedmen. But
the cognomen Marcellus (with variations) is common in the area.[75] In
contrast, the Cornelii have clear Republican associations, and members of the family played a key role in the conquest and organization
of the area in 222, 199, and 197 B.C. Cornelian inscriptions are common at Brixia and Verona, and almost absent from the cities near the
Po and from the centers of the Veneto, with the exception of Aquileia.[76]

Valerii are the most numerous in the area. However, the name Valerius, which is common in other provinces, poses problems for the
historian attempting to reconstruct client relationships. The frequency
with which the name appears on inscriptions sometimes outweighs the
known influence of the family in a particular region, suggesting the
nomen may have had nonfamily associations for the natives.[77] The
Valerian pattern in northern Italy is similar to that of the Cornelii,
with the difference being that more Valerii are found in the Milan-
Como area. Again, there are few Valerii in the Veneto outside of
Aquileia and in the centers nearer the Po. The presence of important
Valerii in the province in the late Republic is shown by the family of
the poet Catullus at Verona.[78] The name, with its martial quality,

[74] In part this is certainly due to the different recovery ratio of inscriptions found in
different areas: P. A. Brunt (1971) p. 178.

[75] *CIL* 5 index for Marcellus and Marcella.

[76] L. B. Brizio (1967–68) pp. 81, 85–86 notes the number of Cornelii near Bergamo.

[77] R. C. Knapp (1978) p. 191.

[78] *CIL* 5 index for Valerius. On the family of Catullus see G. A. Mansuelli (1961).

must have appealed to the Celts. It should not be forgotten, though, that it was L. Valerius Flaccus who in 194 B.C. completed the pacification of the Insubres.

The families less well represented, such as the Caecilii and Cassii, have some of the same general distribution patterns, as well as a few particular ones. Cassii are almost absent from Brixia, which produces large numbers of most other principal Republican names, but are abundant in Verona and have a definite concentration in the eastern part of the transpadana.[79] Perhaps most striking is the relative absence of Pompeii, especially considering the role that Pompeius Strabo played in advancing the cause of Roman citizenship in the north. Pompeii are thinly scattered over the area, and none are found at the obviously Pompeian center of Laus Pompeia.[80] This poor Pompeian showing may be in part because by the first century B.C. many of the native aristocrats had already made their Roman client associations, and they reflected this when assuming citizenship and choosing their family name.

Also associated with the first years of the establishment of the Roman hegemony across the Po is the development of a native coinage. A silver coinage based on types derived from Massilia appeared in parts of northern Italy during the second century B.C. and remained in use until the first century B.C.[81] The derivation from Massilian types is interesting, for there is little other archaeological evidence for an active trade from the Tyrrhenian Sea through the Ligurian passes to the Po. The evidence of the coinage, however, suggests that contacts may have been more frequent than the trade objects suggest and may help to explain the actions of the Carthaginian agents Hamilcar and Mago in Liguria and the Po area at the close of the Second Punic War. The adoption of a common coin type, albeit with variations, suggests a world of shared social, economic, and perhaps political values among many of the groups of northern Italy.

Almost all of the coin finds and certainly all of the mints are located north of the Po and south of the Alps.[82] On the west the heaviest concentration of finds ends around Vercellae, and in the east with Padua.[83] There is a particularly heavy concentration around Vercellae, in the area around Ticino and Como, and in the middle and upper Adige valley. Many of the finds come from areas near the mountains.

---

[79] *CIL* 5 index for Cassius.

[80] Asc. 3.6; P. A. Brunt (1971) pp. 168–72.

[81] H. Rolland (1949); A. Pautasso (1960), (1962–63). A. Pautasso (1960) p. 89 notes that the actual coinage of Massilia is not found in the area.

[82] A. Pautasso (1962–63) pp. 85–87.

[83] A. Pautasso (1960) pp. 81–85, (1962–63) pp. 111–18.

Scholars seem confident in identifying certain coin types with specific tribal groups such as the Insubres and the Cenomani.[84] In several instances the coins bear names written in the northern Italic native alphabet. Some of these appear to be the names of native rulers or officials. The custom of allowing native chiefs to rule their peoples in the area apparently continued to the end of the Republic, since names appear on the latest of the native coinages.[85]

This northern Italian native coinage appears to have started after the establishment of the Roman administration in the area.[86] A similar development seems to have taken place with the appearance of native coinages in Spain and Languedoc during the second century B.C.[87] It is important to note that this coinage had relatively little circulation outside the transpadane and Alpine areas. A few pieces have been found among the Helvetii and around Genoa, but almost none appear to have crossed the northeastern Alpine frontier, despite the developing trade with Rhaetia and Noricum.[88] Even the examples found in the valley of the Athesis stop with the territory of the Anauni.

The coinages can be associated mainly with the Gallic and Lepontic tribal groups, and were issued by peoples both friendly and hostile to Rome. The distribution range of the native coins overlaps considerably with that of the inscriptions of family names with Republican associations. The daily economic role of the coinage must have been limited, since no bronze fractional coinage appears to have been issued. They circulated together with the official Roman coinage.[89] It is curious that the Romans tolerated and apparently even encouraged the development of this parallel monetary system.

Scholars interested in monetary history have increasingly called our attention to the danger of projecting our own notion of the use of coinage back into a period like the Roman Republic, especially when we are discussing groups not even part of the Mediterranean monetary tradition.[90] Among the Gauls, coined money had a display function, which is evident in accounts of the behavior of such Gallic chieftains as Luerius the Arvernian.[91] Although it is difficult to imagine the rapidly Romanizing aristocracy of the interior transpadane region behaving like Luerius, this may well have been the case for groups closer to

---

[84] A. Pautasso (1960) pp. 14–16, (1962–63) pp. 111–18, (1975–76).
[85] A. Pautasso (1962–63) pp. 14–16, 43–48, 59, 62, 68–69, (1975–76).
[86] A. Pautasso (1960) pp. 100–6.
[87] R. C. Knapp (1977b) pp. 1–18.
[88] A. Pautasso (1960) pp. 81–85.
[89] A. Pautasso (1962–63) pp. 59–79; G. Gorini (1971).
[90] R. C. Knapp (1977b).
[91] Strabo 4.2.3.

the frontier where the coinages concentrate. It is possible that this coinage was used for gifts, tribute, or troop payments associated with maintaining frontier stability. This function would also explain the relatively conservative typology of these northern Italian coinages, which anticipate the nineteenth-century Maria Teresa thalers used in Africa.[92] The fact that these coins were apparently locally produced and sometimes bore legends with local associations suggests that the Romans encouraged a degree of tribal self-consciousness on the frontier, providing it did not conflict with the interests of Rome.

The evidence of the inscriptions and the coins provides a glimpse into how the Romans were establishing their hold across the Po. Unfortunately, most of the literary sources are silent about internal development in the area during the crucial first half of the second century B.C. This is mainly because of the slow and essentially peaceful way in which Romanization took place. Only when problems arise, as with the factional fighting at Padua in 174 B.C., do we get a passing literary reference.[93]

One source that would have been invaluable if it had been preserved intact is that pioneering historical work, the *Origines* of Cato the Censor. Cato was familiar with northern Italy. He had fought at the Metaurus in 207 B.C. More important, he was censor in 184 B.C., at a time when the evaluations of the potential resources of the transpadane zone made after the completion of conquest were fresh in everyone's mind, and the political and social adjustments necessary to integrate the zone into the Romano-Italian system would have begun.[94] Cato's interest in making this integration as smooth as possible is shown by his move to expel L. Quinctius Flamininus from the senate for slaying a friendly Boian chieftain.[95] Cato also had a general interest in provincial and frontier matters, and had the access to returning Roman administrators. This allowed him to incorporate the most recent information into his histories, a process that continued until 167 B.C.[96] Pliny, Varro, and Livy all used the *Origines*, and their tantalizing fragments provide some sense of the way Cato and other literate Roman administrators went about investigating a newly conquered area.

Of primary concern was the question of who controlled which territory and which population centers, and what was the historical background for those claims. This information allowed the Romans to impose an administrative order based on native traditions and to settle

[92] R. C. Knapp (1977b).
[93] Livy 41.27.3–4.
[94] J. Heurgon (1974); A. E. Astin (1978) pp. 79–80.
[95] Cf. p. 39.
[96] A. E. Astin (1978) p. 211.

the inevitable border disputes that arose. Thus Cato noted that Novara was founded by the Vertamacori, and that Bergamo and Forum
Licinii belonged to the Orumbivii.[97] The reference to Forum Licinii
is interesting on a number of counts. Since the foundation can most
reasonably be attributed to C. Licinius Crassus, who was in cisalpine
Gaul in 168 B.C., it shows that Cato was using the most recent information. Moreover, it highlights the fact that these fora, common in
the zone south of Po, were rare to the north, where the native centers
were in a better position to develop into local markets. Forum Licinii
does not appear on the later road itineraries, and this suggests that it
did not become a great center.[98] Changes in native settlement patterns
can also be deduced by comparing Cato with later sources. The people
of Bergamum, according to Cato, originally lived at the elevated site
of Parra. By the time of Pliny, the site was in ruins.[99]

Cato provides much information on the tribes of the Alpine and
subalpine zones, no doubt a reflection of the concern of the Roman
administrators in securing the frontier. He mentioned the thirty-four
oppida of the Euganei; included in that group were the Triumpilini,
the Camunni, and some other tribes that, by the time of Pliny, had
been assigned to the administrative jurisdiction of neighboring towns.
The Lepontii and the Salassi are described as having the same origins
as the Taurisci.[100] Less is said about the large tribes behind the Po.
Cato does comment, however, on the size and number of hogs produced among the Insubres, a reference that shows not only the agricultural sophistication of the tribe but also its integration into the market economy of Italy.[101]

Other references similarly suggest a slow integration of the native
culture into the Roman sphere, as well as the resulting tension and
local rivalries. M. Aemilius Lepidus had to be sent to Padua in 174
B.C. to calm factional fighting, showing the same social tensions appearing in northern Italian society that appeared in Republican Etruria
and that would be an element in the Romanization process in much
of the Western Roman Empire.[102] Among the few surviving Republican inscriptions are several that refer to the Roman arbitration of
boundary disputes, another indication of a sometimes painful adjustment to Roman administration.[103]

[97] Pliny *HN* 3.124–25.
[98] J. Heurgon (1974) pp. 242–43.
[99] Pliny *HN* 3.125; J. Heurgon (1974) p. 246.
[100] Pliny *HN* 3.133–4.
[101] Varro *Rust.* 2.4.11.
[102] S. L. Dyson (1971), (1975).
[103] *CIL* 5. 2490–92.

This same impression of gradual integration is provided by the few preserved inscriptions written in the local script and native language.[104] Most important of these is the Gallic inscription found at St. Bernandino di Briona, ten kilometers northwest of Novara. It is written in the local Lepontic dialect and appears to date to the late second century or early first century B.C. It demonstrates the persistence of native forms of literacy well after the Roman conquest.[105] The inscription comes from a funerary monument. The text mentions two generations of two families. Although most of the people recorded bear native names, one person in the second generation is called Kuitos (Quintus) and has the designation of *lekatos* (*legatus*), as though he were some kind of Roman official. The use of the name Kuitos-Quintus implies conscious Romanization. The inscription also mentions the *touta*, which is the native equivalent of the *civitas*. The inscription, though enigmatic, does appear to show the Roman use of acculturated natives for local administration in areas close to the Alpine frontier zone.

Related to this is the inscription found well to the south at Todi in Umbria.[106] The text is bilingual, with Latin and Lepontic versions. It mentions a father named Drutos and a son named Ategnatus, both Celtic names. Again the inscription appears to be from the late second century B.C. It is uncertain what the individuals were doing in Todi, but the combination of native names and language with a Latin text shows the complex process of Romanization that was under way.

A more recent discovery is the bilingual inscription from Vercellae, written in Latin and Gallic. It commemorates the donation of land, apparently for religious purposes, by a certain Acisius and shows people of Libican ancestry still using native names and carrying on native customs in the first century B.C.[107] Some mention should also be made of the Gallic Lepontic inscription found at Prestino near Como, which seems to have been a dedication on a public monument. It dates to the second or first century B.C., and again shows the survival of a prosperous native class continuing its own rites well into the Roman period.[108]

This peaceful integration depended on a secure frontier and a sharply reduced movement of new groups into the transpadane area. Rome

---

[104] J. Whatmough (1933) pp. 170–75; M. Lejeune (1956) pp. 206–11; J. Heurgon (1974) pp. 240–41.

[105] M. Lejeune (1971); E. A. Arslan (1978) p. 83.

[106] J. Whatmough (1933) pp. 175–78 no. 339; C. DeSimoni (1978).

[107] P. Baldacci (1977). On Vercellae as a center of Libici and Salluvii see Pliny *HN* 3.124.

[108] M. G. Tibiletti Bruno (1966); A. L. Prosdocimi (1967).

did not directly control the Alps, let alone land beyond the Alps, and the prevention of new folk movements required vigilance and sophisticated diplomacy. Presumably the system was being continually tested in small ways, but only certain episodes were of sufficient importance to attract the attention of the historians. Such a chain of events started in 186 B.C. The description of the way it was handled reveals much about Roman frontier policy and practice.

Livy notes for the year 186 B.C. a new movement of Gauls into the Veneto area. The passage bears quotation in full:

> Eodem anno Galli transalpini transgressi in Venetiam sine populatione aut bello haud procul inde, ubi nunc Aquileia est, locum oppido condendo ceperunt. Legatis Romanis de ea re trans Alpes missis responsum est neque profectos ex auctoritate gentis eos, nec quid in Italia facerent sese scire.[109]

> In the same year, transalpine Gauls who had crossed over into the Veneto without any devastation or war seized a place to found an oppidum not far from where Aquileia is today. The response was made to the Roman ambassadors sent across the Alps for this matter that they (the Gauls) had set out without the authorization of the tribe and that the tribe did not know what they were doing.

Who the Gauls were and why they came into Italy has been a subject of considerable scholarly dispute.[110] Apparently they belonged to one of the northeastern Celtic groups associated with the Taurisci. They were not the first Celts in the area, for the Friuli area in Italy had in antiquity a Celtic as well as a Venetic caste.[111] It is no surprise that on this ethnically mixed border of Italy, frontier control was loosely applied. What is unexpected is that the area was so thinly populated. One possible explanation for this is provided by Vergil, who as a northern Italian must have known the area and its history. In Book Three of the Georgics, he describes an animal pestilence and is quite specific about where the plague was centered:

> tum sciat, aerias Alpis et Norica si quis
> castella in tumulis et Iapydis arva Timavi
> nunc quoque post tanto videat, desertaque regna
> pastorum et longe saltus lateque vacantis.[112]

---

[109] Livy 39.22.6–7.

[110] F. Sartori (1960) and references cited there.

[111] F. Sartori (1960) cols. 7–14. G. Alföldy (1974) pp. 17–25 notes that Venetic inscriptions have been found all the way up to southern Noricum. F. Cassola (1972) pp. 23–29 mentions traces of a Gallic settlement found at Aquileia itself.

[112] Verg. G. 3.474–77.

Then if anyone should see the lofty Alps and the Norican castles
on their hilltops and the fields of the Iapydian Timavus, let him
know that now after so long he may see the realm of the shepherd
deserted and far and wide the empty meadows.

Vergil states that the disease affected horses. Other sources also comment on the decline of horse-breeding among the Veneti.[113] Although
Vergil does not say when this pestilence occurred, he implies that it
happened long before he wrote. It is possible that an animal disease
could have sharply reduced the population in an area where the inhabitants were dependent on herding. Modern parallels can be found
in places like Africa.

Whatever may have been the cause of its desertion, such a thinly
populated frontier zone would have suited the Roman frontier commander. The arrival of a new Celtic group would not have pleased
them. The Romans quickly dispatched ambassadors to enquire about
the reasons for the folk movement. They were informed that the migrants had acted on their own without higher tribal authority. The
ease with which the embassy conducted its business in the mountains
implies that the Romans had had previous contact with these Alpine
tribes and suggests that the Romans held them responsible for preventing new groups from moving into Italy.[114] This was part of the
Roman policy of using the Alps as a barrier to Italy that was not to
be breached.

It is unclear how the Romans dealt with the original group of settlers. But by the end of 184 B.C. the problem had intensified to the
degree that the senate assigned one of the praetors for 183 B.C.,
L. Julius Caesar, to cisalpine Gaul.[115] Livy notes that the Gauls were
continuing to pass into Italy *per saltus ignotae antea viae* and that they
were building an oppidum about twelve miles from the site of the later
colony of Aquileia. The continued infiltration combined with the establishment of a permanent center disturbed the senate. The praetor
was ordered to hasten his departure for the area and to stop, by peaceful means if possible, the building of the oppidum. If his efforts failed,
he was to call for armed consular support.[116] The task was not easy.
The migrations were continuing, and the Gallic leaders were unable
to stop the flow. Moreover, while the original settlement had been in
sparsely inhabited land and produced few tensions with the indige-

[113] Verg. *G.* 3.498–501; Strabo 5.1.4, 9.

[114] Livy 39.22.7.

[115] Livy 39.45.6–7; T.R.S. Broughton (1951) p. 378; G. Alföldy (1974) p. 29.

[116] Livy 39.45.6–7. This creation of an oppidum with the implication of growing
political centralization may have spurred Roman intervention: Pliny *HN* 3.131.

nous natives, the increasing number of new arrivals brought the Gauls into greater conflict with the Roman allies in the area.[117]

Peaceful persuasion did not work, and the consul M. Claudius Marcellus was forced to intervene with the legions. As the third generation of a family involved in the transpadane area, he had inherited a tradition of rough and ready frontier action better suited to the wars of conquest waged by his father and grandfather than to the needs of a stable but delicate frontier.[118] The Gauls, though numerous, were not well armed and regarded resistance as futile. They surrendered almost immediately. Marcellus destroyed their oppidum and then proceeded to deprive them of their arms and property.

The Gauls, feeling that their rights as a surrendered people had been violated, sent a delegation of protest to the senate. Their ambassadors were introduced by C. Valerius Flaccus, who was in part carrying out his responsibility as *praetor peregrinus*. In contacting him, however, the Gauls may have been drawing upon old Valerian connections with the north. It was Lucius Valerius Flaccus who in 194 B.C. had completed the conquest of the Insubres and thus played a role in the establishment of the frontier system. The widespread distribution of the nomen Valerii in the transpadane area may be partly a result of continuing Valerian influence there.[119] It would be natural for the Gauls to use the services of that family in much the same way that the Allobroges were to use the Fabii in 63 B.C. during the Catilinarian controversies. Moreover, the Valerii would be interested in embarrassing the family of Claudius Marcellus, which was their main rival for power and influence in the north. It is also interesting that a group of newly arrived Gauls had a knowledge of Roman ways sophisticated enough to induce them to send a delegation to the capital. This suggests previous relations with Rome that our sources do not allow us to reconstruct.[120]

Livy states clearly the position taken by the Gauls.[121] They claimed that they had been forced to emigrate from their homeland because of a scarcity of good land needed for their large population. Tempted by the sparsely inhabited territory of the eastern Veneto, they had moved in and settled down. The Gauls strongly emphasized their peaceful intentions. The senate recognized a certain justice in their pleas and restored to the Gauls their goods. At the same time, however, the

---

[117] Livy 39.54.3–4 describes the migrants as including twelve thousand armed men who had acquired weapons locally and were ravaging fields in the area.

[118] Livy 39.54.5–9; T.R.S. Broughton (1951) p. 378.

[119] On L. Valerius Flaccus see T.R.S. Broughton (1951) p. 379.

[120] Sall. *Cat.* 41.4–5; H. H. Scullard (1973) p. 168.

[121] Livy 39.54.5–10.

senators reprimanded them for coming into Roman territory without
the permission of the commanding magistrate of the province. The
principles of Roman border control were firmly stated, and it was
emphasized that the Alps were the *prope inexsuperabilem finem* of Italy.[122]

The Romans again realized that the problem of Gallic migration had
to be addressed at the source, and they dispatched a delegation into
the Alps to speak with the leaders of the offending Gallic tribes. It
was a high-powered embassy, staffed by men with considerable experience in both native diplomacy and the problems of northern Italy.
One member, Q. Minucius Rufus, had been consul in 197 B.C., and
had defeated both the Boii and the Ligurians.[123] L. Furius Purpurio,
the other senior ambassador, had as praetor in 200 B.C. quelled an
uprising of the Gauls and Ligurians and had celebrated a triumph. He
had fought the Gauls again as consul in 196 B.C.[124] The most junior
member of the delegation was L. Manlius Acidinus. While he apparently had no northern Italian experience, he had served as praetor in
Hispania Citerior, an assignment that must have exposed him to border problems similar to those found in the Alps. He evidently impressed his senior colleagues as well as the senate, for he was selected
in the same year to be one of the commissioners for the foundation of
Aquileia.[125]

The exact destination of the embassy is not stated, though it is likely
that they dealt with one of the tribes in the Friulian Alps or just
beyond in Noricum.[126] The Roman legates were well received and
even mildly reprimanded for the lenient treatment the senate had accorded the migrants. The elders of the tribe pointed out that they had
left without tribal permission. The light punishment would encourage
others to follow their example. The implication was that the Gallic
elders felt themselves powerless to stop this outflow of their fellow
tribesmen.

The embassy went well, and the departing Roman diplomats were
sent on their way with gifts. Nevertheless, the Romans must have felt
increasingly uncomfortable with the weak collective leadership represented by the tribal elders. It is possible that they began the process
of encouraging the emergence of stronger tribal leaders among the
Gallic groups. By 178 B.C. a *regulus* Catmelus had been established in

[122] Livy 39.54.12.
[123] A. Degrassi (1947) p. 552; T.R.S. Broughton (1951) pp. 332–33, 379.
[124] A. Degrassi (1947) p. 551; T.R.S. Broughton (1951) pp. 323, 335, 379.
[125] T.R.S. Broughton (1951) pp. 365, 369, 379–80; *CIL* 1.2 p. 621.
[126] Livy 39.55.1–4; F. Sartori (1960) pp. 21–26.

the eastern Alpine lands.[127] Of similar origin might have been the father of Aepulo, the leader of the Istrian revolt in 178–177 B.C., who was described as having held his territory *in pace* from the Romans.[128]

While the embassy was traveling back and forth to the Alps, the ambitious consul Marcellus, by requesting permission to invade the territory of Istria, called the senate's attention to another sensitive frontier zone in the northeast.[129] That peninsula posed frontier problems for the Romans on the northeast similar to those created by Liguria on the northwest. The land was inhabited by a tough warrior folk called the Castellieri by archaeologists.[130] Living in relatively small fortified settlements on the bare Karst limestone hills, they survived by herding and hunting. The large number of these Iron Age oppida suggest a native overpopulation that strained local resources.[131] Crowded and poor, these Istrians easily turned to raiding the eastern plain of the Veneto and the sea lanes along the northern Adriatic. Already in 221 B.C. the Romans had sent the consuls M. Minucius Rufus and P. Cornelius Scipio Asina to fight the Istrians. The Istrians were defeated, but not without some difficulty.[132]

The senate rejected the request of Marcellus. A raid into Istria would stir up a hornet's nest and solve little. They had in mind a more permanent solution for the problems of this insecure frontier and underpopulated plain. It would involve the foundation of a colony that would increase the population base in the area, serve as a watch on the frontier, and provide a springboard for military expeditions into the mountains. It would be the Pisa, Mutina, or Placentia of the northeastern frontier. The site of Aquileia on the Ledra River at the head of the Gulf of Venezia, not far from the recently destroyed Gallic oppidum, seemed ideal. Future developments would confirm the wisdom of the senate's choice. Aquileia grew into one of the most important centers of the Roman Empire.[133]

The great destiny of Aquileia was not manifest to the first settlers. The senate began debating the question of founding the city in 183

[127] Livy 41.1.8; G. Alföldy (1974) p. 30.

[128] Livy 41.1.1.

[129] Livy 39.55.4.

[130] D. Randall-MacIver (1927) pp. 59–60; L. Barfield (1972) pp. 126–27. A. Radmilli (1972) notes this pastoral element and also evidence of long-standing trade among groups closer to the coast. M. Zaninovic (1975–76) pp. 625–26.

[131] C. Marchesetti (1903).

[132] Livy *Per.* 20; Eutropius 3.7; Oros. 4.13.16; Zonaras 8.20; T.R.S. Broughton (1951) p. 233–34.

[133] Cic. *Font.* 1.2; Strabo 5.1.8; A. Calderini (1930); A. Degrassi (1954) p. 17; R. Cessi (1957); S. Panciera (1957); A. Bertacchi (1965).

B.C., but the actual settlement was not made until 181 B.C.[134] To encourage the recruitment of colonists, the initial allotments were more generous than those for other colonies, with 50 *jugera* going to each of the 3,000 infantrymen, 100 to the centurians, and 140 to the knights. It has been estimated that the original *territorium* of the colony embraced some 50,000 hectares of land.[135] These comparatively large land grants suggest that the Romans had trouble attracting settlers to this exposed frontier zone. The colony embraced much of the arable land between the Tagliamento River on the west and the Isonzo on the east.[136] On the north it probably extended to the hills of Buttrio.

The fears of the first settlers were justified, for the Gallic migrations into Italy continued and the Istri did not take kindly to the new settlement bordering their lands. In 179 B.C. another group of three thousand transalpine Gauls moved into Italy and asked for land.[137] By this time the patience of the senate was wearing thin. Permission was refused and the senate instructed the consul Q. Fulvius Flaccus to:

> quaerere et animadvertere in eos qui principes et auctores transcendendi Alpes fuissent.[138]

> seek out and punish those who were the leaders and instigators of crossing the Alps.

More dangerous was the growing antagonism between the new colonists and the Istrians.[139] What had formerly been a sparsely inhabited land held by scattered Veneti and Gauls now was the center of a Roman settlement. The boundaries of the colony pushed up to the Istrian hills. For a pastoral people who presumably had used the lowland pastures during winter months, this extension of agriculture posed a serious problem. Moreover, the presence of the new colonists probably encouraged Istrian raids, for the settlers brought with them a wealth of Roman goods. The large size of the individual tracts must have meant that many colonists were scattered on relatively isolated farms, making hit and run attacks easy.

Already in 181 B.C. the Romans were forced to fight Istrians who were disturbing the new colonists.[140] They also began developing a

---

[134] Livy 39.55.5–6, 40.34.2–4; A. Bertacchi (1965); E. T. Salmon (1970) pp. 106–9; F. Cassola (1972a) pp. 30–33; H. H. Scullard (1973), pp. 167–70.

[135] A. Calderini (1930) p. 13; A. Degrassi (1954) p. 18.

[136] A. Degrassi (1954) pp. 18–19; F. Sartori (1960) p. 26.

[137] Livy 40.53.5–6; Florus 1.19.5; T.R.S. Broughton (1951) pp. 391–92; G. Alföldy (1974) p. 3.

[138] Livy 40.53.6.

[139] Livy 40.26.2.

[140] Livy 40.26.3–4.

protective band of border client rulers. For this approach to succeed, the Romans had to overcome the tradition of local autonomy among the Istrians. Leaders had to be found who could build larger political units loyal to Rome. Aepulo's father, who had held the Istrians in peace for so long, must have been such a figure of the early frontier. But such solutions had their negative aspects. Superior political organizations could be turned against Rome, and the sons of leaders bred in the Roman way could prove among the most effective opponents to Rome. By the first century A.D. the Romans on the German frontier were to become all too familiar with this kind of leader in the person of Arminius. Much earlier they met it in Aepulo, the son of their old Istrian client and friend.

Aepulo organized a rebellion in Istria. The impact on the territory of Aquileia was devastating. As with many other uprisings against Rome, the support came from the younger warriors who were naturally more headstrong, did not have the experience of the previous wars with Rome, and needed loot to build up their power and prestige within the tribe.[141]

To counter the rebellion, Rome sent the consul of 178 B. C., A. Manlius Vulso. Among the troops in his strong army, two contingents deserve special attention. The first is a unit from Placentia.[142] References to the use of troops drawn from military colonies outside of their immediate area are rare. The soldiers from Placentia had presumably been pressed into service because of their experience in mountain warfare developed during years of fighting in eastern Liguria. The second is a large contingent of Gauls led by their *regulus* Catmelus.[143] Livy does not name the specific tribe of Gauls, but it was most likely one of the eastern Alpine Gallic groups with whom the Romans had been establishing diplomatic and military contacts during the preceding decade. The Romans in the war against Aepulo used the bellicose propensities and the surplus manpower of these border natives to defend their colonial interests.

The campaign of Manlius opened in confusion. The Istrians rallied their forces more quickly than expected and in a lightening raid seized the consul's camp. The ensuing panic spread all the way back to Aquileia and showed the insecurity of the newly formed colony. The Romans finally regrouped, and Manlius Vulso was joined by the other consul, M. Junius Brutus. By 177 B.C. they had defeated the Istrians. Aepulo's center at Nessatum in southeastern Istria was besieged and taken along with two other centers at Mutila and Faveria. The Istrian leader

[141] Livy 41.1.1.
[142] Livy 41.1; T.R.S. Broughton (1951) p. 395; F. Cassola (1972b) pp. 56–65; H. H. Scullard (1973) pp. 186–88.
[143] Livy 41.1; G. Alföldy (1974) p. 30.

committed suicide. Those held responsible for the uprising were treated as rebels and beheaded, while 5,632 captives were sold into slavery. The consul of 177 B.C., C. Claudius Pulcher, who had assumed command in the final stages of the war, celebrated a triumph. The defeat dealt a severe blow to the Istrians. Those who survived were forced to give hostages. A relative peace was established on the Istrian frontier.[144] To help secure that peace, the Romans apparently added to the eastern domain of Aquileia. This provided a greater buffer between the city and the Istrians.[145]

We can assume that the lack of reference to Istrian-Aquileian problems in subsequent years reflect the lack of open warfare, and not the absence of subtle but effective frontier diplomacy. Indeed, when the spotlight is again centered on the Istrian frontier, it shows a more complex frontier system in place than had existed in the 180s. What brought this into prominence were the rash actions of the consul of 171 B.C., C. Cassius Longinus.

In 171 B.C. the prize in the consular selection of provinces was Macedonia. It promised spectacular military action and showy diplomacy, and access to the wealth and sophistication of the Roman east. Longinus lost this competition to his rival consul, P. Licinius Crassus, and received instead the unrewarding task of guarding the northeastern frontier.[146]

Longinus, however, was not to be frustrated in his quest for *gloria*, and conceived the idea of taking his army through Illyria and the Balkans to Macedonia. It seems unlikely that he had a clear idea of the formidable nature of such an undertaking. The overland road from Aquileia to Macedonia was long and tortuous. Much of it went through unconquered land. He probably started up the valley of the river Frigidus with the intention of entering the Save river system near Ljubljana. The route up to the Save was undoubtedly well known to the Romans and their allies; connections between the Veneto and Slovenia had existed since the days of the situla trade with Este. But beyond that point, Longinus presumably had only the most rudimentary sense of the country that lay ahead and visualized the distances as being much shorter than they really were. In any case, this expedition was an exercise in pure folly and certainly counter to the wishes and instructions of the senate.

The Aquileians viewed the departure of the Roman frontier forces with undisguised horror. As they told the senate, the colony was still weak and insufficiently fortified, and was now exposed to the attacks

---

[144] Livy 41.11.1–9. Nesattium seems to be the Nesation listed on later Roman road itineraries: K. Miller (1916) col. 313. A. Degrassi (1947) p. 555.

[145] A. Degrassi (1954) pp. 23–24.

[146] T.R.S. Broughton (1951) p. 416; H. H. Scullard (1973) pp. 195–98.

of both the Istrians and the Illyrians. Protest delegations were immediately dispatched to Rome.[147] The senate received the report of the Aquileian ambassadors with incredulity. They could not believe that the consul had embarked upon such an unauthorized and foolish enterprise. When the fact of his departure was confirmed, the senate supported the position of the Aquileians. the vainglorious actions of the consul that had left open *viam tot nationibus in Italiam* were condemned. A mission was immediately dispatched to warn Cassius not to wage war on any people without a directive from the senate.[148]

The more shocking news was yet to come. Delegations began to arrive from allied native groups with complaints about the treatment they received from Cassius as his army passed through their territory. First came the brother of a certain Cincibilis who was described as *rex Gallorum*. He protested the fact that *Alpinorum populorum agros, sociorum suorum depopulatum C. Cassium*. Cincibilis was apparently one of the founders of the client state of Noricum, and he was clearly a person of importance to the Romans.[149]

The territory of Cincibilis had not been affected directly, but the Romans has passed through lands of his allies. The people who suffered most from the advance of Longinus are described as the Carni, Istri, and Iapodes. The territory of the Carni and Istri lay northwest and southeast of the Frigidus. The Iapodes presumably dwelt directly on the route up the Frigidus in what was later Pannonia. The allies of Cincibilis immediately affected were most likely eastern Carnic groups who inhabited the mountain valleys leading down to the plain of Aquileia.[150] The Romans would have wanted these potentially dangerous groups directly under the control of a strong friendly client king. They probably allowed the ruler in Noricum to expand his power eastward to include them. Cincibilis was becoming for the mountain areas north of Aquileia the kind of frontier protector that the father of Aepulo had been for the Istrian hills to the east of the colony.

Making the complaint of Cincibilis even more serious was that the Romans had not only inflicted the damage normal for a passing army but had taken a large number of slaves as well.[151] This is the same period in which the Romans were forced to take action to restrain

---

[147] Livy 43.1.5–6; A. Bertacchi (1972) pp. 43–44.
[148] Livy 43.1.9–12. See T. P. Wiseman (1971) p. 40 for clients of Longinus whose families continued in Istria.
[149] Livy 43.5.1–3; G. Alföldy (1974) pp. 30–31.
[150] G. Alföldy (1974) p. 30; G. Dobesch (1976).
[151] Livy 43.5.2–3. Strabo 5.1.8 describes slaves as one of the regular elements in Istrian-Aquileian exchange. M. Crawford (1977) discusses the shifts in slave trade during this period.

slaving on the Ligurian frontier. One would have thought that the
eastern wars of this period had glutted the Roman slave markets, making unnecessary illegal and disruptive operations on the northeastern
frontier that would only recalcitrant mountaineers. The effect of slaving in a friendly mountain frontier could only be disastrous. Hostility
to Rome would increase, while into the vacuum created by the en-
slavement of border natives would come new groups that were not
under Roman control. A socially and politically balanced frontier system would be destroyed.

Cincibilis had to be mollified, and a senatorial embassy was dispatched immediately to carry out this delicate assignment. The importance that the Alpine king had for Rome is clearly demonstrated
by the prestige of the men chosen for the delegation. The senior senator was M. Aemilius Lepidus, whose *cursus honorum* was by this time
awesome. He had been twice consul, and was *princeps senatus* and *pon-
tifex maximus*. Moreover, he was a veteran of the Italian frontier, equally
skilled in the arts of warfare, consolidation, and conciliation. Twice
as consul, he had fought the Ligurians. In other years he had helped
direct the foundation of the colonies of Parma, Mutina, and Luna and
the division of the Ligurian lands. In 187 B.C. he was called to the
delicate task of restoring relations with the Cenomani after the illegal
disarming of that tribe by M. Furius Crassipes. In 174 B.C. he was
entrusted with the responsibility of settling factional fighting at Padua.
No man was better suited for the task ahead.[152] The second man was
C. Laelius, consular and old friend of Scipio Africanus who had fought
in the north in 190 B.C.[153] The gifts they brought with them were
lavish. They included money, torques of gold, vessels of silver, horses,
horse trappings, and armor. Moreover, the Gauls of Noricum were to
be permitted to buy horses in Italy and export them over the Alps.
The Romans had evidently restricted this practice, probably to prevent the development of groups of mounted raiders in the frontier
zone.[154]

The aim of the embassy was to pacify the client king, to restore the
amicitia he had with Rome, and to ensure that the king clearly understood the frontier policy of Rome. The expansion of trade seems to
have been an indirect result of the mission and of the growing strength
of Cincibilis. The first considerable group of Roman coins in Noricum
dates to the 170–150 period.[155] Sometime around 150 B.C. gold was

[152] T.R.S. Broughton (1951) pp. 368, 380, 399, 401–2, 409; G. Radke (1964) pp.
304–5.
[153] T.R.S. Broughton (1951) pp. 356, 421.
[154] Livy 43.5.8–10.
[155] G. Alföldy (1974) pp. 33–34.

found in Noricum, and Italians flocked north to mine it. The foreigners were soon expelled, however, and the Taurisci of Noricum continued the mining themselves.[156] Nevertheless, trade and generally good political relations continued. In 169 B.C., at the time of the Third Macedonian War, the *regulus* Balanos sent offers of assistance to Rome. He was thanked and rewarded with gifts including gold torques and bowls, and horse trappings and cavalry weapons. It is possible that he was the son of Cincibilis.[157]

The Carni, Istri, and Iapydes also needed to be placated, but their relative unimportance (in comparison with the Noricans) is revealed by the composition of the embassy sent to them. None of the three members was a consular, and only one is known to have had frontier experience. This was Cn. Sicinius, who had served in Sardinia as praetor and had also aided C. Licinius Crassus in freeing the unjustly enslaved Statelliates in 172 B.C.[158] The latter experience would be useful since illegal slaving was one of the complaints made by the tribes of the northeastern frontier.

During this period steps were taken to strengthen and consolidate the position of Aquileia. The population of the colony was reinforced in 169 B.C. with the addition of 1,500 new families. This may have involved additions to the *territorium*.[159] Other actions were initiated to strengthen Aquileia's role as the defender of the northeast. The first apparently involved placing free tribes under the administrative jurisdiction of the colony, the process known as *attributio*. Most affected by that action would have been the tribes on the southern Alpine slopes between Noricum and the borders of Aquileia, and other native groups to the east of the colony. At present, we do not know the extent of this attribution or specifically when it took place.[160]

Equally important in the strengthening of Aquileia's hold on the area was the creation and encouragement of what appear to have been satellite communities. In 52 B.C. at Tricesimo, thirty miles to the north of Aquileia, the senate of Aquileia made provision for building gates and walls at the center threatened by raids from the Giapidi. There had been previous occupation at the site going back at least to 115 B.C., when M. Aemilius Scaurus was fighting against the Carni. Tricesimo stands at a transition point between plain and mountains, and thus had an important role in protecting the approach to Aquileia through the Alpine pass from Noricum.[161]

[156] Polyb. 34.10.10; Strabo 6.12; G. Alföldy (1974) p. 34.
[157] Livy 44.14.1–3; G. Alföldy (1974) pp. 32–33.
[158] Livy 43.5.7, 10; T.R.S. Broughton (1951) pp. 379, 411, 421.
[159] Livy 43.17.1.
[160] A. Degrassi (1954) pp. 19–26.
[161] *CIL* 1.2 2648; A. Calderini (1930) p. 29; A. Degrassi (1954) pp. 29, 34, 37.

Another approach to Aquileia from the mountains was down the Frigidus. This was probably the route taken by Cassius Longinus. There is a later reference to a place called Castra, the modern Aidussina, which is located in the Frigidus valley at the very foothills of the Carnic Alps.[162] The name implies a military origin, and it could go back to the Republic. One thinks of parallels in Spain, such as Castra Aelia, Castra Caecilia, and Castra Servilia. These generally date to the second century B.C. The use of fortified outposts is evident in Liguria by 179 B.C. It seems reasonable that the Romans would have used similar institutions on the Carnic frontier.

The final community that should be considered in this context is Concordia.[163] This center was located some forty kilometers west of Aquileia between the Livenza and the Tagliamento rivers. In later times it stood at the juncture of roads coming from Altinum and Opitergium. Ptolemy states that the ancient inhabitants of Concordia were the Carni.[164] An updated Republican inscription refers to four *magistri* from the town. One bears the name of Fulvius, while the others have such non-Roman names as Muttenus and Trosius.[165] Another affirmed use of the name Concordia for a town comes from Lusitania.[166] This kind of name recalls such places as Potentia and Pollentia. The examples in Italy and the western provinces date to the second century B.C. Similarly, the Aquileian Concordia can be viewed as an expression of Roman policy that aimed at continuing the peaceful interaction of different ethnic groups in the Veneto.

These fragmentary literary references and scattered pieces of other evidence allow us to reconstruct in moderate detail the Roman frontier policy on the northeast. Aquileia was intended to be a key nodal point, providing a base for Romanization in the area, a staging point for military expeditions, and a center for trade. In all these roles it appears to have served admirably, and it became one of the great cities of the Empire. Nevertheless, the colony was a part of a larger system. The second most important element was the group of friendly native tribes. Aquileia could not provide mobile frontier defense forces, and the Romans did not want to station garrison troops in the area. Therefore, the client princes formed the first line of defense. They also served as an early warning system that alerted the Romans to movements and changes beyond the Alps. In return, the chiefs received the prestige of Roman support, as well as a privileged trading status and whatever

---

[162] A. Degrassi (1954) pp. 25–26.

[163] Strabo 5.1.8; Pliny *HN* 3.126; *CIL* 5.1 p. 178; G. A. Mansuelli (1965) p. 14.

[164] Ptol. 3.1; K. Miller (1916) cols. 259, 311.

[165] *CIL* 5. 1890. W. Schulze (1933) pp. 193–94 suggests that the name Muttenus might have an ultimate Etruscan derivation. G. A. Mansuelli (1971) p. 75.

[166] Ptol. 2.4

direct aid Rome could provide. This is similar to the system that the
Romans were later to create on the upper Rhone and is the ancestor
of the elaborate client networks of the Empire. Smaller groups located
between the outer tribal ring and the hub at Aquileia fell into one of
the two spheres, and were either allied to client rulers such as Cincibilis or attributed to Aquileia. The whole system was sufficiently low
key to escape the notice of later historians, but its success is demonstrated by the nearly fifty years of relative tranquility that followed
the peace mission to Cincibilis.

The distinguished Italian historian of the cisalpina, Guido Mansuelli, has commented that the hundred and fifty years of Roman occupation in the area before Caesar should be considered primarily as
social history. It is the story of a rapid Romanization taking place
behind a relatively calm frontier.[167] This process, as much as it can be
reconstructed from the paltry evidence, will be discussed at the end
of the chapter. First it is necessary to review the limited references we
have on frontier activity in the century preceding Caesar, and to consider what they tell us about the way the system was working and the
strains that were imposed upon it.

Much of the frontier activity involved local police work or the preparation of expeditions directed beyond the border. In 156 B.C. the
consul C. Marcius Figulus set out from Aquileia for his campaign
against the Pannonians.[168] Aquileia must have served a similar role for
the expedition of C. Sempronius Tuditanus against the Iapydes in
Pannonia, though Tuditanus was also concerned with problems closer
to the northeastern frontier. A fragmentary inscription implies that he
was fighting the Taurisci, and another reference mentions a victory
over the Istrians. The victory in Pannonia was impressive enough to
bring him a triumph and for his defeat of the Histrians to be recalled
in an Augustan elogium.[169] His efforts in fostering frontier peace were
appreciated locally. Dedications were erected to him both at Aquileia
and in the Diomedes sanctuary on the Timavus near the provincial
border.[170]

These actions in areas north, northeast, and east of Aquileia show
that not all was calm on the border. The praetor L. Caecilius Metellus
Diadematus was involved in frontier fighting around Aquileia in 120
B.C. In 115 B.C. M. Aemilius Scaurus was forced to campaign against

[167] G. A. Mansuelli (1963) p. 57.
[168] T.R.S. Broughton (1951) p. 447.
[169] Livy Per. 59; Pliny HN 3.19.129; App. Ill. 10; A. Degrassi (1947) p. 559; R. F.
Rossi (1972) p. 68; G. Alföldy (1974) p. 34.
[170] Livy Per. 59; Pliny HN 3.129; App. Ill. 10; CIL 5. 8270 (ILS 8885); AE (1953) no.
95; A. Calderini (1930) pp. 24–26; A. Degrassi (1947) p. 559.

the Carni to the north of Aquileia, again in wars of sufficient intensity to win him a triumph.[171]

Still, the situation was basically one of peace, and it was due in no small measure to the client kings of Noricum. They continued to help preserve the border peace and in turn to strengthen their own position within Noricum. In 113 B.C. the Roman consul could describe the relationship between Rome and Noricum as one of mutual hospitality.[172] No better expression of the importance of Noricum can be cited than the Roman intervention there in 113 B.C. to expel the Cimbri. This action also brought out the ambiguities of Roman frontier policy and the tensions and problems that the uncertainties of policy created for Roman generals operating on the border.

The Cimbri were a Germanic group who probably originated in the Jutland area and during the second century B.C. were progressively moving southward. By 113 B.C. they had reached Noricum and were ravaging its territory. The terms of Rome's official relationship with the kingdom did not oblige intervention. The devastation of Noricum, however, would reduce its effectiveness as a border guardian, a watch over central Europe, and a growing entrepot for Roman trade. A system that the Romans had been developing since the early part of the century would be destroyed. Moreover, if the Cimbri were successful in Noricum, they might be tempted to move into Italy.[173]

The Roman consul Cn. Papirius Carbo took the most judicious steps possible. He occupied the Alpine passes and dispatched legates to the Cimbri to inform them of the friendship that existed between Noricum and Rome. All went well up to that moment. The Cimbri accepted the Roman arguments and prepared to withdraw. At that point, Carbo attempted to ambush the Germans and decimate their forces before they could escape. The plan backfired; the army of Carbo was defeated, and his career ended in disgrace and suicide.[174] Fortunately the Cimbri did not follow up their success, and in fact the Germanic groups disappeared from the Noricum area for a decade. In the final stage of the coordinated Germanic advance toward Italy at the end of the second century B.C., the Cimbri appeared again. They initially wanted to use Noricum as their entry point into Italy, but instead they turned south before reaching the area and entered through the

[171] For Diadematus see App. Ill. 10; M. G. Morgan (1971) pp. 299–301. On Scaurus see Frontin. Str. 4.3.13; Auct. Vir. Ill. 72.7; A. Degrassi (1947) p. 561; T.R.S. Broughton (1951) p. 531.

[172] App. Celtica 13.

[173] App. Celtica 13.

[174] Livy Per. 63; Strabo 5.1.8; Plut. Vit. Mar. 16.5; T.R.S. Broughton (1951) p. 535; G. Alföldy (1974) pp. 36–37.

Brenner pass and the Adige valley. There they defeated the army of
Q. Lutatius Catulus.[175] Their allies, the Helvetian Tigurini, did move
into southern Noricum, however. With the defeat of the Germanic
armies by Marius, the Tigurini fled and peace returned to the Noricum.[176] Sulla brought several of the now restless Alpine tribes to submission, and Romano-Norican relations entered a new golden era.[177]

A lonely tombstone has been found in the East Tyrol in the upper
Tyrol valley. It bears the image of a Roman portrait and the name
Popaius Senator. If the generally proposed date of 100 B.C. is true, it
is the oldest Roman tombstone in Austria.[178] The explanation of the
name is debated, but the man appears to have been a trader, perhaps
from Aquileia, who was seeking his fortunes in the metal-rich area of
the East Tyrol.

An even better expression of the degree to which conditions in Noricum had returned to normal after the Germanic interlude is the growth
of the oppidum at Magdelensberg.[179] The native settlement on the hill
began to develop during the late second century B.C. By the first century B.C. it had grown into the most important native center in Noricum. The timber structures of the Roman trading settlement appeared in the area below the oppidum by the 80s B.C. Houses, shops,
and a forum similar to the Agora of the Italians at Delos were constructed. Later, the wooden houses were rebuilt in stone and wall
painters imported from Italy to decorate them. Perhaps the best testimony to Mediterranean influence at Magdelensberg is the life-sized
statue of a youth in the tradition of Praxiteles discovered there. It was
set up as a dedication to the Celtic god Latobius by a group of Aquileian freedmen and a native Celt.[180]

The expansion of the center and its trade strengthened the ruling
family of Noricum. During the mid-first century B.C. the ruler Voccio
married into the family of the German chieftain Ariovistus. He also
remained on friendly terms with Caesar, supplying him with cavalry
during the Civil Wars.[181] By 70 B.C. a local coinage had appeared. The
native population became increasingly acculturated, and mixed on equal
terms with the Italians in the culturally blended world of Magdelensberg.[182] The most comparable situation on any other frontier would

[175] Livy Per. 68; Plut. Vit. Mar. 15.4, 23–4; T.R.S. Broughton (1951) p. 567.
[176] Florus 1.38; Plut. Vit. Sull. 4.2–4; G. Alföldy (1974) pp. 38, 294 n. 59.
[177] Plut. Vit. Sull. 4; G. Alföldy (1974) p. 294 n. 59.
[178] G. Alföldy (1974) p. 44; G. C. Susini (1978).
[179] G. Alföldy (1974) pp. 44–51.
[180] G. Alföldy (1974) p. 46.
[181] Caes. BGall. 1.53.4, BCiv. 1.18.5; G. Alföldy (1974) pp. 40–41.
[182] G. Alföldy (1974) pp. 43–44.

be that of the late Republican Aedui on the Rhone, who had a frontier responsibility similar to the Norici and whose chief city at Bibracte had become Mediterraneanized in a similar manner.

The northeastern frontier was, of course, only one element in a system that stretched from the Adriatic to the headwaters of the Po. Along much of the northern mountain frontier, the tribal populations were relatively small. The valleys were not the transmontane passes that would allow the migration of groups from the heartland of Europe, and there was little in the way of natural resources to tempt the Romans to conquer the mountains. Frontier action consisted mainly of minor raids, the occasional reduction of a hill fort, and the steady process of integrating the mountain people into the Roman system.

Some sense of this stable if not always peaceful frontier is obtained from scattered episodes found in the literary record or in the occasional well-excavated archaeological site. Such an episode took place in 143 B.C.[183] The consul Appius Claudius Pulcher had been charged with the responsibility of settling a dispute over water rights between the Salassi and Libici, two tribes in the Val d'Aosta. The Salassi wished to use the waters of the river Dora to wash gold mined in their area. This reduced the flow for the tribes downstream who needed water for agricultural purposes.[184] It was a basic mountain-plains dispute with the added complication of the mining of precious metals. It seems obvious that the Romans intended to consul to seek a peaceful solution. Claudius, however, saw this as an opportunity to win a triumph at a time when such possibilities were becoming more limited.

Claudius attacked the Salassi and was defeated. The setback was serious enough for the Romans to consult the Sibylline books on what they should do to expiate the defeat. The reply was that here, as in any Gallic war, the Romans should make a sacrifice within Gallic territory. This provided Claudius with the pretext to take the offensive again and compensate for the losses of the preceding year. The claims that Claudius made for a triumph were unconvincing to many. He was finally forced to celebrate one at his own expense and to use his daughter, a Vestal Virgin, as a shield against any attempt to stop the procession.[185] The Salassi were pushed back into the hills and driven from the gold works, but they still controlled the mountain passes and to some extent the water. Those who would exploit the

---

[183] Livy *Per.* 53; Dio Cass. 22 fr. 74.1; T.R.S. Broughton (1951) p. 471; I. Beretta (1954) pp. 9–15; A. Pautasso (1960) pp. 72–73 notes destruction levels in number of Alpine sites.

[184] Dio Cass. 22 fr. 74.1; Strabo 4.6.7.

[185] Cic. *Cael.* 34; Val. Max. 5.4.6; Suet. *Tib.* 2; Dio Cass. 22 fr. 74.1; Oros. 5.4.7; Macrob. *Sat.* 3.14.14; A. Degrassi (1947) p. 558; E. S. Gruen (1968) pp. 22–23.

mines or pass through the Alps still had to reckon with the Salassi, until Augustus completely subdued them.[186]

A sense of these semi-independent, semi-Romanized mountaineers is provided by some of the late Republican native cemeteries. Especially illuminating is the cemetery of San Bernardo in the Val d'Ossolo.[187] Most of the graves are from the late second and first centuries B.C. Swords are present in many graves, indicating a continuing warrior mentality, while occasional sheepshears show the importance of herds and the transhumant life. Roman coins, black-glaze pottery, and signs of rudimentary literacy in the form of graffiti inscribed on pots demonstrate that the tribesmen were increasingly being integrated into Roman society.

The tension and insecurity of this frontier is evident from the fragmentary information we have on the history of the settlements in the border districts. One of these was Eporedia, founded in 100 B.C. at the point where the river Dora Baltea emerged from the mountains.[188] The name of the town was derived from a Celtic word meaning one who was good at breaking horses. Pliny notes that it was founded at the instruction of the Sibylline books, which is evidence of a consultation similar to that of Appius Claudius Pulcher in 143 B.C. It was apparently the last colony founded before the Social Wars, and its establishment was probably in part a result of the increasingly acerbic land politics of the late second century B.C.[189] Whatever propaganda value the colony may have had, its effectiveness as a control of the mountain tribes was limited. Not until the enslaved warriors of the Salassi were paraded through the streets of Eporedia by the officers of Augustus did the inhabitants feel safe from the raids of that people.[190]

The situation at Comum must have been similar. It too was a community that straddled the border between plain and mountain. The natives in the area had a strong cultural identify rooted in the Golaseccan tradition, yet they were vulnerable to the peoples in the mountains above them. Pompeius Strabo attempted to reinforce the position of the loyal natives by a colonial foundation. It proved inadequate and required reinforcement of three thousand colonists about 85 B.C. Caesar again had to add five thousand new settlers.[191] This need for new colonists suggests that the frontier zone was still dangerous and un-

[186] Strabo 4.6.7.

[187] P. R. Agostinetti (1972).

[188] G.E.F. Chilver (1941) p. 7.

[189] Pliny *HN* 3.123 calls it an oppidum. P. Fraccaro (1919) pp. 96–102; U. Ewins (1952) pp. 70–71; E. T. Salmon (1970) pp. 121–23.

[190] Strabo 4.6.7–9.

[191] Strabo 5.1.6; P. A. Brunt (1971) p. 199.

pleasant and the turnover rate of settlers at Comum was high. Strabo clearly stated the problem of Comum when he noted:

ὑπέρκεινται δὲ τοῦ Κώμου πρὸς τῇ ῥίζῃ τῶν Ἄλπεων ἱδρυμένου⁵ τῇ μὲν Ῥαιτοὶ καὶ Οὐέννωνες ἐπὶ τὴν ἕω κε-κλιμένοι, τῇ δὲ Ληπόντιοι καὶ Τριδεντῖνοι καὶ Στόνοι καὶ ἄλλα πλείω μικρὰ ἔθνη κατέχοντα τὴν Ἰταλίαν ἐν τοῖς πρόσθεν χρόνοις, λῃστρικὰ καὶ ἄπορα.[192]

Lying above Comum, which is situated near the foot of the Alps, are on one side the Rhaeti and the Vennones, located toward the east, and on the other side the Lepontii, the Tridentini, the Stoni and many other small tribes that occupied Italy in former times, and are now impoverished and live by brigandage.

Whatever other problems of insecurity there were on the frontier were largely local in nature and affected mainly communities close to the mountains. Large sections of the Po drainage remained at peace, and there emerged in the second and early first centuries B.C. a distinctive, loyal, and successful Romano-native society. A complex blend of local roots and outside stimuli, it was the world of Catullus, Vergil, and Livy. Although the information we have is scanty, some effort must be made to reconstruct the currents that were active in this creative process of Romanization.

In addition to the colonies of Cremona and Placentia on the southern margins of the transpadana and frontier communities at Eporedia and Comum, there is the Pompeian settlement at Laus Pompeia in the Lambrus Valley on the road between Mediolanum and Cremona. The center's foundation has been associated with the actions of Cn. Pompeius Strabo in 89 B.C. in extending the citizenship.[193] Pliny, however, credits the town with a Boian origin, and it is indeed significant that no Pompeian inscriptions have been found there.[194]

More important for the Romanization of the area was the development of the road network.[195] Although the region is blessed with a fine river system, the rivers flow toward the southeast, away from the centers of Roman power. Moreover, the Po system did not directly link communities that had grown up on its individual tributaries. A complementary system of roads was necessary to unify the area. The

---

[192] Strabo 4.6.6.
[193] G. A. Mansuelli (1964) p. 253. Asc. *Pis.* 2–3 says the settlers were natives who received citizenship under the Lex Julia.
[194] Pliny *HN* 3.124; G. A. Mansuelli (1961) p. 116.
[195] G. A. Mansuelli (1961) p. 114, (1971) pp. 56–60; G. Uggeri (1975).

course of roads determined, as elsewhere in the Empire, to some degree which towns would prosper and which would stagnate.

The first main road in the transpadana was constructed around 175 B.C. by the consul M. Aemilius Lepidus, that crusty veteran of northern frontier politics.[196] Strabo describes the road as running from Bologna along the base of the Alps and around the coastal marshes to Aquileia. This must be the route that crossed the Po at Hostilia and passed through Ateste, Patavium, and Concordia to reach Aquileia. In 132 B.C. came the Via Popilia linking the coastal area between Ravenna and Adria.[197] In 148 B.C. the Via Postumia was extended from Verona to Concordia, linking Verona, Vicetia, and Opitergium with Aquileia.[198] Other roads followed, and by the end of the second century B.C. the important centers in the transpadana were integrated into the Roman communications system.[199]

The primary aim of the road building was military, but it also expedited the peaceful movement of men and goods. Trade networks had been well developed in the pre-Roman periods, and there is no reason to think that the Roman intervention did anything but improve them. For many items of a fragile or bulk nature, water remained the best means of transport, and centers such as Adria with access to both the Adriatic and the Po remained important. Cemeteries around Adria stress the continuity from pre-Roman to Roman.[200] Before the arrival of the Romans, Adria had a mixed population that included Venetians, Etruscans, and Gauls.[201] No doubt this cosmopolitan mix expanded under the Romans. The presence of the name M. Aimil on a bronze situla found in one tomb shows the influence of that Roman family at Adria.[202]

The archaeological reconstruction of Republican trade in northern Italy is still in its infancy, but certain studies done in recent years provide a sense of both its quantity and its complexity. The two types of objects most easily traced are the black-glaze pottery that was the standard decorated tableware of the third to the mid-first century B.C., and the amphorae that were sufficiently distinctive in shape and material to allow for pinpointing their place of origin. Black glaze is abun-

[196] Strabo 5.1.11; K. Miller (1916) cols. 205–10; G.E.F. Chilver (1941) p. 34; G. Uggeri (1975) pp. 56, 155–57.

[197] K. Miller (1916) cols. 307–8; G. Uggeri (1975) pp. 57, 158.

[198] *CIL* 1.2 n. 624; K. Miller (1916) cols. 257–59; P. Tozzi (1974) pp. 65–66.

[199] G. Fogolari (1940); G. Gorini (1971) p. 502. L. Bertacchi (1972) p. 44 dates the Via Annia to 131 B.C.

[200] G. Fogolari (1940).

[201] G. Fogolari (1940) pp. 436–42; G. Fogolari and G. B. Pellegrini (1958).

[202] G. Fogolari (1940) pp. 439–440.

dant at Republican sites in the transpadana.[203] Some of it appears to have been produced at Adria, suggesting that the centers of production moved to serve developing local markets. This phenomenon repeats itself many times in later Roman economic history, especially with the ceramics industry.

The wine trade represented by the amphorae underwent an evolution whose outlines are just beginning to be understood. By the late third century B.C. Rhodian wine was coming up the Po to Cremona and to the local settlement that preceded Laus Pompeia. In the period 150–100 Greek imports declined, and those from southern Italy increased. The disturbances in southern Italy during the early first century B.C. in turn undercut that source and spurred the development of a northern Adriatic industry. By the mid-first century B.C. Istrian wine was becoming a common drink of northern Italians.[204]

The importation of these goods and the social rituals that attended their use imply growing Mediterraneanization of the native population, especially the ruling elite. Beyond the Po, as elsewhere in Italy, the Romans based their power on the local aristocracy. Our understanding of this ruling class, and of the Romanized center it helped to develop, is thwarted not only by the limitations of the evidence but also by our misconceptions of the pre-Roman population and its fate during the early centuries of Roman rule. Thin strands of evidence do exist, however, and they can be woven into a general, though imperfect, picture.

Among the centers of the north, that where urban continuity is best documented is Padua. Livy records several episodes in his native town's early history, and other sources indicate that the memory of such events as the expulsion of Cleonymus remained strong.[205] No evidence exists for any large formal settlement of Romans or cispadane Italians during the Republic. What is known is that by the end of the Republic the town had become prosperous. It boasted a vigorous wool and cloth trade. The herdsmen could combine use of the Euganean hills and the mountains north of Padua with the low-lying valleys of the Po and the Brenta to satisfy the seasonal needs of their flocks. Some of the roads north of Padua may have originated from these transhumant routes.[206] By the end of the Republic, Padua had five hundred knights on its census, a number greater than any other city in Italy except

[203] G. Fiorentini (1963); V. Righini (1970) pp. 59–65.

[204] P. Baldacci (1967–68), (1972) pp. 18–19 feels that the third-century B.C. Greco-Italic-type amphorae may have come through Genoa.

[205] Cf. nn. 9, 10, 16.

[206] G.E.F. Chilver (1941) pp. 164–65; Mart. 14.143.

Rome.[207] The character of the city was conservative, with a strong loyalty to the Republic and a certain frugality.[208] Continuity in culture and population was expressed by such cults as that of the water deity Aponus and by devotion to hero Antenor.[209]

The city whose territory bordered Patavium on the southwest was Ateste. The only Republican historical references to it come in 135 B.C. and 116 B.C., when boundary disputes erupted with Vicetia to the northwest and with Patavium.[210] Inscriptions provide evidence of the slow but smooth absorption of the Venetian aristocracy into the Roman orbit. Epitaphs of the family of the Ostialii begin with Venetian names and scripts and end with one member of the family, Ostialia Gallenia, who in the first century B.C. was married to a Roman.[211]

Similar in its social complexity and pride in its past was Mantua. While there appears to have been some truth in the city's claim of continuity from the Etruscan period to the second century B.C., Mantua had a heavy Gallic element. Vergil, her famous native son, probably had no Celtic blood but would have had exposure to rural Celtic traditions.[212] His family appears to have typified the elements of continuity and change in the area. The family name may well be Etruscan, and there is even stronger reason for thinking that the cognomen had Etruscan associations.[213] Since Vergil took the *toga virilis* in 55 B.C., six years before Caesar had extended the citizenship widely in the area, his father must have been part of the select group that possessed the franchise early. His father's property was substantial, and he was able to provide his son with the best education in the north.[214] His mother's name was Magia. The frequency of the name around Cremona and the fact that Vergil undertook his first studies in the colony suggests that Magia came from there and that Vergil was the product of the mingling of the old colonial and native transpadane aristocracy.[215]

The position of Catullus, who came from Verona, must have been similar. Catullus was born about 84 B.C. into a distinguished family

---

[207] Strabo 5.1.7; P. Fraccaro (1919) pp. 87–90.

[208] Pliny *Ep*. 1.14.6; Mart. 11.16; G.E.F. Chilver (1941) pp. 216–21.

[209] Dio Cass. 62.26; G.E.F. Chilver (1941) pp. 188–89; C. B. Pascal (1964).

[210] *CIL* 5. 2490, 2492; U. Ewins (1955) p. 73.

[211] *Padova Preromana* (1976) pp. 35–36.

[212] H. W. Garrod (1912); T. Frank (1922) pp. 5–7; G.E.F. Chilver (1941) pp. 212–16.

[213] M. Gordon (1934) pp. 4–6; A. McKay (1971) pp. 55–58; *RE* ser. 2.8.A.1 cols. 1037–38. On Roman Mantua in general see P. Tozzi (1972) p. 55–72.

[214] M. Gordon (1934) pp. 1–2; A. McKay (1971) pp. 62–64; *RE* ser. 2.8.A.1 cols. 1039–41.

of the region.[216] Valerius is one of the most common names in the
Verona area, and there is reason to associate its spread to the first
stages of Roman conquest. Again, the population around this area was
mixed. Raetian elements were present, and there are traces of an
Etruscoid population.[217] Some Cenomanic Celts must have remained,
too.[218] Whatever the mix that went into it, the family of Catullus was
ultimately native to the transpadane area, though highly Romanized
by the second century B.C. and even possessing citizenship by the turn
of the first century.[219]

The Verona that Catullus knew was an important city.[220] Located
on the river Athesis, it controlled a large and diverse *territorium*. Its
position on the road network allowed close contact with the Roman
world to the south. Its art of the late first century B.C. was directly
shaped by Rome and showed little regional influence.[221] Land under
Verona's control extended at least forty kilometers up the Athesis and
embraced much hill country.[222] The city must have benefited from the
Roman policy of attributing to growing political centers the less organized hill tribes.[223] The hill people immediately behind Verona
probably had longstanding associations with the city and had undergone acculturation. The native shrine of the Arunsnates shows a mixture of Roman, Raetic, Celtic, and even Etruscan influences.[224] The
acculturated buffer may have meant that Verona was less exposed
than other centers to frontier depredations.

A similar development appears to have taken place at Brixia (modern Brescia), another town located at the base of the mountains. By
the time of the Empire, Brixia had under its administrative control a
large section of the mountainous territory immediately to its north,
including the land of the Triumpilini, the Camunni, and the Sabini.[225]
The date of this attribution is not known but is generally assumed to
have taken place relatively early. The policy of attribution had been
employed in Liguria in the late second century B.C. In fact, as a strat-

[216] G. A. Mansuelli (1961).
[217] Pliny *HN* 3.130.
[218] V. Bonuzzi (1971) p. 98; G. Gorini (1971) p. 498–501.
[219] G. A. Mansuelli (1961).
[220] Strabo 5.1.6
[221] B. Tamaro (1965) pp. 12–13.
[222] G.E.F. Chilver (1941) pp. 46–47. G. Gorini (1971) p. 504 notes that coin hoards
appear more to the south of the city.
[223] U. Laffi (1966) feels that Arusnates at least may have been a rural district rather
than strict attributi.
[224] G.E.F. Chilver (1941) pp. 183–85.
[225] G.E.F. Chilver (1941) pp. 24, 46; P. Tozzi (1972) pp. 108–11.

egy of frontier control it better suits the period of the later Republic, when the Alps were not really under Roman control.

It should be noted that while attribution implied a degree of administrative subordination, it did not mean the end of native institutions. Both tribes assigned to Brixia still had indigenous *principes* during the Empire.[226] Place names and family names show the persistence of native elements in the Brixian hills even under the Empire. The same situation existed at Bergamo, another center that grew up in the Celtic zone. The epigraphical evidence there suggests the same social pattern found in other northern cities. Roman and Italian names are common, but both cults and nomenclature show that the old Celtic *populus* survived.[227]

The final center that should be mentioned in this review of the transpadane towns is Mediolanum, the modern Milan.[228] It first appears in history as an Insubrian oppidum that was stormed by the Romans in 221 B.C. One is tempted to think of the center as the third-century B.C. equivalent of Bibracte or Magdelensberg. Unfortunately, the growth of later Milan has destroyed most traces of the Celtic settlement and prevents an assessment of Mediolanum as an oppidum. Strabo mentions its growth under the Republic from a village to a city.[229] Its degree of sophistication by the first century B.C. is demonstrated by Vergil's going there to complete his education. By the late second century B.C., it was producing its own local black glaze.[230]

Scattered literary references suggest some acculturation of the Insubres even before conquest. The playwright Statius Caecilius Insuber was taken from Insubrian Mediolanum as a war captive.[231] Although it can be assumed that the bulk of his education took place in Rome, it is difficult to imagine a completely un-Romanized Gaul becoming a pioneer on the Roman stage. Puzzling, too, is Cicero's story of the Insubrian merchant whose daughter was married to the son of the consul L. Calpurnius Piso Caesoninus.[232] It is generally assumed by scholars that Cicero was being insulting in describing the young lady as a Gaul, and that she was a perfectly respectable Roman from Cremona. But the idea of a Calpurnius Piso taking a rich Gallic wife does not seem too absurd. After all, earlier in the second century B.C.

[226] *CIL* 5. 4910, 4893; G.E.F. Chilver (1941) p. 24; P. Tozzi (1972) pp. 146–49.

[227] L. B. Brizio (1967–68).

[228] M. M. Roberti (1973–74).

[229] Strabo 5.1.6.

[230] G. Fiorentini (1963) pp. 38–40.

[231] Gell. *NA* 4, 20, 12–13; Hieron *Chron.* 179 B.C.; D. O. Robson (1938).

[232] Cic. *Pis.* 53. Cic. *Fam.* 15.16.1 mentions a Catius Insuber, an Epicurean philosopher who had recently died (45 B.C.).

Cato could take the daughter of a freedman as his wife. Furthermore, the leading families of places such as Cremona (a Roman colony), Patavium (an old Venetian center), and Mediolanum (a rising Celtic town) all mingled and intermarried.[233]

The fragmentary evidence suggests a wide variety of cities and their roles in the transpadane area. Towns like Mediolanum, Patavium, and Cremona that are relatively removed from the frontier and safe from disturbance became centers of commerce and education, blending native and Roman traditions and providing models for the area. Cities closer to the frontier such as Verona and Brixia with a tradition of interaction with the mountain peoples could serve as active agents in the development of a frontier buffer zone. Most vulnerable were centers like Comum and Eporedia that could not develop and maintain symbiotic relations with the natives, and that hung on tenaciously but marginally in the face of the hostile mountain forces.

Punitive expeditions could be mounted, and the Romans might bring frontier groups into informal and semiformal relations with itself and with the great centers of the north. But the non-Italian area of the peninsula beginning with the Po and extending into the mountains was large and the formal instruments few. Rome ultimately depended on personal relations between itself and the peoples of the north. This brings us to the problem of the nature of the transpadane population in the second and early first centuries b.c., before the colonization of the Civil War period.

I have already argued that the presence of the names of the great Republican consular families beyond the Po is deceptive. It does not imply large-scale movement of Romans into the area and may in fact show the reverse, that is, the assumption of great Roman names by native aristocrats. More suggestive of migration are the typically Italic family names such as Sertorii. These names have been used to demonstrate immigration from southern Italy.[234] We have little evidence, however, suggesting a Roman policy supporting such moves. Some Italians who had fought in the north may have settled down, either buying land or receiving a portion of confiscated territory. But this well-populated country with a stable and respected native populace had little to offer the farmer-immigrant until the large-scale colonization of the Civil War period, when many of the Italic names may have appeared on the scene.[235]

[233] One has to recall the remark of Tacitus (*Hist.* 3.34) on Cremona: *adnexu conubiisque gentium adolevit*. It has been suggested that the family of the important early Imperial figure L. Verginius Rufus was of Celtic origin: A. Sherwin-White (1966) p. 144.

[234] D. O. Robson (1934); L. B. Brizio (1967–68) p. 85.

[235] G.E.F. Chilver (1941) pp. 82–83; P. A. Brunt (1971) pp. 192–98.

It is more sensible to regard the area north of the Po during the Republic as being inhabited by the same native groups that had been there before the Roman conquest. Some communities probably changed little. The native population continued its old ways, especially in the countryside. The distinctively Celtic necropoleis do not die out until the first century B.C.[236] The native religious imprint was strong, and even the scattered Celtic settlement patterns may have their later reflections in the development of dispersed villae.[237] Traces also remain of natives in transition. In an early first century B.C. tomb near Bergamo, a wealthy Celt was buried with a combination of Greco-Roman toilet articles and native weapons and jewelry.[238] At Vercellae, in a recently discovered inscription of the first century B.C., a certain Akisios, a native of some importance, set aside land for cult purposes.[239] At the other end of the scale must have been people with Roman names, Roman political status, and Roman habits whose native origins had been obscured and, as far as possible, discreetly forgotten.

The hypothetical and sparsely documented picture I have drawn of an evolving native population in the northern Italian frontier zone will be familiar to students of later imperial history. It recalls the efforts of Agricola in Britain and probably most closely the picture we have of social and economic evolution in transalpine Gaul in the first century A.D. The strong conservative flavor the north had in the late Republic and early Empire is also familiar. Acculturated inhabitants of the fringes of any empire have good reasons to emphasize their connections with the central power. The Republican poets of Verona and Mantua have in some respects descendants on the cricket pitches of Karachi and Jamaica.

[236] E. Arslan (1975–76) pp. 46–49.

[237] The falera of Manerbio near Brescia dated to 100–50 B.C. has a severed head decoration: E. A. Arslan (1978) p. 113. See G. A. Mansuelli (1961) p. 107 on the relation between villa development and earlier settlement patterns.

[238] R. De Marinis (1978) pp. 95–100.

[239] P. Baldacci (1977).

CHAPTER 3

THE DEVELOPMENT OF
THE LIGURIAN FRONTIER

By 187 B.C. the power of the Boian Gauls had been crushed and the
rest of cisalpine Gaul brought into the Roman system. Under construction was the Via Aemilia, which would unite the cisalpine colonies and connect them with the potentially rich lands across the Po.
Urban centers were beginning to prosper. Across the Mediterranean,
Rome was expanding her conquests in Sardinia and Spain. However,
one frontier remaining within Italy itself—that of the Ligurian mountains—had already proved to be one of the most intractable in Roman
history.

In the northwest of Italy, Alps merge unbroken into the Apennines.
The mountains rise almost directly out of the sea along a stretch of
coast that extends from the area just north of Pisa to the approaches
of the Rhone valley. Tribesmen dwelling in these mountains could
effectively control communications along a narrow coastal road. The
mixed environment of mountains, small river valleys, miniature harbors, and coastal plains discouraged political and social unity. The
limited agricultural and pastoral resources and a seemingly overabundant population encouraged the natives to try their fortunes by raiding
land and sea. The Ligurian coast remained until the end of the Republic a potential and often real den of pirates and highwaymen. The
Ligurians in their mountain strongholds threatened the security of any
power that wished to unite central coastal Italy with the northwestern
part of the Mediterranean, especially since Mediterranean seamen have
always relied on coastal navigation and avoided, whenever possible,
the open sea.[1]

The Ligurian frontier also had its landward extensions. On the south
it faced the Arno valley and the northernmost advance of Etruscan
power.[2] The northeastern flank of Liguria faces on the Po valley, with
the upper part of the drainage extending like an enormous cul-de-sac

[1] F. Braudel (1976) vol. 1 pp. 103–8.
[2] L. Banti (1973) pp. 158–60 notes that in the sixth and fifth centuries the Etruscans
pushed north of upper Arno without difficulty and formed prosperous farming communities. Polyb. 2.16.2 called Pisa the first town in western Etruria. Other sources
place Pisa in Liguria. For a discussion see W. V. Harris (1971) p. 2; RE Pisae (1950)
col. 1769.

into the narrowing tongue of plain between the Apennines and the Alps. Any power that wished to bring unity and order to the Po valley had to confront the prospect of Ligurian raids on land similar to those experienced on the coast.

Liguria, however, was not just an impenetrable mountain mass to be contained or ignored. The most direct route between the northwestern Mediterranean, the rich lands of the Po valley, and ultimately the eastern and central Alps and lands beyond lay through the Ligurian mountains. A combination of river valleys and mountain passes did allow penetration at certain points. Whatever the dangers of these passages were, they were evidently more than compensated for by the rewards of trade across the mountains. These routes had been open for centuries before the appearance of Rome, and they were to play a significant role in the acculturation of key elements among the Ligurians.[3]

We are not well informed about the social and economic structure of the Ligurians, especially those groups relatively unchanged by contact with Mediterranean high culture.[4] The terrain and the hostile populace did not encourage ethnographic investigation in antiquity, and the area has, up to the present, seen only relatively limited archaeological research. Nevertheless, the scattered fragments of evidence that are preserved can be unified into a coherent picture of a mountain society.

The quality of the land and the nature of the terrain encouraged the development of pastoralism and transhumance among the Ligurians. Strabo describes them as living mainly on shepherding, pasturing their flocks sometimes by the sea, sometimes in the mountains in classic transhumant patterns. Diodorus, probably deriving his account from Poseidonios, gives an even more dismal picture with the Ligurians living in huts and caves and surviving mainly by hunting.[5] Questions of pasturage rights between Genoa and its mountain Ligurians arise in one of the earliest written testimonies we have on Liguria, an inscription known as the Tabula Polcevera.[6] The continuous pastoral movement and regrouping of herds, while encouraging small and sometimes unstable settlement units, provided the Ligurians with an intimate knowledge of a diverse and difficult countryside. It also served as a means for exchange of information among the mountain folk. As

[3] G. F. Lo Porto (1952); E. Sereni (1971); A. Ambrosi (1972) pp. 11–12.
[4] E. Sereni (1971).
[5] Strabo 4.6.2; Diod. 5.39.
[6] *CIL* 5. 7749 ll. 32–35.

more modern examples show, news in a pastoral society tends to travel quickly over long distances.[7]

Although pastoralism was important to their way of life, the Ligurians were not completely dependent on herding. Some agriculture was possible in their territory. In 180 B.C. the Roman consul A. Postumius Albinus was able to bring the Ligurians to heel by destroying their crops and vines.[8] Those who could not grow their own vines or who preferred better Italian wine to the wretched Ligurian product could obtain Italian wine by trading wool, hides, honey, and even wood products from their forested mountainsides.[9]

Rigorous estimates of the population level in the mountains must await archaeological surveys of Ligurian sites there, but recent research in the French sector of the Ligurian mountains suggests that the area may have had a relatively high density in pre-Roman times.[10] This is also supported by finds in the geographically similar area of Istria on the northeastern frontier of Italy, and by the accounts of the Roman wars.[11] The figures on casualties inflicted by the Romans and on the numbers involved in mass deportations, though exaggerated, suggest a relatively large population. Indeed, overpopulation in relation to the limited resources of the area appears to have been a real problem. In that respect, Liguria was in a position similar to that of Switzerland in early modern European history. Raids and mercenary service became necessary outlets for an abundant and militant population.

In the interior mountains, political and social development remained at a relatively simple level. The classical sources speak of *vici* and *castella*. A few of these are beginning to be investigated archaeologically.[12] Large concentrations of warriors could be assembled for war and raiding, and some of the Ligurian armies mentioned by the Roman historians, even allowing for exaggeration, were of considerable size. The mechanism for forming these temporary armies is not explained in detail by the ancient authors but can be partly reconstructed from passing references and from a general knowledge of how mountain societies function. Even the shifting world of pastoral man has certain fixed points, and among Ligurians these related to religious

---

[7] For an account of the mobility and communications networks characteristic of such pastoral societies see P. Arbos (1923); E. LeRoy Ladurie (1978).

[8] Livy 40.41.5–6. *CIL* 5. 7749 l. 27 mentions the vines of the Ligures Langenses.

[9] Strabo 4.6.2.

[10] J. E. Dugand (1970); E. Sereni (1971) pp. 181–82, 379.

[11] C. Marchesetti (1963).

[12] M. C. Cervi (1969); L. Barfield (1972) p. 145.

sanctuaries and the burial places of the dead. Shrines were located on such mountains as Penna, Antola, and Gottero. Livy at one point refers to a Ligurian army as *lege sacrata coacto exercitu*.[13] When the Romans began deporting Ligurians, the natives raised the plea that they not be removed from their ancestral shrines and cemeteries. Burial places and shrines can serve as regular assembly places during the annual cycle, helping to unify an otherwise dispersed pastoral society.[14]

The movement was aided throughout the year by an intimate acquaintance with the mountains and the existence of tracks and paths known almost exclusively to the natives. The ease with which the Ligurians could move booty from the settlements they had raided in the plain to their mountain strongholds supports the image of sophisticated communication networks. Some scholars have even claimed to have discovered traces of these tracks in the mountains.[15] This ability to rally forces was apparently aided by a system of intercommunicating hill forts positioned to allow signal fires to be passed from one to the other.[16] Still, the ability of the Ligurians to unite their forces should not be exaggerated. The Carthaginian captain Mago experienced the painful slowness of the process, and the Romans were able to block these aggregations of Ligurian troops.

Several lines of evidence support the notion that the permanent political structure of the mountain Ligurians was a relatively simple one. One scholar has made the perceptive point that despite the many wars the Romans fought with the Ligurians, the name of not a single Ligurian leader is preserved.[17] This is in sharp contrast to the nearby Gallic frontier, where many of the native leaders are specifically identified. Ligurian chiefs themselves commented on the difficulty of controlling their own followers. References to *principes* and to fomenters of rebellions and conspiracies do occur but are scattered.[18] Whatever problems the Romans faced on the Ligurian frontier, strong leaders and a chieftain-style structure was not among them. On the other hand, the lack of complex political systems made the task of frontier management and postconquest control difficult. No person or group

[13] Livy 36.38.1; U. Formentini (1949) pp. 217–18; E. Sereni (1971) pp. 353, 358; A. Ambrosi (1972).

[14] Livy 40.38.4-6; A. Fleming (1971) pp. 154–64.

[15] E. Sereni (1971).

[16] M. C. Cervi (1969).

[17] E. Sereni (1971) pp. 146–47, 161–62.

[18] E. Sereni (1957) pp. 65–66, (1971) pp. 161–62. Similar problems arose in dealing with the Plains Indians of the United States: C. A. Milner (1981) pp. 146–47.

could guarantee the peace of more than a limited number of followers. Again, it is probably significant that we do not have reference to a single client ruler among the Ligurians. The Romans would have attempted to develop a client system similar to that in the Alps and Istria if the means had been available.

Despite their social, economic, and political limitations, the Ligurians should not be considered a static society. In every direction, they were open to contact both peaceful and bellicose with more developed groups, and that was bound to introduce change. Of these outside contacts, the impact of seaborne trade is the most important. It has been noted that Liguria provided passages through the mountains to the rich lands of the Po plain, which led to the early development of emporia and mixed foreign-native centers. The earliest of these coastal centers is Chiavari, between Genoa and La Spezia. A cemetery there that has been excavated dates to the eighth century B.C. and had been in use to the sixth century B.C. Cremation graves contained an abundance of grave goods and were arranged in enclosures suggesting family units. The items in the graves show outside contacts, including some across the Apennines with Bologna and the culture of Este.[19]

More important to the development of coastal Liguria in the pre-Roman period was the emporium at Genoa. The site provided an excellent harbor and starting point for routes leading through the passes of the mountains to the Po drainage. The rich cemetery of pre-Roman Genoa begins in the early fifth century and reveals a wealth of imported Greek and Etruscan goods.[20] Craters and amphorae attest to the rituals of wine-drinking, while the strigils suggest Greek notions of exercise and cleanliness. The bulk of the material appears to date to the fifth and fourth centuries B.C. Greeks and Etruscans were certainly present as settlers, although much of the population had remained Ligurian. Greek influence did not cease with the fourth century. The spread of a Massilian-derived coinage up the valleys behind Genoa into the Po area attests the continuing influence of the Greek colony into third century B.C. Strabo, writing in the first century A.D., still considered Genoa a Ligurian emporium. Its position and its friendly relations with Massilia led naturally to association with Rome.[21]

The growth of these rich and sophisticated coastal centers in the face of poor mountaineers must have engendered social problems. The

[19] N. Lamboglia (1960b); P. Zucchi (1967).

[20] N. Lamboglia (1939) pp. 196–99; L. Bernabo Brea and G. Chiappella (1951); L. Barfield (1972) p. 145. Most of the material dates from the 450–300 period.

[21] Strabo 4.6.2 discusses the emporion role of Genoa. L. Bernabo Brea and G. Chiappella (1951) p. 198 note the amount of native pottery in Genoa cemetery.

scholars who published the Genoa cemetery stressed the contrast between their rich finds and the poverty of contemporary Ligurian centers and cemeteries.[22] The poorer mountaineers probably increased the
number of raids on their rich neighbors. Livy reports that by the end
of the third century the prosperous coastal tribe of the Ligurian Ingauni near Ventimiglia was being harassed by its less fortunate kinsmen up in the hills, and this practice was no doubt repeated at other
points along the coast.[23] But equally common must have been more
peaceful symbiotic arrangements in which the emporium served as a
focus for mountain and coastal relations. The Tabula Polcevera shows
interaction between Genoa and its *retroterra*. The Romans found such
associations in places they could develop, and it is no accident that the
first example we have of the practice of *attributio* (the linking of politically underdeveloped peoples to a more sophisticated center) comes
from Genoa.[24]

Another important frontier for Liguria was that with Etruria on the
south. For the Etruscans, control of the Arno valley was essential for
maintaining close communications with their transapennine settlements around Bologna.[25] The mountains of Liguria pressed closely
around the Arno valley, however, and it is doubtful that the Etruscans
extended their control much beyond the valley slopes. Some Etruscan
objects and place names are found along the tributaries flowing into
the Arno from the north as well as along the valley of the Serchio.[26]
Livy noted that the territory of Luna was once Etruscan but that it
later became Ligurian.[27] When the Romans came on the scene in the
second century B.C., they found Pisa, a frontier town, and the Etruscans, a beleagured folk subject to the raids of Ligurians who carried
the *praeda etrusca* back to their mountain hideouts. Nevertheless, the
frontier relationship cannot have been completely hostile, and some
interdependence must have developed similar to that of the Genoese
and their backcountry neighbors.

A second force for change among the Ligurians was mercenary service. Ligurians fought with the Carthaginians at the battle of Himera
in 480 B.C. are mentioned several times during subsequent centuries
serving Greek and Carthaginian generals.[28] It is expected that the Car-

[22] L. Bernabo Brea and G. Chiappella (1951) pp. 198–99.
Livy 28.46.9–10.
    [23] Livy 28.46.9–10.
    [24] *CIL* 5. 7749.
    [25] H. H. Scullard (1967) pp. 168–70.
    [26] L. Banti (1931) p. 179.
    [27] Livy. 41.13.5.
    [28] Herod. 7.165; E. Sereni (1971) pp. 181–82. Diod. 21.3 says that Ligurians were

thaginians would have employed the Ligurians as they employed other
poor warrior folk of the western Mediterranean. A network of contacts
and agents must have been developed to tap the supplies of warriors
in the mountain valleys. Returning mercenaries brought with them
Mediterranean wealth and goods and the experience of contact with a
larger world, not only classical but also Gallic and Spanish. Perhaps
the tomb discovered at Ligurian La Spezia prepared in the local manner but with Celtic arms is that of a returning warrior strongly influenced by contacts with Celtic mercenaries.[29]

These opportunities for mercenary service were seriously damaged
by the Carthaginian loss of maritime hegemony during the First Punic
War. Some contacts must have remained open however, since Mago
and Hamilcar depended on Ligurian support during their daring raids
at the close of the Second Punic War. One would like to know more
about the impact that the final closing of the Punic mercenary markets
had here as well as elsewhere in the Mediterranean. In Liguria it helped
to create a surplus warrior population that had developed a taste for
Mediterranean goods but was bottled up in the mountains with no
outlet other than herding, scratch farming, or raiding Etruscan and
developing Roman settlements. This combination of ecological, social,
and economic factors helped to turn Liguria into one of the most complex and difficult frontiers faced by Rome. In many ways it was a
Spain in smaller scale, with the difference that it was closer to home
and therefore more vital to the interests of Roman Italy. Although
large-scale assults from the mountains were not generally a problem,
raiding was probably continuous, and with it came the uneasiness of
a frontier dominated by guerrilla warfare. Hit and run attacks and the
destruction of isolated farms and settlements were countered with reprisal raids, burning, massacre, and torture. The settlers would have
developed toward the Ligurians an attitude similar to that of the
American frontiersmen toward the Indians. For them, the only good
Ligurian was a dead one.[30]

The Roman field commanders, even with an enraged frontier population urging them to action, faced the prospects of a Ligurian campaign with decidedly mixed feelings. For Livy, Liguria seemed an
ideal field for Roman *virtus*, a tough training ground for later wars.[31]

---

serving in the army of Agathocles in 299 B.C. Diod. 11.1–5 mentions Ligurians serving
with the Carthaginians in 480 B.C.

[29] A. Frova (1968).

[30] As early as Cato the Ligurians are described as *omnes fallaces* (fr. 32) and *inliterati
mendacesque* (fr. 31).

[31] Livy 39.1.2.

The problems were great and the temptations small. The Romans had to deal with rough terrain and a wily enemy. Ambushes were the normal way of starting battles. The land and the people were poor, and the main booty was spoil that the Ligurians themselves had taken from Roman-controlled territory. The results of each victory were soon erased as the enemy regrouped, came down from their almost inaccessible retreats, and resumed raiding. Moreover, the successes achieved by Roman generals brought little recognition at home. Ligurian victories, which often required the greatest skill of a commander and courage and endurance on the part of the army, became the source of derision and rebuff. Ligurian triumphs were regarded as something of a political joke by the late Republic. It is hardly surprising that Roman commanders preferred the more lush assignments to the east.[32]

As the Ligurian frontier was moved north and west and the Romans realized the necessity of relating Ligurian policy to Alpine security, commanders were denied even the small amount of glory and the modest booty that an attack on a mountain tribe could bring. The senate at Rome increasingly restrained the generals in the field and sought limited victories or stalemates in the interest of larger strategic and political gains. This is a situation familiar to modern colonial and neocolonial commanders and their superiors at home. In all its aspects, the Ligurian frontier provides an excellent illustration of the complexities and problems of Roman frontier development.

Three initial factors caused the Romans to keep a wary eye on the Ligurians. The first was Rome's old alliance with Massilia, a Greek city that knew the Ligurians well and had fought them often on both land and sea.[33] Second, by gaining control of Etruria in the early third century B.C. and advancing into north-central Italy, the Romans developed an increasingly long border facing the Ligurian mountains.

It was the third area of interaction that led to Rome's first war with the Ligurians. As a result of the First Punic War, Rome had not only established hegemony in the western Mediterranean but had seized the islands of Sardinia and Corsica. Rome had to assume responsibility for the protection of the northern Tyrrhenian Sea, and that brought her face to face with the problem of Ligurian piracy and the funneling of Ligurian mercenaries into the armies of Carthage. Sardinia and Liguria had formed part of a Carthaginian sphere of influence, and their mariners had always cultivated piracy as a way of life. The connection

[32] Cic. *Brut.* 255–56; Livy 39.1.
[33] H. Rolland (1949).

between problems in Liguria and on the islands is suggested by a cryptic passage from the historian Zonaras:

μετὰ ταῦτα δὲ ἔπεισαν τοὺς Σαρδονίους οἱ Καρχηδόνιοι κρύφα τοῖς Ῥωμαίοις ἐπαναστῆναι. καὶ τούτοις οἱ Κύρνιοι προσαπέστησαν, καὶ οἱ Λίγυες οὐχ ἡσύχασαν.[34]

Afterwards the Carthaginians secretly persuaded the Sardinians to revolt against the Romans. In addition to this the Corsicans also revolted and the Ligurians did not stay quiet.

It was probably no accident that in 238 B.C. Ti. Sempronius Gracchus, who occupied Sardinia, also waged war on the Ligurians.[35] And in 236 B.C. we find the consul P. Cornelius Lentulus in action against the Ligurians while his colleague C. Licinius Varus was engaged in pacification in Corsica.[36]

These victories did not end the wars. In 234 B.C. the consul L. Postumius Albinus marched into Liguria while other military actions were carried out in Corsica and Sardinia.[37] In fact, these first Ligurian wars only ended with the victories and triumph of Q. Fabius Maximus in 233 B.C. He defeated the Ligurians in battle, drove them back into the mountains, and claimed to have ended their plundering and harrying of nearby territories. Fabius considered his successes of sufficient importance not only to deserve a triumph but also to be commemorated with the dedication of a temple to Honor. Again, it is probably no coincidence that the other consul of the year was fighting in Sardinia.[38]

The short, scattered references to these wars do not allow us to locate the theater of action with any precision. The principal aim seems to have been to defend Italian lowland territory under Roman protection. In the late third century this must have meant the northern Tuscan frontier. The concern for the safety of the Etruscan border probably prompted the decision to bring Pisa into the Roman frontier system. Pisa provided the Romans with a military base near the sea and a staging ground for campaigns through the coastal plain to the valley of the Serchio, as well as the support of a people whose warlike spirit

[34] Zonaras 8.18.

[35] Livy *Per.* 20; Zonaras 8.18; N. Lamboglia (1932).

[36] Zonaras 8.18. Lentulus received the first Ligurian triumph: A. Degrassi (1947) p. 549.

[37] Zonaras 8.18.

[38] Cic. *Nat. D* 2.23.61, *Pis.* 58; Plut. *Vit. Fab.* 2.1; Zonaras 8.18; A. Degrassi (1947) p. 549.

had been continually sharpened by combat with the Ligurians.[39] Of
equal importance in land like Liguria was the intelligence that the
Pisans could provide. Trade and warfare had given them a knowledge
of the tribesmen in the vicinity.

The years between the triumph of Fabius Maximus and the Second
Punic War saw other Ligurian actions that reflected an increasingly
complicated frontier situation. In 223 B.C. P. Furius Philus triumphed
over both the Gauls and the Ligurians.[40] This combination of Ligurians and Gauls reflected the changing nature of Roman control in central Italy. The legions had by this time advanced to the Po, creating
an increasingly long frontier on the eastern slopes of Liguria. Furius'
wars with the Ligurians probably developed when he tried to outflank
the Gallic Insubres by advancing through the territory of the Anares
in the upper Po valley. It is certainly tempting to associate with Furius
Philus a place called Cameliomagus, which is mentioned in the later
itineraries.[41] It was located in the area where Philus was campaigning.
The name Camillus was one intimately associated with the Furii family.

The Romans at the same time had not forgotten their growing responsibilities in the west and the need to control land and sea routes.
In 218 B.C. the consul P. Cornelius Scipio stopped along the Ligurian
coast on his way to Spain. The emporium of Genoa probably became
a Roman ally at this time. Scipio also began to investigate the routes
that connected coastal Liguria with the Po valley.[42]

By the outbreak of the Second Punic War, Rome had defined the
nature and problems of its Ligurian frontier. The struggle with Hannibal left Romano-Ligurian relations largely in limbo. Fortunately for
Rome, the Carthaginians did not exploit an area of potential trouble
for Rome until it was too late for their actions to have any great impact.

A change in Carthaginian policy began when their general Mago
landed in Savona, a center located northwest of Genoa.[43] His expedition had two main strategic aims. The first was to win the friendship
of the local Ligurian tribe Ingauni and thus gain a secure foothold on
the coast. From there, friendship networks could be developed with
Ligurians to the west and east. To the west this initiative would threaten

---

[39] Strabo 5.2.5; N. Lamboglia (1932) p. 18.
[40] Polyb. 2.32.1; Zonaras 8.20; A. Degrassi (1947) p. 550.
[41] R. Miller (1916) col. 232. The sources give different spellings for the name.
[42] Livy 21.32.5.
[43] On strategic importance of Savona see E. Pais (1918) pp. 495–96; A. J. Toynbee
(1965) vol. 2 p. 263.

Rome's ally Massilia, a city that had a long history of contact with the Ligurians on both land and sea. To the southeast the threat would be against Genoa and the important passes it controlled across the mountain to the Po. Additionally, Carthaginian-directed Ligurian forces could harass by land and sea Rome's newly developing communications with Spain.

To accomplish the first part of his mission, Mago had to demonstrate his usefulness to the Ingauni. The tribe had two main enemies. The first was the more primitive Ligurians of the hills who constantly raided the territory of the Ingauni. Mago joined the Ingauni in a successful campaign against them. The second rival was, of course, the emporium of Genoa. With Genoa gone, the Ingauni would become the strongest power on the northwestern coast of Italy. Mago had temporarily resolved the problem even before arriving at Savona. On his way to the territory of the Ingauni, he destroyed Genoa.[44]

The more important aim of Mago's mission was probably to establish communications with the Gauls of the Po valley. Savona provided access to routes that led to the upper reaches of the Po and to tribes not subdued by Rome. These could be rallied to attack the developing Roman interests in the Po area. The Gauls did respond to the blandishments of Mago, and Rome felt herself seriously threatened.[45]

The Roman reaction was swift. In 203 B.C. the propraetor Sp. Lucretius was instructed to rebuild the town of Genoa. At the same time, the Romans turned against Mago and his gathering Gallic forces. The Gauls were defeated, and Mago, mortally wounded, was forced to withdraw his army from Liguria.[46] The Romans came to an understanding with the Ingauni and thus brought some peace to that stretch of the coast and the passage to Massilia and Spain.[47]

A short interval of relative tranquillity followed, but new wars were inevitable. The continued existence of an unpacified Liguria was unacceptable to the Romans, and the road to Spain along the Ligurian coast was assuming increasing importance. Although the nature of the narrow, twisting coastal road precluded its use for large troop and supply movements, couriers and small groups moved along it. Sea travelers followed the coast closely and depended on friendly Ligurian ports. The tribesmen and pirates of Liguria could threaten both of these routes. Perhaps even more dangerous to the Romans was the long Ligurian land frontier facing the cisalpina. Rome was about to

[44] Livy 28.46.7–12, 30.1.10–11.
[45] Livy 29.4–5.
[46] Livy 30.18–19; N. Lamboglia (1933) pp. 9–10.
[47] Livy 31.2.11; A. J. Toynbee (1965) vol. 2 p. 268.

open the final phase of her long and bloody Gallic wars in Italy. Both Gauls and Ligurians saw an enemy in Rome, and the Ligurians could hinder the Roman effort to pacify cispadane Gaul by harassing new settlements and diverting Roman military resources to their defense.

The renewal of campaigns against the Gauls was followed closely by new fighting with the Ligurians. In 200 B.C. the praetor L. Furius Purpurio defeated a rising of both Gauls and Ligurians.[48] The year 197 B.C. saw an intensified Ligurian war and new Roman tactics. C. Cornelius Cethegus continued his Gallo-Ligurian war in the northwestern cisalpina. The other consul, Q. Minucius Rufus, started his campaign from Genoa. He appears to have used the opportunity to establish personal and familial relations with the leading families of Genoa. The role the Minucii assumed as the patrons of Genoa is attested by such later evidence as the Tabula Polcevera. From Genoa, Minucius advanced through the mountains and emerged to attack the Ligurians and Gauls on the flanks and rear. One aim was to reduce pressure on the colony of Placentia, whose *territorium* had a long Ligurian frontier and whose vulnerability the Romans realized all too well. Minucius Rufus accomplished his basic goals and was awarded a triumph on the Alban Mount.[49]

Yet the campaigns of Rufus hardly ended the war. In the following year, the consul L. Furius Purpurio attacked Ligurians who were aiding the Boii.[50] In 195 B.C. the praetor P. Porcius Laeca was assigned to Pisa so that he could harry the Ligurians from the rear.[51] In 194 B.C. the consul Ti. Sempronius Longus was again fighting both Gauls and Ligurians.[52] But despite these punitive campaigns, the Ligurians were able in 193 B.C. to descend from the mountains and carry the war right up to the walls of Placentia itself.[53] Moreover, troubles was developing on another frontier. In 193 B.C. the prefect at Pisa reported that the Ligurians had formed a universal conspiracy (*coniuratione per omnia conciliabula universae gentis facta*). The use of the word *coniuratio* implies a degree of coordinated political and military action not normal among the Ligurians. It suggests that the Roman attacks, rather than cowing their spirits, were forcing them to respond with more sophisticated political and military organization.[54]

[48] Livy 31.10.–31.11.3, 31.21–31.22.3.
[49] Livy 32.31.3–5; *CIL* 5. 7749; A. Degrassi (1947) p. 552.
[50] Livy 33.37.4–5.
[51] Livy 33.43.5.
[52] Livy 34.46–34.48.1
[53] Livy 34.56.9–11.
[54] Livy 34.56.2–3; N. Lamboglia (1932) pp. 11–12.

Buoyed by this new sense of strength and unity, the Ligurians took the offensive. Again they moved down from the hills, attacking Luna, then Pisa, and finally the whole neighboring coast. Pisa itself came under siege. With the regular Roman frontier staging center under assault, the consul. Q. Minucius Thermus was forced to assemble his army at Arretium, far from the Ligurian frontier. The Ligurians, their number swollen by compatriots anticipating rich spoils, systematically pillaged the *ager Pisanus* and shipped the booty back to their mountain *vici* and *castella*. The Roman army finally advanced and entered Pisa in battle array. But their efforts nearly led to disaster. They were trapped in a narrow valley. Only the skillful use of Numidian cavalry that raided Ligurian villages and forced the enemy to defend their homelands prevented another Caudine Forks.[55] The main Ligurian camp was finally captured, but it yielded little booty. The seizure of neighboring *castella*, however, did result in the recovery of some of the lost *praeda etrusca* during the following year. L. Quinctius Flamininus followed these successes with an offensive against the Ligurian *castella* that were menacing Placentia. Roman prisoners were freed and booty recovered. A short-lived peace was established on the two frontiers of Liguria.[56]

The year 187 B.C. saw the revival of fighting in Liguria. Livy opens his account with a passage that emphasizes the military virtues of the enemy and the role these wars played in the larger scheme of the developing empire: *Is hostis velut natus ad continendam inter magnorum intervalla bellorum Romanis militarem disciplinam erat.*[57] His attitude, of course, reflected the late downgrading of the Ligurian wars. But the idea of these campaigns as a conditioning exercise for the great wars in the east would have seemed strange to the commanders as they fought to extricate their armies from mountain ambushes, or to the farmers of Placentia as they watched their homesteads burned.

By 187 B.C. the whole frontier was again in flames. The consul C. Flaminius planned a campaign against the Friniates, a Ligurian tribe located in the mountains southwest of Mutina. He soon discovered the frustrations of mountain warfare. The Roman army took the war into the Friniates' own territory and forced them to surrender. When Flaminius tried to enforce the provisions of the surrender agreement that required the Ligurians to surrender their arms, the Liguri-

---

[55] Livy 35.3.1–6, 35.11.1–13.
[56] Livy 35.21.7–11, 35.40.4–5. The actions of Minucius roused considerable controversy, and he was vigorously attacked by Cato: F. della Corte (1969) pp. 43–44; H. H. Scullard (1973) pp. 133–34, 258; A. E. Astin (1978) pp. 63–65.
[57] Livy 39.1.2.

ans balked and fled into the mountains. The Romans pursued them and succeeded in subduing a substantial part of the tribe.[58] Nevertheless, although the Friniates were cowed, Flaminius had to face the prospect of campaigning against yet another Ligurian group: the Apuani.

The Apuani were probably at this time the most powerful group in southeastern Liguria. Their territory was large and their manpower resources abundant. They could threaten the lands of Bononia, the recently founded colony on their east, and those of Pisa to their southwest. They raided both of these Roman frontier settlements in 187 B.C., forcing concerted consular action.[59]

The responsibility for the main attack against the Apuani was assigned to M. Aemilius Lepidus. It was the beginning of a long and illustrious career in the north for this most capable Roman general. His basic plan of attack was similar to that used by Flaminius against the Friniates. He took the war into the land of the enemy, probably from Pisa through the Serchio valley. The lower settlements of the Ligurians located in the valleys and on the edge of the plain were devastated, while the bulk of the enemy fled into the mountains. Finally, systematic destruction of communities and the advance of the Roman army forced them into regular battle. The Romans emerged victorious.[60] Lepidus then turned against those remnants of the Friniates that Flaminius had been unable to reach. They were defeated, disarmed, and forced down into the plain.[61]

The relocation of the mountain-dwelling Ligurians into lower areas, where they could be better policed, marked an innovation in the administration of the area. The Romans had of course in earlier military campaigns moved populations from highly defensible locations to lower, more exposed settlements.[62] By now they had come to realize that Liguria would never be secure while so many unpacified natives lived in the mountains and while the hill forts of the Apennines provided safe retreat for the enemy forces.

By bringing the natives down from the hills and settling them on new lands, the Romans could begin the process of integrating them into their social and economic system. Peaceful farmers on good land with access to markets and an increasing taste for Mediterranean goods would have a stake in maintaining the Pax Romana. Over time, they

[58] Livy 39.1.5–6, 39.2.1–5.
[59] Livy 39.2.5–6.
[60] Livy 39.2.7–9.
[61] Livy 39.2.9–11.
[62] Zonaras 8.18; T. W. Potter (1979) pp. 98–101.

would become like the Ingauni and other acculturated Ligurians. These first steps taken by Lepidus were cautious, but it began a process that was ultimately to tip the balance in Liguria toward Rome.

Another important step that Lepidus took was to initiate the construction of the great road that was to bear his name.[63] Like the first lowland resettlement schemes, the first stretch built from Arretium to Bononia represented a cautious beginning. It not only aided the movement of Roman forces to the still raw colony but also encouraged the importation of trade goods and the integration of the Ligurian natives with the commerce of the road that passed so close to their hills. Detailed archaeological investigations in southern Etruria have shown how nearby trunk-road construction reshaped native settlements. It is likely that future research will demonstrate similar shifts in Liguria.[64]

Any hopes that the Romans might have had that the Apuani had been completely subdued were quickly dashed. In the year following the victories of Flaminius and Lepidus, the consul Q. Marcius Philippus was ambushed by those same tribesmen.[65] His successor, M. Sempronius Tuditanus, avenged the defeat, ravaging the land of the Apuani, burning their *vici* and *castella*, and dislodging them from their *sedes maiorum*.[66] This, however, did not end the unrest. Two consuls had to be assigned to Liguria in 184 and 183 B.C.[67] In 182 there were still rumors that the Apuani were planning new attacks against the territory of Pisa. Again the consuls were sent to Liguria. They did achieve some victories, but most of the Ligurians faded into the mountains. The frontier remained sufficiently insecure for the senate to order a Roman army to winter at Pisa.[68]

The senate increasingly realized the need for long-range steps that would strengthen the Roman position. The year 183 B.C. saw the foundation of large colonies at Parma and Mutina. Although they were planted in confiscated Boian territory, the colonies were positioned to block the Ligurians as well as to watch over the recently decimated Gauls. Their *territoria* extended up to the mountain slopes, and each colony controlled a key communication route down from the Apennines. They would ideally not only help contain the raids of the Ligurians but also keep watch on the seasonal movement of the Ligurian herds. A significant force behind this colonial movement was

[63] Livy 39.2.10–11.
[64] J. B. Ward-Perkins (1962) pp. 397–99; T. W. Potter (1979) pp. 101–20.
[65] Livy 39.20.5–10.
[66] Livy 39.32.1–3.
[67] Livy 39.38.1,7, 39.45.3; T.R.S. Broughton (1951) pp. 374, 378.
[68] Livy 40.1.3–8, 40.16.4–6, 40.17.6–7.

M. Aemilius Lepidus, the consul of 187 B.C. who a few years before
had defeated the Ligurians and started the road-building program in
the area.[69]

One of the traits of the Ligurian frontier during the second century
B.C. was that no zone could be considered permanently secure. Just as
the tide appeared to be turning in Rome's favor in the south, the
northwest erupted. In 189 B.C. the praetor L. Baebius Dives, while
trying to take any army overland to Spain, was ambushed by Ligurians and staggered mortally wounded into Massilia.[70] By 185 B.C. the
tension had made it necessary for a consular army to be sent against
the Ingauni.[71] Specific causes are not given for the renewal of hostilities with this long-peaceful tribe, but one can suggest reasons. Twenty-
six years had passed since the last hostilities. The warriors who had
fought with Mago and had felt the force of Roman arms were fading
from the scene. The decimated ranks of fighting men were once again
filled. The closing of the Carthaginian mercenary market and the steady
advance of the Pax Romana removed most outlets for the warriors'
military energies. Piracy and banditry were increasingly tempting as
the land and sea routes through Liguria became more heavily traf-
ficked. The Romans failed to garrison the area, and the power and
prestige of Massilia declined.[72]

Ap. Claudius Pulcher, the consul of 185 B.C., marched against the
Ingauni. Six oppida and a number of warriors were captured. As an
example to the vanquished and a deterrent to other Ligurians who
might have been contemplating rebellion, forty-three *belli auctores* were
beheaded.[73] The campaign was less successful than the Romans had
hoped, and the mass executions were not a sufficient deterrent. Within
three years, the Massilians were complaining about Ligurian piracy.
The consul L. Aemilius Paullus, a veteran of frontier warfare in Spain,
was assigned the task of once again bringing under control the northwest of Liguria. The appointment of *duumviri navales* showed that his
task was to bring peace on sea as well as on land.[74]

The mission of Paullus was a delicate one. Order had to be restored
on the Ligurian coast and the scourge of piracy removed, but the

[69] Livy 39.55.7–8. On herding in this area see Mart. 4.37.5 (*ex pecore redeunt ter ducena
Parmensi*), 5.13.8 (*innumeros Gallica Parma greges*); F. DePachtere (1920) pp. 22, 26.

[70] Livy 37.57.1–2; Oros. 4.20.24; N. Lamboglia (1933) pp. 11–12.

[71] Livy 39.32.4.

[72] H. Rolland (1949) pp. 145–46 notes the lack of imitation of later Massilian coinage
among the natives.

[73] Livy 39.32.4.

[74] Livy 40.18. On Paullus in Spain see Livy 37.2.11, 37.46.7–8, 37.57.5–6.

Ingauni were not to be exterminated or so badly weakened that they could not defend their hinterland. If they were weakened, less acculturated Alpine groups could come down the valley of the Albegna and wreak havoc with communications to the west. Paullus must have learned from his Spanish experience the importance of avoiding frontier vacuums.[75] Unfortunately, his restraint almost resulted in disaster for the Romans.

Paullus entered the territory of the Ingauni and demanded their surrender. The tribal leaders requested a delay to consult their scattered fellow tribesmen. They also asked the general to restrict the movements of his army in order to avoid damaging crops.[76] Their requests were granted, but the limitations on mobility seriously hindered the scouting and intelligence-gathering of the Romans. The Ingauni used this respite to mass their troops and assault the consul's camp. Only after a tense siege did Paullus break through the encircling forces and defeat the Ingauni.

Near disaster did not change the basic approach of the Romans. The instigators of pirating were systematically rounded up and hostages demanded.[77] At the same time, Paullus took special care not to disturb the existing settlement patterns of the Ingauni. His only demand was that they tear down the ramparts of the communities where he allowed them to remain.[78] This prohibition on oppidum fortifications was similar to Cato's demand for the destruction of hill-fort defenses in Spain and the prohibition issued by Ti. Sempronius Gracchus against the construction of newly defended oppida in Spain. It reflected a desire on the part of the Romans to limit the defensive capabilities of the natives without changing their basic way of life. The Ingauni were left in control of their land and strong enough to be sentinels on the Ligurian road, but too weak to be a serious enemy of Rome.

In 181 B.C. Paullus received a triumph *de Liguribus Ingaunis*.[79] But, his successes did not end the trouble in northern Liguria. The consul A. Postumius Albinus in 180 B.C. felt compelled to watch the shores of the Intemelii and the Ingauni, and in 176 B.C., during renewed wars against the Ligurians, *duumviri navales* were again appointed to patrol

[75] Plut. *Vit. Aem.* 6.5. Polyb. 18.37 records a similar buffer policy in discussing Flamininus's dispositions in Macedonia.

[76] Livy 40.25.

[77] Livy 40.28.7–8.

[78] Plut;. *Vit. Aem.* 6.

[79] A. Degrassi (1947) p. 554. Perhaps to be associated with this triumph is the Ligurian monument on the Capitoline: *AE* (1948) no. 56.

the coast. Sometime during this period, a Roman garrison appears to have been placed at Ventimiglia.[80] The ultimate solution to the insecurity of this section of the coastal zone did not come until the Romans made the decision to assume direct responsibility for the sphere of influence of Massilia to the west. This was postponed until the second half of the second century B.C.

Meanwhile, the pacification of central and southern Liguria went on, and the battles in the mountains became a grim and perpetual treadmill for the Romans. Livy remarks that *nec tamen in discrimen summae rerum pugnabatur*.[81] The raids, especially on the eastern side of the Apennines, threatened the important colonial settlements in the Po drainage area. Brutal campaigns repeated almost yearly failed to restrain the Ligurians. The Romans increasingly realized that here, as in the similar Spanish frontier, the origins of conflict lay both in the life of the natives, with their mobile pastoral economy and a warrior ethos, and in the economic realities of poor land and overpopulation. The cycle of raid and reprisal would continue unbroken until radical new solutions were found.

One prerequisite for new solutions was improved Roman intelligence on both the terrain and the people of Liguria. The wars of the previous decades had taught the Romans to operate more effectively in the interior of Liguria. They had studied the annual cycle and movements of the natives. The passes and byways were no longer a secret and secure refuge for the tribesmen. By 180 B.C. A. Postumius Albinus could effectively block the passes of Liguria, cutting off the movements of supplies to the inhabitants and bringing them to bay.[82] The more radical steps in frontier control adopted during the following years would have been impossible without an ability on the part of the Romans to outmaneuver the Ligurians in their own terrain.

Efforts were made in the 180s to change the fundamental way of life of the Ligurians. As early as 187 B.C. the Romans had attempted to disarm the Friniates. In 182 B.C. disarmament was again stipulated as one of the provisions of Ligurian surrender.[83] Enforcement was not easy, however. Weapons could be hidden in the caves and caches of the interior. Moreover, weapons were intimately linked to the way of life of a Ligurian warrior and were in fact necessary for survival against the host of human and animal enemies that inhabited the mountains. More fundamental changes had to be made in the very nature of Ligurian society before the disarmament could be effective. One step

[80] Livy 40.41.6, 41.17.5.
[81] Livy 39.1.8.
[82] Livy 40.41.2, 40.41.5–9.
[83] Livy 40.16.4–6.

was the physical movement of populations down into the plain area, where they could be more closely watched. This was attempted in 187 B.C. But men of the mountains are not easily turned into men of the plain. With the native mountains in sight, it would be tempting to flee and return to old haunts and old ways. More radical steps were needed, and seven years later the new policy emerged that was to lead the pacification of Liguria.

P. Cornelius Cethegus and M. Baebius Tamphilus had accomplished little of note during their consulship of 181 B.C.[84] When the consuls elected for 180 B.C. were delayed at Rome, they took advantage of this extension of command to attack the Ligurians earlier in the year than was normal for Roman campaigns. Their move caught large numbers of the Apuani by surprise and forced them to surrender. The effectiveness of these early attacks was related to the partly pastoral economy of the Ligurians. During the summer, when most Roman commanders launched their assaults, the Ligurian herds were in the mountains and less vulnerable to attack. During the early spring, though, they were still in their winter lowland pastures, and quick Roman action caught them in a less defensible position.[85] The number of Ligurians seized was large enough for the two proconsuls to think it prudent to consult the senate on next steps. The decision was made to take the captives to an area well removed from Liguria. Without such an action, the senate felt that *nullum alium ante finem rati fore Lingustini belli*.[86] Apparently the Romans had already undertaken this kind of movement in transferring natives of Picenum in northern Italy to the Paestum area and were happy with the results.[87] The Ligurians recognized the significance of this policy decision. They, more than the migratory Gauls, had a special relationship with their mountain homeland, and they pleaded not to be removed from their ancestral shrines and tombs. The Romans undoubtedly saw this as a positive step. A disrooted people become a disoriented one, and therefore more controllable. Modern imperialism offers its parallels.[88]

It was important for the success of the action that the Ligurians be removed to an environment similar to their native land where they could continue their combined agricultural and pastoral ways. For this

---

[84] Livy 40.37.9; T.R.S. Broughton (1951) pp. 383–84.

[85] J. E. Skydsgaard (1974).

[86] Livy 40.38.2–3.

[87] Strabo 5.4.13. A. J. Toynbee (1965) vol. 2 p. 119 n. 8 mentions the deportations undertaken by the Romans in Picenum after the insurrections of 269–268 B.C. Zonaras 8.18 notes that the Romans had also forced the Faliscans to move down from higher ground.

[88] Livy 40.38.4–6.

reason the mountainous area of southern Samnium, not far from Beneventum, was selected. The transfer was to be conducted on a massive scale. By the time it began, the number of Ligurians to be moved including women and children had swelled to forty thousand. They were moved by sea and then overland to Samnium. The senate provided land and funds to aid the Ligurians in establishing themselves in this new environment.[89] Baebius and Cornelius, assisted by a commission of five, were in charge of the resettlement program. The success of their mission, their identification with the group, and the ethnic cohesion of the Ligurians even in this new world is evident; in the first century A.D. the Ligures Baebiani et Corneliani were still a distinct group in Samnium.[90] The appreciation of the senate and the Roman people for this imaginative and well-executed application of a new native policy was demonstrated by the voting of a triumph to the two former consuls, despite the fact that *hi omnium primi nullo bello gesto triumpharunt*.[91]

The success of the program led to its application with modification by other Roman generals. Q. Fulvius Flaccus in 180 B.C. transferred another group of seven thousand Apuani to Samnium. In the following year, he adopted a slightly different approach to eastern Liguria. A group of defeated Ligurians was moved down into the plain, where they could be better controlled. Garrisons were placed in the mountains, presumably to prevent the former inhabitants from returning and to stop new tribal groups from occupying the vacated land.[92] A fragmentary reference to the Ligurian wars of 175 B.C. ends with the word *deduxit*, implying another forced mass movement.[93] Even in their efforts to correct the injustices of the illegal enslaving of Ligurians during the 170s, the Romans were careful to settle the freed natives on the other side of the Po far from their home mountains.[94]

The policy of thinning out the inhabitants of the interior of Liguria was matched by the strengthening of the Roman colonies along the Ligurian frontier. In 190 B.C. Placentia had been reinforced.[95] It played a vital role in separating raiding Ligurians from restive Gauls. Placentian auxiliary troops were used in the Istrian wars, suggesting that the

[89] Livy 40.38.6–7.
[90] Livy 40.38.6–7; Pliny *HN* 3.105; *CIL* 9, p. 125, no. 1455–56; A. J. Toynbee (1965) vol. 2 pp. 234–35.
[91] Livy 40.38–39; A. Degrassi (1947) p. 554.
[92] Livy 40.41.3–4, 40.53.1–3.
[93] Livy 41.18.16.
[94] Cf. pp. 110–13.
[95] Livy 37.46.9–11.

colonists of Placentia had become experienced in mountain warfare.[96]
The southern flank of Liguria was also strengthened. Pisa's position
as the eastern anchor of the Ligurian frontier was weakening, as was
that of Massilia to the west. Pisa had a long Ligurian mountain frontier, and river valleys such as the Lima and the Serchio provided easy
access from the mountains to the coastal plain. Pisans were the first to
suffer from the process of raiding and counterraiding that characterized the accelerating Romano-Ligurian conflict. Aware of her increasing vulnerability, a desperate Pisa in 180 B.C. offered land to the Romans for the foundation of a colony.[97]

The territory of Pisa offered two logical places for the foundation
of a colony. The first was the area of the increasingly important but
vulnerable coastal port of Luna. This center guarded the northern end
of the thin coastal plain that extended north from Pisa, and it watched
over several valley routes from the interior. It had become in the second century B.C. an increasingly important point of embarkation for
sea voyages to Spain.[98] The second potential location was the plain of
Lucca, which controlled the entrance to the Serchio valley. Separated
by rough hill country from the territory of Pisa, this plain was an
ideal place for a colony modeled on the pattern established along the
Via Aemilia.

The evidence for the sequence of events following the Pisan offer
of land in 180 B.C. is confusing and contradictory, and has been the
subject of considerable scholarly dispute. It has centered on the question of whether two colonies were founded in the 170s or whether
only the colony at Luna was founded, with that at Lucca coming
much later.[99] Current interpretation seems to favor the idea of the two
colonies being founded about 177 B.C, with Luna entrusted with the
protection of the coastal frontier and Lucca watching over the interior
mountain frontier.[100] Lucca appears to have been given an extensive
territory that included mountain land as far as the border of Veleia.[101]

The founding and reinforcing of colonies, combined with the movement and deportation of increasing numbers of Ligurians, provoked

[96] Livy 41.1.6.

[97] Livy 40.43.1.

[98] Livy 34.8.4–6; L. Banti (1931).

[99] E. T. Salmon (1933) p. 30; L. Banti (1937) pp. 61–62; N. Lamboglia (1939) p. 152;
P. Sommella (1973–74).

[100] A. J. Toynbee (1965) vol. 2 pp. 533–40. M. Clavel-Leveque (1973–74) pp. 30–34
suggests a mixed population of colonists, natives, and traders at Luni. This conclusion
is based on the Republican inscription *CIL* 11. 1347, which refers to *coloni et incolae*.

[101] F. G. DePachtere (1920) p. 11; E. T. Salmon (1933) pp. 3–35; L. Banti (1937);
U. Formentini (1949) p. 214; F. Castagnoli (1952). Cic. *Fam.* 13.13 refers to Lucca as a
municipium.

the natives to a final, desperate uprising. As is often the case with
native revolts, the extent of the uprising came as a surprise and caught
the Romans off guard. Confident that their problems were behind
them, they had disbanded their field army and had even withdrawn
the legion from Pisa.[102] Meanwhile, the Ligurians rallied an army and
succeeded in capturing Mutina. The psychological impact of this event
on those living along the frontier must have been like that of the seizure of Placentia by the forces of Hamilcar. Colonies were supposed
to be the bastions of any Roman frontier, and the revelation of their
vulnerability could not help but raise the spirit of the Ligurians. The
mountaineers proceeded to vent their hatred and frustration on their
unfortunate victims. This was not limited to human bloodshed; booty,
both animal and material, was ritually destroyed and the meat of the
slain beasts placed in religious shrines. The pattern of behavior suggests a type of fanatical religious activity often associated with nativ-
istic uprisings.[103]

One of the consuls of 177 B.C., C. Claudius Pulcher, was dispatched
to Liguria. He came directly from Istria, where he had suppressed the
similar frontier uprising of Aepulo. After a siege of three days, he
succeeded in recapturing Mutina. Some eight thousand Ligurians per-
ished within the walls of the city, a total that suggests the size of the
Ligurian force and the havoc that the fighting must have wreaked
within the city. Claudius boasted in his dispatch to the senate that
there was no longer an enemy of the Roman people on this side of the
Alps. He also noted that a large amount of land had been seized that
could provide farms for many thousand settlers.[104] His judgment on
frontier peace and stability proved premature.

Reports of continued resistance continued to arrive in Rome. Both
consuls of 176 B.C. were assigned to Liguria, although the death of
one left only Q. Petillius Spurinus to carry out the campaign.
C. Claudius Pulcher remained as proconsul, watching Liguria from
the frontier post at Parma. With the opening of the campaigning sea-
son, he moved into the enemy homeland. The Ligurians made their
stand at two mountain strongholds, Letum and Ballista. Claudius slew
many of the mountaineers before they could reach the safety of their
fortresses, but he was forced to turn over the command to his successor Spurinus before the final assaults on the strongholds could be

[102] Livy 41.14.1–3; L. Banti (1937) p. 111.
[103] Livy 41.18.3–5. For parallels in other native revolts see S. L. Dyson (1971).
[104] Livy 41.16.7–8; A. Degrassi (1947) p. 555; T.R.S. Broughton (1951) pp. 397–98.

mounted.[105] The Roman army, led by Spurinus, overran the Ligurian defenses, but the commander fell in the battle.[106]

This victory did not end the war, and again in 175 B.C. the two consuls were assigned to Liguria.[107] One of these was M. Aemilius Lepidus, the tough and sagacious veteran of war and peace in the north. The fragmentary historical record does not allow a detailed reconstruction of their campaigns. Mention is made of fighting against the Friniates and new tribes such as the Garuli, Lapicini, and Hergates. This was presumably the action of Lepidus. Lepidus' colleague, P. Mucius Scaevola, defeated those Ligurians that had been ravaging the lands of Pisa and Luna. The double campaign seems to have finally ended the Ligurian resistance. Calm settled in on this frontier area, and the two consuls were awarded a triumph *de Liguribus*.[108]

One indication of the new security was the growing interest in the use of the Ligurian lands for the settlement of individual farmers outside the protection of the colonial system. C. Claudius Pulcher had already proposed this in 176 B.C., but the frontier was still troubled and his suggestion was clearly premature.[109] The Roman government waited until the peace was secure, and in 173 B.C. they assigned to Roman and Latin settlers large sections of Gallic and Ligurian land that had been seized in the recent wars.[110] Among those elected to the commission entrusted with carrying out this task were M. Aemilius Lepidus, the northern veteran, and P. Cornelius Cethegus, the man partly responsible for the successful movement of Ligurians to Samnium.[111] Much of this land was located along the Via Aemilia and filled the interstices between the great colonial foundations. Evidence of these assignments may be found in the traces of centuriation still visible along the line of the old Via Amelia and the distribution of citizens assigned to the voting tribe of the Pollia.[112]

Two results of easing tension on the Ligurian frontier were intercity rivalry, a luxury not possible when the cities and colonies were fighting for survival, and the provocation of natives by Roman commanders. The main recorded example of the first is the boundary dispute

---

[105] Livy 41.17.9–41.18.6.
[106] Livy 41.18.6–14.
[107] Livy 41.19.1–2; T.R.S. Broughton (1951) pp. 401–2.
[108] A. Degrassi (1947) p. 555.
[109] Livy 41.16.8.
[110] Livy 42.4.3–4; P. A. Brunt (1971) pp. 192–93. U. Ewins (1952) p. 59 associates many of the settlers later assigned to the tribe of Pollia with these 173 B.C. allotments.
[111] T.R.S. Broughton (1951) pp. 409–10.
[112] U. Ewins (1952) pp. 59–63; L. R. Taylor (1960) pp. 90–91.

between Pisa and Luna, the colony founded from a detached section of Pisan territory. In times of Ligurian attack the Pisans had begged the senate to found a protective colony in her territory, but now, with the frontier relatively calm, border disputes between the two cities reached such a high pitch of acrimony that in 168 B.C. a special senatorial commission had to be dispatched to settle the differences.[113]

More serious and more interesting are the examples of frontier provocation, for they reveal a great deal about tension in the Roman governmental system and value differences among the Roman leaders. The most notorious of these episodes involved the tribe of the Statielli and the consul M. Popillius Laenas. The Roman advance into Liguria and cisalpine Gaul had left largely untouched the northwestern section of the area between the Apennines and the Alps. This included much of the modern Piemonte. We are not told the reasons the Romans had for leaving this land outside of their area of direct control; but perhaps they found it easy to establish a working relationship with the tribes in the area and realized that the tribes could form a buffer against the raids of Alpine peoples. One of these groups was the Statielli. Their territory, which centered on northern Acqui on the northwestern flank of the Ligurian Apennines, was suitably located to protect the western side of the trade routes crossing the mountains from Genoa and to watch movements down such river valleys as the Bormida, the Belbo, and even the Tanarus. They were one of the few Ligurian groups that had not attacked the Romans. Inhabiting fertile land and evidently quite numerous, they were an ideal frontier buffer tribe.[114]

In 173 B.C. the peaceful arrangement was ended when the consul M. Popillius Laenas attacked the Statielli. He claimed that they had been assembling warriors, but this was most likely an excuse designed to justify his provocation and turn it into a *bellum iustum*. The real reason for his attack and his later defiance of the senate is obscure. In part he was engaged in simple triumph-hunting. It has also been claimed that Laenas was attempting to free land for new settlers.[115] This seems unlikely. The Statielli were well removed from the line of intermeshed colonial and *ad viritim* settlements farther south, and their land was surrounded by untamed natives. It was hardly the place where the Romans would place scattered farmsteads. Most of the actions of Laenas can best be explained by political rivalries at Rome and the growing ambitions of the Popillian family.[116]

[113] Livy 45.13.10–11.
[114] P. A. Brunt (1971) p. 189. Some have argued for a war with the Statielli in 179 B.C.: G. Corradi (1939) p. 22; N. Lamboglia (1939) pp. 142–43.
[115] A. J. Toynbee (1965) vol. 2 pp. 206–8; W. V. Harris (1979) pp. 226–27.
[116] E. Pais (1918) pp. 514–15; W. V. Harris (1979).

The military actions were quickly over. The Statielli centered their resistance on the town of Carystus, where they were attacked by the Romans and defeated in a bloody battle with heavy Roman casualties. Despairing of military victory, the survivors surrendered expecting relatively mild treatment from the Roman commander. Instead they were sold into slavery.[117]

When the dispatches announcing the victory were read in Rome, the senate reacted with fury. An attack on a relatively peaceful Ligurian group was a needless provocation that would disrupt a delicate frontier.[118] Moreover, selling into slavery a people who surrendered to the mercy of the Romans only compounded the problem. It is true that the Romans had disarmed, deported, and even enslaved Ligurians, but this policy had been applied only to groups that had created repeated problems for Rome. The attack of Popillius Laenas against a tribe that had done no harm to Rome meant that natives would hesitate to surrender to Roman commanders in the future.

The issue rapidly became caught up in the internal politics of Rome. Both the senate and the popular assembly brought pressure to bear on Laenas to restore the freedom and property of the Ligurians. Laenas bluntly refused, and in 172 B.C., buoyed by his brother's election to the consul, he apparently attacked the Statielli again.[119] The war was characterized as being against both *ius* and *fas*. The tribunes proposed a bill setting a deadline for freeing the Ligurians, which the *consilium plebis* passed enthusiastically.[120] Finally a *senatus consultum* was approved that ordered the freeing of all Ligurians who had not been enemies of the Roman people since 179 B.C. Those freed were to be given land across the Po. In the end, a compromise was reached by which the Ligurians were liberated, but Popillius Laenas escaped any punitive action. Livy states that many thousand Ligurians were freed by the senatorial decree and settled in their new lands.[121]

The case of Laenas is a fascinating study in the imperial politics of the period. We do not know enough about the details of the power struggle to understand how the Popillii could sustain their position against strong senatorial and popular opposition. But the case provides some insight into frontier dynamics. M. Popillius Laenas was not a novice to the Ligurian scene. He had been one of the commissioners sent in 180 B.C. to assess the possibilities of a colonial foundation near

[117] Livy 42.7.3–42.8.3.
[118] Livy 42.8.
[119] Livy 42.8–10, 42.21.2–3; H. H. Scullard (1973) pp. 194–96.
[120] Livy 42.21.4–8.
[121] Livy 42.22.5–7.

Pisa and probably participated in the establishment of Lucca.[122] The
Pisans, after generations of conflict with the Ligurians, would have
provided him with vivid ideas on the best way of dealing with frontier
natives. Moreover, Laenas was in southern Liguria at a time when
Cornelius and Baebius were carrying out their massive deportations,
and could have judged the effectiveness of that policy and the whole
principle of the depopulation of frontier zones.

Policy considerations for northern and southern Liguria were different, however. The Roman government regarded the northern frontier as stable and the natives as essentially peaceful. This especially
applied to the Statielli, who at this time were not considered a front-
line group. The actions of Popillius Laenas were pure adventurism.

The attitudes and actions of the senate and the Roman people are
also of interest. The policy considerations in the minds of the senators
have already been discussed. More surprising is the apparently sympathetic attitude of the *plebs Romana* toward the Ligurians. After the
long series of wars, one might have expected a general attitude of
Ligurophobia among the Roman populace to which jingoistic politicians like Laenas could appeal. But relatively few frontiersmen would
have been present at the popular assembly. Moreover, the heavy casualties of the campaign of Laenas must have cost him much sympathy.
These were factors that politicians hostile to the Popillii could exploit.

The whole episode suggests a positive attitude toward the cause of
illegally mistreated natives and a willingness to uphold the traditional
values of Roman international behavior. It compares well with attitudes found among the citizens of later imperial powers. Also of interest is the difference between the actions of the plebeian assembly
in passing decrees sympathetic to the Ligurians and the election of
Laenas' brother as consul by the centuriate assembly. It is possible
that more prosperous northerners came to Rome for the centuriate
assembly and supported an aggressive frontier policy. However, this
must remain mere speculation.

The final decree on freeing the Ligurians provides another insight
into a persistent frontier problem. It freed not only the Statielli but
also all other Ligurians who had not been *hostes* of the Roman people
since 179 B.C. The stress on freeing only those who had not been
official enemies of Rome shows that the decree was not intended to
abrogate any legitimate actions of victorious Roman generals. Instead
it implies that a number of Ligurians were being enslaved illegally.
(Historically, this has often happened in frontier zones where juridical
refinements are not particularly well observed.) The number of the

---

[122] T.R.S. Broughton (1951) p. 390.

illegally enslaved ran in the thousands, which suggests well-organized slaving operations. This inevitably led to social unrest and disruption among frontier groups.[123]

When the Ligurians had been restored to freedom, they were carefully settled on the other side of the Po, well away from their native mountains. One can imagine that the liberated Ligurians would have harbored considerable bitterness toward Rome. This, combined with knowledge of Roman ways acquired during their period of slavery, could have laid the groundwork for skillful and fanatical opposition to Rome, especially if those involved had been resettled in their old haunts. This kind of "inner frontier" of Romanized natives was already beginning to develop in Spain, and leaders drawn from this group were to spark the great Spanish Wars of the mid-second century B.C. Similar conditions might have arisen in northern Italy. By resettling the Ligurians across the Po, the Romans may have hoped to prevent this.

The actions of Popillius Laenas do not seem to have had negative repercussions. Rome was, of course, distracted by the war with Macedonia. The consul of 170 B.C., A. Atilius Serranus, was assigned the area, but neither Roman nor Ligurian was eager for war.[124] With the defeat of Perseus, however, the Romans showed renewed interest in Liguria. In 167 B.C. M. Junius Pennus was sent to Pisa and his colleague Q. Aelius Paetus to Gaul. Some raids were conducted against the Ligurians, but nothing decisive was accomplished.[125]

The situation changed dramatically in 166 B.C. Both consuls were assigned to the northern frontier. Livy's epitome states that M. Claudius Marcellus fought the Alpine Gauls while C. Sulpicius Galus attacked the Ligurians. The entry in the Fasti Triumphales credits Marcellus with a victory over the Galli Contrubri and the Ligures Eleiates, and Galba with one over a group of Ligurians whose fragmentary name is Ta[..]rni.[126] It is unfortunate that the full text of Livy is not preserved, for the award of a double triumph indicates a campaign of considerable importance.

The exact identification and location of the tribes involved has been a matter of much scholarly debate, but the general direction of the campaign seems clear. The mixture of Ligurian and Gallic peoples places the action in the northwest of Italy, where those two ethnically distinct groups were intermingled. Most firmly identified among the

---

[123] Livy 42.22.5–8. On the comparative impact of slaving across frontiers see W. S. Cooter (1976), (1977) with the references to the Roman and medieval frontiers.

[124] Livy 43.9.1–3; T.R.S. Broughton (1951) pp. 419–20.

[125] Livy 45.16.3, 45.17.6, 45.41.1.

[126] Livy Per. 46; A. Degrassi (1947) pp. 556–57.

natives involved are the Eleiates.[127] This was a group that inhabited
the northeastern part of the Ligurian mountains between Parma and
Placentia. Their main center later became Veleia. They had not previously been mentioned in the context of the Ligurian wars, which
probably means that they enjoyed reasonably good relations with the
Romans. It is possible, though, that they became increasingly hostile
after viewing the treatment of the Statielli to their northwest. Firm
control of this large and important group was necessary if the Romans
were to dominate the upper Po and its tributaries. The location of the
other groups is not so easy to determine. Ta[..]rni might be associated
with the Taurini near modern Turin, but the Taurini are generally
described as Gauls rather than Ligurians.

The victories of Marcellus did not end the wars against the Eleiates.
In 159 B.C. M. Fulvius Nobilior was sent as consul against the Eleiates
and remained there in 158 B.C. as proconsul, suggesting a prolonged
campaign. He was awarded a triumph *de Liguribis Eleatibus*.[128] Although the campaigns of 159–158 took place in the north, problems
arose a few years later around Luna and Pisa, where the remnants of
the Apuani again became restless. The old generational cycle was operating again as the mountains became filled with warriors who had
little direct experience of the wars with Rome. By 155 B.C. the situation had became sufficiently serious for M. Claudius Marcellus, the
victor over the Eleiates, to be elected consul for a second time and
sent to the Luna-Pisa front. He evidently made short work of the
Apuani and returned to Rome to celebrate a triumph.[129] The grateful
citizens of Luna, pleased with his pacification of the frontier, erected
a statue in his honor.[130] The recorded wars against the Ligurians came
to an end with the victory of Q. Marcius Rex in 118–117 B.C. over
the Ligures Stoeni, a group on the fringes of the Alps near the Lepontii to the north.[131]

With the wars of pacification ended, it is time to turn to the more
peaceful steps that the Romans had been taking to insure control in
Liguria. Some of these have been discussed already in consideration
of the resettlement schemes. Two other actions that played an important role were the building of roads and the establishing of either
native or colonial settlements.

The mountains of Liguria do not lend themselves to road-building
and even in imperial times the Ligurian communication network was

[127] A. J. Toynbee (1965) vol. 2 p. 281.
[128] A. Degrassi (1947) p. 557.
[129] A. Degrassi (1947) p. 557.
[130] *CIL* 11.1339.
[131] A. Degrassi (1947) p. 560.

not highly developed. Men and goods had to move around and through the mountains, though, and by the end of the Republic the basic road system had been established. The key elements were the Via Aemilia, which paralleled the mountains on the northeast; the Via Aurelia, which ran up the coast in the direction of Gaul; an extension of the Via Aemilia that ran from Dertona down to the sea at Vada Sabatia; the Via Postumia from Genoa through the mountains to Dertona; and the road that branched off the Aurelia at Forum Clodi and went from Lucca to Florence along the south flank of Liguria. In some cases, the construction of these roads can be dated precisely. At least a general picture of the development and significance of the road network can be assembled.

By the time the wars in Liguria began in earnest, the Romans had probably constructed a series of trunk roads leading from the city in the direction of the southern border of the mountains. The Via Aurelia ran up the coast and by the mid-second century had reached the city of Pisa.[132] For the important staging base at Arretium there was the Via Cassia, and for the area of cispadane Gaul the Via Flaminia.[133]

The first main addition to the trunk system that affected Liguria was the Via Aemilia. It was started in 187 B.C. and eventually led all the way to Placentia. Flanking the mountains, it allowed the lateral movement of troops and provided a focus for settlement and a means of encouraging trade.[134] The origin of the roads along the southern flank of Liguria is more obscure. In imperial times one led from Pisa along the southern bank of the Arno to Florence.[135] It probably followed old Etruscan trade routes up the valley. More specifically related to military developments was the road that went from Luna through Forum Clodii to Lucca and then on to Pistoia and Florence.[136] The Luna-Lucca link must be placed after the colonization of 177 B.C. A reasonable candidate for the man responsible for the development of this route between Luna and Lucca would seem to be M. Claudius

[132] K. Miller (1916) col. 233. P. A. Brunt (1971) p. 569 suggests 157, 144, and 111 B.C. as possible years. In those years there were consuls of the Aurelian family who could have been involved in road construction. A. J. Toynbee (1965) vol. 2 pp. 660–61 suggests 200 B.C. but is willing to settle for a later date.

[133] P. A. Brunt (1971) p. 568 feels that the Via Cassia dates to 164, 127, or 124 B.C. and doubts a third-century origin. A. J. Toynbee (1965) vol. 2 p. 665 notes the lack of Cassian consuls or censors before the second century B.C.

[134] G. Radke (1964) pp. 301–5 has Lepidus constructing the road in 187 B.C. T. P. Wiseman (1970) p. 126 has him building the road to Placentia in 187 B.C. and in 175 B.C., continuing it from Placentia to Caesina and from Bologna to Aquileia.

[135] K. Miller (1916) cols. 233, 241–42 k.77.

[136] K. Miller (1916) cols. 241–42 k.77 cols. 286–88.

Marcellus, who in 155 B.C. had driven back the Apuani for apparently the last time and won the gratitude of the people of Luna.

In contrast to flank roads that would have aided the pacification of the mountains, the roads through the mountains had to wait until relatively firm Roman control. The first of these came in 148 B.C. with the construction of the Via Postumia. A milestone testifies that Sp. Postumius Albinus Magnus built this road, which ran from Genoa through Libarnum to Dertona.[137] Here again the road followed old trade routes that connected Genoa and Dertona. Few communities are mentioned along the route. This contrasts sharply with the Aemilia or even with the coast road. It suggests that whatever the importance of the Postumia for long-distance trade and communication, the road did not become a magnet for local settlements and therefore a significant instrument of Romanization.

The second great road-builder in Liguria was the censor of 109 B.C., M. Aemilius Scaurus. He was concerned with both coastal and interior communication.[138] Along the coast he continued the line of the Aurelia from Pisa to Vada Sabatia beyond Genoa. From there the road turned inland to pass through Aquae Statiellae to Dertona. It not only provided another link with the Po but also completed the encirclement of Liguria with a road network. In a period of Germanic danger from transalpine Gaul, the road provided a better means of moving troops over the Alps.

Complementing the roads as instruments of consolidation and Romanization were the various settlements either planted or encouraged by the Romans. The role of the great colonial foundations along the line of the Via Aemilia has already been stressed. They were "janus-like," looking toward both the *ager Gallicus* and the Ligurian hills. They served as listening posts, protective bastions, and, to a certain degree, lightening rods in the Roman defense of the two frontiers.

The official colonies were not the only settlements that grew up under Roman auspices. A study of the ancient itineraries shows a number of communities whose names have a distinct Roman origin. They are concentrated along the Via Aemilia and in the northwest, and seem to bear a direct relationship to the pacification of Liguria. The origin and nature of these communities has often been debated, and the evidence for them is generally slight. Nevertheless, they deserve whatever detailed consideration is possible.

---

[137] K. Miller (1916) cols. 252–53; *CIL* 5. 2045; *ILS* 5806, *CIL* 1.2. 624; T.R.S. Broughton (1951) p. 461.

[138] G. Radke (1964) p. 307; Strabo 5.1.11; *De Vir. Ill.*, *Aem*, 85. N. Lamboglia (1937) feels that the Via Aemilii Scauri probably ran from Luna to Dertona to Vado and is related to the Cimbric wars.

The first group of these settlements is located in the interstices between the great colonies of the Aemilia. Between Bononia and Placentia were to be found Forum Gallorum, Regium Lepidum, Tannetum, Forum Novum, Fidentia, and Florentia. It is easiest to begin with the settlements that bear family names since they can provide some chronological anchor. Regium Lepidum would appear to have clear association with the great molder of the northern frontier, M. Aemilius Lepidus.[139] It probably dates to 175–173 B.C. and served as a center for the *ad viritim* settlements in the area. Its territory extended in the direction of the hills controlled by both Friniates and Eleiates, and it is located at the point where the river Crostolo moves out into the plain. Regium is a local name and implies a preexisting native settlement. It possibly developed as a market center and helped link the ethnically, ecologically, and economically diverse hill and lowland zones with the main trunk road.

Two other fora are mentioned for this area. Forum Gallorum would appear to be associated with the Gauls to the northeast. In contrast, Forum Novum (modern Fornovo) was very much linked with Liguria. Located some twenty-three kilometers southwest of Parma, it was placed right at the border of the colonial territory in the valley of Taro, at an entry point into the mountains.[140] Since it was surrounded by the Eleiates on three sides, the settlement must date after the pacification of that tribe in the 150s and should relate to Roman steps to integrate Eleiates into the Roman system. It has even been proposed that Forum Novum is identical with one of the several Fora Clodii, which would bring a closer association with the actions of Claudius Marcellus.[141]

The names of Florentia and Fidentia, two settlements between Parma and Placentia, have a familiar second-century ring. During this period the Romans liked to found communities named after *numina* or propitious conditions. Several had native associations. Florentia (modern Florenzuola) is known mainly from passing references on the itineraries and a few inscriptions.[142] Fidentia is mentioned by Pliny, and there are clear traces of centuriation in its territory, to the north of the Via Aemilia.[143] It seems likely that these two communities had some association with the *ad viritim* settlements of 173 B.C. They are also well located for service as periodic markets. They would be con-

[139] Festus 332L calls it Forum Lepidi. P. A. Brunt (1971) p. 574. A. J. Toynbee (1965) vol. 2 pp. 272, 656, dates it to 175 B.C., as does U. Ewins (1952) pp. 56, 59.

[140] A. J. Toynbee (1965) vol. 2 pp. 281, 656, 669–70; P. A. Brunt (1971) p. 574.

[141] U. Ewins (1952) pp. 64–65.

[142] *CIL* 11. 1146; K. Miller (1916) col. 205; L. Grazzi (1972) pp. 194–97. On the use of names of this type see H. J. Wolf (1968).

[143] Pliny *HN* 3.116; P. A. Brunt (1971) pp. 575–76; L. Grazzi (1972) pp. 192–94.

venient not only for the Ligurians but also, being close to the borders of Placentia and Parma, for the outlying inhabitants of Placentia and Parma who must have found the long journey to the markets of the central city most arduous.

The line of settlements along the Via Aemilia was developed as much to service the needs of the individual settlers in the redivided Ligurian and Gallic lands as to integrate the Ligurians into the Roman system. The centers to the northwest must be related more to native needs. They are numerous and appear to corroborate other evidence that the inhabitants of the area had relatively amicable relations with Rome and could be brought into the Roman system. Again we have the two basic types of named communities, with some variations.

The only forum in the area that bears a Roman family name is Forum Fulvii. Pliny designates it as *Foro Fulvi quod Valentinum*. It is the modern town of Valenza, located just west of the juncture of the Po and Tanarus rivers. At some point the town was connected with the road system that linked Ticinum with Asti.[144] The route went ultimately to Turin. Its final extension must be Augustan, but the Dertona-Forum Fulvii-Hasta section could well be Republican. The strategic importance of the location for the control of access to the lower Po is shown by the significant role played during the Middle Ages by the nearby fortress at Casale and by the growth of the city of Alessandria.[145]

The name Valentia was used several times for frontier settlements during the second century B.C. The most famous example is the Valentia in Spain founded in 138 B.C. in part as a center for the warriors who had fought with Viriathus.[146] Another Valentia was located in Narbonese Gaul and was the focal point for the rebellion of the Allobroges in 61 B.C. It was probably founded in 123–121 B.C. and had a largely native population. Another Valentia is known from Sardinia.[147] The exact date of foundation is not recorded, but it seems reasonable to associate it with the pacification measures of the second century B.C. Thus, a Valentia in northern Italy would fit into a pattern of frontier communities designed to promote settled life. The difference in spelling between Valentia and Valentum should be noted, however, and parallels used with caution.

The relationship between the designations Forum Fulvii and Valentum in the text of Pliny is uncertain. Both fit a second-century B.C.

[144] Pliny *HN* 3.49; K. Miller (1916) cols. 231-32; U. Ewins (1952) p. 67; A. J. Toynbee (1965) vol. 2 pp. 672–75.
[145] C. J. Burckhardt (1967) pp. 310–62.
[146] C. Torres (1951); H. Galsterer (1971) p. 12.
[147] Cf. pp. 262–63.

context. Two phases of foundation are possible from the title.[148] What is clear is that the location in the northwest must date the Roman organization of the community to the period after campaigns had begun against such groups as the Eleiates and the Statielli. Of the Fulvii who campaigned in this area, the person most logically identified with the forum's foundation would seem to be M. Fulvius Nobilior, who triumphed over the Eleiates in 158 B.C. The details of his campaigns are not known, but he was certainly in the northwest at a time when the Romans were seeking to consolidate the frontier.[149]

Another person who has been suggested is M. Fulvius Flaccus, who was sent in 125 B.C. to protect the Massilians from the transalpine Ligurians.[150] Although the main theater of his operations was beyond the Alps, it has been suggested that he was also interested in improving communications through the Alps, as well as imitating the Gracchan land reforms by planting *ad viritim* settlements along an advancing frontier.[151] But the time seems premature for the development of the Alpine roads up through the Dora Baltea and the Durance, and there is no evidence that Flaccus used the route. Moreover, no evidence survives of land confiscation in this area. The forum's location seems better suited to changing native ways of life than providing a focus for scattered Roman farmers.

The two other fora located in the northwest, Forum Vibii Caburrum and Forum Germanorum, are probably quite late and reflect the developments of the post-Caesarian frontier. Forum Vibii is generally identified with the proconsul of 45 B.C., C. Vibius Pansa. Forum Germanorum, placed even farther into the mountains, seems to be later.[152] The area has a whole series of towns with other "*numina*" names, and they can be associated with activities of the second century B.C.

Perhaps most important was Hasta (modern Asti), which occupied a strategic location at a bend of the River Tanaro at a transition point between plain and mountain.[153] Several tributaries join the Tanaro at this point and have helped make the center an important road hub in

---

[148] U. Ewins (1952) pp. 68–69 sees two phases with a Valentia being built in 173 B.C. and a Forum Fulvii in 125 B.C. The whole phrase in Pliny (*HN* 3.49) is *Correa quod Potentia cognominatur Foro Fulvi quod Valentinum.*

[149] P. A. Brunt (1971) pp. 575–76 inclines toward Nobilior.

[150] A. J. Toynbee (1965) vol. 2 pp. 672–75 reconstructs a whole series of events for which there is no real evidence.

[151] A. J. Toynbee (1965) vol. 2 pp. 674–75.

[152] *Forum Vibii*: Pliny *HN* 3.117; *RE* 7.73–74. *Forum Germanorum*: *CIL* 5. 7832; *RE* 7.68. Pliny notes that the stream that forms the source of the Po emerges from underground in the territory of Forum Vibii. The proximity to the mountain spring suggests a possible association with an active cult center.

[153] Pliny *HN* 3.49; *CIL* 5.2 pp. 856–61; A. J. Toynbee (1965) vol. 2 p. 668.

ancient and modern times.[154] It has been suggested that the settlement owes its origins to M. Popillius Laenas and was designed to protect the frontier after his decimation of the Statielli,[155] though we have no real evidence for such an early settlement in this area. Before the campaigns of Marcellus and Fulvius Flaccus, it would have been isolated and surrounded by natives made unfriendly by the atrocities of Popillius Laenas. Hasta is the name used for a native settlement in Spain, and it seems more reasonable to regard the Italian example as part of a group of basically native communities where development was encouraged by the Romans.

Further up the Tanaro were the closely spaced settlements of Alba Pompeia and Pollentia. Alba is associated with the activities of Gn. Pompeius Strabo in the early first century B.C.[156] Pollentia, a few kilometers to the west, is definitely earlier.[157] Its position is again important. The center is located at the point where the Tanaro breaks out of the mountains into the plain above Cuneo. The praise of Pollentian wool in the classical authors suggests the importance of shepherding and transhumance in the territory of the community.[158] By the end of the Republic, a road linked Pollentia with Aquae Statiellae in the mountains.[159] There is another Pollentia in the Balaerics founded in 123 B.C., with a population drawn from Romans born in Spain.[160]

The first of two final towns in this series is Industria, located just south of the Po near its juncture with the Dora Baltea. Pliny notes that the town bore the original native name of Bodincomagum, a designation that is attested even under the Empire.[161] The double name again suggests a native center that had been given some support and perhaps reorganization by the Romans. Pliny also notes that the Po at this point becomes especially deep, placing Industria at a key transi-

[154] K. Miller (1916) cols. 184, 238.

[155] A. J. Toynbee (1965) vol. 2 p. 668 dates Hasta to 173 B.C. and the actions of Popillius Laenas. This is probably too early for such a foundation in still unsecured country.

[156] Pliny HN 3.49; CIL 5.2 pp. 863–66; G.E.F. Chilver (1941) p. 7. Alba was on the Roman road that ran from Aquae Statiellae through Pollentia ultimately to Augusta Taurinorum.

[157] Pliny HN 3.49; Suet. Tib. 37; CIL 5.2 pp. 866–68; A. Ferrua (1948); U. Ewins (1952) p. 70.

[158] Columella Rust. 7.2.4; Pliny HN 8.191; Sil. Pun. 8.599; Mart. 14.157–58.

[159] Cic. Fam. 11.11; K. Miller (1916) col. 253.

[160] Strabo 3.5.1; Pliny HN 3.77; A.J.N. Wilson (1966) pp. 22–24; M. G. Morgan (1969).

[161] Pliny HN 3.122; CIL 5.2 pp. 845–48, no. 7464. U. Ewins (1955) p. 73 sees the double name as indicating a separate Ligurian community near a Roman one. There is no reason to regard these centers as enclaves of Roman citizens as does A. J. Toynbee (1965) pp. 674–76.

tion site in the navigation of the river. Another double-named town was Carrea, probably located at Chieri south of the Po where the Vajorce River emerges from the mountains. Pliny says that it also bore the name of Potentia.[162] In both these instances, we seem to have native centers that the Romans rebaptized with names of good omen, but that retained their indigenous flavor.

The development of Aquae Statiellae is quite likely related to this policy of native acculturation. M. Popillius Laenas decimated but did not exterminate the Statielli tribe. The center of Aquae Statiellae must have been in existence by the end of the second century B.C., since the Via Aemilia Scauri was designed to pass through it. It is located well up the Bormida River where the river enters the rugged interior uplands of Liguria.[163] The name recalls the strongpoint Aquae Sextiae, founded by C. Sextius Calvinus in the 120s in transalpine Gaul. That center replaced in part the destroyed native oppidum at Entremont. Aquae Statiellae may also have replaced the oppidum Carystus destroyed by Popillius Laenas, and may have been intended to be a center of native trade and a vehicle for ensuring loyalty and acculturation. Its placement at a key mountain-plain transition point would have also made it accessible for a transhumant society.

The group of settlements in the northwest with *numina* names is interesting in several respects. Although this kind of name is used elsewhere in Italy and the west, no other area of the Western Empire has such a concentration. Several of the centers were later placed in the voting tribe of the Pollia, which was also used for the *ad viritim* settlements along the Via Aemilia. This has led some scholars to see them as extensions of the Roman settlement policy.[164] The Pollia seems also to have been used as a convenient voting unit for indigenous groups in the north when they acquired full Roman citizenship.[165] Considerable care appears to have gone into placing the settlements; it has already been noted that most are located at a key geographical point. Fora were by Roman definition designed to be primarily markets, and geographers note that successful markets are often located at the meeting place of two ecological zones. There is also a regular spacing to the group Industria, Hasta, Pollentia, Valentia, and Aquae Statiellae that would delight the abstract geographer, and it suggests that at least

[162] Pliny *HN* 3.49; *CIL* 5.2 pp. 848–49. *CIL* 5.2 no. 7496 has what seems to be the twin names *Karreae et Industriae*.

[163] *Pliny HN* 3.49; *CIL* 5.2 pp. 850–53; K. Miller (1916) col. 253. Strabo 5.1.11 mentions a road connecting Clastidium, Dertona, and Aquae Statiellae. Cf. also Cic. *Fam.* 11.11.

[164] L. R. Taylor (1960) pp. 90–91.

[165] P. A. Brunt (1971) p. 576 n. 2.

subconsciously the Romans were aware of the need for more or less equal market territories.[166]

The colonies and fora do not include all of the kinds of communities that grew up in the northwest. Several of the most important belong in neither category. Libarna (Serravalle) is a good example. Located on the river Scrivia where it begins its descent from the mountains, Libarna became in 148 B.C. a mid-point between Genoa and Dertona on the Via Postumia. Pliny describes it as a flourishing town in the first century A.D.[167] At the site have been found impressive imperial remains as well as coins dating to the Republic.[168]

Farther down the Scrivia where the Via Postumia joined the Aemilia was the town of Dertona (Tortona). The city is described in an ancient reference as a colony, but if true that probably applies to a later period. It is also designated as a city of the Ligurians, and it was most likely a native center in origin that prospered because of its location.[169] Less is known about Iria (Voghera), but it too was located on a river (the Iria) at a point accessible to the plain and mountains, and was on an important Roman road.[170] The name Forum Julii associated with the center implies a Caesarian settlement, but there is nothing to suggest that it was not built on a native base.

Final mention should be made of market centers that never acquired the status of formal community but served to link Romans and natives. Sometimes located at shrines or at the juncture of colonial and indigenous territory, they brought the native economy into juncture with Rome and encouraged acculturation. Representative of this is Campi Macri, southwest of Mutina, which operated as a market center from at least the second century B.C. at a location convenient for the herders coming down from the mountains.[171]

When the settlement picture of Liguria is viewed as a whole, a pattern that emerges was the result of the encouragement of natural geoeconomic trends by sympathetic Roman authorities. Few substantial settlements apparently developed in the interior mountains. The people there were eliminated, moved, assigned to the nearest com-

[166] Festus Paulus 33, 74L; F. DePachtere (1920) p. 46; N. Lamboglia (1939) p. 18; P. A. Brunt (1971) pp. 570–71. On the application of geographical systems to Chinese market development cf. G. W. Skinner (1964).

[167] Pliny HN 3.49; CIL 5.2 pp. 838–40; N. Lamboglia (1939) pp. 16–17.

[168] G. Moretti (1914).

[169] Vell. Pat. 1.15.5; Pliny HN 3.49. Artemidorus of Ephesus (c. 120 B.C.) cited in Stephanus of Byzantium s.v. Derton describes it as polis Liguron. CIL 5.2 pp. 831–38; U. Ewins (1952) pp. 68–70; A. J. Toynbee (1965) vol. 2 pp. 675–81.

[170] Pliny HN 3.49; K. Miller (1916) col. 232; P. Tozzi (1976) pp. 298–99.

[171] F. G. DePachtere (1912); G. C. Susini (1977); Columella Rust. 7.2.3; Livy 45.12.11, 41.18.5. Strabo 5.1.11 mentions the annual festival held there. B. D. Shaw (1979) discusses markets in Roman North Africa and the relevant anthropological literature.

munities, or left to their own rather primitive devices. Strabo notes a sprinkling of small towns and villages in the area.[172] Along the communication routes and especially on the flank where plain and hill could be united, centers were developed, sometimes by colonization and *ad viritim* settlements, but more often by the encouragement of larger native communities that emerged with the imposition of the Pax Romana. The most striking testimony to its success are the *nobilia oppida* described by Pliny.

In closing the discussion of Liguria, it is fitting to refer in greater detail to two pieces of evidence that illuminate key elements in the pacification. The first of these is the Tabula Polcevera, an inscription relating to disputes between Genoa and neighboring Ligurians, and the second is a cadaster of Veleia that provides some insight into the development of a native mountain town.

The bronze tablet found in the Polcevera valley a few miles outside Genoa in the early sixteenth century is one of our longest early Roman inscriptions. Its subject is a controversy over rights and obligations between Genoa and a neighboring Ligurian tribe called Langenses Viturii. The year is 117 B.C. Serving as mediators are two members of the Minucii family whose association with Genoa and the area went back to the campaigns of Q. Minucius Rufus in 197 B.C., when the arrangements described in the tablet were probably put into effect.[173] The Ligurians had been placed under the partial control of Genoa by the process later known as attribution. The obligations included payments by the Ligurians. The initial arrangements may have been informal, but by 117 B.C. a more regular administrative system had become necessary. The Via Postumia had been cut through the territory in 148 B.C. The Roman commissioners were now careful to define boundaries using the road as one of their guides. Traditional elements remained in the Ligurian society. A tribal assembly of some kind was still in existence, and it controlled the use of public land.[174] Herding was still a large element in the Ligurian economic structure, and the use and control of pastures was mentioned in the inscription. There was also private land with citizens of Genoa evidently settling in the territory of the Ligurians.[175] Reference to the cultivation of vines provides another indication of a stable life.[176] Perhaps most Roman of all is the use of mediation like that which took place between such urban centers as Ateste and Patavium to replace the world of raid and counterraid so typical of Liguria. The Romans certainly used

[172] Strabo 5.1.11.
[173] *CIL* 5.2 7749; E. Sereni (1971).
[174] *CIL* 5.2 7749 ll. 30–31.
[175] *CIL* 5.2 7749 ll. 5–6, 32–34; E. Sereni (1971) pp. 21–22.
[176] *CIL* 5.2 7749 ll. 27; Livy 40.41.5–6.

attribution in other instances, for example with the acculturated Ingauni.[177] If it was as successful in other places as it was around Genoa,
the institution must have played an important role in the Romanization of Liguria.

The second document is a land register from the town of Veleia.
Located on the opposite side of the Apennines on the upper Ciavenna,
it was, according to Pliny, *citra Placentiam in collibus oppidum*. Veleia
today still has impressive remains that testify to its imperial prosperity.[178] It lies in the territory of the Eleiates conquered by the Romans
in the first half of the second century B.C. As a native center it might
be compared with Aquae Statiellae. Pliny mentions that the Veleiates
had the old name of Regiates.[179] Perhaps it is not too bold to suggest
that the name derives from some client *regulus* backed by the Romans
in an effort to control the area around Veleia.

The land register dates to the time of Trajan and is mainly of interest to economic historians of the Empire. But it also sheds some
light on past eras around Veleia.[180] Ligurian names remain, and it can
be presumed that much of the local Roman-sounding nomenclature
hides acculturated Ligurians.[181] Small holders are still important even
though by the first century A.D. they were under increasing pressure.[182] Veleia seems to have been a typical Roman hill community
with every indication of almost total integration into the world of the
Empire.

We would naturally like much more evidence on the Roman accul-
turation of Liguria. For instance, the special festivals founded by the
Romans at Campi Macri on the border of southeastern Liguria hint at
the use of a combination of religion and commerce to integrate the
Ligurians.[183] The information we do have shows that the conquest of
Liguria not only involved some of the most difficult campaigning faced

---

[177] *CIL* 5 2490–92.

[178] *CIL* 11.1 pp. 204–239; Pliny *HN* 7.163; S. Aurigemma (1940); G. Radke (1955);
L. Grazzi (1972) pp. 219–30.

[179] Pliny *HN* 3.116, 7.163; G. Radke (1955) p. 623.

[180] *CIL* 11.1 1147; F. G. DePachtere (1920).

[181] F. G. DePachtere (1920) pp. 47–49. S. Dardaine (1969–70) stresses the possible
role of migrants from nearby colonies such as Placentia in the settlement of Veleia, as
well as the probability of some Ligurian continuity.

[182] F. G. DePachtere (1920) pp. 60–62, 67–93. R. P. Duncan-Jones (1976) p. 15 feels
that estates worth less than fifty thousand HS may have been systematically omitted
from the list. For the general distribution of estates by value see R. P. Duncan-Jones
(1976) pp. 15–17 and figs. 2–4.

[183] Strabo 5.1.11; G. Barruol (1969) p. 103; G. C. Susini (1977). For Ligurians in
Roman military service during the Republic see Sall. *Jug.* 38.6, 77.4, 93.2, 100–2.
E. Pais (1918) pp. 588–89 comments on the lack of major literary figures from Liguria
in the Roman period. This contrasts sharply with Venetia and the Transpadana.

by the Roman army but also required some of the most imaginative use of more peaceful frontier policies. The variety of devices used and the imagination evident in their application speaks well for Roman frontier strategists. Liguria was very different from the other two Italian Republican frontiers. Its kinship was with the frontiers developed by the Romans in the west, especially Gaul and Sardinia. It is to those frontiers that I will now turn.

CHAPTER 4

THE REPUBLICAN FRONTIER
IN GAUL

Linking the Roman frontiers of northern Italy and Spain was the southern coast of France. Geographically and historically, its development was closely connected with that of its neighbors. The mountain masses on its eastern and western borders were continuations of those of Italy and Spain, and posed similar problems of frontier control. The coastal strip of the Riviera was the main connection between the Roman homeland of Italy and the Iberian peninsula. But although the frontier needs of Spain and Italy should have forced an early Roman involvement in Gaul, Rome did not intervene militarily until the late second century B.C. Even then the Romans disciplined their advance toward the interior until 58 B.C., when C. Julius Caesar changed rapidly the frontier of Gaul as well as the historical geography of Europe.

This relatively short period of Republican frontier development in Gaul is interesting for a variety of reasons. The Romans assumed control over a mixed society that had evolved from the complicated long-term interaction between Greek colonists and sophisticated native groups. The late date of the intervention allowed the Romans to apply experience derived from success and failure on other frontiers. It made the Gallic frontier the most evolved and subtle example of Republican border management.

Sources for this period are mixed in nature and extremely uneven in quantity. In the literary sources such events as the invasion of the Cimbri and Teutones and the governorship of Fonteius are fully (though not impartially) described, while other events of equal or greater importance are practically neglected. The loss of Livy's history for most of the period is especially unfortunate. Republican epigraphical material is rare indeed, although some useful material is preserved and important information can be extracted from the more abundant imperial inscriptions. Most significant is the archaeological material. Greek, Roman, and native sites in the south of France have been the object of increasingly sophisticated archaeological investigation.[1] The coinage has been well studied,[2] and high-quality regional works are beginning

[1] Some good recent reviews of the evidence are P. A. Février (1973); G. Clemente (1974); R. Chevallier (1975).
[2] S. Scheers (1969); J. B. Colbert de Beaulieu (1973).

to appear.[3] Problems of evidence and interpretation are still manifold, but the archaeological finds from Gaul can now be used for frontier reconstruction in a way that is not possible for any other section of the western Republican frontier.

Roman policy and action in Gaul, as in the other frontiers, cannot be understood without a consideration of geography and pre-Roman social development. The varied terrain of southern France helped to shape distinct frontier units. East of the Rhone the mountains that slope down to the sea were an extension of those on the Ligurian and northern Italian borders and presented similar problems of control and conquest. The coastal groups were ethnically related to the Ligurians of Italy. Like their Italian neighbors, they threatened peaceful communications along the narrow coastal road and at times on the sea lanes themselves. Not surprisingly, the first Roman military intervention in Gaul was a continuation of the frontier wars in Liguria. The

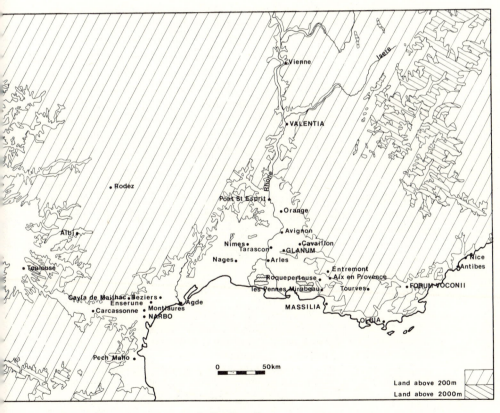

2. Southern France

[3] M. Labrousse (1968); G. Barruol (1969); J.C.M. Richard (1973).

Alpine mass itself defied total conquest, and in Gaul, as in Italy, the
Romans relied on their diplomatic skills to keep open the passes that
connected Italy with the Rhone.

The heart of southern Gaul was the Rhone valley and its delta. The
lower Rhone provided attractive land for settlement. The Rhone also
united the Mediterranean with the heart of Europe, by way of such
tributaries as the Durance, the Isère, and the Saône. The river valley
was used for trade but also for the invasion of people wishing to reach
the inland sea.

The geography to the west of the Rhone is similar to that found to
the east. The Massif Central blocks the western side of the Rhone.
This large mountain area harbored raiding tribes, but also provided a
protective barrier against bellicose groups farther north. The first
opening through it was to the west in the Aude region where the pass
between Carcassonne and Toulouse united the Mediterranean with
Aquitania and the Bay of Biscay. The importance of this area for
Rome is shown by its foundation of a colony at Narbo Martius (modern Narbonne) on the Etang de Bages. On the extreme west the Pyrenees provided a final mountain barrier between southern Gaul and
the Roman province of Hispania Citerior. This geographical assort-
ment has through the ages given rise to an ethnic and historical variety
that is central to the history of the entity known today as Provence.[4]

My consideration of pre-Roman cultural development in the area
begins with the first local interaction with the larger Mediterranean
world. The seventh and early sixth centuries B.C. saw considerable
Etruscan and some Punic contacts along the coast.[5] The Etruscans in
particular had more extensive connections than was formerly believed.
It was, however, the Greeks and especially the Phocaeans who from
the sixth century increasingly dominated the commerce of the area.
The basis of Hellenic hegemony was laid by the foundation of the city
of Massilia around 600 B.C.[6]

Archaeological evidence shows precolonial Greek contact with the

[4] M. Cary (1949) pp. 243–52.

[5] F. Villard (1960) pp. 74–75; H. Rolland (1963) pp. 84–89; F. Benoit (1965) pp. 29,
35–36, 51–56, 64, 75; M. Clavel (1970) pp. 54–55, 87–89; J. J. Jully (1975). M. Py
(1968) pp. 61–63 has distribution maps of Etruscan finds on the coast and up the lower
Rhone. Py argues that by the sixth century B.C. Etruscan goods may actually have been
distributed by Greek merchants. For the Etruscan shipwreck off Antibes dated 570–
560 B.C. see C. A. Livadie (1967); P. Arcelin (1976) p. 670. A number of Punic bronze
coins have been found in France, either in the northwest or in the coastal areas east of
the Rhone. These seem to be late and are of uncertain origin: J. B. Colbert de Beaulieu
(1973) pp. 337–42. Y. Solier (1968) discusses the Punic amphorae.

[6] G. Nenci (1958) pp. 47–63; F. Villard (1960) pp. 76–81; M. Euzennat (1980);
V. Jolivet (1980).

area, and it can be presumed that this was reflected in the selection of the colonial site at Massilia.[7] The settlers avoided the Rhone delta for a bay area slightly to the east that offered good harbor facilities but a limited *retroterra* hemmed in by mountains. The Greeks probably felt they could control the local mountaineers and develop communication routes along the coast while avoiding the larger tribes in the Rhone valley. Trade networks evolved that linked Massilia with the plain around Aix to the northeast and with the east-west route known to the Greeks as the Road of Heracles and to the Romans as the Via Domitia. In Roman times another road led south of the Etang de Berre through Fossa Mariana to Arles and the Rhone. The location suited a city that was to flourish by land and sea trade. In many ways, Massilia was to southern Gaul and the Rhone what Naucratis was to Egypt, Spina to the Po, and Istria to the Danube Valley.[8]

Stories relating to the foundation of Massilia preserve the spirit if not the detailed history of the first settlement.[9] They apparently derived from local traditions, since the basic account came from Pompeius Trogus, a member of the southern Gallic tribe of the Vocontii.[10] Even if the account of the wedding festival of Gypsis is dismissed as an archetypical foundation legend, the account of the grant of land from the king of the Segobriges, the continual early fighting with the neighboring Ligurians, and the hostile actions of the son of King Nannus against the developing Massilian colony ring true.[11]

Massilia increased its impact on southern Gaul by establishing secondary foundations along the coast. They ranged from Emporion, Rhode, and Agde on the west to Nice, Antibes, and later Olbia on the east.[12] Generally small in size (the fortifications of Olbia measure only 175 meters on a side) and located on isolated points of land, they controlled limited enclaves.[13] Their survival in the face of an often numerous native population depended on the cultivation of trade and good native relations. A bronze hand found at Vaugrenier bearing a

---

[7] M. Py (1968) pp. 61–63 notes that the precolonial Phocaean trade contacts were more concentrated than those of the Etruscans.

[8] F. Benoit (1965) p. 91. On Roman roads around Massilia see K. Miller (1916) cols. 87–89, 132-33.

[9] Strabo 4.4–5; G. Barruol (1969) p. 208.

[10] Just. *Epit.* 43.5.11; O. Hirschfeld (1913) p. 64.

[11] Just. *Epit.* 43.3–4; E. Sereni (1957) pp. 71–73, 78–87.

[12] F. Benoit (1965) p. 109. The site had Etruscan, Ionian, Phocaean, and Attic pottery of the first half of the sixth century B.C. J. Coupry (1968) p. 237 and G. Clemente (1974) pp. 36–37 have Ὄλβια founded in the fourth century B.C. On Nice, see P. A. Février (1973) pp. 6–7. On Emporion see Livy 34.9. On Agde see J. Sagnes (1970); A. Nickels (1976).

[13] J. Coupry (1968) pp. 240–42.

legend referring to alliance with the Velauni illustrates this process at work.[14] At Emporion a native compound grew up in proximity to the walls of the Greek center, while the Ligurian oppidum of Vaugrenier has yielded quantities of imported pottery, Massiliote coins, and even graffiti that are written in Greek.[15] In general, the natives still largely controlled the nearby land.[16]

The territorial limits of Massilia need to be emphasized, since the impression is sometimes created by modern historians that the Greek city exercised extensive political control in the south of France. This impression derives in part from the abundance of Greek goods in the oppida of Provence.[17] Also common is the Massilian coinage. There is no doubt that Massilia controlled the trade in imported Mediterranean luxury goods and that its coinage played an economic role in the area.[18] However, the superficial Hellenization of such centers as Entremont, Vaugrenier, and Nages can be deceptive. Economic influence does not imply political control. Indeed, as has been stressed by K. Polanyi and others, centers like Massilia can often best function by acting as ports of trade, linking two zones like Celtic Gaul and the Greco-Roman Mediterranean, enhancing their economic influence while tempering their pretensions to political domination.[19]

The Hellenization of the natives around Massilia needs to be placed in perspective. Massilia's role as the school of southern Gaul is often emphasized, but the Greek geographer Strabo noted that before the Roman conquest the Massilians considered themselves fortunate if the Celtic natives understood the Greek language enough to write contracts. The persistence of such grisly customs as head-hunting at sites like Entremont and Les Pennes raises doubt about the depth of Hellenization.[20] This matter will be discussed in more detail. What be-

[14] J. Carcopino (1957) pp. 103–4; G. Barruol (1969) pp. 372–73.

[15] Strabo 3.4.8; J. E. Dugand (1970).

[16] Strabo 4.1.9. J. E. Dugand (1970) pp. 25–27, 128ff. stresses the density of the native population behind Nice and Antibes.

[17] J. Brunel (1945); J. Jannoray (1955) pp. 298–302; J. DeWever (1966); C. Ebel (1976) pp. 26–40. F. Benoit (1965) discusses the distribution of Greek goods and influence.

[18] At Montfo near Beziers, 117 of 120 coins are Massilian: M. Clavel (1970). J. Brunel (1945) regarded the area of Massilian hegemony as very extensive. For a more balanced view see L. Chabot (1968).

[19] K. Polanyi, C. Arensberg, and H. Pearson (1957); C. Crumley (1974) p. 79; P. Wells (1980b). Just. *Epit.* 43.3.13, 43.5.1 notes the isolated position of Massilia. J. Jannoray (1955) pp. 286–302 stresses the limits of Massilian control in its hinterland.

[20] Strabo 4.4.5; F. Benoit (1970) pp. 17–22. R. Chevallier (1975) p. 712 states "L'hellénisation a certes précédé et préparé la romanisation mais à la différence de ce qu'a fait et réussi Rome, la Grèce n'a pas tenté d'helléniser la Gaule." C. Rostaing (1973) pp. 308–12 notes the limited number of Hellenic place names in Provence and regards this

comes clear is that the Romans brought fundamental changes to the culture of southern Gaul by integrating the Celtic and Greco-Roman societies.

Control of the neighboring sea lanes and a combination of trade, diplomacy, and limited military action were the keys to Massilian survival and prosperity for the early five centuries between the establishment of the colony and the development of the area into a Roman sphere of influence. The trade of Massilia has been the object of considerable study.[21] Only the general outline of its history is relevant to this volume. Much of the trade was centered along the coast and in the lower Rhone valley. The area was flooded first with Greek and later with Italian goods. Longer-range trade networks developed, taking advantage of the river valleys and mountain passes that linked the coast with the interior of Gaul. The Vix crater found near Mt. Lassois at the headwaters of the Seine is the most famous example of this trade connection.[22] Much of the commerce went up the Rhone, although some passed through Carcassonne into Aquitania.[23] The first period of widespread trade seems to have been the sixth and early fifth centuries B.C. Then, after interruptions brought by changes in the ethnic and political organization in interior Europe, a revival came in the late fifth and fourth centuries B.C. The later trade was apparently directed more at the natives closer to the coast.[24]

Much is still to be learned about the mechanisms of this trade. Underwater archaeology has provided considerable information on the use of sea lanes.[25] More important for the development of a Gallo-Greek society in the south and a Greek-influenced society in the north was the land trade and the shipment of imported goods to the interior.

---

as an indication of a relatively low level of Hellenization. At Les Pennes-Mirabeau, less than fifteen kilometers from Massilia, were found two skulls with iron attachments, indications of the severed-head cult: *Gallia* (1972) p. 520. For this question of Celtic cultural survival see also H. de Gerin Richard (1929) pp. 81–83; G. Barruol, U. Gilbert, and G. Rancoule (1961); J. Charmasson (1972) pp. 112–14; C. Rostaing (1973) pp. 308–12; P. Arcelin (1976) pp. 674–75.

[21] W. Kimmig (1958); F. Benoit (1963) pp. 362–86. R. Joffroy (1960) pp. 149–52 notes the lack of sixth-century Greek pottery north of Avignon and suggests that Massilian trade may have been overrated. J.V.S. Megaw (1966) pp. 38–44; P. Wells (1977) (1980b).

[22] J. Carcopino (1957); J.V.S. Megaw (1966).

[23] J. J. Hatt (1959) pp. 20–31. R. Etienne (1962) p. 71 n. 67 notes Attic black figure found around Agen. *Gallia* (1976) p. 479 mentions Attic red figure at Toulouse. S. Scheers (1968) notes that coins of the Ambioni in the Seine valley imitate those of Tarentum of the third century B.C. and suggests a possible direct sea link.

[24] J. Jannoray (1955) pp. 343–45; F. Villard (1960) pp. 91–95, 113–20; F. Benoit (1965) p. 219; J. DeWever (1966); J.M.C. Richard (1973) pp. 104–10; M. Euzennat (1980) p. 138.

[25] A. Tchernia (1969); J. Sagnes (1970) pp. 53–54; B. Liou (1973).

Here the archaeological finds are useful, but they can also be misleading. The Massilians, like the Phoenicians, were salesmen for the products of other people. The presence of Attic and later Campanian pottery in the oppida of Provence does not necessarily mean that their
merchants had penetrated the area.[26] Moreover, it is difficult to determine how far the Massilians themselves carried the goods they imported or at what point they turned them over to Celtic middlemen.[27]
The spread of Greek writing and the availability of Massilian military
intelligence and practical knowledge to the Romans suggest that the
Massilian Greeks became familiar figures in the oppida all along the
coastal plain and up into the middle Rhone valley.[28] Trade and diplomacy were probably indistinguishable as Massilian agents sought to
maintain peace with local groups, facilitate the flow of trade goods,
and protect their small and vulnerable centers.

This Massilian trade expansion involved a dynamic interaction that
brought changes to the local native societies. Since Massilia lacked the
military capability to control physically much of the native area, the
Celts and Ligurians were left largely independent. Among those natives one finds every indication of a high level of social vitality and
little evidence of the degeneration often characteristic of rapid acculturation.[29] In fact, one Roman observed that in some respects the Massilians themselves were being affected by the culture of the natives
who surrounded them.[30] The opportunity to control lucrative trade
routes and to accumulate foreign goods was bound to have a profound
effect on the cultural outlook and economic development of the natives, and especially of their ruling elite. The economic interaction
brought political and social change, which in turn led to an uneasiness
that outsiders could exploit. A new native society was emerging in
southern and central Gaul that was distinct from both the Greek enclaves and the less Mediterraneanized tribes in northern Gaul. The
natives of this new society, along with the Greek colonials, were the
basis for the Roman *provincia*.

Our two sources for the Greco-native interaction are the archaeological remains and the literary texts. Both provide much information,
but also raise a host of problems. The archaeological evidence is the

[26] M. Py (1968) pp. 69–70.

[27] P. Wells (1980a). J. Charmasson (1972) pp. 123–25 discusses the production and
distribution of pseudo-Ionic ware.

[28] P. M. Duval (1958); F. Benoit (1962). Isid. Etym. 15.1.163 mentions that Massilians became versed in Greek, Latin, and Celtic.

[29] The works of both G. Barruol (1969) and G. Clemente (1974) summarize well the
evidence for this complex development.

[30] Livy 38.17.12.

most abundant and is expanding rapidly. Oppida-digging, along with
eating and wine-drinking, has become a regular activity in the south
of France.[31] Hundreds of these forts have been identified. Oppidum
is an omnibus word used for a native settlement usually raised on a
hill or bluff and at least partly fortified.[32] They are excellent places
for the study first of Hellenization and then of Romanization.

Dating the initial occupation at these oppida and identifying breaks
in habitation allow the reconstruction of local political dynamics as
well as the impact of outside forces such as the invasion of the Cimbri
and Teutones or the arrival of the Roman army. The interpretation of
the evidence is, however, often problematic. The contemporaneous
development of a series of oppida at key strategic points in a zone may
indicate the appearance of a complex political system with diverse but
unified clan and tribal groups.[33] But it may also represent the simul-
taneous response of independent groups to new trade opportunities or
a common outside danger.

Destruction levels can also be ambiguous. Entremont, with its ground
peppered by Roman ballista balls, can easily be placed in the historical
context of the initial Roman conquest.[34] But less clear is the significance of the group of third-century B.C. destruction levels in the
Languedoc.[35] They might have been caused by the arrival of the new
Celtic tribe of the Volcae, the passage of Hannibal, or just the Iberian
equivalent of Mrs. O'Leary's cow. Archaeological evidence does not
ordinarily allow the degree of chronological precision necessary to
connect archaeological catastrophe with specific historical events.
Nevertheless, general trends can be reconstructed, and these studies
provide useful information on changes in native society.

A second question often raised in oppidum excavations is the degree
to which the native culture is influenced by outside forces. Archaeologists working on these sites have been greatly impressed by the amount
of Greek pottery, Massilian coins, and even Hellenic-inspired urban
design. This indicates the incorporation of many Hellenic forms into
native life. Yet, it is probable that the degree of Massilian penetration
and even the amount of Hellenization have been exaggerated. The
social, political, and structural role of hill forts in Iron Age Western
Europe is just beginning to be considered from the point of view of

---

[31] P. A. Février (1973); G. Clemente (1974).

[32] In Provence, the term is rather loosely applied to all hill forts rather than just to
more complex native settlements like those in northern France: B. Cunliffe and
T. Rowley (1976).

[33] Cf. p. 136.

[34] Cf. p. 149 n. 138.

[35] Cf. pp. 143–44.

modern archaeological technique and anthropological theory, and more thought needs to be given to the kinds of native societies the hill forts represent.[36] The presence of Greek pottery several hundred miles from Massilia should be balanced against the persistence of native religious cults and practices at oppida less than ten miles from Massilia.

The literary sources provide some of the context missing from the archaeological record, although they pose problems of their own. The authors give some accounts of political and military events, but neither Greek nor Roman writers were particularly interested in the west. References are limited in quantity, often fragmentary, and usually compiled long after the events described. They lack the immediacy of a broken Attic pot or an archaeological destruction level with late third-century coins. Furthermore, unlike the archaeological record, the literary one is quantitatively fixed. The texts will not be markedly increasing in number or improving in precision. The future lies with archaeology as the main historical tool in reconstructing the flow of events in pre-Roman and early Roman Western Europe.

Another caution about the evidence should be entered. During the period under discussion, southern Gaul was an ethnically mixed and changing native society. Much consideration has been given in the literature to the degree of Ligurian and Iberian, as opposed to Celtic, elements in the culture.[37] Although it is always dangerous to equate linguistic and cultural differences, Ligurians and Celts do appear to have been ethnically distinct. Moreover, the Celts were changing constantly with the forces of acculturation and the arrival of new tribal elements. In the early fourth century B.C. we find one newly arrived group of Gauls under Catumandus besieging Massilia.[38] Later the Celtic Volcae were to penetrate and settle in the Languedoc.[39] In the late second century B.C. the Germanic Cimbri and Teutones invaded the Rhone Valley, and by the mid-first century B.C. the Germans of Ariovistus were an important presence among the client groups of the Gallic frontier.[40] The changing ethnic picture should be kept in mind when evaluating the literary and archaeological material. Information about natives in one part of Gaul at one time may have little to do with those in another time and place.

The changing face of southern Gallic society would provoke Massilian anxiety and finally Roman intervention. An early concern of Greeks and Romans alike was the appearance of developing political and social systems among the natives. This posed a threat to the small

[36] R. Chevallier (1970); B. Cunliffe and T. Rowley (1976).
[37] N. Lamboglia (1959) (1972a); R. Chevallier (1975) pp. 704–5.
[38] Just. *Epit.* 43.5.5.
[39] Cf. p. 144.
[40] Cf. p. 170.

Greek settlements and later to the Roman system of informal political control. The most obvious expression of this was the appearance of the institution known to anthropologists as the chieftainship. This meant that certain individuals and lineages, having gained special access to sources of wealth and prestige (often through control of outside trade), attained a dominant position within the native society. Their rule was still largely personal and nonbureaucratic, and was normally transitory. Nevertheless, it allowed a temporary concentration of wealth and political power.[41] The Gauls, with their large population, good land, and long-range trading networks, seem throughout the Iron Age to have been prone to the formation of chieftainships.

The first example of a chieftainship that affected Mediterranean traders was the *regnum* that developed around Naro near later Narbo in the Languedoc. The geographer Avienus, drawing upon early Greek sources, describes it as *gens Elesycum prius / loca haec tenebat atque Narbo civitas / erat ferocis maximum regni caput.*[42] Naro is generally identified with the oppidum site of Montlaurés near Narbo.[43] The literary and the archaeological evidence both suggest a society developing under the twin stimuli of mercenary service and trade. Herodotus mentions Helisycians fighting with the Carthaginians in Sicily in 480 B.C., and the term *ferox regnum* implies a formidable military reputation. Those returning from mercenary service would have brought home not only a knowledge of Mediterranean military skills but also a taste for Mediterranean luxury goods.[44] Archaeological evidence from Montlaurés and other nearby sites shows the penetration of Etruscan and then Greek goods during the late seventh and early sixth centuries. Abundant Greek pottery as well as some Punic material appeared during the fifth and fourth centuries.[45] The trade extended through the Carcassonne passes into Aquitania and the Atlantic coastal area. Attic black- and red-figure pottery has been found at Agen beyond Toulouse, while La Tène I and II fibulae from interior Gaul appear at coastal sites.[46] This developing trade explains the establishment of a Massilian trading center at Agde during the sixth century B.C. Its placement at the margin of the rich coastal area of the Hérault suggests

[41] D. Nash (1978); P. Wells (1980a) pp. 4–6.

[42] Avienus *Ora Marit* 584ff.; J. Jannoray (1955) pp. 378–80.

[43] G. Clemente (1974) pp. 61–66.

[44] Herod. 7.165; J. Jannoray (1955) pp. 294–95, 335–37.

[45] O. and J. Taffenal (1956) p. 103, (1960); Y. Solier and J. Giry (1972) pp. 90–95; G. Clemente (1974) pp. 56–58. J. J. Jully (1976) notes the considerable number of Greek graffiti on pottery in this area, which is an indication of the presence of Greek traders, especially in the fifth and fourth centuries B.C.

[46] H. Martin-Granél (1944); R. Etienne (1962) p. 71; M. Labrousse (1968) p. 108; Y. Solier and J. Giry (1972) pp. 95–98; G. Clemente (1974) p. 61.

that the founders wanted to avoid the central areas of the growing native power.[47]

The natives that controlled the area were ethnically Iberians. Inland they appear to have developed a group of linked oppida at such centers as Pech Maho and Cayla de Mailhac that protected the trade routes to the northwestern Atlantic and the valleys leading down from the Cevennes.[48] Their main center at Montlaurés has provided no evidence yet of marked status differentiation like that which developed at Tartessos in Spain or among the tribes of the interior. Some sites, however, such as Pech Maho and Cayla de Mailhac, have produced relatively rich burials that show the developing power of frontier leaders.[49] The history of the rise and fall of this Iberian society in Languedoc cannot yet be reconstructed in detail, but it seems to have lasted for several centuries, with the breakup coming in the wake of the appearance of new Celtic groups in the third century B.C.[50] The traditions of native trading networks and political organization must have been very much alive when the Romans established control in the area. It is no coincidence that Narbo Martius was founded so close to Montlaurés.

The developments in the Languedoc did not markedly affect Massilia or arouse Roman concern. But it was another matter with the Salluvii, who were also concentrating local political and military power and developing a differentiated social order. Massilia and Rome both felt seriously threatened. The Romans ultimately intervened, starting a chain of events that led to permanent Roman occupation in the south of Gaul.

Drawing on his fifth-century B.C. sources, Avienus described the Salluvii as *atroces*. During the fifth century they were a small tribal group who controlled an important east-west route through the valley of the Arc. By the time of the Second Punic War, they controlled areas as far south as the coastal mountains. In the late second century B.C. they built up a confederation of tribes and extended their power

[47] M. Clavel (1970) pp. 90, 106–14; G. Clemente (1974) p. 44.

[48] J. Jannoray (1955) p. 414–40; O. and J. Taffenal (1956); J. Campardou (1957) pp. 62–65; Y. Solier (1968a); G. Clemente (1974) pp. 52–53.

[49] Y. Solier (1968a) pp. 7–37 suggests a 300–250 B.C. date for Pech Maho. It may have been a hero shrine. Iberian inscriptions have been found there. O. and J. Taffenal (1960) pp. 27–28, 117–20 discuss the c. 300 B.C. chieftain tomb at Mailhac. O. and J. Taffenel (1961) pp. 7–13, 34–35 describe tombs of the late sixth and mid-fourth centuries at Corno-Lauzo. *Gallia* (1971) pp. 377–79 mentions a Pech Maho *ustrinum* of c. 200 B.C. that seems associated with a warrior cremation during the last phase of occupation. The site was occupied from 600 to 200 B.C.

[50] M. Clavel (1970) pp. 140–41.

from the Rhone on the west to the Loup on the east and the sea on the south.[51]

The Salluvii were a mixture of Celts and Ligurians, with the Celts apparently forming the ruling class. The literary sources mention several chieftains. King Toutomotulus, a Celt, led the tribal forces against Massilia and the Romans.[52] He was not the first Celtic warleader whom the Massiliotes had met. During the fourth century B.C. the tribes that were neighbors of Massilia had allied and elected a warrior named Catumandus as their leader. In the words of Justin, *dux consensu omnium Catumandus regulus eligitur.*[53] The phrase implies that here tribal assemblies still had considerable power. Elsewhere Gallic groups were increasingly dominated by aristocratic factions and charismatic leaders.[54] Toutomotulus did not rule unchallenged. Another leader called Crato is mentioned. The name has a Greek sound to it. His advocacy of the interests of Massilia and Rome, his mistreatment by the followers of Toutomotulus, and his rescue by the Romans suggest that he supported Greco-Roman interests among the Salluvii.[55]

The best expression of the power of the Salluvii is the remains at the oppidum of Entremont. Located three kilometers northeast of Aix at a height that dominates the surrounding countryside, Entremont is an obvious control center for the area. Finds by antiquarians and recent excavations by French archaeologists have revealed a settlement with contradictory evidence of intense Hellenization and strong survival of native ways.[56] Greek, Italian, and even Iberian trade goods were found in abundance. The coins, including a hoard of 1,435 obols, reflected the overwhelming monetary influence of Massilia, although the issues of other centers including Rome and the Allobroges were represented.[57] The layout of the oppidum, with regular blocks of streets, clearly reflects the influence of Hellenistic city planning.[58] However, this must be contrasted with the religious monuments and iconography that were overwhelmingly native. Most striking is the abundance of evidence for the continuation of the cult of the severed head down to the time of the sack of the city by Roman forces.[59]

---

[51] Livy 21.26.3; Strabo 4.1.6, 4.1.9, 4.1.11; G. Barrruol (1975) pp. 187–88.

[52] Cf. pp. 149–50.

[53] Just. *Epit.* 43.5.5; C. Jullian (1920) vol. 1 pp. 393–96.

[54] Livy 21.20.

[55] Diod. 34.23.

[56] F. Benoit (1947), (1954), (1957), (1968).

[57] F. Benoit (1947) pp. 83–84, (1950) pp. 117–19, (1958) p. 414, (1968) pp. 31–32; G. Clemente (1974) p. 31.

[58] F. Benoit (1968) pp. 13–17; *Gallia* (1972) pp. 511–14.

[59] Strabo 4.4.5; F. Benoit (1947) pp. 88–94, (1954) pp. 290–94.

It would be helpful to have more information on the social and political structure of the tribal group of which Entremont was the center. Entremont was in a position to control the main east-west routes between the Alps and the Rhone, as well as important north-south routes leading from the Durance to Massilia.[60] The oppidum developed relatively late, with most of its growth coming in the third and second centuries B.C. Apparently Massilia had little power to stop the consolidation of native forces nearby.[61] This is made more clear by the development in the area between Aix and Massilia of the Salluvian oppidum of Baou Rouge.[62]

The Salluvian confederacy not only controlled smaller neighboring groups but developed links between its ruling class and that of neighboring Gallic tribes like the Allobroges.[63] How unity was preserved within the confederacy is difficult to determine. The ties were loose ones, and individual oppida must have retained considerable freedom of action. This is shown by the rapidity with which the confederacy dissolved when the Romans destroyed its political center and its ruling family.

The Salluvii was not the only group in the south of France that was forming an alliance system. Their territory marched with that of the Cavares. This people controlled the east bank of the Rhone between the Isère and Durance, as well as the fertile lower portion of the small river valleys that flow from the east into the Rhone. They were in an ideal position to benefit from trade moving up the valleys, and seemed to have formed a close relationship with Massilia and later with Rome.[64] In 218 B.C. they attempted unsuccessfully to stop Hannibal from crossing the Rhone.[65] Located between the restless Salluvii and the Allobroges, they formed an important frontier client group for Rome. Benefiting from their connection, they prospered and by the end of the Republic were highly Romanized.[66]

The final tribal group on the eastern shore of the Rhone was the Allobroges. Linked by trade relations with Massilia and by political connection with the Salluvii farther south, the Allobroges were conquered by Rome in the 120s and incorporated into the newly established province. They had a history of close ties with tribes farther

---

[60] Arist. [Mir. Ausc.] 85–86; G. Barruol (1969) pp. 63–65.

[61] The role of the oppida immediately around Massilia has been disputed. Some see them as native centers threatening Massilia. Others view them as Massilian outposts: J. DeWever (1966) pp. 111–12; G. Barruol (1969) pp. 81–83.

[62] G. Clemente (1974) pp. 32–33.

[63] Cf. pp. 149, 152.

[64] Strabo 4.1.11; G. Barruol (1969) pp. 231–42.

[65] Livy 21, 27, 28; G. Barruol (1969) p. 233 n. 2.

[66] Strabo 4.1.12.

north such as the Arverni, however, and remained until the wars of
Caesar one of the most restless of the southern Gallic groups.[67] On
the south their territory reached to the Isère, except for a section of
the delta where Segovellauni, clients of the Cavares, were in control.
The Segovellauni—well armed, well organized, and bellicose—held
the Allobroges at bay.[68] On the north the Allobroges' boundary reached
to the bend of the Rhone and on the east extended into the Alps.
Their principal center was at Vienne. Greek pottery dating to the
fourth century has been found there, and the site has produced ample
indication of contact with Mediterranean traders during the third and
second centuries B.C.[69]

On the west bank of the Rhone, another alliance system developed
around Nimes. Strabo mentions that twenty-four communities had
been placed under the political jurisdiction of Nimes.[70] It is likely that
this tradition of political unification goes back before the Roman period. The territory was fertile, and the numerous oppida commanded
trade and transhumance routes coming down from the Massif Central.
Many reached a high level of prosperity by the first century B.C.[71] At
the oppidum of Nages a grid network of streets was laid out and
sophisticated fortifications built by the second quarter of the second
century B.C. Greek imports were common, but more than seventy
percent of the pottery found was native. Evidence for the persistence
of the cult of the severed head also shows the strength and continuity
of Celtic culture at the site.[72]

A blend of Greek and Celtic elements characterized both Entremont
and Nages. Similar traits are found at the center of Glanum. Located
between Cavaillon and Tarascon, Glanum developed around the nearby
sacred spring.[73] By the second century B.C. the sanctuary and the
nearby settlement had acquired a strong Hellenistic flavor. Both ar-

[67] G. Barruol (1969) pp. 296–305. Strabo 4.1.11 notes their general change from
warlike to peaceful agricultural people.

[68] Polyb. 3.49.5–13.

[69] Strabo 4.1.11; A. Pelletier (1966); G. Chapotat (1970); G. Clemente (1974) pp. 40–
41.

[70] Strabo 4.1.12. Although extensively rebuilt in Roman and later times, Nimes has
preserved some pre-Roman material. Trade goods going back to the sixth century B.C.
have been found, and there are remains of fortifications probably of fourth century B.C.
as well as evidence of continuity of occupation into the Roman period: A. Robert (1965b)
pp. 219–20.

[71] A. Robert (1965a), (1965b).

[72] H. Rolland (1936); A. Robert (1965b); M. Py (1968) p. 83; F. Benoit (1970) pp.
51–64. Pliny HN 11.240 in praising the cheeses of the area shows the community's link
to the pastoral economy. M. Aliger (1967) p. 58 describes the period 100–30 B.C. as one
of great prosperity.

[73] H. Rolland (1960) p. 22; P. A. Février (1973) p. 13 notes Bronze Age pottery on
site.

chitecture and coinage reflected this.[74] Again the question arises as to
whether Glanum was basically a Greek or a native city. There is no
doubt that Greeks were to be found there, probably in considerable
numbers, but the cult itself was definitely native. The blend of Hellenic and native in the sanctuary is well illustrated by the discovery
of fine Hellenistic architectural blocks with holes for severed heads or
individual head sculptures hollowed into them.[75] The persistence of
native traditions is shown by the representation of native deities in a
column capital from the first-century B.C. shrine; in addition, in the
shrine to Valetudo built by M. Vipsanius Agrippa, the victory goddess is shown wearing a torque.[76] Presumably Celts, too, lived in the
fine porticoed Hellenistic houses of Glanum. The extent of the Celtic
population on the lower Rhone can be gauged by the great number of
La Tène III incineration burials in the area below Orange.[77]

Another indication of a continuing native presence around Glanum
is the large concentration of Gallo-Greek inscriptions in the area. These
inscriptions, Gallic in language but Greek in writing, are another sign
of the growth of a sophisticated native population in such areas of
interior Provence as the central Gard, northern Bouches du Rhone,
Vaucluse, and central Hérault.[78] Most are difficult to date. One seems
to date to as early as the third century B.C.[79] Most probably date to
the period of the Roman occupation. Significantly fewer are the Gallo-
Latin inscriptions. Other information suggests that the natives of the
area preferred the Greek alphabet, although it may be going too far to
see this as an affirmation of Greek values in the face of Rome.[80] In
addition, Gallo-Greek money was issued by native centers in imitation
of the ubiquitous Massilian coinage.[81] Communities with these native
mints included Avignon, Cavaillon, Nimes, and Glanum. Cavaillon,
Nimes, and Glanum are all places where large numbers of Gallo-Greek
inscriptions have been found, and there is a significant overlap between these two manifestations of native Hellenization.

The Hellenic-native cultural interaction in southern Gaul from the
fourth to the second century B.C. is important background for understanding Roman policy and actions. Far from losing their cultural vi-

[74] H. Rolland (1958), (1960), (1962); G. Clemente (1974) pp. 38–39.
[75] H. Rolland (1958) p. 122, (1960) pp. 55–63, (1968) pp. 26–34; P. Arcelin (1976) p.
674. G. Barruol (1976) p. 404 describes Celtic deities on capitals of the first century
B.C. H. Rolland (1968) pp. 24–25 mentions actual skulls found at Glanum.
[76] G. Barruol (1969) pp. 68–72 fig. 36; F. Benoit (1970) pp. 50–64.
[77] J. J. Hatt (1970) pp. 130–31.
[78] P. M. Duval (1958); J.C.M. Richard (1973) p. 127.
[79] P. M. Duval (1958) pp. 66–67.
[80] P. M. Duval (1958) pp. 68–69.
[81] H. Rolland (1949).

tality in the face of Greek influence, these Celts, Iberians, and Ligurians developed a dynamic social system that used Greek elements
to articulate and develop native forms. Greek architecture graced native shrines. Greek letters expressed the native language. Political and
military institutions were emerging that employed territorial concepts
larger than the Greek polis and its outlying emporia. The developments were not unlike those that characterized the emergence of the
Roman system in the Italian peninsula. Moreover, despite folk movements and tribal separation, there was among the Celts some tribal
intercommunication and sense of ethnic identity. Gauls in southwestern France knew of Roman attacks on Gauls in northern Italy.[82] In
197 B.C. when a delegation from the Greek city Lampsacus in Asia
Minor was headed for Rome, it first went to Massilia and from there
to the Volcae Arecomaci near Nimes to pick up communications that
were brought back to the Volcae in Galatia.[83] In one of the Greek
Romances a man who had lost his wife during a Celtic raid on Miletus
sought her among the Gauls in the hinterland of Massilia.[84]

The Hellenized natives of Provence were not the only indigenous
groups that played an important role in the development of the Republican frontier. Upstream were other tribal agglomerations that represented a transition between the Gallo-Greek culture of the south and
the Celtic culture of central and northern Gaul. Tribes like the Aedui,
Sequani, and the Arverni were true buffer groups.

The Aedui and Sequani, located on opposite banks of the river Saône,
were traditional rivals for the control of the important trade connecting with northern Gaul.[85] The territory of the Aedui centered on the
modern French departments of Saône and Loire, and touched not only
the Rhone-Saône river system but also the headwaters of the Loire.
Thick settlement from the Neolithic period onward suggests the importance of the area. Traded goods changed from flint and amber to
metals, and by the second century B.C. Greek amphorae and Mediterranean pottery were common among the Aedui.[86]

The land of the Sequani stretched to the northeast, with its principal center at the modern city of Besançon This provided them with
access not only to the Saône but also to the Rhine drainage and to the
German tribes of the area. The latter connection served the Sequani
as a trade outlet and as a source of allies with whom to fight their
rivals, the Aedui. Those contacts were apparently of long standing.

[82] Livy 21.20.5–8.
[83] M. Holleaux (1957).
[84] Parth. 8.
[85] Strabo 4.3.2; E. Thevenot (1969) pp. 33–36.
[86] E. Thevenot (1969) pp. 21–28.

The Sequani were accused of aiding the Germans at the time of the invasion of the Cimbri and Teutones. They made their peace with Rome by turning over to Marius several German chieftains who had taken refuge in their land. By the time of Caesar the Germans had tipped the balance heavily in favor of the Sequani, although they were proving to be somewhat burdensome guests in Celtic lands.[87]

The literary sources provide little evidence for the social structure of these two tribes during this period. The lack of distinctive personalities in the historical record suggests that charismatic leaders or strong rulers had not yet appeared. The archaeological finds do not indicate any heavy concentrations of population.[88] While the evidence suggests that before the Roman conquest the Aedui and Sequani preserved a relatively undifferentiated ruling class, the same was not the case with the Arverni. Located in the modern Auvergne on the northeastern shoulder of the Massif Central, they represented the most significant concentration of political power in Gaul during the second century B.C. Controlling important trade routes leading toward the Loire, the Arverni had the potential of becoming what anthropologists call a "gateway community" determining access to important trade networks and reaping the subsequent advantages.[89] Such popular pre-Roman trade goods as amphorae and black-glaze pottery are found in their territory but do not seem to have circulated beyond it.[90] By the eve of the Roman conquest, a dominant ruling family had emerged whose extravagant style impressed even the Romans. The first known ruler is Luerius, who was noted for his exhuberent displays and lavish distribution of money, practices designed to win clients.[91] His rituals of control included not only granting largess but also holding elaborate feasts and patronizing a group of bards whose role was to sing his praises.[92] Bituitus, his son, continued these customs.

The accounts of the activities of Luerius and Bituitus show all the elements of an emerging chieftain system.[93] Solid achievement as well as elaborate ceremonies underpinned their position. There is evidence of systematic drainage and organized agricultural development in the land of the Arverni.[94] The Arverni appear to have been the tribe that

---

[87] Caes. *BGall.* 1.31.3–4, 6.12; Plut. *Vit. Mar.* 24.4; *RE* 2R. 2A. 1639.

[88] J. B. Colbert de Beaulieu (1973); D. Nash (1975).

[89] K. Hirth (1978).

[90] D. Nash (1976) pp. 114–15, 122.

[91] Strabo 4.2.3; Ath. 4.152 D.

[92] Ath. 4.152 D.

[93] The limited evidence both literary and archaeological suggests that these Gallic leaders stood somewhere between the "big man" and the chieftain type of government: M. D. Sahlins (1962–63).

[94] J. P. Dauggs and F. Malacher (1976) p. 744.

introduced into central Gaul gold coinage based ultimately on types of Philip II, although the extent of their monetary hegemony has been exaggerated.[95] Also debatable is the extent and nature of the Arvernian political control. Strabo describes their dominion as reaching as far as the ocean and the territory of Narbo. Much of this must have represented alliance systems like that binding the Allobroges and the Arverni in the Rhone valley, and probably joined the Volcae and Arverni toward the southwest.[96] There is no evidence for the emergence of a truly bureaucratic state system. Nevertheless, the Arverni, their clients, and their allies did represent a political and military power that was bound to make the Gallo-Greeks of Provence, Massilia, and ultimately Rome extremely nervous.

Important changes were also taking place in the southwest of Gaul. The emergence of the chieftainship at Naro has already been discussed. This phase ended with the arrival of the Volcae, a Celtic group with links to the interior of Gaul in the third century B.C.[97] Although the Volcae caused some intitial disruption, they appear to have left the Iberian ethnic base intact and to have adjusted to life along the Mediterranean.[98]

A key center for the developments during this period in southwestern Gaul is Ensérune.[99] The oppidum was first occupied at the beginning of the sixth century B.C., but began its period of importance during the fourth century B.C. Fortifications were built, and evidence of literacy appeared. The population was basically Iberian. By the mid-third century imports at the site included pieces of black-glaze pottery produced near the city of Rome. This suggests the beginning of Roman contacts with the natives of the area that were to lead to the Roman diplomatic missions during the Second Punic War and the later foundation of the city of Narbo.[100] A destruction level at Ensérune dated to the late third century probably relates either to the arrival of the Volcae or to the passage of Hannibal.[101] The break was minor, and the center continued to prosper. Building techniques be-

[95] M. Clavel (1970) pp. 131–32, 194–95 decribes Arvernian staters found at Beziers. D. Nash (1975) p. 212; E. Wightman (1976).

[96] Strabo 4.2.3.

[97] H. Gallet de Santerre (1962) p. 167; J. Jannoray (1955) pp. 404–13; N. Lamboglia (1960) p. 314.

[98] M. Clavel (1970) pp. 140–41; J.C.M. Richard (1973); G. Clemente (1974) pp. 53–55, 47. Y. Solier (1964-65) p. 30 connects the lack of occupation during the second century B.C. at the former Elysian frontier posts to the arrival of the Volcae.

[99] J. Jannoray (1955) pp. 418–40; G. Clemente (1974) pp. 50–51.

[100] J. Jannoray (1955); H. Gallet de Santerre (1962); Clemente (1974) p. 50

[101] J. Jannoray (1955) pp. 269–72; G. Clemente (1974) p. 50. Pech Maho has a destruction level of similar date: J. Campardou (1956) pp. 62–65.

gan to show Greek influence. Ensérune weathered smoothly the transition to Roman rule, and of Roman-style houses from the first century B.C. testify to the thorough acculturation of at least the native ruling class.[102]

Livy's account of the Roman embassy in 218 B.C. gives us some sense of the political and social organization of the territory of the western Celts.[103] The Gauls are described as still assembling in the traditional armed meeting of their people. This assembly was controlled by the elders, although Livy notes that they had a difficult time keeping the younger warriors in line. The Celts were knowledgeable about the fate of their kinsmen in the north of Italy. The seeds of future political and social change were evident. When the Romans reported the results of their mission to the Massilians, they were told that the only way to make progress with those people was to bribe the principal men of the community with gold. That probably reflects a longstanding practice of the Massilians in dealing with the Celts. It also explains in part the accumulation of wealth by certain members of the leadership class who emerged as "big men" in their dealings, first with the Greeks and then with the Romans.[104]

The settlement of the Celtic Volcae in Languedoc reinforced connections with the interior of Gaul through the Carcassonne gap. New oppida sprang up along these trade routes.[105] At La Lagastre, between Carcassonne and Limoux, a new oppidum was settled around 180 B.C., and at Eburomagus (modern Bram) the first occupation seems to date to the mid-second century B.C.[106] The distribution of the silver coins known to numismatists as *monnaies à la croix* demonstrates the growing complexity of commercial relations during the period.[107] Derived from the coin types of the Greek center of Rhode on the northeastern Spanish coast, they had their principal circulation between Languedoc and Bordeaux, although scattered examples are found elsewhere, including sites in Spain. They appear in dated coin hoards as early as the late third century.[108] Their persistence shows the relative independence of the southwestern area from the growing Arvernian power.[109]

---

[102] H. Gallet de Santerre (1962) pp. 163–64, (1968); P. A. Février (1973) p. 11; C. Vatin (1968–70). J. Jannoray (1955) pp. 441–59 has the site abandoned c. A.D. 30.

[103] Livy 21.20. J. Campardou (1956) pp. 63–65 dates the destruction at Pech Maho to Hannibal.

[104] Livy 21.20.8–9.

[105] G. Clemente (1974) p. 58.

[106] G. Clemente (1974) pp. 59–61.

[107] D. F. Allen (1969) pp. 33–61; A. Soutou (1969); J.C.M. Richard (1972).

[108] D. F. Allen (1969). J. B. Colbert de Beaulieu (1973) pp. 279–88 argues for a date after the collapse of the Arvernian confederacy.

[109] D. F. Allen (1969) p. 49.

Although in many respects these Celts and Ligurians shaped the pattern of Roman conquest in southern Gaul more than the Massilians did, it was Rome's relationship with Massilia that provided the initial cause for intervention. Contacts between Rome and Massilia extended back into the sixth century B.C. perhaps in part as a result of Etruscan trade in the south of France, and they were certainly active by the fourth century B.C.[110] Justin mentions a treaty between Roman and Massilia in 386 B.C. and notes that spoil from the Roman conquest of Veii was dedicated in the Massilian treasury at Delphi.[111] Several factors drew Rome and Massilia closer during the later fourth and early third centuries. Both had the Etruscans, Ligurians, and Gauls as enemies. Massilia, with its location and experience in Gallic diplomacy, was an invaluable source of intelligence on events in the interior of Europe. Moreover, Massilia increased its trade with Celtic northern Italy and Magna Graecia during this period and, in doing so, came into closer contact with developing Roman power there.[112]

As noted above, the Roman merchants seem to have been familiar with parts of the Gallic coast before the Second Punic War. The ease with which the Roman ambassadors moved through Gaul in 218 B.C. and the way Scipio managed to position Roman troops around the Rhone and obtain guides and Gallic auxiliaries from the Massilians suggest that Roman contacts with the area may have been more frequent than the historical sources reveal.[113] There is no denying, however, that the Second Punic War marked a turning point in Rome's relations with southern Gaul. The growing Roman involvement in Spain increased the need to control land routes and ports along the coast of France.[114] The final conquest of the peninsula below the Alps brought the Romans into an area where the coin types show considerable Massilian and Celtic interaction.[115] Their advance up the Ligurian coast brought the Romans into Massilia's sphere of influence and gave the two states the problem of controlling the land-sea depredations of the Ligurian tribes.

As a result of these mutual interests, Romano-Massilian contacts accelerated during the first decades of the second century. The Mas-

[110] Livy 5.25.7–10; Diod. 14.93.4–5; N. DeWitt (1940); F. R. Kramer (1948); G. Nenci (1958) pp. 63–80; M. Sordi (1960) pp. 97–98; C. Ebel (1976) pp. 5–15.

[111] Just. *Epit.* 43.5.10.

[112] G. Nenci (1958) pp. 80–97.

[113] G. Clemente (1974) pp. 11–14. Central Italian black-glaze pottery circulated in southern Gaul by the mid-late third century B.C.: G. Clemente (1974) pp. 23–24.

[114] The expeditions of both Hannibal and Hasdrubal were of major importance in increasing this Roman involvement: Livy 27.36.1–4.

[115] J. E. Dugand (1970) pp. 26–27.

silian role in the Greco-Gallic diplomacy of the Lampsacan delegation to Rome in 197 B.C. has been mentioned. In 189 B.C. the praetor L. Baebius was attacked by Ligurians on his way to Spain, and staggered mortally wounded into Massilia.[116] In 181 B.C. *duumviri navales* were appointed to protect the Ligurian coast as far as Massilia, a reminder that the Ligurians were a menace by sea as well as by land.[117] The complaints that led to this action came directly from Massilia.[118]

By the 150s the time was ripe for direct Roman intervention. Roman forces had pushed up the Po to the southeastern fringes of the Ligurian mountains. In 155 B.C. the Ligurian Apuani north of Luni had staged a revolt that required the intervention of the experienced general M. Claudius Marcellus. The Romans were coming to regard the Ligurian problem as one that involved the French as well as the Italian coast. Florus expresses this well:

> Ligures, imis Alpium iugis adhaerentis inter Varum et Magram flumen inplicitosque dumis silvestribus, major aliquanto labor erat invenire, quam vincere. Tuti locis et fuga durum atque velox genus ex occasione latrocinia magis quam bella faciebant. Itaque cum diu multumque eluderent Salluvii, Deciates, Oxubii, Euburiates, Ingauni, tandem Fulvius latebras eorum igni saepsit, Baebius in plana deduxit, Postumius ita exarmavit ut vix reliquerit ferrum quo terra coleretur.[119]

> It was considerably more difficult to find than to conquer the Ligurians who kept close to the lower part of the mountain ridges between the Varus and the Magra and were entangled in their wooded thickets. Protected by their locale and the possibility of flight, this tough and mobile people engaged in banditry rather than wars as the opportunity presented itself. And since the Salluvii, the Deciates, the Oxubii, the Euburiates, and the Inguani for so long and so often slipped away, Fulvius finally trapped them in their hiding places with fire, Baebius moved then down onto level ground and Postumius so completely disarmed them that there was hardly iron enough left with which to plough the land.

The dynamics of geography and demography combined with outside commercial contacts and the larger issues of Mediterranean geopolitics complicated life for the Ligurians. The land is rugged and

---

[116] Livy 37.51.1.
[117] Livy 40.18.7–8, 40.26.8.
[118] Livy 40.18.4–5; C. Ebel (1976) pp. 60–62.
[119] Florus 1.19.4–5.

provides limited opportunity for a stable agriculture. Strabo described the tribesmen living between Monaco and the Tyrrhenian as pastoralists who evidently used the numerous small valleys that flow down to the coast and moved seasonally between winter coastal and summer mountain pastures.[120] Their migratory habits and their control over key mountain passes encouraged raiding. The pressures of a growing population were also intensifying. Young males often had to seek livelihood elsewhere in activities like piracy. Many oppida have been counted in the rugged country between Nice and Antibes,[121] and warfare was endemic among these groups crowded into lands with limited resources. An apparent by-product of this was slaving, which helped to reduce population but also brought more serious social disruptions.[122] Increased trade contacts with the Greeks heightened the natives' social and political sophistication as well as their desire for Mediterranean goods. Vaugrenier—a Greco-Ligurian site with much imported pottery, Massilian and other coins, and even graffiti written in Greek—has already been mentioned.[123] Despite trade contacts and the development of friendship links between the Greeks and the mountain tribes, the balance of power was shifting against the small Greek communities of the coast. This represented a potential danger for Roman interests in the area.[124]

The first Roman military intervention came in 154 B.C.[125] Members of the Ligurian tribes of the Oxybii and Deciates had been raiding the lands around the cities of Nice and Antibes. Massilia, unable to bring effective aide to its dependencies, complained of the Ligurian actions to the Roman senate. Antibes and Nice were described as being under siege and the Ligurians as well established on the shore. The senate dispatched a legation to determine what was happening and "to attempt by remonstrances to correct the misconduct of the barbarians."[126] On arriving at Aegitna, the chief center of the Oxybii, the Roman and Massilian delegation was attacked and one of the Roman ambassadors wounded.[127] Roman retaliation was inevitable. One of the consuls, Q. Opimius, was dispatched from Placentia with an army.

[120] Strabo 4.6.2.
[121] J. E. Dugand (1970) pp. 25–27.
[122] An ostracon with the inscription ἀποστελῶ σοί ἐπιστολὴν περὶ τῶν σωματίων dating from the third century B.C. was found at Olbia: J. Coupry (1968) p. 244.
[123] J. E. Dugand (1970).
[124] J. E. Dugand (1970) pp. 25–27.
[125] J. Prieur (1968) pp. 65–66; G. Barruol (1969) pp. 212–17; G. Clemente (1974) p. 17; C. Ebel (1976) pp. 58–59.
[126] Polyb. 33.8.3.
[127] Polyb. 33.9.

The Oxybii and the Deciates were defeated at battle.[128] The Ligurian
center was sacked, and the ringleaders responsible for the attack were
sent to Rome in chains. The Romans may have also attacked other
oppida. The site at Vaugrenier, which was either a fort or a shrine,
seems to have been assaulted at this time.[129]

By this period of their history the Romans had plenty of experience
in dealing with raiding Ligurians, and they adopted some of the approaches they had used in Italy. Polybius notes that the Ligurians
were forced to give hostages to the Massilians and that certain territory
was turned over to the Greek city.[130] The tribesmen were disarmed.
A reference in Strabo may be associated with these events. The Greek
geographer states that after eighty years of war the Romans succeeded
in opening up a safe route twelve stadia wide through the Ligurian
mountains for those traveling on public business. Because the first
Roman intervention in Liguria came in the 230s, roughly eighty years
before the attacks of Opimius, it is possible to associate the actions
described by Strabo with the intervention of Opimius. The archaeological evidence for native-site abandonment, however, suggests a later
date.[131] The enhancement of the territorial responsibility and control
of Massilia reflects the general Roman policy of building friendly local
forces.

The Roman defeat of the Deciates and the Oxybii marked the culmination of the process of conquest of coastal Liguria that had begun
in Italy many years before. If the Massilians carried out their responsibility and the natives were sufficiently cowed, the road to Spain as
far as the Rhone would remain relatively clear and the disaster of
Lucius Baebius not repeated. Less secure was Massilian control west
of the Rhone, and here the Romans may have intervened more force-
fully than the sources suggest. Polybius, who probably passed through
the area in the late 130s, notes that the road between Narbo and the
Rhone had been carefully measured and marked by the Romans. Unless the composition of this passage is dated much later than generally

---

[128] Polyb. 33.10; Livy *Per.* 47; G. Barruol (1969) pp. 10–11.
[129] J. E. Dugand (1970) pp. 128ff.
[130] Polyb. 33.10.11–14.
[131] Cic. *Rep.* 3.16; Strabo 4.6.3. J. Coupry (1968) dates the abandonment to the period
of Calvinus. E. Badian (1967) pp. 20–21 believes the famous passage in Cicero concerning prohibition on vine and olive culture among Gauls dates to this period and relates
to Roman desire to enhance the economic position of Massilia. A similar forced clearing
of a coastal zone took place in Dalmatia c. 135 B.C.: Strabo 7.5.6; M. G. Morgan (1969)
p. 228 n. 49.

thought, it suggests that the Romans were involved in securing the coastal road well before the arrival of Domitius Ahenobarbus.[132]

In 125 B.C. Massilia again called for Roman direct intervention in Gaul. This time the danger came from the Salluvii, the tribal group whose central oppidum was Entremont. The specific *casus belli* is not known, but the general problem is evident. A tribe with growing centralized power was threatening not only the coastal route but also the main interior road down the Durance from the Alps to the Rhone. Massilia, with its limited military power, was unable to cope with this new threat.[133]

The Romans themselves viewed the new war as a watershed. Florus linked the conquest of the Salluvii with the pacification of the other Ligurians.[134] The Salluvii, however, also had close relations with the more organized interior tribes. M. Fulvius Flaccus, the first Roman general sent against them, soon found himself fighting the Vocontes as well as the Ligurians.[135] Hoping for a quick and limited campaign, the Romans found themselves drawn more and more deeply into the politics of southern Gaul.

M. Fulvius Flaccus had sufficient success to be awarded a triumph, but he did not complete the conquest of the Salluvii.[136] This was left to his successor, C. Sextius Calvinus, who remained in Gaul until 122 B.C.[137] His first objective was to destroy the Salluvian capital at Entremont. The excavations have produced vivid evidence of the Roman assault. It can be presumed that some of the severed heads found in the sanctuary were those of Romans slain by the natives in encounters before the final attack.[138]

The king of the Salluvii, Toutomotulus, fled to the Allobroges. Calvinus followed up his victory at Entremont with a carefully designed policy aimed at breaking the power of those elements in the tribe hostile to Rome and Massilia, while strengthening the hand of potentially friendly groups and individuals. He defined the policy as a "clear demonstration of Roman thoroughness whether in dispensing mercy

[132] Polyb. 3.39.7–8; C. Ebel (1976) pp. 62–63. F. Walbank (1957) p. 373 believes Polybius inserted this passage after the creation of Via Domitia.

[133] For evidence of Massilian outposts being burned at this period see L. Chabot (1968) pp. 212–13.

[134] Florus 1.19.5. M. Euzennat (1980) p. 36 dates some fortification activity at Massilia to the mid-second century B. C.

[135] G. Clemente (1974) pp. 76–77.

[136] Livy *Per.* 60; Vell. Pat. 2.6.4; A. Degrassi (1947) p. 559; C. Ebel (1976) pp. 64–66.

[137] T.R.S. Broughton (1951) pp. 511, 515, 518; C. Ebel (1976) pp. 68–70.

[138] F. Benoit (1947) p. 88, (1968) pp. 4–8.

or exacting reprisals."[139] Toutomotulus' followers were slain, enslaved, or driven into exile; but Crato, the leader of the pro-Roman
faction, was allowed to save nine hundred of his fellow citizens from
slavery. This assured a grateful and loyal population in the area.

The same selectivity was applied to the treatment of the various
oppida near Entremont. Roquepertuse, an important native sanctuary,
was sacked, suggesting that the Romans saw the indigenous religion
as a rallying point for local resistance.[140] Nearer to Massilia, the center
at Baou-Rouge shows similar signs of Roman attack.[141] At the same
time, however, the oppidum at Saint Marcel (Constantine, twenty
kilometers west of Roquepertuse), which controlled important communication routes toward the Etang de Berre, was spared.[142] The same
was true of the settlement at Les Pennes Mirabeau, which was located
close to Massilia.[143] The Salluvii as a group were not exterminated.
Strabo describes their territory as still stretching to the Rhone and to
the sea, and they remained sufficiently powerful to raise a revolt in 90
B.C.[144] There is no reason to think that the Romans wanted them eliminated. A single strong tribal unit was much easier to manage than the
numerous Ligurian mountain bands. Moreover, this tribe controlled
key interior and coastal routes from the mountains to the Rhone, and
its positive integration into the new Roman system would be advan-
tageous. The geographic position of the Salluvii was similar to that of
the Insubres and the Cenomani on the southern slopes of the Alps,
and it is not surprising that they were treated in similar ways.

Calvinus quickly grasped the impressive potential that the interior
Durance route had for connecting the Alps and the Rhone. To protect
this communication route and to prevent native settlement around the
destroyed capital at Entremont, a Roman garrison was placed at Aquae
Sextiae (Aix-en-Provence).[145] The sources are confusing in their description of the status of this settlement. Despite what Livy's epitome
states, it probably was not a colony.[146] Native as well as imported
Roman pottery has been found in levels dated to the early years of

[139] Diod. 34.23.

[140] H. de Gerin Richard (1929); G. Clemente (1974) p. 33.

[141] *Gallia* (1964) pp. 576–77; J. DeWever (1966) pp. 108–9; G. Clemente (1974) pp.
32–33.

[142] G. Clemente (1974) p. 35; J. Gourvest (1956) pp. 61–62.

[143] *Gallia* (1972) pp. 511–12. The end of occupation is associated with Caesar. Castellas de Rognac also does not seem to have been destroyed: L. Chabot (1968).

[144] Strabo 4.1.3, 4.1.6, 4.1.12.

[145] Livy *Per.* 61; M. Clerc (1916). See J. Soyer (1973) pp. 224–31 on centuriation
around Aix that does not conform to direction of *cardo* of city.

[146] Livy *Per.* 61; Strabo 4.1.5. Pliny *NH* 3.36 calls it an *oppidum Latinum*. C. Benedict
(1942) p. 41; P. A. Brunt (1971) p. 216; C. Ebel (1976) p. 69.

the settlement, suggesting an ethnic mix in the population.[147] The settlement was probably intended to be a center for friendly or pacified natives. The name recalls Aquae Statiellae in Liguria.

The fragmentary sources suggest that Aix did not get an official road link until the late first century, when the Via Aurelia was put through.[148] However, Aix lay on a long-used route into Italy. Marius appreciated this when he retreated to the area and then fought his decisive battle with the Cimbri and Teutones nearby, preventing their advance into Italy. The rugged nature of the Riviera route made the passage through Aix attractive. The later road followed the coast to Frejus and then used the valley of the Argent to cut inland toward Aix. This route must have been in use by 43 B.C., for L. Munatius Plancus followed it. Moreover, three place names on the later itineraries suggest communities that developed along the Republic supply and transport route to Spain. The first is Ad Horrea, a name suggesting a grain resupply point. Another, Ad Turrem (Tourves), is located in the upper Argens valley and might be the kind of fortified way station a Republican road system would need.[149]

The third settlement was Forum Voconi,[150] seventy-two miles northeast of Massilia on the middle Argens. It is already attested in 43 B.C., when it was the forum of the Vocontii. That tribe had been conquered in the wars of Flaccus and Calvinus, but was apparently treated better than other groups in the area. Strabo noted that although the Allobroges and Ligures were subject to the praetor at Narbo, the Vocontii were autonomous. Pliny describes them as a *civitas foederata*.[151] Most of their territory lay north and west of the Durance. The forum seems to have been established on their southeastern border to let the mountain people tap the trade potential of the newly developing route.

Another indicator of the steps that the Romans took to gain control of the area and assure the loyalty of the native aristocracy is a funerary monument of the first century A.D. erected at Rognes, northwest of Aix. The family that built it was the Domitii, who appear to have been the local magnates of Rognes. There seems no doubt that we have here a native, Romanized aristocracy. The name suggests an as-

---

[147] M. Clerc (1916) pp. 129–197; *Gallia* (1974) pp. 501–2.

[148] I. König (1970) pp. 28–36.

[149] Cic. *Fam.* 10.17; K. Miller (1916) cols. 130-32.

[150] K. Miller (1916) col. 131; G. Barruol (1969) p. 281. R. Boyer and P. A. Février (1959) pp. 168–78 note that the site is well watered and located at the juncture of the mountains and a small plain along the main east-west road. P. A. Février (1973) p. 18 locates Forum Voconi at Le Baies (Var).

[151] Strabo 4.6.4; Pliny *HN* 3.37.

sociation with Domitius Ahenobarbus, who did so much to create a Roman entity in Gaul. Any such system must have been based on the loyalty of such prominent natives as Crato and the Domitii.[152]

The defeat of the Salluvii and the foundation of Aquae Sextiae were followed by even greater changes in the Roman position in Gaul. By the end of the war the Romans had been drawn into the larger alliance systems of the Rhone valley. Not only had the Salluvian king fled to the Allobroges: sometime during the course of the war, the Romans had established friendly relations with the Aedui. The action was perfectly sensible. The Romans must have known of the ties between Salluvii and Allobroges. A pro-Roman tribe on the northern border of the Allobroges would be a most convenient counter. Sensing that the wars and problems of organization were beginning rather than ending, the Romans dispatched a consul of 122 B.C., Cn. Domitius Ahenobarbus, to Gaul.

Two causes were given for the new round of wars that involved the Romans first with the Allobroges and then with the Arverni. The first was the harboring of Toutomotulus. The second was the attack of the Allobroges on the Aedui, a tribe now officially friends of the Romans. The Allobroges had not regarded the defeat of the Salluvii as marking an end to the war. Instead their forces marched south, crossed their tribal boundary, and joined battle with the Roman forces at Vindalium, a center near the juncture of the Rhone and Sulgas rivers, about eight kilometers south of Orange.[153] The Allobroges did not act alone. While Ahenobarbus was crossing the territory of the Salluvii to meet the new challenge, ambassadors came to him from Bituitus, ruler of the Arverni, asking mercy for the leaders of the Salluvii. The embassy was rejected, and Ahenobarbus advanced to meet the Allobroges.[154]

Domitius defeated the attacking army of the Allobroges but hesitated before invading their territory. The potential involvement of the powerful Arverni must have given him pause. The senate appreciated the extent of the danger and sent one of the consuls of 121 B.C., Q. Fabius Maximus, to Gaul, presumably with a new army.[155] Ahenobarbus awaited his arrival. With an enlarged force, consul and proconsul advanced up the Rhone to meet the forces of tribal Gaul.

In a second decisive battle, the Arvernian and Allobrogan armies were defeated. The ancient sources placed this battle at the juncture of the Rhone and Iser (Isère), between Valence and the Allobrogan

[152] Y. Burnand (1975) esp. pp. 214–40.

[153] Livy *Per.* 61; Strabo 4.1.11, 4.2.3. G. Barruol (1969) p. 242 places it at Mourre de Seve where a destruction level dated to the period.

[154] App. *Celtica* 12; C. Ebel (1976) pp. 70–71.

[155] T.R.S. Broughton (1951) p. 520.

center at Vienne.[156] The testimony of Pliny is especially useful here, since he had served in Gallia Narbonensis and had seen the trophy erected on the site of the battle. Some modern authorities have disputed this location of the battle site, arguing that it should be placed farther south at modern Point St. Espirit, where the trade routes down the Ardeche from the territory of the Arverni reached the Rhone.[157] The revision seems unnecessary. The principal object of the Roman attack appears to have been the Allobroges, and a location near the Isère just south of their chief oppidum would have been a logical place for a battle. The initial attitude of Bituitus had been one of reconciliation, and he probably joined the war only when the territory of the Allobroges was directly threatened. Orosius says that the Arverni were decimated while crossing the Rhone. The Isère area of the Rhone with the island west of St. Georges Chau seems a logical place for such a crossing.[158] Both of the Roman generals were involved in the fighting. In the final triumph, Fabius received credit for a victory *de Allobrogibus et Rege Arvernorum Betuito*, while Domitius received his *de Galleis Arverneis*.[159]

At this point Bituitus again sought peace, but his efforts ran afoul of the rivalries of the two Roman commanders. Domitius feared that Bituitus would surrender the Allobroges and Arverni to Fabius, thus enhancing the reputation of his rival. To prevent this, Domitius summoned Bituitus to a conference, where he imprisoned him and shipped the king and his son to Rome. The senate was faced with a dilemma. It could hardly approve of the actions of Domitius, which violated so many canons of Roman diplomatic behavior. On the other hand, they realized the role of Bituitus and his family in holding together the Arvernian confederacy. In the words of Valerius Maximus, *cuius factum senatus neque probare potuit neque rescindere voluit ne remissus in patriam Bituitus bellum renovaret*. Bituitus remained in captivity in Italy.[160]

Despite the controversy over the treatment of Bituitus, the reaction at Rome to the victories over these ancient Gallic enemies was most enthusiastic. The trophies set up on the site of battle became the prototype for many other such monuments. At Rome the Fornix Fabiana, erected in the forum near the Regia, started a long line of such trium-

---

[156] Strabo 4.1.11, 4.2.3; Pliny *HN* 7.166; Florus 1.37.2.

[157] Hannibal made his crossing in the Allobrogan territory at a place called *insula*: Poly. 3.49; Livy 21.31. F. Benoit (1965) pp. 280–81 argues for a crossing further south. G. Barruol (1969) pp. 16–24 discusses Pliny and Gaul.

[158] Oros. 5.14; C. Ebel (1976) pp. 72–74.

[159] A. Degrassi (1947) p. 560.

[160] Val. Max. 9.6.3.

phal monuments. A temple to Fever, vowed at the time of the battle, was built; as were temples to Mars and to Hercules, who was becoming increasingly identified with Rome's conquest of the northern barbarians.[161]

Much organizational work had to be done after the victory if the conquests were to be truly consolidated. Breaking the Allobroges and the Arverni had removed a threat to the emerging Roman system in Gaul. At the same time, though, a too serious weakening of their power could create a vacuum into which new groups from central and northern Gaul would move. A new frontier system had to be created that would involve a balance of forces capable of meeting most outside threats, allowing minimal direct Roman involvement while providing no danger to the territories farther south.

The first line of defense developed by the Romans relied on the friendship of the Aedui. The protection of their interests had been one of the causes of war. They remained firm *amici populi Romani* and generally prospered because of the association. Their coinage issued in silver became linked to the Roman monetary system rather than to the coinages of central Gaul,[162] and their leaders became Romanized. The new prosperity and power are best reflected in their center at Bibracte, which grew to be a massive 333.6-acre site with a Romanized aristocracy, an active industrial quarter, and trade links with much of Gaul.[163] The importance of this part of the frontier for trading networks is also shown by the oppidum site at Essalois on the upper Loire, where Campanian pottery and amphorae of the period 180–130 B.C. were found, along with pottery of neighboring Gallic tribes and bronzes of Massilia.[164]

If the Aedui were to be fully incorporated into the Roman frontier system, it would be prudent to do the same with the Sequani, their neighbors and rivals across the Saône. We are not certain when the Sequani became friends of the Roman people, but they had achieved this status by the time of the Cimbric-Teutones invasion. It seems reasonable to suppose that the arrangement dates to that period.[165]

The two main protagonists in the war received different treatment at the hands of the Romans. The Allobroges were fully integrated into the Roman administrative system and were by the first century B.C. part of the *provincia*. It is not clear how much of their political and social structure was changed. Occupation continued at their oppidum

[161] Florus 1.37.5; E. Nash (1961) pp. 398–99.
[162] S. Scheers (1969) pp. 176–79; J. B. Colbert de Beaulieu (1973) p. 229.
[163] J. Déchelette (1904); C. Crumley (1974) p. 61–68.
[164] C. Crumley (1974) p. 68; J. P. Preynat (1962); J. Renaud (1962).
[165] E. Wightman (1976) p. 411.

of Vienne, where imported amphorae and black-glaze pottery have
been found along with native wares. A Celtic name written in Greek
letters on an Italic black-glaze pot illustrates the cultural crosscurrents
active among the Allobroges at this time.[166]

Our sources do not provide information on how much territory was
removed from the jurisdiction of the Allobroges. The decision to found
the settlement named Valentia certainly seems related to the Roman
desire to keep watch on the Allobroges. Pliny describes it as located
in agro Cavarum, but Ptolemy has it belonging to the Segovellauni.[167]
Apparently border land was detached from the Cavares and granted
to the small group of Segovellauni. The name had also been used for
other non-Roman settlements during the second century B.C. Most
famous is the Valentia founded by D. Junius Brutus in Hispania Ulterior in 138 B.C.[168] Unfortunately the exact date of the foundation of
Gallic Valentia is not known. An inscription of 46–45 B.C. dedicated
to L. Nonius Asprenas mentions the *coloni et incolae* of Valentia.[169] A
corrupt textual reference in Dio appears to refer to a Valentia in connection with the revolt of the Allobroges in 62 B.C. This implies that
it was a center with a strong native population.[170] Members of the
settlement were perhaps enrolled in the tribe of the Pollia, the same
one used for settlements of the Valentia type in northwestern Italy
during the second century B.C.[171] All the threads of evidence suggest
that the foundation of the native center of Valentia was part of the
initial frontier arrangement by the Romans, and that the community
was designed to be a focus for Romanization and a watch on the Allobroges.

The Arverni were not included within the new frontier, but they,
along with other groups northeast and north of the Massif Central,
had to be kept under Rome's watchful eye. These arrangements seem
to have been left in the hands of Fabius Maximus, while Ahenobarbus
dealt with groups in the coastal zone to the southwest. Caesar mentions that Fabius subdued the Ruteni as well as the Arverni.[172] It is
reasonable to assume that the Romans advanced along the northern
flank of the Massif Central through the land of the Arverni in the
direction of Rodez and the Ruteni. Like the Arverni, the Ruteni were

---

[166] G. Chapotat (1970) pp. 121–23.
[167] Pliny *HN* 3.36; Ptol. 2.9.13.
[168] Cf. pp. 213–14.
[169] *CIL* 12.1748.
[170] Dio Cass. 37.47. For centuriation around Valence see A. Blanc (1953); A. Grenier
(1958) pp. 281–84.
[171] *CIL* 12. 207.
[172] Caes. *BGall.* 1.45.2.

not included within the province itself. Some groups were detached
from the control of the Arverni, especially the Vellavii to their south.[173]
Special efforts were also made to win the friendship of the Helvii,
who controlled the northern bank of the Ardeche, a main route down
from the land of the Arverni. Their chief, Cabur, was a Roman citizen
by 83 B.C.[174]

The Arverni accepted their new client status reasonably well. Coins
from before 52 B.C. found at Alesia show that the Arverni had most
of their contracts with Roman-controlled march tribes such as the Lingones, Aedui, and Sequani and had almost no association with the
tribes of Gallia Comata.[175] The Arverni remained at peace with Rome
until the rise of the new charismatic leader Vercingetorix.

Fabius apparently made his own settlement arrangements. Later
sources mention a center called Fabia that was located among the Cel-
togalatians, probably in the Rhone valley.[176] Like Aquae Sextiae and
Valentia, such a settlement would have provided a focal point for
native acculturation. The continuing interest of the Fabii in the area
is shown by their role as patron in later Romano-Gallic affairs.[177]

In the meantime, Domitius Ahenobarbus was consolidating the Roman position to the south and southwest. Suetonius mentions that he
moved through Gaul on an elephant with an escort of soldiers. The
elephants, which had been used previously in the battle at the Sor-
gues, were undoubtedly employed to awe the natives not only by their
size and unfamiliarity but also by their association with Hannibal,
who had passed through the area.[178] Domitius was not a totally sympathetic figure. Contemporaries described him as having a face of iron
and a heart of lead. He was certainly a practical administrator, however, who left his mark on the province.[179]

Domitius' principal aims were developing the communication route
between Italy and Spain and establishing a local base of support that
would insure the safety of that route. His first efforts must have centered on the eastern part of the province. The important family of
native Domitii near Aix testifies to his development of clients in the
area. The greatest memorial to the efforts of Domitius was, of course,

[173] Strabo 4.2.2.
[174] Caes. *BGall.* 1.47.4.
[175] J. Colbert de Beaulieu (1958), (1966).
[176] Apollodoros *apud Suidas* describes it as city of Celtogalates: C. Ebel (1976) p. 87.
G. Barruol (1976) p. 395 n. 10 places it in the mid-Rome valley.
[177] The *CIL* 12 lists thirty-three Fabii from southern Gaul. There are fifty-eight Domitii. E. Badian (1958) p. 309 has fifty Fabii and eighty Domitii.
[178] Suet. *Ner.* 2; Florus 1.37.4.
[179] Suet. *Ner.* 2; G. Clemente (1974) pp. 77–78; N. Lamboglia (1973) p. 68; C. Ebel
(1976) pp. 76–85.

the Via Domitia.[180] His work on that road is attested by a milestone bearing his name found in 1947 at Treilles (Aude).[181] The most controversial aspect of the text is that the miles are numbered from Narbo. That colony was supposedly not founded until after Ahenobarbus had left Gaul.[182] It appears likely, however, that even before the campaigns of Domitius the Romans had started to develop a coastal road system using the area of Narbo or Montlaurés as one of its reference points.[183] A tradition of cooperation between native and Roman would explain why the advance of Domitius through the area was little more than a progress with no real combat.

For much of its length, the new road followed the line of the ancient Via Herculis. Most clearly associated with Domitius himself was the section west of the Rhone. Turning slightly inland, it passed through such centers as Arles, Nimes, and Beziers before reaching Narbo. Then it continued onto the Pyrenees. The Massilian outpost at Agde was bypassed much as Massilia itself had been bypassed when the road east of the Rhone was laid out.[184] As was customary in Roman road-building, Domitius memorialized his achievement with the foundation of a forum near the site of modern Montbazin.[185]

This Roman activity appears to have disturbed only slightly the pattern of native life. Such oppida as Ensérune and Montlaurés show no evidence of destruction like that found at Entremont.[186] In fact, finds at Ensérune show increased acculturation of its ruling class during the first decades of Roman administration. The local leaders who supported Rome received strong backing. This is shown by local coinages that appear in southwestern Gaul in the wake of the conquest. They bear the names of local rulers and even the title of *basileus*.[187]

Much of this frontier area was protected from the larger tribes of central Gaul by the slopes of the Massif Central. With the acquisition of Languedoc, however, Rome became involved with the trade and communication routes that extended through the passes of Carcassonne to Aquitania and the Atlantic. Before the conquest, the Romans

[180] Cic. *Font*. 18; G. Clemente (1974) pp. 127–30.

[181] P. M. Duval (1949), (1968).

[182] P. M. Duval (1949), p. 216. A. Grenier (1959) pp. 59–68 notes that centuriation in the area is based on the Via Domitia and that the road into Aquitania bypasses the colony. I. König (1970) pp. 57–66.

[183] Polyb. 3.39.78; A. Degrassi (1962) pp. 512–13.

[184] J. Sagnes (1970).

[185] J. Heurgon (1952) pp. 46–47; J. Jannoray (1955) p. 442; M. Labrousse (1968) p. 123 n. 18.

[186] Y. Solier and J. Giry (1973) pp. 99–109; G. Barruol (1976) p. 397.

[187] J. Jannoray (1955) pp. 324–29; M. Labrousse (1968) pp. 152–60; J.C.M. Richard (1972); J. B. Colbert de Beaulieu (1973) pp. 210–13, 306.

had become aware of the trade. Scipio Africanus the Younger had questioned the merchants of Narbo about the trade routes to Britain. Stories about mineral resources of the interior also circulated. The territory of the Volcae Tectosages was known to be rich in gold, while that of the Ruteni had silver.[188]

The imperatives of frontier control forced the Romans to extend their domain inland. The Volcae, who were a dominant power in the coastal area, also had connections with the interior. Toulouse was emerging as an important native center.[189] Roman generals fighting on the northern slopes of the Ebro were increasingly aware of the way native groups used the passes of the Pyrenees to harass pro-Roman Iberians and escape Roman retaliation. Contacts on the northern as well as the southern slope would facilitate Roman control of that mountain zone.

Details on the first steps taken by the Romans to control this north-western corridor are not provided by our fragmentary sources. Fabius did subdue the Ruteni and possibly joined with Ahenobarbus in bringing order to the Toulouse frontier. Some elements in these early arrangements can be projected backward from the events of 107 B.C. that suddenly brought the Toulouse–Carcassonne frontier into sharp focus.

In 107 B.C. the army of the consul L. Cassius Longinus was defeated at Agen while returning from an expedition that had apparently carried Roman forces as far as the Atlantic. The expedition appears to have been caused by rumors of tribal migrations into the area in the wake of the Cimbric-Teutonic movements. The actual perpetrators of the ambush were an offshoot group of the Helvetii. Slain along with Longinus was L. Calpurnius Piso Caesoninus, who was accompanying the expedition as a consular legate. In general, the post of consular legate was used to attach an experienced advisor to a delicate and important mission. The fragmentary evidence suggests that Piso was given the assignment because he had played an important role in the creation of the frontier system in the area. The main pieces of evidence for this can be reviewed briefly.[190]

Caesar mentions a certain Piso Aquitanus whose grandfather had been designated an *amicus populi Romani*. The younger Piso died in 55 B.C., placing the naming of his grandfather as an *amicus* during the first years of the Roman administration in western Gaul.[191] The name Piso suggests an association with Caesoninus. The reference is not

---

[188] Strabo 4.1.3, 4.2.1, 4.2.3.

[189] Strabo 4.1.14. On Toulouse in general see M. Labrousse (1968).

[190] Livy *Per.* 65; App. *Celtica* 1.3; Oros. 5.15.23–24. See S. L. Dyson (1970) for a review of sources and background for the campaign.

[191] Caes. *BGall.* 4.12.4–5.

unique. Diodorus mentions a certain Contoniatus who is described as a chieftain of the Gallic city known as Iontora or Laktora. He was a friend and ally of the Roman people who "had previously spent much time in Rome and had come to share their ideals and way of life, and through Rome's support had succeeded to his chieftainship in Gaul." The passage is placed in the text of Diodorus at around 110 B.C. Iontera has been generally located in Aquitania.[192]

A third reference to this area, also in Caesar, mentions a Teutomatus, king of the Nitiobriges, whose father had been hailed as a friend of the Roman people. Again, the establishment of these ties of friendship can be pushed back to the early years of Roman domination.[193] It was in the supposedly friendly territory of the Nitiobriges that Cassius and Piso were attacked. Each of these scattered fragments speaks to the Roman foundation of their traditional frontier system based on alliances with native rulers backed by limited military force. The latter was provided by the garrison of Toulouse that was imprisoned by the natives after the disaster of Longinus and Piso.[194] This system was apparently developed by Piso sometime between the departure of Fabius and Ahenobarbus and the disaster of 107 B.C.

The final step in establishing Roman control in the southwest of Gaul was the foundation of the Roman colony at Narbo. The settlement began in controversy. The use of the colony as an instrument of Roman imperial policy had waned by the late second century B.C., and overseas colonies were especially unpopular. The recent aborted colonial attempts of Gaius Gracchus were a fresh memory for most Roman politicians in 118 B.C., when a commission was selected to establish Narbo.[195] One of the founders, L. Licinius Crassus, identified the move to create the colony as a *causa popularis*, and there was senatorial opposition to the scheme. The official procolonial arguments were presumably those voiced by Cicero several decades later. It was to be a *specula populi Romani ac propugnaculum istis ipsis nationibus oppositum et obiectum*. Undoubtedly the equestrians thought of the rich trade they were soon to tap so effectively.[196]

The opponents had reasons other than purely political ones for their fears. The settlement of a body of Roman citizens in Gaul meant that Rome's responsibilities in the area were enormously increased. Moreover, a large settlement in a well-populated native area was bound to

[192] Diod. 34.35.36; O. Hirschfeld (1913); J. Carcopino (1957).
[193] Caes. *BGall.* 7.31.5.
[194] Dio Cass. 27 fr. 90.
[195] Vell. Pat. 1.15.2; E. Badian (1967) pp. 23–24; E. T. Salmon (1970) pp. 112–23; C. Ebel (1976) pp. 81–82.
[196] Cic. *Brut.* 160, *Clu.* 140, *Font.* 13; G. Clemente (1974) pp. 119–21.

cause problems like those that had developed in connection with the *ad viritim* settlements in the north of Italy. Despite these fears, the colony was established.[197] Extensive traces of centuriation, probably for the colony, have survived around modern Narbonne. Narbo soon became the hub of Roman commerce in the area.[198] The displacement of the natives may not have been as severe as anticipated. Occupation at Montlaurès continued, while the presence of names like *prata Liguriae* in the area suggests continued native settlement elsewhere.[199]

The foundation of Narbo and the consolidation of the Toulouse frontier completed the first cycle of Roman administrative intervention in southern Gaul. What is striking about the initial stage of Roman frontier development is the sophistication of planning and the strong grasp of overall strategic and administrative problems. Once the initial decision had been made to become deeply involved in Gaul, a whole series of actions followed with relative rapidity. The main centers of native military resistance were broken. Alliances were formed to hedge in potential enemies like the Arverni and Allobroges, and to provide a barrier and intelligence network in dealing with tribes in the interior. Within the territory brought directly under Rome's supervision, the sphere of control of Massilia was enlarged on the east and a new urban entity at Narbo was established as a counterbalance on the west. And yet, the importance of these two centers should not be exaggerated. All evidence indicates that the Romans relied heavily on the emerging, acculturated native ruling class for maintaining frontier and interior control. It was a complicated system, but the Romans were used to such arrangements. It was typically Roman.

This reconstruction of the frontier and internal arrangements makes somewhat irrelevant the recent debates over the precise date for the formal establishment of the province itself.[200] At the beginning the Romans appear to have decided in general terms whom and how they were to administer. The limitations of the Republican system hindered the creation of too formal an organization, but it was clear from the victories and actions of Domitius and Fabius Maximus who was in charge in southern Gaul and what the general outlines of that control were to be.

The frontier arrangements of Fabius, Domitius, and their succes-

[197] H. B. Mattingly (1962) dates the founding around 110 B.C. G. Clemente (1974) pp. 78–79.

[198] M. Guy (1955) pp. 103–8.

[199] N. Lamboglia (1959); Y. Solier and J. Giry (1973) pp. 99–109. O. and J. Taffanel (1956) p. 125 place the burning of the oppidum at Cayla in this period and associate it with the foundation of the colony.

[200] E. Badian (1966); C. Ebel (1976) pp. 76–81, 92–95.

sors were designed to deal with the military and political situation in
Gaul as it existed in the 120s and 110s B.C. As such, they were effective and imaginative. Almost immediately, however, the arrival of the
Cimbri and the Teutones from the north of Europe altered the whole
situation. The changes produced by the presence of these people affected the development of the frontier in Gaul as well as many other
aspects of Roman history.

The causes of those folk movements were a subject of controversy
in antiquity and remain so today.[201] One tradition had a natural disaster in their northern homeland provoke the folk movement. Others
stated that the Germans were mere freebooters, seeking loot in rich
Roman-controlled areas. The sources do not allow a precise reconstruction of the nature and motives of the migration. One theme of
repeated requests for land suggests that the Germans were more potential settlers than raiders.[202]

The new menace first appeared on the northeastern frontier of Italy.
In 113 B.C. Germans moved into the Roman client state of Noricum.
The consul Cn. Papirius Carbo moved north to meet the threat and
forced a military showdown. He was badly defeated.[203] The Germans,
now designated as Cimbri by Livy and Strabo, did not press their
temporary advantage by trying to cross the mountains into Italy. Instead, they turned westward into Gaul.[204]

The Germans reappeared in 109 B.C., this time in the central section
of the Gallic frontier. A consul, M. Junius Silanus, was dispatched
against them. He engaged them in battle and was apparently defeated.[205] Again the Germans did not try to exploit their advantage,
but sent an embassy to the senate requesting *sedem et agros in quibus
consisterent*.[206] The senate followed its normal policy of not allowing
the movement of new people into Roman-controlled territory and refused the request. The Germans then retreated into the interior of
Gaul.

Silanus did not come out of the episode unscathed. Cn. Domitius
Ahenobarbus, son of the conqueror of Gaul, charged him with responsibility for the defeat and for mistreating a Gaul, Aegritomarus,
who was a *hospes* of the Domitii. The charges clearly indicated the web
of connections and interests that the Domitii had with the province of
Gaul. The trial did not come until 104 B.C. In spite of the scandal of

---

[201] J. J. Tierney (1960) p. 200; H. Schutz (1983) pp. 339–41.
[202] Florus 1.38.1–2; Strabo 7.2.1.
[203] App. *Celtica* 13.
[204] Livy *Per.* 63; Strabo 5.1.8.
[205] Asc. 60, 71; Livy *Per.* 65; Vell Pat. 2.12.2; Florus 1.38.4–5.
[206] Livy *Per.* 65.

the gold of Toulouse and the wave of hysteria that spread over Rome after the defeat of Orange, Silanus was acquitted.[207]

One result of the Germanic movements in the interior of Gaul was the displacement of the Helvetian Tigurini and their encounter with the expedition of Piso and Longinus at Agen. In the aftermath of that disaster, the people of Tolosa revolted and placed the Roman garrison in chains. Their hopes of German assistance proved false. The consul Q. Servilius Caepio soon arrived to suppress the revolt and stabilize the northwestern frontier of the province. Caepio already had experience with frontier warfare in Hispania Ulterior, where he won a triumph for his actions in Lusitania. The dispatch of a man of this rank and experience to the Carcassonne area again shows how seriously the senate regarded events in this section of the border.[208]

Caepio made quick work of the revolt at Tolosa. The center was sacked, and the treasures that had been stored in the important native sanctuary were confiscated by the Romans. The Romans may well have wanted the shrine destroyed as a potential focus of native resistance, much as they had destroyed Roquepertuse and later were to sack the center of Mona at Anglesey in Wales. The Romans always felt a certain ambiguity about the desecration of such sacred places, and their uneasiness was compounded when much of the treasure from Tolosa mysteriously disappeared during its journey to Rome. The sacking of the shrine, followed as it was by the disappearance of the treasure and the disastrous defeat suffered by Caepio at Orange, made the *aurum Tolosum* a *cause célèbre* in Roman history and the subject of an enquiry set up in 104 B.C.[209]

Meanwhile, in 105 B.C., the Germans reappeared on the Rhone frontier. Again they claimed solely peaceful intentions, *pacem volentes et agros petentes frumentumque quod serent*.[210] The Romans, however, did not want them in the already densely populated Rhone valley. This time the Germans did not accept the rejection of their request, and moved south. They had penetrated as far as Orange before they were met by the combined armies of Caepio and the consul Cn. Mallius Maximus. Divisions among the army commanders helped turn the battle into a disastrous defeat for Rome, one that would be remembered as a *dies ater* in Roman history.[211]

---

[207] Cic. *Div. Caec.* 61; C. Ebel (1976) p. 85.

[208] M. Labrousse (1968) pp. 129–36. For Caepio in Hispania Ulterior see T.R.S. Broughton (1951) pp. 546, 549, 552.

[209] Strabo 4.1.13; Gell. *NA* 3.9.7; Dio Cass. 27.90; Just. *Epit.* 32.3.9–11; G. Bloch (1913); E. S. Gruen (1968) pp. 162–63; S. L. Dyson (1970).

[210] Granius Licinianus 33.8 (Criniti).

[211] Livy *Per.* 67; Oros. 5.16.1–7; Plut. *Vit. Luc.* 27.7; C. Jullian (1920) vol. 3 pp. 65–69.

At this point, the Germans seemed uncertain about their objectives. Advancing down the Rhone, they initially turned westward toward the Languedoc and Spain. The Roman colonists around Narbo and friendly natives in southwestern Gaul must have felt the full fury of their attack. Some site destruction, including that at Ensérune, can probably be associated with their passage.[212] Land was apparently seized, for in the aftermath of the German wars the politician Saturninus urged that "Germanic" land in Gaul be used for Italian colonization.[213] Despite the disastrous defeat of the Roman armies, however, the natives of Gaul felt no real desire to join the German invaders. The ethnic and cultural barriers were too great. Only the recently pacified Volcae Tectosages appear to have collaborated. The rising young Roman officer Sulla helped reduce that danger by capturing the warleaders of the Volcae Tectosages.[214] Resistance on the part of the locals is not surprising. The presence of the Germans strained limited land resources and disturbed the peaceful and prosperous life that was developing in the new Roman territory. In the end Celtiberian resistance stiffened significantly, and the Germans turned eastward to attack Italy.[215]

The initial decision of the Germans to move westward had provided the Romans with a much needed respite. They found a capable general in the person of Marius. He not only developed a confident army but surrounded himself with clever officers who appear to have shown great skill in dealing with the natives. The exploits of Sulla in the capture of Copillus have already been mentioned. A house owned by a native named Cornelius Sulla at Glanum suggests that Sulla developed his own client network in Gaul.[216] Equally famous were the exploits of Sertorius, whose ability to speak local languages and blend in with native customs provided invaluable intelligence for Rome.[217] The activities of such officers helped assure that there would be no massive defections among the natives.[218]

Marius initially moved the Roman army up the Rhone valley to the juncture of the Isère and the Rhone. No doubt he was attempting to assure threatened and wavering Roman allies on the northern frontier. In part it was successful. The Sequani turned over to him leaders of

[212] Livy *Per.* 67; M. Clavel (1970) p. 153.

[213] App. *BCiv.* 1.29.

[214] Plut. *Vit. Sull.* 4.1.

[215] Plut. *Vit. Mar.* 15.4–5. H. Rolland (1968) pp. 22–23 discusses the destruction of Glanum.

[216] Plut. *Vit. Mar.* 16–17. J. B. Colbert de Beaulieu (1966) pp. 53–56, (1973) pp. 230–31 describes coin types of the Lingones based on the P. Cornelius Sulla coin type of 148–45. B.C. F. Benoit (1966) pp. 297–98.

[217] Plut. *Vit. Sert.* 3; G. Barruol (1969) p. 225.

[218] Frontin. *Str.* 1.2.6.

the Teutones.[219] The selection of the Isère area for a stand may have
been intended to restore Roman morale by recalling victories of Fabius
and Domitius. The identification was not to end there. After the war,
Marius erected his famous trophies in the Velia near the place where
Fabius Maximus had built his temple to Fever.[220]

Marius was not prepared to fight the barbarians at that point. Instead he followed on their heels as they moved south and then turned
east to follow the line of the Roman road toward Italy. Finally, in the
plain around Aquae Sextiae, the decisive battle was fought, ending
the German menace in Gaul.[221]

The victories of Marius were wildly celebrated and played an important role in Roman domestic and frontier politics down to the period of Caesar.[222] Gaul, which had been the battleground for much of
the war, must have suffered terribly. The frontier system seems to
have been restored without too much difficulty. More serious was the
social and economic damage caused by the passage of undisciplined
hordes.[223] The destruction, combined with the normal stress of acculturation, produced severe social strains. Those in privileged positions
sought to benefit from the suffering of others. Certainly Romans and
Italians were involved. The demagogue Saturninus tried to exploit the
possibilities of open land in Gaul for colonization, and the movement
of Italians into Gaul that is so obvious in the period of Fonteius must
have accelerated during these years. Native discontent was widespread. The Salluvii, who had remained quiet ever since the sacking
of Entremont over thirty years before, now rose in revolt.[224]

Strabo cites an incident from the Greek historian Poseidonius, who
traveled in Gaul during this period, that provides a vivid sense of the
exploitation of the local populace.[225] A Massilian named Charoleon
described to Poseidonius the fortitude of a Ligurian woman engaged

[219] A. Donnadieu (1954) pp. 282–86.
[220] A. Donnadieu (1954) pp. 284–85, 294–95.
[221] Livy *Per.* 68; Vell. Pat. 2.12.4–5; Plut. *Vit. Mar.* 18–21; C. Jullian (1920) pp. 83–
84; A. Donnadieu (1954) pp. 286–94.
[222] Plut. *Vit. Mar.* 27.5–6. G. Pascucci (1956) discusses the way Caesar used images
of Cimbri and Teutones in his propaganda.
[223] A. Pelletier (1966) pp. 151–54 associates the destruction level at Vienne with the
Germanic invasions. E. Wightman (1976) p. 411 notes that in parts of Gaul to north,
there is a decline of richer graves in the 100–75 B.C. period. S. Scheers (1969) p. 178
relates the collapse of the gold stater among the Aedui and their conversion to coinage
in silver to the economic problems they developed in the wake of the German invasions.
[224] Livy *Per.* 73; C. Ebel (1975) p. 363. E. Badian (1964) pp. 90–93, (1967) p. 60 talks
about extensive land confiscations.
[225] Strabo 3.4.17; M. Laffranque (1964). On Poseidonius in Gaul during this period
see M. Truscelli (1934) pp. 623–35; J. J. Tierney (1960). For a parallel enserfment of
local native population by Greeks in Black Sea area see S. M. Burstein (1979).

in digging ditches on his land who left her work only long enough for childbirth and immediately returned for fear of losing a day's wages. This suggests that the Massilians who had escaped the Germanic attacks relatively unscathed were concentrating land holdings. The land was worked by a class of free but impoverished rural laborers whose condition was in part the result of destruction and displacement brought by the recent invasions. Moreover, land speculation was not limited to the Massilians. Cicero, in his *Pro Quinctio*, paints a picture of considerable Italian investment in land in Gaul. This included the development of large-scale pastoralism. Although herding had long been an element in the economy of Gaul, this new emphasis suggests its extension in the wake of devastation, depopulation, and land speculation caused by the passage of the Germans.[226]

The Germanic invasions were soon followed by the Social and Civil Wars, which had a considerable impact on the rapidly evolving province. As in most of the western provinces, personal allegiance here counted for much among both the native leadership and the new Italian arrivals. A man like Marius would naturally have had a considerable following that he and his successor Sertorius could exploit. Joined to them would be the followers of the Domitii.[227] The *optimates* were not without their followers, too. Sulla had been assiduous in developing a base of support, especially among the native leadership. Cornelii Sullae are prominent in places like Glanum, and native coins bearing the name of Sulla are common.[228] Unfortunately, before the arrival of Fonteius and the direct involvement of Pompey, we cannot follow these developments in any detail.

A figure of considerable importance in Gaul during this period was C. Valerius Flaccus. In 81 B.C. he received a triumph *ex Gallia et Celtiberia*. Much of his activity as consul and proconsul took place in Spain.[229] His activity on the Rhone frontier is illustrated by his granting citizenship to the family of the Helvian chieftain Cabur.[230] The concern for the Helvii and the Rhone frontier must be related to problems with the Arverni. Sometime during this period, the father of Vercingetorix was executed for aiming at the kingship of the tribe. The Romans would have looked with apprehension on the revival of the tradition of Luerius and Bituitus among the most powerful of cen-

[226] Cic. *Quinct.* 12, 15, 79, 80. On pastoralism in general in the area see J.C.M. Richard (1973) p. 10.

[227] E. Badian (1964) pp. 94–96; C. Ebel (1975) pp. 363–65.

[228] F. Benoit (1954) pp. 296–97; cf. n. 216.

[229] Gran Licinianus 39 B; A. Degrassi (1947) p. 563; C. Ebel (1975) p. 363, (1976) pp. 94–95.

[230] Caes. *BGall.* 1.47.4, 7.65.2; A. Blanc (1975) p. 18.

tral Gallic tribes.[231] The northwestern frontier of Gaul was also far from peaceful. In 78 B.C. the army of L. Manlius was ambushed during an attempt to push into Aquitania.[232]

Our clearest picture of the condition of Gaul during this period is from the governorship of M. Fonteius, in 74 to 71 B.C.[233] Gaul had assumed a special importance because of the uprising of Sertorius in Spain. Fonteius had the complicated task of controlling the spread of Marian-Sertorian sentiment in Gaul, supplying the Roman armies fighting in Spain with both men and supplies, and controlling an increasingly unstable internal social and economic situation that had been developing over the preceding two decades.

Gaul does not seem to have experienced the kind of Roman settler and exile wars that erupted in Spain. Some people, such as L. Valerius Flaccus, son of the consul slain by Fimbria in Asia, took refuge in Gaul, but no evidence exists for uprisings like those promoted by Crassus and Sertorius across the Pyrenees.[234] In part this was the result of the relative newness of the Roman administration. The Roman and Italian settlers in Gaul were just not present in the numbers found in the Iberian peninsula.

Ethnic hostilities did exist, and Pompey and his agents had to work to assure the peace and loyalty of the natives. Pompey used the term *recepi Galliam* to describe his exploits in the area. His monument at the height of the Pyrenees recorded among 876 captured oppida, those *ab Alpibus ad fines Hispaniae ulterioris*.[235] Reference is made to discontent among the Allobroges, Vocontii, and Volcae.[236] Caesar mentions that land had been confiscated from the Helvii and the Volcae Arecomaci. A leader of the Allobroges Indutiomarus was one of the most important witnesses against Fonteius.[237] The *Pro Fonteio* refers to demands for troops and money. Cicero also mentions large debts and individuals expelled from their land for opposition to Fonteius. The two winters of 77 and 76 B.C. passed in Gaul by the Roman armies would hardly have helped to ease tensions.[238]

Pompey, however, did work to strengthen his native base of support in the area. The most vivid testimony to this is the widespread pres-

[231] Caes. *BGall.* 7.4.1–2.
[232] Caes. *BGall.* 3.20.1.
[233] Cic. *Font.*; H. De la Ville de Mirmont (1904); G. Clemente (1974); C. Ebel (1975), (1976) pp. 97–98.
[234] Cic. *Flac.* 63, 100.
[235] Sall. *H.* 2.22, 3.46; Livy *Per.* 93; App. *BCiv.* 1.109.
[236] Sall. *H.* 2.98.9; Pliny *HN* 3.18, 7.95–97.
[237] Cic. *Font.* 27; Caes. *BCiv.* 1.35.4.
[238] Cic. *Font.* 11, 13–14.

ence of the Pompeian name.[239] Representative of this growing pro-Roman native elite was the family of the historian, Pompeius Trogus, whose grandfather obtained citizenship from Pompey. Most likely the reward came for his assistance suppressing unrest among the Vocontii.[240]

Possibly the most important contribution of Pompey to the development of Gaul was the consolidation of Roman influence on the northwestern Gallic frontier. Fonteius had his problems with the Celtic tribes in the area. The Volcae Tectosages resisted the Romans, and much of their land was confiscated.[241] The Ruteni seem also to have been reorganized about this time. Caesar speaks of a group known as the *Ruteni Provinciales* who controlled the more fertile lands of the tribe around Albi.[242] This extension of provincial control is probably attributable to Fonteius and Pompey. The expansion of coinages bearing the names of local tribal chieftains during this period suggests that the Romans were strengthening these smaller units at the expense of the larger tribal agglomerations.[243]

On the flank of the Pyrenees, Pompey's most important contribution was the settling of displaced Spanish mountaineers at Lugdunum Convenarum. Pompey realized that control of the Pyrenees meant clear access to the passes on both sides. The settlement at Lugdunum was described as consisting of *de latronum et convenarum natus est semine*.[244] The community guarded the upper Garonne and the routes leading toward the crossroads center of Toulouse. It also provided a focus for trade and acculturation among the Pyrenees tribesmen.[245] The widespread presence of the Pompeian name in the area testifies to the personal loyalties that these actions inspired.[246]

The ancient sources on the development of Gaul between the departure of Pompey and the arrival of Caesar stress ongoing social unrest. This was manifested by delegations to Rome, accusations against governors, and occasional rebellions. They also note a fluid power

---

[239] C. Jullian (1920) pp. 108–17; F. Benoit (1959) pp. 293–94, 297–98; J. J. Hatt (1959) pp. 46–47; R. C. Knapp (1978) p. 196. *CIL* 12 records 164 Pompeii from Gaul, considerably larger than the number of Fabii and Domitii. E. Badian (1958) p. 310 notes a total of 223.

[240] Just. *Epit.* 43.5.11; E. Hirschfeld (1913) p. 64; C. Ebel (1976) pp. 7–9.

[241] M. Clavel (1970) pp. 155–56 dates the first appearance of *aes* coinage in sites of Tectosages to c. 75 B.C. and sees it as an effort to favor local chiefs.

[242] Caes. *BGall.* 7.7.4.

[243] M. Clavel (1970) pp. 155–56.

[244] Hieron. *Adv. Vigilitantium II* p. 357 cols. 389ff.

[245] R. Lizop (1931) pp. 5–22. R. Gavelle (1960) pp. 139–40 and pl. 2 notes trans-Pyrennic connections of the coins found at Lugdunum Convenarum.

[246] R. Lizop (1931) pp. 5, 9–10.

situation that existed on and beyond the frontier. This concerned Roman officials, but never seemed beyond their control. Along with these problems also emerged a developing province with increasing trade and Romanization. The base of peace and prosperity so obvious in the Gallia Narbonensis of the early Empire was being laid during these years. Some scattered references indicate that internal security was not complete. The reappearance of widespread piracy in the Mediterranean during the early 60s B.C. tempted some of the coastal Ligurians to return to their ancestral vocation. Pompey had to station two lieutenants in the area, one along the Gallic coast and another off the Ligurian coast. The settlement of Pomponiana on the Iles d'Hyères may well represent a move by Pompey's legate to protect the coast and even settle pirates.[247]

The demands of the Roman administration and the strains caused by a changing social and economic scene also affected the tribes of interior Gaul. The assignment of the consul of 67 B.C., C. Calpurnius Piso, to transalpine Gaul is an indication of anticipated trouble.[248] In 66 B.C. L. Licinius Murena was in Gaul *summo cum imperio*. His vigorous collection of debts received the strong praise of Cicero.[249] No doubt the main debtors were the native tribal aristocracy, the Allobroges. A delegation of Allobroges was in Rome in 63 B.C., and the Catalinarian conspirators obviously regarded them as ripe for rebellion.[250] Although Cicero praised their loyalty, the Allobroges received no relief and in 62 B.C. they rose in revolt.[251]

The exiguous evidence does not allow a detailed reconstruction of the causes of the revolt. Taxes, debt, and extortion probably figured among the reasons. Underlying it all was the strain produced by a change from a Gallic to a Roman way of life. In this respect, the Allobroges stood in a middle position between the more Hellenized natives farther south and the more slowly evolving groups such as the Aedui to the north. Unfortunately the excavations at Vienne have not allowed the detailed reconstruction changes that can be seen in some of the acculturating oppida such as Nages and Ensérune to the south

[247] App. *Mith.* 95; Florus 1.41.9; T.R.S. Broughton (1952) pp. 148–49; J. Coupry (1968) p. 238 n. 3.

[248] Cic. *Att.* 1.13, *Flac.* 98; Dio Cass. 36.37.2–3; T.R.S. Broughton (1952) pp. 142–43, 154, 159. Caesar accused him of unjustly killing a native: Sall. *Cat.* 49.2.; C. Ebel (1976) p. 100.

[249] Cic. *Mur.* 42, 68–69, 89, *Har. Resp.* 42; T.R.S. Broughton (1952) p. 163; C. Ebel (1976) p. 101.

[250] Sall. *Cat.* 40–41.

[251] S. L. Dyson (1975) pp. 153–54 provides relevant sources.

or Bibracte to the north.[252] We can assume, however, that similar changes were taking place among the Allobroges and that the new ways of life led to debt. Moreover, as new power groups emerged within the tribes, the old leaders probably felt themselves increasingly threatened. The situation was not unlike what would appear in central Gaul during the first century A.D. or in Britain in the generation after the Claudian conquest.[253]

The governor of Gaul was C. Pomptinus. In the previous year as praetor, he had helped arrest the Allobrogan ambassadors in Rome. He should have had a sense of the state of unrest in the province, but he seems to have initially underestimated the extent of the outbreak.[254] He dispatched one of his legates, Manlius Lentinus, to the rebellious center at Valentia. Lentinus was on the point of capturing the city when his efforts were thwarted by large groups of hostile natives coming in from the countryside. This cooperation between town and country showed the depth of resistance to Rome. Catugnatus, the leader of the Allobroges, threw his forces behind the revolt, and Pomptinus himself was forced to intervene. An Allobrogan center at Solonium was sacked, but Catugnatus escaped. Unfortunately the fragmentary sources fail completely at this point, and we have no evidence on the Roman mopping-up operations or the steps taken to avoid a repetition of the troubles.[255]

The internal unrest was matched by tension between the Roman border tribes and the groups immediately beyond the Roman sphere of influence. In 61 B.C. the Aeduan Diviciacus was in Rome, where his druidical connections aroused considerable interest. Undoubtedly he was there to raise support for the Aedui in the face of hostile neighbors.[256] In 60 B.C. the Helvetians defeated the Aedui, causing some concern for the safety of the Roman frontier. By March of that year, a delegation was sent out from Rome to see that the Gallic states did not join the Helvetii. The group included the senior consular Q. Caecilius Metellus Creticus and L. Valerius Flaccus. The latter had already served as *tribunus militum* in Gaul under C. Valerius Flaccus and had been involved in the arrest of the Allobrogan ambassadors in 63 B.C. His connections served to rally clients to Rome.[257] The dele-

[252] C. Crumley (1974) pp. 67, 71 calls attention to sharp differences in the quality of housing at first-century B.C. Bibracte.

[253] S. L. Dyson (1971) pp. 258–64, (1975) pp. 155–58, 167–68.

[254] Cic. *Prov. Cons.* 13; Livy *Per.* 103; Dio Cass. 37.47–48; T.R.S. Broughton (1952) pp. 167, 176.

[255] G. Chapotat (1970) p. 150 n. 269 on location of Solonium.

[256] Cic. *Div.* 1.41.90.

[257] Cic. *Att.* 1.19.2–3; T.R.S. Broughton (1952) pp. 185–86.

gation's task was made more difficult by the outbreak of fighting between the Aedui and the Sequani, both *amici populi romani*. This was
undoubtedly brought about by the continuing dispute over the control
of the increasingly lucrative trade routes up the Saône.[258] The Sequani
had called in the Germans under the leadership of Ariovistus to aid
their cause. Possibly to be placed at this period is the meeting between
a *rex Sueborum* (probably Ariovistus) and a certain Q. Metellus Pius
(most likely a mistake for Metellus Creticus, who was on the delegation), at which merchants of Indes were turned over to the Romans.[259]

The governor and the embassy used the standard Roman Republican diplomatic tactics with good results. Orgetorix, the leader of the
main hostile faction of the Helvetii, was killed. This stopped the development of a strong central leadership among the Helvetii.[260] Ariovistus and his warriors were recognized as a permanent frontier reality. Ariovistus was honored in 59 B.C. with the title of *amicus populi
romani*, an action that drew him into the frontier administrative system. No doubt the ties with tribes such as the Sequani and the Arverni were also strengthened.[261] The frontier balance was restored. This
was to change dramatically, however, with the arrival of C. Julius
Caesar.

Before reviewing the Gallic frontier as Caesar found it in 58 B.C.,
some mention should be made of the changing economic and social
scene in interior Gaul. One most striking feature is the relative continuity of occupation at the native oppida. There is little sign of forced
Roman evacuation and increasing indication of native prosperity based
in part on the substantial growth of trade along the Aquitanian and
Rhone corridors. The best excavated oppida of the Languedoc, for
instance, provide considerable evidence of this prosperity and acculturation. Romanized native names and even Roman names appear.
The same was true of the native centers of the Rhone.[262]

Also important was the growth of trade with Gaul beyond the frontier. Both the literary sources and the archaeological remains testify to
its expansion. From the north came tin, slaves, and a variety of other
items.[263] In return went Roman finished products and large quantities

---

[258] Cic. *Att.* 1.19.2; Caes. *BGall.* 1.3.4–5, 6.12.1; Strabo 4.3.2; W. Hoffmann (1952)
pp. 16–18; E. Wightman (1976) p. 412.

[259] Caes. *BGall.* 1.44.1–5; Pliny *HN* 2.170.

[260] Caes. *BGall.* 1.2–4, 9, 26.

[261] Caesar mentions an Epasnactus of the Arverni who is described as *amicissimus
populo Romano* (*BGall.* 8.44.6), and a Catamantaloedis of the Sequani who was also designated an *amicus* by the senate (*BGall.* 1.3.4).

[262] G. Barruol (1976) pp. 398, 684–85.

[263] Diod. 5.22.4, 5.26.2; M. Labrousse (1968) pp. 111, 148–49; G. Rancole and
O. Taffanel (1972) pp. 131–33; D. Nash (1978) pp. 458 fig 2, 470–71. Cic. *Quinct.* 24

of wine. Some of this trade must have been in the hands of native intermediaries, some under the control of Mediterranean merchants of the sort whom Caesar found estalished in Gallic centers. Late Republican wine amphorae and Campanian pottery are found at sites such as Toulouse, Bordeaux, and Agen.[264] The native center at Lagaste expanded dramatically at the end of the second century B.C. It was producing local Campanian pottery that it marketed between Carcassonne and Limoux.[265] In the Rhone corridor, the La Tène III sites (100 B.C. onward) enjoyed a flourishing trade.[266] Caesar describes Bibracte as a prosperous community, and the coin finds show that it was an important marketplace for trade. Other centers such as Essalois and even Allobrogan Vienne benefited.[267] The wealth produced by trade undoubtedly encouraged rivalry among the different native aristocracies. The slave trade probably brought further instability, although the extent of it may have been exaggerated.[268] The native coinages suggest a concentration of political power in a smaller number of centers.[269] If this meant stability, the Romans would want to encourage the trend.

With the arrival of C. Julius Caesar as governor in 58 B.C., a new era in the history of the Gallic frontier began. In the early sections of his *Commentaries*, Caesar provides a final impression of the workings of the Republican frontier system in Gaul as he found it. In many ways, it is the last picture we have of the traditional Republican frontier in the west.

Caesar took over a province with minimal military forces. He found no more than one legion and few other regular garrison troops.[270] The first line of defense was the border client groups whose loyalty Rome had so carefully cultivated. Guarding key approaches to the lower

---

mentions a slave dealer in Gaul. For general observations on shifting patterns of slaving in this period see M. H. Crawford (1977). D. Nash (1978) pp. 459–60, 470–71 believes Pompey's suppression of piracy may have stimulated the slave trade in Gaul.

[264] For the distribution of black-glazed pottery and amphorae see F. Benoit (1954) pp. 288–90. The relation between trade and alcohol consumption has parallels in other frontiers . For anthropological considerations see D. Wishart (1976) pp. 325–28. On the distribution of amphorae of the Sestius type in the Rhone and Toulouse corrider area see E. L. Will (1979) p. 342 fig. 2. Diod. 5.26 describes the relation between wine trading and slave trading.

[265] S. Rancoule (1970) pp. 33–34, 53–54, 65.

[266] G. Barruol (1969). M. Perrin and R. Perichon (1974) describe a site with amphorae and black glaze near Tournus.

[267] Caes. *BGall.* 7.55.4; J. Déchelette (1904).

[268] Diod. 5.26.3.

[269] M. J. Rowlands (1973) pp. 598–99 discusses the growing complexity of coin usage among the Gallic tribes of this period.

[270] Caes. *BGall.* 1.7.

Rhone valley, the Aedui and Sequani were the most important of these. Although Rome made every effort to win the support of the tribal leadership, it does not appear to have interfered in any public way in internal tribal affairs, unless Roman interests were directly affected. The shifting balance of power between Sequani and Aedui was watched carefully, and some effort at mediation was made. Rome did not actively intervene, however. New groups such as the Germans of Ariovistus were worked into the client network. Native rivalries, if channeled and controlled, prevented the emergence of a unified native group just beyond the frontier.

The border client tribes were useful for their contacts with groups within the unconquered regions of Gaul. Here the Aedui were especially helpful. Intelligence was vital to a Roman commander who needed time to get instructions from Rome, maneuver diplomatic levers, and gather armies from distant and scattered points. Client leaders and Roman traders were constantly interrogated and events to the north carefully watched.

Of special concern were new population movements that could threaten Roman-controlled areas. The memory of the Cimbri and the Teutones was fresh, and it is a theme that Caesar often used to explain his actions. The Germans were not the only perceived danger. In justifying his actions against the Helvetii, Caesar recalled wars in Aquitania during the last years of the second century B.C.

Traditional Roman patterns of thought and concerns relating to the frontier appear in the narrative of Caesar. The poverty of the land and the overabundant population gave rise to instability and tempted natives to enter the richer, more stable provincial and border areas. The Helvetii left their homeland because their expanding population could not be sustained within their confined territory. They sought to move to the area of the Santones, where they would pose a threat to the agriculturally rich and relatively unprotected border area around Tolosa.[271]

Vacuums along the frontier were to be avoided. As in Italy, one of the concerns of a victorious Roman general was that the vanquished tribe's territory not be deserted and provide a temptation to a new group. Caesar required the defeated Helvetii to return to their homeland and rebuild their native villages so that excellent farmland on the border of the province would not be left vacant.[272] Moreover, to assure stability during the initial period of resettlement, the Allobroges were required to provide the Helvetii with grain.

---

[271] Caes. *BGall.* 1.2, 1.10.
[272] Caes. *BGall.* 1.28.3–5.

One traditional feature of Roman native policy that Caesar stressed was the notion of barriers and boundaries that could not be crossed by native forces. As early as Cato, the Alps played this role in Roman frontier thinking. Caesar appears to have been developing the Rhine as a similar barrier even before his full conquest of Gaul. Among his initial demands of Ariovistus was one that no more Germans be allowed to cross the Rhine. This was probably behind his tendency to exaggerate the ethnic difference between the two sides of the river.[273]

The final aspect of the frontier in Gaul that Caesar emphasized was support provided for Rome by natives within the province. Earlier in this chapter I stressed the relative importance of the emerging Romano-native society that gradually overshadowed Massilia. This is evident in Caesar. No native of Massilia is mentioned in the *Bellum Gallicum*. The people of Gaul who do appear are the Romanized native aristocrats such as the sons of tribal leaders G. Valerius Procillus and Piso Aquitanus, who served as both soldiers and interpreters of Caesar.[274] The persistence of a warrior tradition among the leaders of southern Gaul is shown by the number of graves containing the armaments of warriors, especially among the Volcae Aremaci. These were often marked with stelae bearing the name of the deceased in Gallo-Greek.[275] The respect and affection that Caesar felt for these men is evident in his chronicle. This was in part because of military needs, but it also reflects a social connection that can be seen in the rise of other families such as the Pompeii Trogi and the Domitii Aquenses. The dominant element in the province was becoming the powerful, loyal native aristocracy. There is no better indication of this than Caesar's use of the father of Pompeius Trogus, not only as a soldier but also *epistularumque et legationum simul et anuli curam habuisse*.[276]

The Roman frontier in southern Gaul, short-lived though its evolution was, drew on the experiences of the third and second centuries on other fronts. In part, the training ground was Italy. But it was also Spain and Sardinia. It is to those frontiers that I will now turn.

---

[273] Caes. *BGall.* 1.43; G. Walser (1956); S. L. Dyson (1968).

[274] Caes. *BGall.* 1.47.4, 4.12.3–6. The importance of local native organization in the Caesarian period is shown by the inscription *T. Carisius T. F. Pr.(aetor) Volcarum Dat.*, which was found at Avignon. S. Gagniere, J. Granier, and R. Perrot (1962) pp. 70–71 dated it to the Caesarian reorganization of Gaul. For a general discussion of the title of praetor in the first-century B.C. Gallic inscriptions see M. Lejeune (1968–70).

[275] G. Barruol and G. Sauzade (1969).

[276] Just. *Epit.* 43.5.11.

CHAPTER 5

THE BEGINNINGS OF
A ROMAN FRONTIER IN
THE IBERIAN PENINSULA

No place better revealed the problems, ambiguities, and agonies of the Roman frontier experience than the Iberian peninsula. The Romans inherited a complicated frontier with a long, involved history. For two hundred years they carried on their military conquest and political, social, and economic development in an effort to bring peace and stability to the region. The Iberian provinces became a source of military disillusionment, imperial ambition, and growing resistance at home to Roman foreign policy. They also became a place of refuge from the growing political strife in Italy. At the same time, ironically, they became Rome's first overseas success story where things Roman and Hispanic became inextricably blended.

A detailed consideration of the Roman involvement in Iberia would make a book in itself. My first inclination was to omit Iberia from this study and deal with its frontier in a separate work, but the Spanish frontier experience was too closely bound up with the Roman experience elsewhere. For two centuries frontier soldiers and administrators moved back and forth between Iberia and other frontiers. The peninsula added significantly to the pool of ideas and experiences that made the overall Republican frontier development possible. I have opted for a compromise solution that will outline what seem to me the most salient aspects of Iberian development. The peninsula will be considered as a whole, without separate provincial divisions. This reflects the reality of the way the frontier developed from both the Roman and the native point of view.

No discussion of the Roman frontier in Iberia can begin without a consideration of the geography. The constraints of geography have always operated strongly on any people seeking to conquer and develop the peninsula. Today the area presents sharp contrasts between fertile river valleys and coastal plains, and stark uplands and rugged mountains. The contrasts certainly existed in antiquity, although ecological changes such as deforestation have since altered the balance in the Spanish landscape.[1] The history of these changes and the role of

---

[1] A. Schulten (1914) pp. 112–15, (1974) pp. 155, 199, 422–42; G. Nicolini (1974) pp. 15–16, 30–31.

3. *The Iberian Peninsula*

the Roman and pre-Roman settlers in bringing them about is an area
of palaeoecological research that is just beginning.[2]

The coastal plains were the first foci for outside settlement. They
differ widely in size and potential for development. Some plains, such
as that around Ampurias, are mere pockets of relatively flat land hedged
in by the mountains.[3] In both Andalusia and southwestern Lusitania,
however, the coastal area is large and fertile and the areas were proverbial in antiquity for their wealth.[4] The security and peaceful development of these areas became a mission of the Roman frontier plan-
ners.

The uplands, often heavily forested, appeared grim and hostile to

[2] A. Schulten (1914) p. 161; M. Cary (1949) p. 234; A. Schulten (1974) pp. 200–2;
A. Arribas (1964) pp. 37–39. Pliny *HN* 33.67 refers to the dry and barren hills of the
Iberian peninsula.

[3] A. Schulten (1974) pp. 224–25.

[4] Strabo 3.3.4; J. Caro Baroja (1968) pp. 180–83; M. Cary (1949) pp. 234–35.

Roman commanders.[5] The Romans had always been a "people of the plain," and the rough *macchia* and woods of Iberia made them no more comfortable than did the woods and hills of Etruria and Liguria. These areas supported a substantial population and were places of refuge. Frontier peace was impossible without some control of the interior. Moreover, some areas had long been famous for their mineral wealth, and the Romans wanted to obtain secure access to these mines.[6]

The great river systems of the peninsula linked these two disparate zones. The most important areas during the early period of frontier development were the Ebro in the northeast and the Guadalquivir (the Roman Baetis) on the south coast. Both had provided passage for trade goods and Mediterranean cultural influences long before the Romans.[7] Their broad and fertile valleys were prime land for settlement. As the frontier developed, rivers farther west such as the Guadiana, Tejo, and Douro became key factors in Roman conquest plans.

Even before the arrival of the Romans, Iberian society was far from static. The indigenous population had to adjust not only to a diverse environment but also to the periodic appearance of new groups both overland from the European continent and from the sea. The invasion hypothesis in Spanish prehistory may have been overstated, but the existence of groups like the Celtiberians in the north shows that the peninsula was not hermetically sealed.[8] More important for the Roman experience were the traders and colonists who arrived from the Mediterranean.

Scholars are still uncertain about the time of the first trade contact between Iberia and the eastern Mediterranean,[9] but by the eighth century B.C. natives in the southern peninsula had regular dealings with the Phoenicians.[10] At this stage the number of Phoenicians involved in trade and settlement was probably not large. They typically estab-

---

[5] For general information on vegetation patterns of Iberia see A. Schulten (1974) pp. 521–38.

[6] Population estimates for pre-Roman and Roman Spain will remain highly tentative until more systematic archaeological surveys are conducted. Research like that of F. Wattenberg (1959) has demonstrated the intensity of settlement in certain areas. For mineral resources see M. Cary (1949) pp. 235–36; A. Schulten (1974) pp. 469–517.

[7] A. Balil (1955) p. 50 notes that Eratosthenes mentions that Greek merchants ascended the Ebro to trade wine in Celtiberia.

[8] P. Bosch-Gimpera (1940); T.R.S. Broughton (1959) pp. 645–51; H. N. Savory (1968) pp. 240–42.

[9] A. García y Bellido (1952) pp. 318–26; J. M. Blazquez (1975) pp. 22–35; C. Renfrew (1976) pp. 94–101.

[10] Diod. 5.35.3–4; Paus. 6.19.2–4; A. García y Bellido, H. Schubart, and H. G. Niemeyer (1971) pp. 145–50. W. Culican (1970) argues for a Phoenician penetration of the western Mediterranean in the period 700–675 B.C.

lished coastal entrepôts that became the foci for regular contact with the natives. The recently excavated settlement of Toscanos in Andalusia, with its mixture of colonial and indigenous elements, is representative of this kind of foundation.[11]

The Phoenicians did not limit themselves to the coast. The fertile lands of the Baetis valley were attractive to them, and the river provided access to the silver-mining regions of the interior. Recent excavations have demonstrated the presence of either Phoenicians or highly Punicized natives in the rich silver areas of the Río Tinto in the eighth and seventh centuries B.C. Mediterranean goods had a wide circulation in the lower peninsula, traveling as far as the upper Guadiana.[12]

The presence of the outside traders stimulated development toward more complex social and economic organization similar to that already observed in Gaul. The clearest historical manifestation of this was the emergence of the kingdom of Tartessos during the seventh and sixth centuries B.C.[13] The kingdom was centered on the Río de Huelva area.[14] The metal trade was the base of its prosperity. Tartessos was the funnel through which passed the mineral resources of the interior to the merchants of the Mediterranean. The trade produced local wealth and social and political differentiation.[15] The personification of this developing chieftain society was the shrewd Arganthonius, who was said to have ruled the Tartessians for eighty years.[16]

Arganthonius owed part of his success to his ability to exploit the competition between Phoenicians and Greeks for access to the Iberian trade. The number of Phoenician and later Carthaginian settlers was increasing. The center at Gades was probably founded by the eighth century B.C., and Ibiza in the Balearics was established in 654 B.C.[17] Greeks were also appearing on the scene. Arganthonius welcomed Phocaean traders as a counterbalance to the Phoenicians and even tried to encourage colonization. These Greek colonial schemes in southern Iberia were aborted by changing power balances in the western Med-

---

[11] J. Ferron (1970); J. M. Blazquez (1975) pp. 310–32; H. Schubart and H. G. Niemeyer (1969). A. García y Bellido, H. Schubert, and H. G. Niemeyer (1971) pp. 150–60 place the high point of the trading center at Toscanos in the seventh century B.C.; ninety-seven percent of the pottery is of Phoenician type.

[12] A. Blanco and J. M. Luzón (1969); J. M. Blazquez (1975) p. 79. C. Fernández-Chicarro y de Diós (1969) pp. 10–11 discusses Punic objects at El Carambolo. For indications of native-Tyrian fighting see Strabo 3.2.13, 3.4.5; Vitr. De Arch. 10.13.

[13] Strabo 3.1.6, 3.2.11; Just. Epit. 44.4.16; Paus. 6.19.3; A. Schulten (1914) pp. 32–34; A. Tovar (1974) pp. 18–23, 28–29; J. M. Blazquez (1975).

[14] M. Guerrero (1969).

[15] Paus. 6.19.2–4.

[16] Herod. 1.163; Strabo 3.2.14.

[17] A. García y Bellido (1952) pp. 338–42.

iterranean, and the area remained basically a Phoenician-Carthaginian zone.[18]

More successful was the development of the Greek sphere in northeastern Iberia. The Phocaeans established a colony at Ampurias in the early sixth century B.C. This, as well as the nearby settlement at Rhode, represented the most extreme extension of Greek interests on the southwestern coast of Europe.[19] Here, as in Gaul, the main competition was between the Greeks and the Etruscans. Etruscan pottery has been found both at Ampurias and at the Iberian center of Ullastret, as it has in Languedoc and along the Riviera.[20]

Ampurias was relatively small and isolated, and controlled only a small coastal plain. Trade with the locals was obviously its main function. These interactions were apparently successful. Native dwellings crowded around the city, and by the beginning of the Roman period Ampurias had become a dual city with a Greek and a native quarter.[21] It also maintained trade contacts with the Punic zone. This flexibility helps explain the survival and continuing prosperity of this farthest Greek outpost.[22]

The interaction with the larger Mediterranean world had profound, long-term effects on the native Iberian society. Tartessos as a unified political entity seems to have declined by the early fifth century, although the natives of Turdetania in the Baetis valley appear to have been decendants of the Tartessians. At the time of the arrival of the Romans, they were the most sophisticated people of Iberia, with their own literary and historical traditions. They became the backbone of Romanization in the south.[23]

The development of more complicated native cultures was not limited to the Baetis valley and the old area of Tartessos. In the regions behind the Punic centers of the southeast and the Greek emporia of the northeast, the culture designated Iberian by the archaeologists was emerging. As with Tartessos, part of the stimulus was the trade in mineral resources. Centers like Castulo expanded into major oppida, and their prosperity is reflected in the archaeological finds that include Punic and Greek wares.[24]

[18] Herod. 1.163, 165; Strabo 3.2.11–14; G. Lopez Monteagudo (1977).

[19] M. Almagro (1943) pp. 22–23; C. A. Livadie (1967) pp. 304, 312–14; G. Lopez Monteagudo (1977) p. 7.

[20] E. Sanmartí Grego (1973).

[21] M. Almagro-Basch (1969); N. Lamboglia (1973).

[22] A. Arribas (1964) pp. 53–59, 127–29; J. Maluquer de Motes y Nicolau (1969); Y. Solier (1968b) pp. 149–50; G. Lopez Monteagudo (1977) pp. 10–11.

[23] Strabo 3.2.15.

[24] G. W. Schule (1969); G. Nicolini (1974).

Another factor in the development of the indigenous cultures was the growing importance of the Iberian peninsula for the mercenary market of the fifth and fourth centuries B.C. Both Celts and Iberians participated.[25] A combination of overpopulation and limited opportunity made mercenary service popular. Moericus, one of the few individuals named in the accounts of Iberian mercenary activity, switched from the Punic to the Roman side after being given a promise of land and a place of settlement.[26] Those mercenaries who did return brought back with them more sophisticated Mediterranean ways. The wealth and cultural sophistication they had accumulated in military service helped them play an elite role in their native communities. A Spanish scholar has compared their position with that of the *tercios*, veterans who returned from the wars of the Spanish Empire[27] in the sixteenth and seventeenth centuries.

A string of sites in eastern and southeastern Iberia make manifest the increasingly complicated nature of the native culture. Perhaps most representative is the center of Ullastret near Ampurias. There archaeologists have found sophisticated fortifications, well-built houses, and an abundance of imported Greek goods. Nevertheless, it seems to have been a basically native, rather than Greek, community.[28] Its development was probably similar to that of Saguntum, which played a pivotal role in the early history of the Roman involvement in Spain.[29]

In addition, the Iberians had sanctuaries with large-scale stone sculptures, an opulent personal style that reflected itself in elaborate dress and jewelry, and finally elite burial customs. Expressive of this world is the sculptural piece known as the Dame de Elche, which shows a female figure dressed in rich garments and bedecked with much jewelry.[30] Other statues of both people and animals have been found at sanctuaries and burial sites.[31] The Iberians who produced these were among the most sophisticated natives that the Romans met during their expansion in the western Mediterranean. Social stratification and the presence of wealthy and powerful elites are reflected in the tombs, especially those of upper Andalusia. The tumuli recall the burial places of the Etruscan magnates of Cerveteri, while items like

[25] G. T. Griffith (1935) pp. 225–27; L. Pericot Garcia (1952) p. 202. A. García y Bellido (1945) pp. 27–28 describes the mercenary market as a "valvula de escape."
[26] Livy 25.30.2, 26.21.12–13.
[27] P. Bosch Gimpera (1966) pp. 141–48.
[28] A. Arribas (1964) pp. 102–4.
[29] A. Arribas (1964) p. 99.
[30] A. Arribas (1964) pp. 23–26, 160; G. Nicolini (1974) pp. 123–31; R. R. Fernández (1975) p. 102. M. Almagro-Basch (1977) stresses the oriental over the Greek contribution during the formative period of Iberian art.
[31] A. Arribas (1964) pp. 155–62.

the complete chariot entombed at Toya remind one of the Celtic aristocrats farther north.[32] These individuals were the ancestors of such
powerful frontier figures as Astolpas, who was to play an important
role in the development of the second-century B.C. Roman frontier.

Literacy among the Iberian groups was widespread. The earliest
inscriptions in an Ionic alphabet date back to the sixth century. They
became abundant by the fourth century and show dialectal variations.
The widespread use of a written language is made evident not only
by the coins and large monuments but also by decorated ceramics and
graffiti scratched on individual vessels.[33]

The remains in the peninsula also reflect the changing balance of
forces in the Mediterranean. During the fourth century B.C. Greek
trade was revitalized. This is reflected in the greater flow of Hellenic
goods into native Iberian sites.[34] By the third century these were com-
plemented by imports from Italy. Most interesting for the future of
the peninsula was the appearance of ceramics produced in Latium and
Rome. Black-glaze pottery of the *petites estampilles* type was, during the
first half of the third century B.C., widely distributed along the northeastern coast of Iberia. It documents the Latin traders going before
the flag into Spain.[35]

Carthage, heir to the old Phoenicians' interests in the western Mediterranean, was the power most involved with Iberia. A development
of special concern was the growing strength of the interior Iberian
groups that by the fourth and third centuries were threatening Carthaginian access to the mining areas.[36] The situation was complicated
by the outbreak of the First Punic War, which forced Carthage to
draw more heavily on the Iberian mercenary markets. This increased
the long-term flow of riches and acculturated warriors into the interior
Iberian communities.[37] Events like the mercenary revolt in North Africa involved Iberians and put pressure on the Spanish frontier. Even
the core Punic center at Gades felt itself threatened.[38]

The loss of Sicily and Sardinia that resulted from the First Punic
War increased the importance of Spain for Carthage. The peninsula
provided continued access to mercenaries and the mineral resources

[32] A. Arribas (1964) pp. 146–51. A. M. Amilibia (1968) p. 132 notes the large quantity of Greek pottery of 375–350 B.C. date found around Castulo.

[33] A. Arribas (1964) p. 53. A. M. Amilibia (1968) p. 129, however, notes a crisis in
the southeastern Greek sphere around 340–330 B.C. This is related to the Rome-Car-
thage treaty of 348 B.C.

[34] A. Arribas (1964) pp. 87–96; M. Tarradelli (1968).

[35] J. M. Blazquez (1967) p. 211; E. Sanmartí Grego (1973).

[36] A. M. Amilibia (1968) pp. 133–34.

[37] Polyb. 1.17.4–5, 1.67; A. Schulten (1974) p. 74.

[38] Polyb. 1.67.7; Just. *Epit.* 44.5.2–4.

needed to pay the indemnities owed to Rome.[39] For a great family like the Barcids it offered a field of action and a power base relatively free from interference by the government at Carthage. With these and perhaps greater ambitions, Hamilcar Barca crossed over to Spain.[40]

Hamilcar's first concern was the restoration of Punic control in the south. The Turdetani were attempting to assert their independence, and they had apparently been joined by Tartessians, Iberians, and Celts. The revolt was led by a man named Indortes.[41] The name suggests a Celtic warlord and shows the cooperation of several ethnic groups against the common Punic enemy. The revolt failed. Indortes was treated with great cruelty, but the bulk of his warriors were incorporated into the Carthaginian army.

Hamilcar then turned to the task of creating a stable, Carthaginian-oriented order for the Iberian centers of the southeast. Access to the silver-producing region was a primary concern. This meant moving against some of the most powerful oppida in the area. Hamilcar attacked the center at Helice (probably modern Elche), but soon found himself facing relief forces from the Orissi (probably the later Oretani). In the ensuing battle Hamilcar's army was defeated, and Hamilcar himself was killed.[42]

The death of Hamilcar produced no real change in Punic strategy or Barcid ambition, and his son-in-law, Hasdrubal, assumed the command of Carthaginian forces in Spain. With a combination of force and diplomacy, he set out to master the Iberian frontier. Twelve centers allied with the Orissi were taken, and the defeat of Hamilcar was avenged.[43] The Iberian sanctuaries were apparently also attacked. They were probably eliminated as potential foci of resistance.[44]

Hasdrubal realized that force alone was not sufficient to pacify Iberia. The Carthaginians had become skilled native diplomats, and Hasdrubal brought this long experience to bear on winning loyalties among the Iberians. Such relationships in peninsular society always

[39] Dio Cass. 12 fr. 48; B. H. Warmington (1964) pp. 205–6; J. M. Blazquez (1961) p. 24–28.

[40] Polyb. 2.1.5–9; App. *Hisp.* 5; J. M. Blazquez (1961) pp. 23–24, 34–35. A. M. Amilibia (1968) p. 137 speaks of the foundation of a Hellenistic-type monarchy by Hamilcar in Spain. E.G.S. Robinson (1956) comments on the independent quality of the Barcid coinage in Spain.

[41] Diod. 25.10; A. García y Bellido (1952) pp. 365–68.

[42] Polyb. 2.1.5–9; Diod. 25.10.3–5; Zonaras 8.19; Nepos *Hamilcar* 4; Just. *Epit.* 44.5.4; F. Walbank (1957) pp. 151–53; A. García y Bellido (1952) pp. 368–69. M.A.Beltrán (1964) feels that the defeat of Hamilcar should be placed somewhere around the Ebro.

[43] Diod. 25.12; B. H. Warmington (1964) pp. 207–8.

[44] A. Arribas (1964) pp. 136–37.

had their personal element, and Hasdrubal acknowledged this when he took the daughter of an Iberian chieftain as his wife.[45]

The Carthaginians began the development of new centers to serve their growing sphere of influence. Hamilcar had established a new city at Akra Leuce (modern Alicante). Hasdrubal now followed with his own foundation at Carthago Nova (modern Cartagena).[46] Both were on the east coast and had access to the Punic centers of North Africa. They also flanked the delta of the Segura River. The valley of the Segura and that of the Sanganera slightly to the south provided access to the silver regions around Castulo. The later Roman road linking Carthago Nova with the interior traversed the Sanganera valley to reach the headwaters of the Guadalquivir. This must have followed earlier trade routes that linked coast and interior.[47]

Hasdrubal was assassinated in 221 B.C. The succession passed to Hamilcar's son, Hannibal, and with him began a new phase in Mediterranean history. Hannibal's first concerns were with the Barcid frontier in Spain. He followed Hasdrubal's example by marrying a chieftain's daughter from Castulo.[48] This helped to pacify the immediate Iberian hinterland. It also served as a springboard for a more wide-ranging venture that took him into the central part of the peninsula.

The long-term impact of Hannibal's expedition, impressive though it was, should not be exaggerated. It did involve victories over tribes such as the Carpetani and Vaccaei located well beyond the borders of Iberia proper, and it took him as far as Salamanca. But this was a lightning campaign, and Hannibal was never able to consolidate his conquests. His thoughts were on bigger adventures.[49]

In 219 B.C. Hannibal faced a challenge from Rome to his growing ambitions for hegemony in the peninsula. The complicated question of Rome's relation with Saguntum is not a concern here. What is worth noting is that the *casus belli* was a local frontier dispute typical of the east coast of Spain. Saguntum controlled a small fertile coastal enclave, which was harassed by the Torboletae who lived in the hills beyond. In the face of Saguntum's efforts to control the situation,

[45] Polyb. 2.13.1; Diod. 25.12; Livy 21.2.5–6; E.G.S. Robinson (1956) pp. 37–38; F. Walbank (1957) pp. 167–68.

[46] Polyb. 2.13.1–2; Diod. 25.10.3–13; E.G.S. Robinson (1956) pp. 37–38; A. García y Bellido (1952) pp. 368–69; G. V. Sumner (1967).

[47] K. Miller (1916) cols. 179–80; J. M. Blazquez (1975) pp. 14–15 fig. 1.

[48] Livy 24.41; Sil. *Pun.* 3.97; J. M. Blazquez (1975) pp. 24–25.

[49] Polyb. 3.13.14; Livy 21.5.2–17; Plut. *De mul. vir.* 248 C. A. García y Bellido (1952) p. 374 sees evidence for centers in the Avila region being abandoned during this period.

Hannibal took the side of the natives. The result was his seizure of the city, and his war with Rome.[50]

Hannibal, as he moved east to Italy, left a mixed frontier legacy behind. The Carthaginians had strengthened their links with the Iberian tribes of the southeast. Meanwhile, loyalty of other groups was secured by the taking of hostages or by the activities of Punic agents working among them. However, the Turdetani were restless, the loyalty of most Iberians was uncertain, and coastal centers like Emporion were more closely linked to Greco-Roman interests. The actions of Hannibal had inspired fear but hardly affection among the natives of both coast and interior. Not surprisingly, the Scipios saw in Iberia an opportunity to use the frontier situation to strike at a vital Carthaginian resource base to counter Hannibal's invasion of Italy.

This strategy of disrupting Carthaginian interests in Spain meant that the Romans had to join with the inland groups and exploit weaknesses in the Carthaginian frontier system. The approach became obvious in 217 B.C., when P. Cornelius Scipio joined his brother at Emporion, where the Romans had established their base.[51] The brothers realized that the key areas for the Carthaginians lay in the south and especially in those Iberian areas just behind the coast. Roman control of that zone would mean a denial of minerals to the Carthaginians. It would also provide a staging platform for raids down the river valleys to the coast. With these objectives in mind, Cn. Scipio had already probed the direction of Castulo.[52]

As has been noted, the Carthaginians had carefully cultivated their links with the ruling elite at Castulo and had enhanced Castulo's power. When the Romans arrived, the ruler of Castulo, Culchas, controlled twenty-eight oppida.[53] A tradition of independence ran strong in the area, however, and the former brutal campaigns of the Carthaginians must have left bitter memories. The appearance of an outside force could easily turn local loyalties. The Romans did just that. Celtiberians began raiding the Punic zone, and the Carthaginian commander, Hasdrubal, who had been moving toward the Ebro, had to return to defend his own territory.[54] The success of the raids increased the restlessness of natives near the coast. The Romans were learning to use the other side of the frontier to undermine the Carthaginian position.

The next two years saw continued native and Roman exploitation

---

[50] Polyb. 3.29–30; Livy 21.6; Zonaras 8.21; App. *Hisp.* 10; J. M. Blazquez (1967) pp. 214–19; W. V. Harris (1979) pp. 201–3.

[51] Livy 21.41.1–2, 21.19.1–21.22.1.

[52] Polyb. 3.97; Livy 22.20–21.

[53] Livy 28.13.3. Polybius designates this ruler as Kolichas.

[54] Livy 22.21.

of Punic weakness. In 216 B.C. the Tartessians revolted and seized the
Punic garrison center at Ascua. Hasdrubal suppressed the revolt only
with difficulty. In 215 B.C. the natives of the oppida at Iliturgi and
Intibili rebelled, and the Carthaginians were prevented by Roman action from regaining control.[55] In the following year Castulo went over
to the Romans, while the Scipios felt sufficiently secure of their position in southern Iberia to pass the winter on the frontier.[56] This
prolonged stay provided time for diplomacy and the cultivation of
those important bonds of personal friendship. The Scipios began recruiting among the Celtiberians and even dispatched three hundred
Spanish leaders to Italy to try to tempt their fellow tribesmen away
from the forces of Hannibal.[57]

The Spanish frontier was never truly stable, however, and the Carthaginians were masters of border politics and border warfare. Gradually, they regrouped their forces and reestablished links with the
interior. In the northeast they persuaded their old ally, Indibilis, to
raise a pro-Punic army among the Suesetani and attack the areas around
Emporion. Roman support in the south also wavered. Finally, the two
Scipio brothers were defeated and killed near Ilurgia.[58] The Roman
power south of the Ebro dissolved.

The situation remained a stalemate until the arrival of the younger
Scipio, who reanimated the Roman cause. His bold stroke of attacking
Carthago Nova not only dealt a near fatal blow to Punic prestige but
also provided the means for developing new native strategies. The
Iberian hostages freed at Carthago Nova were treated with exemplary
kindness by Scipio.[59] He also used his great diplomatic skills to win
over such ambivalent native chieftains as Indibilis and Mandonius.[60]

The war between Scipio and the Carthaginians now centered on
control of the coastal hinterland and the interior mining areas. Alliances among the Iberian peoples were constantly shifting. The victory
of Scipio over Hasdrubal at Baecula resulted in some defections to
Rome.[61] Meanwhile, centers such as Iliturgi and Castulo remained
outside the Roman camp. The Carthaginians undertook new recruitment among the Celtiberians and Lusitanians, and dispatched Masi-

[55] Livy 23.26–27, 23.48.4–23.49.14; App. *Hisp.* 15.
[56] Livy 24.41–42; App. *Hisp.* 16.
[57] Livy 24.49.7–8.
[58] Polyb. 10.7.1; Livy 25.32–39; Pliny *HN* 3.9; H. H. Scullard (1930) pp. 50–51,
(1970) p. 264–65 n. 70; G. V. Sumner (1970) pp. 86–89.
[59] H. H. Scullard (1930) pp. 92–93, 98, 100–1, (1970) pp. 48–63. E.G.S. Robinson
(1956) pp. 40–43.
[60] Polyb. 10.18; Livy 26.49; Dio Cass. 16.42–43; H. H. Scullard (1930) pp. 102–3.
[61] Polyb. 10.38.7–10.40.12; Livy 27.19; H. H. Scullard (1970) pp. 68–75.

nissa to harass the Romans. Scipio found the frontier so insecure during the winter of 208–207 that he returned to quarters at Tarraco.[62]

The balance shifted strongly to the Romans in 207 B.C. The Carthaginians were defeated at Ilipa (Alcalá del Rio) on the Baetis. This left the Romans dominant in Turdetania and prompted new defections from the Punic cause. One native leader, Culchas, brought his twenty-eight oppida over to the Romans. Attenes, *regulus* of the Turdetani, followed and left only limited pockets of resistance.[63] The inhabitants of Ilurgia and Castulo had played important roles in the betrayal and destruction of the earlier Scipionic army. Expecting no mercy from the Romans, they fought on. Castulo was taken by treachery, and Iliturgi was razed. Even here, the Romans attempted to build a local power base. Cornelian names are common in the area around Castulo and probably testify to the efforts of Scipio to establish client connections.[64]

With the Carthaginians routed, the role of Rome on the Iberian frontier changed dramatically. Up to that time, the Romans in the southern peninsula had acted as disrupters of a frontier system that the Carthaginians had long labored to develop. Now they were the dominant power charged with defending the settled groups located on the coast and in the river valleys against threats from the hinterland.

In adjusting to this new role, the Romans faced two main problems. The first was the personal nature of alliances in the Iberian area. Among the natives, personal loyalty to a leader was a strong bond within the community. The same concept was extended to intercommunity relations. The Barcids had ruled in Iberia as a dynasty largely independent of their home city. They had every reason to encourage personal loyalties rather than loyalties to the state. Rome was also a state in which clan allegiance still meant much and the Scipios had used this approach effectively in the Spanish area. At the same time, however, Rome was an oligarchic state with the beginnings of bureaucratic organization. The senate had a healthy fear of families becoming too strong, and it rotated governors on a regular basis. The problems that the Iberians had in understanding this new system was demonstrated by their attempt to salute Scipio as king after the battle of Baecula and by the revolts that took place upon the false rumor of Scipio's death.[65]

[62] Polyb. 10.40.12; Livy 27.19.1–27.20.8; H. H. Scullard (1970) pp. 75–85.

[63] Polyb. 11.20; Livy 28.13.3–5; H. H. Scullard (1970) pp. 86–96.

[64] Polyb. 11.24.10; Livy 28.15, 28.19–20; App. *Hisp.* 32; J. M. Blazquez (1975) p. 29; H. H. Scullard (1970) pp. 95–98, 264 n. 70; S. L. Dyson (1980–81).

[65] Polyb. 11.25–30; Livy 38.24–29; J. M. Blazquez (1967) p. 238. On the notion of *fides iberica* in general see F. Rodríguez Adrados (1946).

An even greater obstacle to effective frontier control was the sense of independence that the Romano-Punic struggle had engendered in the native groups. The Barcids had built a system of alliances designed to ensure minimal peace, while the Romans encouraged renewed raiding and the breaking of those bonds. The process was not easily reversed. Soon reports reached the Romans that the tribesmen of Astapa (Estepa) had begun raiding Roman allies in the Baetis area and had been capturing Roman stragglers. L. Marcius Septimius, the legate of Scipio, had to be sent to restore order.[66]

The Romans could not afford an extended garrison system, and here, as in northern Italy, they had to create a stable frontier based on powerful, friendly border magnates.[67] Some figures, such as Culchas, Mandonius, and Indibilis, carried over from the Carthaginian period; however, these men had ambitions of their own.[68] Gradually the older leaders would be replaced by other rulers of firmer loyalty. Appian describes what must have been a typical solution.[69] At Castax (Castulo) a garrison was installed, and the government was placed under the control of a prominent citizen, no doubt one of proven loyalty to Rome.

The Iberian peninsula was too far distant for the Romans to attempt a true colonial system. Nevertheless, Roman settlements would provide a model for acculturation and a counter to the major Punic communities such as Gades and Carthago Nova. Scipio, in one of his final acts, settled some of his veterans at a place called Italica in the Ebro valley. It is significant that this was not a coastal entrepôt but an agricultural settlement set amidst the most Mediterraneanized natives of Iberia. It provided both a bulwark and a model for the Romanization process.[70]

The years between the departure of Scipio and the arrival of Cato are obscure ones for Roman Spain. Some of the governors are names only in the historical record, and their actions are sparsely recorded. Certain trends are evident, though, that were to be important in the later history of the province. The first was the realization that even the limited section of the peninsula under Roman control needed two separate administrative districts. The northeastern areas centered on the Ebro and the southeastern on the Baetis were just too divided by

[66] Livy 28.22–23; App. *Hisp.* 33.
[67] R. C. Knapp (1977) pp. 16–18 discusses evidence of garrisons in Iberia at this time.
[68] Livy 28.24.
[69] App. *Hisp.* 32; E. Badian (1958) p. 118.
[70] Strabo 3.2.2; App. *Hisp.* 38; H. H. Scullard (1930) p. 157; E. Badian (1958) p. 119; A. García y Bellido (1960) pp. 18, 69, 156; H. H. Scullard (1970) pp. 104–5; A. Tovar (1975) pp. 163–66; R. Nierhaus (1966).

history and geography to allow effective unified administration. The basis of the later province of Hispania Citerior and Hispania Ulterior was laid during this period.[71]

The Romans also soon realized that Iberia could be a considerable source of wealth both to the state and to those who represented it on the peninsula. The first post-Scipionic governors returning from the area deposited 43,000 pounds of silver and 1,200 pounds of gold. Naturally, such possibilities for wealth prompted abuse. In 199 B.C. a delegation arrived from the old Punic city of Gades asking that they be spared the presence of a Roman prefect. Their protests were presumably made in response to administrative abuses.[72]

The problems intensified as the Romans attempted to impose more regular taxation. In 199 B.C. Lucius Stertinius was sent out to Hispania Ulterior. He is a shadowy figure from a relatively unknown family.[73] Little is said about his role in Spain, but it can be assumed that his principal task was the regularization of fiscal administration. When he returned to Rome after a relatively short stay in Iberia (199 to 196), he brought back fifty thousand pounds of silver. Moreover, he was immediately sent off to Macedonia to help Flamininus organize that area after the victory at Cynocephalae.[74] These incidents suggest a proven administrator who could guarantee a good return for the Roman *fiscus*.

Rising discontent over an increasingly heavy financial burden, combined with wavering loyalty on the part of border magnates, sparked a series of revolts. The revolt cycle coming at a critical juncture in administrative and cultural change would appear again and again in Roman history and in later imperialism.[75] The year 196 B.C. saw trouble in both provinces. Cn. Cornelius Blasio received an *ovatio* for his actions against the Celtiberians and brought back over 1,500 pounds of gold, 20,000 pounds of silver, and 34,500 silver coins.[76] His successor and the first non-Cornelian governor of Citerior found the province still in turmoil and was mortally wounded trying to suppress the revolt. The border defenses then broke, and the natives of the hinterland swept down to the coast. Only a few strongpoints such as Emporion remained in Roman hands, and large numbers of Latins, Ro-

[71] Livy 29.1.19–29.3.7, 29.13.7–8, 30.2.7, 30.27.9, 30.41.4–5. App. *Hisp.* 38; W. V. Harris (1979) p. 32.

[72] Livy 31.20, 32.2.5–6, 32.7.4; E. Badian (1954).

[73] Livy 31.50.11; T.R.S. Broughton (1951) pp. 328, 331, 334.

[74] Livy 33.27.3–4; R. Thouvenet (1940) p. 106.

[75] S. L. Dyson (1975).

[76] Livy 31.50.11, 33.27.1–3; A. Degrassi (1947) p. 552.

mans, and friendly Iberians fell captive to the raiders.[77] In Ulterior
the situation was similar. The successor of Stertinius, Marcus Helvius, also faced a rebellion. Livy stresses its local origin, noting that
it was carried off *sine ullo Punico exercitu aut duce*.[78] One of the revolt
leaders was Culchas.

We have more information about Culchas than about most other
native leaders faced by Rome, He had earlier brought his twenty-eight
oppida over to Scipio, and apparently benefited from this timely change
of allegiance. In 190 B.C. the Romans, who were trying to win the
support of Prusias of Bithynia, used the following argument:

οὐ γὰρ μόνον ὑπὲρ τῆς ἰδίας προαιρέσεως ἔφερον ἀπολο-
γισμούς, ἀλλὰ καὶ περὶ τῆς κοινῆς ἁπάντων Ῥωμαίων, δι᾽
ὧν παρεδείκνυον οὐχ οἷον ἀφῃρημένοι τινὸς τῶν ἐξ ἀρχῆς
βασιλέων τὰς δυναστείας, ἀλλὰ τινὰς μὲν καὶ προσκατε-
σκευακότες αὐτοὶ δυνάστας, ἐνίους δ᾽ ηὐξηκότες καὶ πολ-
λαπλασίους αὐτῶν τὰς ἀρχὰς πεποιηκότες. ὧν κατὰ μὲν τὴν
Ἰβηρίαν Ἀνδοβάλην καὶ Κολίχαντα προεφέροντο.[79]

They were describing not only their particular plan but that which
was shared by all the Romans; and they showed that they [the
Romans] had not removed from power anyone who belonged to
the original kingly lines, but they had created a number of king-
ships and had added to others to make them much larger than
before. They cited Andobales and Kolichas in Iberia.

Other sources suggest, however, that the Romans were not interested
in enhancing the position of Culchas. Only seventeen oppida joined
his revolt in 197 B.C. Although this evidence should not be pushed too
far, it does not suggest a waxing power.[80] Later the chieftains of Julio-
Claudian Gaul were similarly to feel their position threatened and rise
against Rome.[81] The exact location of Culchas' sphere of influence is
not certain. It was probably in the hinterland behind the upper Baetis.
This would suggest a union of the three most Mediterraneanized groups
of southern Iberia against the new administrative order. Luxinius was
the other *regulus* who revolted. Joining him were the centers of Carmo
and Baldo in the Baetis valley and the coastal tribes of the Malacini
(near modern Málaga) and the Sexteni.[82]

[77] Livy 33.25.8–10, 34.16.7–8; App. *Hisp.* 39; Oros. 4.20.10.
[78] Livy 33.21.6–9, 33.26.6. M. H. Crawford (1969) pp. 82–84 associates the revolt
with imposition of taxes based on newly developed Iberian coinages.
[79] Polyb. 21.11.5–7.
[80] Polyb. 21.11.6–7; Livy 33.21.8; E. Badian (1958) p. 122.
[81] S. L. Dyson (1975) pp. 156–58.
[82] Livy 33.21.6–9; A. Tovar (1974) pp. 76–78, 81–82.

Helvius defeated some of the rebels, but he hardly completed the pacification. In 195 B.C. the governor of Ulterior, Q. Minucius Thermus announced that at the oppidum of Turda he had defeated two enemy leaders named Budares and Baesadines. Turda was presumably in the territory of the Baetis valley in Turdetania.[83] The victory was not decisive, and fighting continued in Turdetania in 195 B.C.

The new praetor, P. Manlius, gathered a veteran army and moved against the rebels. The Turdetani were defeated, even though they had resisted more fiercely than their reputation of being the *omnium Hispanorum maxime imbelles* might suggest. Their allies, the Turduli, continued the fight and called in ten thousand Celtiberian mercenaries.[84] These connections were presumably not new. The movement of herds had previously brought together inhabitants of the Celtiberian uplands and the Baetis valley, and the richer groups of the Baetis must have needed paid warriors to defend them against neighboring tribes. Nevertheless, for the Romans they were largely a new element. Warriors from the interior threatened both frontiers.

The consul, M. Porcius Cato, was sent to Iberia in 195 B.C., which suggests the gravity of the situation. Cato had already proved his worth as a frontier administrator in Sardinia. His new assignment centered on the stabilization of the frontier in the northeast, although he was also to assist his colleague, the praetor P. Manlius Vulso, in the south. Cato was a superb self-publicist, and his pioneering history, the *Origines*, described in full his accomplishments in Spain.[85] Moreover, his personal qualities made him a suitable object for later moralistic and historical commentary. These sources allow an understanding of events in Spain during the period, even though they may lead to an exaggeration of Cato's role.[86]

When Cato arrived, the Roman cause in the northeast of Spain was almost totally lost. He first had to expel the natives from the old Greek center at Rhode and secure the immediate hinterland of Emporion. His first winter camp was only three miles from that city.[87] At least minimal support had to be brought to the remaining Roman allies. In the words of Cato himself, *interea ad socios nostros sedulo dispertieram aliis frumentum aliis legatos aliis littera aliis praesidium.*[88] Only after vigorous

---

[83] Livy 33.44.4–5, 34.10.1–5. A. Degrassi (1947) pp. 552–53 presents the arguments for Q. Minucius Thermus serving in Hispanic Ulterior rather than in Citerior as stated in Livy 33.26.2.

[84] Livy 34.17.1–4.

[85] A. E. Astin (1978) p. 28.

[86] F. della Corte (1969) pp. 29–36; A. E. Astin (1978) pp. 47–48.

[87] Livy 34.8–9, 34.11, 34.13.2.

[88] Cato fr. 34 (Malv.).

campaigning, the storming of hill forts, and the systematic disarming
of natives did a modicum of peace and order return to the hill region
northeast of the Ebro.[89]

All peace was relative, however, as Cato soon learned. While his
attention was attacted elsewhere, the bandits of the northern mountains increased their activities. Livy describes one such group:

> Lacetanos deviam et silvestram gentem cum insita feritas conti-
> nebat in armis tum conscientia, dum consul exercitusque Turdulo
> bello esset occupatus, depopulatorum subitis incursionibus so-
> ciorum.[90]

Not only their natural savagery kept the Lacetani, an isolated,
woodland group, in arms but also the realization that while the
consul and his army were engaged in the war in Turdetania they
had devasted the allies with sudden attacks.

These events revolved around an oppidum called Bergium. For once,
the sources are sufficiently full for the historian to understand the
interactions at work. Bandits (*praedones*) had seized control of Bergium
with the assistance of some of the inhabitants. Others had opposed
the takeover. Cato recaptured the center and then carefully distinguished among the various groups in his postconquest dispositions.
The bandits who had been captured were executed. Those of the Ber-
gistani who had aided them were sold into slavery. The natives who
had remained loyal to Rome retained their homes and possessions.[91]

Cato appreciated that the Roman territory in the northeast was too
limited and that the border had to be advanced if the Romans were to
create a stable frontier. Expansion into the Ebro valley seemed natural. The natives in the area had a developed culture and could easily
be incorporated into the Roman system. Their position was similar to
such groups as the Turdetani in the Baetis valley. Moreover, as people
holding some of the best land in the northeast of the peninsula, they
were the target of raiders from the proper territories north and south
of the river. Such natives might well appreciate the protection and
assistance that Rome could provide.

Cato advanced with his army well up the valley. Progress seems to
have been relatively easy in contrast to the difficult fighting he had
experienced in the hill country behind Emporion.[92] His army eventually reached Numantia in the central Ebro area. Geographical and

[89] Livy 34.16; App. *Hisp.* 41.
[90] Livy 34.20.2–3.
[91] Livy 34.21; R. C. Knapp (1980) pp. 34–35.
[92] A. E. Astin (1978) pp. 43–46.

ethnographic references derived ultimately from Cato's *Origines* indicate that the consul made extensive inquiries concerning the geography, resources, and peoples of the Ebro area.[93]

By this time it had become clear that frontier events in both Citerior and Ulterior were linked, and that the Romans could not hope for peace and security without better control of the central Meseta area. Cato made forays into this territory with the hope of relieving Celtiberian pressure on the borders of Ulterior. He had at best marginal success and left to his heirs the grim task of bringing the Celtiberians to heel.[94]

The wars in Celtiberia forced the commanders of both provinces to concentrate on the Meseta area, even if they did not always promote cooperation. This common focus can be seen in the wars of the late 190s. P. Cornelius Scipio Nasica was sent to Ulterior in 194 B.C.[95] The selection of a Cornelius was probably not accidental, since the connections of his family in the province would have been useful in rallying the local elites after a period of revolt. Scipio's sensitivity to local problems was demonstrated in another way. Frontinus notes that he tried to keep his troops busy with make-work tasks so that in their idleness they did not harass the locals.[96]

Reconciliation within the province had to be matched by vigorous campaigning beyond the frontier. Scipio is described as fighting *trans Iberum*. This presumably means Celtiberia south of the Ebro. Another uprising was nipped, and some fifty oppida surrendered to him. At the same time, Scipio had to think about another frontier. Lusitanians were raiding the Baetis valley northwest of Seville. Scipio turned to face them, and intercepted and defeated their booty-laden forces near Ilipa (Alcalá del Rio).[97]

Hispania Citerior received C. Flaminius in 193 B.C. He was the son of the man who had done so much to develop the frontier system in northern Italy, and thus he was familiar with the problems of border warfare in a partly pacified province. He was joined in 193 B.C. by a new colleague in Ulterior, M. Fulvius Nobilior, who had been sent out with instructions to wage new wars. The anxiety of the senate was certainly justified. New groups farther north, such as Vaccaei and

---

[93] Cato in fr. 93 discusses mineral resources in Iberia, and in fr. 110 the sources of the Ebro. Gell. *NA* 16.1.3; A. Schulten (1914) p. 117. R. C. Knapp (1980) p. 43 places this episode as part of the return journey of Cato from Turdetania.

[94] A. E. Astin (1978) pp. 34–50. R. C. Knapp (1980) pp. 39–54 is skeptical, probably rightly, about too great a penetration by Cato into the south.

[95] Livy 35.1.3–4.

[96] Front. *Str.* 4.1.15.

[97] Livy 35.1.3–12. See A. Tovar (1974) pp. 162–63 on the location of Ilipa.

Vettones, are mentioned as fighting alongside the other Celtiberians. Moreover, the natives appear to have been developing more sophisticated forms of political, social, and military organization. Mention is made of *reges* such as the *rex* Hilernus captured by Nobilior. Toletum (Toledo) was emerging as the central point of resistance and the focus of a coalition of tribes.[98]

The two governors apparently divided their spheres of action in such a way as to allow complementary attacks. This would have hindered native cooperation. In 193 and 192 B.C. Nobilior concentrated on breaking the resistance around Toletum itself.[99] This involved fighting such groups as the Oretani, the Toletani, and the Vettones. His actions culminated in the capture of Toletum in 192 B.C. We do not know the dispositions made by Nobilior to ensure peace after his victory, but presumably a network of *amici* was established. The arrangements seem to have worked. That section of the frontier enjoyed relative peace for a long period of time.

Flaminius meanwhile appears to have followed the plan of Cato and moved directly south to reduce pressure on the northeastern border of Ulterior. Centers captured included Illucia (Illugo, northeast of Castulo) and Licabrum (probably to be identified with later Igabrum and modern Cabra).[100] At Licabrum he captured the *nobilem regulum Conribilonem*, apparently the political equivalent of the *rex* Hilernus seized by Nobilior.[101]

The tribes in the territory bordering the middle and upper Baetis continued to resist Roman pacification. The country was rugged and well populated, and the silver trade had given the natives extensive contacts with Mediterranean ways. They were effective warriors who could not only use their own resources but also call in neighboring groups like the Lusitanians. Archaeological evidence indicates that cultural exchange had long taken place between the Bastetani and other groups southeast of the river and the tribes in the mountains across the Baetis.[102]

This frontier provided a rude initiation for the next governor of Ulterior, L. Aemilius Paullus.[103] Near a place called Lycho, in the territory of the Bastetani, he suffered a defeat at the hands of tribes-

---

[98] Livy 35.2.1–9, 35.7.6–8. T.R.S. Broughton (1951) p. 347; P. Bosch-Gimpera and P. Aguado Bleye (1962) p. 65.

[99] Livy 35.7.8, 35.20.11, 35.22.5–8.

[100] Livy 35.7.6–8; P. Bosch-Gimpera and P. Aguado Bleye (1962) pp. 66–67; A. Tovar (1976) pp. 121-22.

[101] Livy 35.22.5–6.

[102] A. Arribas (1967).

[103] Plut. *Vit. Aem.* 4.

men identified as Lusitanians. Lycho is generally placed near Castulo on the upper Baetis.[104] The Lusitanians may have just been raiders, but they may also have been assisting groups to the southeast in the face of the common Roman enemy. Aemilius Paullus went on to avenge his defeat and obtain the submission of two hundred and fifty oppida. Most of these oppida must be placed in the Andalusia area southeast of the river.[105]

An inscription from Lascuta near Hasta, just east of the mouth of the Baetis, seems to relate to this campaign.[106] Aemilius, the probable author of the decree, is described as *impeirator*. He issued the document *in castreis*, implying that a military campaign was in progress. The text refers to the granting of freedom, land, and an oppidum to the *Hastensium servei in Turri Lascutana*.

The inscription is unique for that period, and the lack of parallels or even a clearer context makes interpretation risky.[107] Nevertheless, a few inferences can be made about Hasta and its probable role in the campaigns. Located between the Baetis and the Guadalete rivers, midway between the coast and the hill country, Hasta was in a good position to mediate between the Punicized coast and the Iberian interior. It had a long pre-Roman history. Occupation went back to the Bronze Age, and Attic red-figure pottery has been found there. During the Punic period Hasta remained important. It has even been suggested that it was the center of one of the native monarchies developing the area.[108] The Lascuta inscription would seem to confirm this picture of extensive territorial control. Lascuta, where the *Hastensium servei* were located, was about sixty kilometers east of Hasta. Hasta retained its importance under the Empire, when it became the meeting place of the *conventus* of Gades.[109]

Paullus may well have been attempting to reduce the power of Hasta by freeing dependents of the city. The people of Hasta continued to resist and turned elsewhere for help. In 186 B.C. the governor C. Atinius defeated an army of Lusitanians near Hasta and stormed the city itself.[110] The pattern of cooperation between obdurate oppida and warriors from the interior was repeating itself.

[104] Livy 37.46.7–9, 37.57.5–6.

[105] Plut. *Vit. Aem.* 4.2–3.

[106] *ILS* 15; E. Hübner (1869); A. Tovar (1974) pp. 55–56. Pliny *HN* 3.15 places Lascuta in the Gaditan *conventus*; Asta seems to be an older Turdetanian center with occupation going back to the third millennium B.C.: M. Guerrero (1969).

[107] E. Badian (1958) p. 122.

[108] M. Guerrero (1969) pp. 116–18.

[109] Strabo 3.2.2; K. Miller (1916) cols. 178–84; M. Guerrero (1969) p. 115; A. Tovar (1974) pp. 149–50.

[110] Livy 39.7.6–7, 39.21.2–6.

For several years the situation did not change markedly. Our limited sources suggest that governors in both Citerior and Ulterior were attempting to keep local hill tribes at bay and disrupt any coalitions that may have been developing in the interior.[111] Only with the appearance of major figures do we get a sense of developing frontier strategy. Two such people are Q. Fulvius Flaccus, who went out to Citerior in 182 B.C., and his successor Ti. Sempronius Gracchus.

It is clear that one purpose of the campaigns of Flaccus was breaking resistance in Celtiberia and assuring Roman access to the area.[112] Detailed reconstruction of his strategy is hindered by the lack of agreement on the location of some key places mentioned in the ancient authors. However, the location of others seems secure. One attack was directed against Carpetania, an area east of Toledo and west of Ercavica, the later Cabeza del Griego.[113] The goal here would presumably be to control the central Meseta and the headwaters of the Tagus and the Guadiana.

Another place mentioned is Contrebia, which is described as an *urbs*.[114] This was probably the same Contrebia that became an important road junction under the Empire. Not only did the main north-south road of eastern Iberia pass through Contrebia, but two roads to the coast branched out from there, one going to Saguntum and the other to Intibili. Its position was similar to that of Teruel on the modern road network of Spain. Roman control of Contrebia would both help assure north-south communication between the two provinces and assist in checking raiding down the river valleys to the east coast. Flaccus captured the center and inflicted a series of defeats on the Celtiberians, who then scattered *in vicos castellaque*. Flaccus used their former central place as his base as he reduced a number of the neighboring *castella*.[115]

While Flaccus was occupied with large moves on distant frontiers, problems created by groups closer to the center of Roman control also continued to plague him. The Lusones on the middle Ebro revolted.[116] That uprising was suppressed, but it was not the end of the unrest. As Flaccus returned to Tarraco at the end of his governorship, rebellious natives ambushed his army in the *saltus Manlianus* not far south

[111] Livy 39.7.7, 39.21.6–10, 39.29.4–7, 39.30.1–8, 39.31.1–18, 39.42.1, 39.56.1–3, 40.1.4; A. Degrassi (1947) p. 554; P. Bosch-Gimpera and P. Aguado Bleye (1962) pp. 69–71.
[112] P. Bosch-Gimpera and P. Aguado Bleye (1962).
[113] Livy 40.30.
[114] Livy 40.33; K. Miller (1916) cols. 174–76.
[115] Livy 40.33.
[116] Diod. 29.28; App. *Hisp.* 42.

of the Ebro. Only with difficulty did he extricate his army.[117] He
emerged victorious, but the problems of land-hunger and banditry
that had helped spur the revolts remained. His successor, Gracchus,
described the province as having *paucae civitates . . . quas vicina maxime
hiberna premebant, in ius dicionemque venerunt; ulteriores in armis sunt.*
Meanwhile Flaccus, defending his accomplishments, had to admit that
it was a situation with *pacatos barbaros nondum satis adsuetos imperio.*[118]

No figure played a greater role in creating the Roman frontier in
Iberia than Ti. Sempronius Gracchus.[119] When he arrived in Citerior,
three frontier problems faced him as governor. The central part of the
peninsula needed to be pacified, as did the northeastern part of Ulterior. The main hill forts of the central Ebro had to be brought into
more secure relations with Rome. Finally, the underlying causes of
banditry and unrest in the fringe areas of Roman control needed to be
addressed. Gracchus made progress in all three areas.[120]

Evidence of Gracchus' campaigns to the south is clear, though some
of the details of geography are uncertain. One known location is Ercavica (Cabeza del Griego), which places some of the fighting in the
Meseta area. Gracchus' object was to break newly reformed tribal coalitions. Fortunately, the sources are sufficiently full to allow us to
understand some of the means he used to ensure long-term frontier
peace. In the attack on Alce, the Romans captured the two sons and
a daughter of a man named Thurrus. He *regulus hic earum gentium erat,
longe potentissimus omnium Hispanorum.* Gracchus, in a gesture that recalls Scipio the Elder, received Thurrus under truce and promised to
spare him and his family. The action secured Thurrus' loyalty to Rome.
In the words of Livy, he *secutus est inde Romanos, fortique ac fideli opera
multis locis rem Romanam adiuvit.*[121] The Romans had recruited a client
king who could secure the north-central frontier of Hispania Ulterior.
Similar thinking was evident when the Romans took Certima. As part
of the surrender terms there, the Romans required the military service
of forty of the *nobilissimi equites* of the community *nec obsidum nomine
nam militare iussi sunt et tamen re ipsa ut pignus fidei essent.*[122]

Gracchus took other steps to assure local loyalty. An inscription
recently found at Iliturgi claims a Gracchan origin for the town.[123] It

---

[117] Livy 40.39–40.
[118] Livy 40.35.13–40.36.2.
[119] P. Bosch-Gimpera and P. Aguado Bleye (1962) pp. 75–78.
[120] P. Bosch-Gimpera and P. Aguado Bleye (1962) p. 77.
[121] Livy 40.49.4–7.
[122] Livy 40.47.1–10.
[123] A. Blanco and G. Lachica (1960); A. D'Ors (1971) p. 256; R. C. Knapp (1977) pp.
109–11; R. Wiegels (1982).

was possibly, like Gracchuris founded in the Ebro, designed to provide foci of Roman support to the area. Another testimony to his effort
to assure loyalty is the network of inscriptions bearing the Sempronian
family name. A number have been found in the sites of the frontier
region of Ulterior just south of the Baetis and around the key Meseta
community of Ercavica.[124] The result of these actions was relative
frontier peace in Ulterior for two decades.

Similarly bold steps were taken by Gracchus in the middle and
upper Ebro valley. His forces captured one hundred and fifty *urbes* or
oppida.[125] Again, military action was combined with the careful cultivation of client networks. Treaties were established with such groups
as the Arevaci, Belli, and Titthi and with centers like Numantia and
Segeda. The equity of these treaties became proverbial. The chief
provisions seem to have been to supply auxiliaries and grain to the
Roman forces.[126] Military service was a means of integrating natives
into the Roman system, putting the Celtiberian warriors to use for,
rather than against, Rome and reducing the need of the provinces for
outside aid. The supply of grain helped make the provincial garrisons
self-sufficient and encouraged a more settled, agriculturally based life.
A similar approach can be observed in Sardinia and was presumably
also applied in Liguria.

Community development was part of Gracchus' plan. The town of
Gracchuris was established on the Ebro at the point where river breaks
out of the mountains.[127] Its population was most likely drawn from
friendly natives, who would provide a watch on the surrounding hills
and establish a market to draw neighboring natives into the developing
Roman frontier economic system. Another settlement named Sem-
proniana is mentioned on the road itinerary from Barcelona to Ge-
rona.[128] It is probably of Gracchan origin and served to bring together
people from the hills and the coastal zone. Evidence of more personal
loyalties is the concentration of Sempronian names in the area of the
middle and upper Ebro valley and its tributaries.[129]

One action of Gracchus that would seem to run counter to the policy of developing communities is the supposed provision placed in the

[124] S. L. Dyson (1980–81).

[125] Florus 1.33.9–10. Strabo 3.4.13 says Polybius gave the number as three hundred.
Poseidonius, however, regarded many of those as not real towns.

[126] Plut. *Vit. Ti. Gracch.* 5.3; App. *Hisp.* 44.

[127] Livy *Per.* 41; Pliny *HN* 3.24; K. Miller (1916) col. 174; P. Bosch-Gimpera and
P. Aguado Bleye (1962) pp. 77, 297; R. C. Knapp (1977) pp. 18–19.

[128] K. Miller (1916) col. 182.

[129] S. L. Dyson (1980–81) pp. 263–66.

Gracchan treaties that prohibited the foundation of new cities.[130] I believe, however, that this clause was aimed at the establishment of fortified hill forts. After storming so many of these, Gracchus could appreciate how they hindered the development of effective administration and a Roman way of life. They were quite different from the more Mediterranean communities whose growth he encouraged.

Gracchus also had to deal with problems of revolt and rising social discontent. His treatment of Complega was typical. Part of the community rose against the Romans and attempted to ambush their army. The uprising was crushed, and the instigators were harshly punished. Gracchus tried to address the underlying causes of unrest. Banditry around Complega arose in part from social inequalities and a shortage of land. After the revolt, he "gave a position in the community to the poorer classes and apportioned land to them."[131]

Gracchus returned to Rome in 178 B.C. to celebrate the triumph *de Celtibereis Hispaneisque* that he so richly deserved.[132] In many parts of Citerior, though, his peace was more illusionary than he thought. His successoor, M. Titinius Curvus, became engaged in heavy fighting and also celebrated a triumph.[133] In turn, Curvus' successor, Appius Claudius Centho, faced another Celtiberian uprising and won an *ovatio* for his victories.[134] Only at this point did a lasting peace begin.

The tightening Roman administrative hold, another legacy of Gracchus, presented its own problems. Military service and forced grain tributes led to official abuses. During the late 170s Spanish delegations appeared in Rome complaining about the malfeasance of Roman officials. A series of extortion trials for governors of Citerior followed. The use of Roman procedures to deal with these problems shows the emergence in the Iberian provinces of a more sophisticated native class that was aware of its rights and sought redress not through the sword but through the use of Roman legal processes.[135]

Another sign of acculturation was the appearance in Rome of a group of Iberians who were the progeny of liaisons between Roman soldiers and native women.[136] They represented a class often found in the history of imperialism. Products of two cultures, they are themselves outside both. The senate, sensing a potential source of unrest, allowed them to found their own community at Carteia. It was designated a

[130] Diod. 31.39; App. *Hisp.* 44; E. Badian (1958) pp. 122–24.

[131] App. *Hisp.* 43; R. C. Knapp (1977a) pp. 19, 46, 108.

[132] A. Degrassi (1947) p. 555.

[133] Livy 41.9.3–4, 41.15.11, 41.26.1, 43.2.6–7; A. Degrassi (1947) p. 555.

[134] Livy 41.26.1–5, 41.28.1–2; A. Degrassi (1947) p. 556.

[135] Livy 43.2.1–12; A. Balil (1955) p. 42.

[136] Livy 43.3; A.J.N. Wilson (1966) pp. 24–25; R. C. Knapp (1977a) pp. 116–20.

Latin colony and included freedmen and natives as well as people of
mixed background. This mingling of conqueror and conquered must
have been widespread in both Citerior and Ulterior, and certainly
helped create the highly Romanized society of the peninsula that
emerged by the late Republic.

A generation of relative peace now began on all frontiers. The word
relative should be stressed; it can be assumed that the Iberian frontier,
like any other border zone, was the scene of constant raiding and
skirmishing. But several characteristics of this zone promoted a certain
calm. The prolonged and bloody wars had exhausted the natives, and
large numbers of Celtiberian warriors had been slain or carried off
into captivity. The Romans had also learned to deal with many of the
social, economic, and administrative problems that had exacerbated
frontier tension in the past. Moreover the Gracchan treaties were acknowledged by both sides to be fair. The extortion trials and administrative reforms provided a warning to potentially venal officials.
Channels of communication were kept open between the increasingly
sophisticated natives and their patrons at Rome. Finally, the treaty
stipulations on grain and troops seem to have been lightly enforced.[137]
This benign neglect had short-term benefits, but created long-term
problems. Lapsed treaty obligations could be reimposed only at the
cost of considerable resentment. Meanwhile, agricultural development
was not being encouraged, and a surplus of warriors was collecting in
the Celtiberian oppida.

[137] App. *Hisp.* 44.

CHAPTER 6

THE POST-GRACCHAN
EXPERIENCE IN SPAIN

Dividing the Roman frontier experience in the Iberian peninsula into phases is a difficult task. In a sense, it was a single, seamless process. The governorship of Tiberius Sempronius Gracchus does, however, mark an important turning point. Not only did it start a generation of peace; it also brought fundamental change in the approach to provincial development and frontier management. The period from the Scipios to Gracchus had seen the establishment of a Roman frontier on the remains of its Greek and Punic predecessors. Some areas were conquered and some territory partly subjected, while large parts of the peninsula remained untouched. The wars that broke out after the Gracchan peace seemed to emerge from new forces that had grown out of the long history of the frontier and the cross-cultural contacts it produced. These involved not only the natives on both sides of the frontier but also the Romans who brought their growing internal political problems to the Iberian borders. The line led directly from Numantia and Viriathus to Sertorius and the Roman Civil Wars.

During the 150s war emerged on the frontiers of both provinces. For convenience, Hispania Citerior will be considered first. There the Romans were concerned about the concentration of power in an oppidum of the Belli named Segeda, located on the Rio Jiloca southeast of the river Jalón.[1] The Segedans had been forcing their neighbors to resettle within the confines of their oppidum and were starting to refortify the newly enlarged center. Those resettled included not only small local groups but also elements of the larger tribe of the Titthi. Fortification of new oppida was expressly prohibited by the Gracchan treaties, although old centers could be strengthened. Segeda was located in a strategic position that threatened the southern banks of the Ebro. A concentration of population there would upset the balance of power along the border. Moreover, the Segedans were not acting alone. Reports reached Rome that the Segedans were forming alliances with such major centers as Numantia.

The senate reacted quickly to the growth of Segedan power and pretension. A delegation was sent to investigate. One result was the

[1] Diod. 31.39 App. *Hisp.* 44; A. Schulten (1914) pp. 139-40.

decision to reinforce the provisions of the Gracchan treaties. To underline its seriousness, the senate dispatched the consul of 153 B.C., Q. Fulvius Nobilior, to bring the Segedans into line.[2] The natives, faced with an approaching consular army and an oppidum whose fortifications were still incomplete, fled to the neighboring center of Numantia.

With that action, Numantia assumed its position as the center of a new round of Celtiberian wars. Subsequent events made that hill fort into a symbol of native resistance to Roman imperialism and to a certain degree a symbol of Spanish nationalism.[3] Excavations undertaken by Adolph Schulten early in this century have made possible an archaeological reconstruction of some of its history.[4] Many of the remains discovered by Schulten, however, dated to the postdestruction Roman rebuilding, and only recently has a clearer picture of Celtiberian Numantia begun to emerge.[5] The oppidum is located southwest of the Ebro at a point where river plain gives way to mountain. It controlled a fertile agricultural area. In the period of the Empire, Numantia was on an important road linking the Ebro with the upper Duero. This road presumably followed Iron Age communication routes.[6] Numantia was the center for the large tribe of the Arevaci. Extensive cremation cemeteries have been found in the area.[7] Finds from the site show a Celtiberian population influenced by contacts with the Iberians near the coast.[8]

Nobilior quickly discovered how formidable his new opponents were. The Roman army was ambushed and mauled by the combined Segedan and Arevacian forces led by a Segedan named Carus. Nobilior's attempt to storm Numantia failed, as did his effort to destroy the supplies of the Celtiberians at a place called Axinium.[9] Moreover, the rebellion spread to areas southeast of the Ebro. The town of Ocilis on the upper Jalón deserted the Roman cause, and the Nertobriges on the lower Jalón joined the rebellion. The route to Hispania Ulterior through the *saltus Manlianus* was now in enemy hands. Nobilior fell

---

[2] Polyb. 35.1; Diod. 31.41; App. *Hisp.* 45; T.R.S. Broughton (1951) p. 452; H. Simon (1962) pp. 18–20.

[3] App. *Hisp.* 45–46; J. Caro Baroja (1968) pp. 28–30.

[4] A. Schulten (1914), (1929).

[5] F. Wattenberg (1963).

[6] K. Miller (1916) col. 157.

[7] L. Pericot Garcia (1952) pp. 263–66.

[8] F. Wattenberg (1963) pp. 27–31.

[9] App. *Hisp.* 45–47; A. Schulten (1917) pp. 336–45; H. Simon (1962) pp. 25–30; H. J. Hildebrandt (1979) pp. 240–45, 265.

back to his winter camp at Renieblas (near Numantia) and waited in misery for his successor.[10]

The senate appreciated the gravity of the situation. Such coordinated activity among the hill-fort inhabitants on the borders of the Roman territory always spelled deep trouble. Another consul was sent out in 152 B.C. He was M. Claudius Marcellus, one of the most distinguished frontier fighters of the era. As praetor he had served in Spain, and as consul in cisalpine Gaul and Liguria.[11] In Citerior his military and diplomatic skills quickly transformed the situation. Roman control was reestablished in the Jalón valley. Ocilis and the Nertobriges returned to the Roman fold. The favorable terms granted to the Nertobriges were made conditional on the surrender of the Arevaci, Belli, and Titthi. They agreed, asking for the restoration of the Gracchan treaties. Marcellus took hostages and referred his peace conditions to the senate at Rome.[12] He then joined the governor of Ulterior, M. Atilius Serranus, in campaigning against the Lusitanians. His successful campaign year ended with a pleasant winter stay in Corduba, where he was lionized by the Romano-Hispanic population. It was a stark contrast to the bitter winter camp of Nobilior the year before.[13]

Meanwhile, the debate at Rome on the actions of Marcellus had unleashed all the forces that were involved in any frontier decision. Among the Iberian delegations that went to Rome were those elements of the Belli and Titthi who had remained loyal to the Roman cause. They had suffered heavily for their fidelity and wanted strong measures taken against the rebels, and especially against the Arevaci, whom they saw as the main cause of their troubles. The Arevaci countered by asking for the restoration of the Gracchan treaties with only a moderate penalty attached.[14]

The senate was divided. Marcellus himself advocated leniency. He understood the importance of an enduring frontier peace based on compromise. Others in the senate wanted harsher terms and a punitive war against the Arevaci. They felt that the interests of loyal allies must be better protected. Under the lenient terms of restored Gracchan

[10] App. *Hisp.* 47; P. Bosch-Gimpera and P. Aguado Bley (1962) pp. 103–4; H. Simon (1962) p. 267.

[11] A. Schulten (1914) p. 345; T.R.S. Broughton (1951) pp. 424, 437, 448, 453.

[12] App. *Hisp.* 48; A. Schulten (1914) pp. 347–49.

[13] Polyb. 35.2.1-3; Strabo 3.2.1; C. Sánchez Albornoz (1949) p. 13 n. 38; A.J.N. Wilson (1966) pp. 16–17.

[14] Polyb. 35.2.3–15; App. *Hisp.* 49; R. C. Knapp (1977a) p. 52.

treaties, the Arevaci would be free to extend their power.[15] In the end the hard-liners won, and the senate decided that the Arevaci were to be punished. Marcellus, on receiving these orders, moved against Numantia and imposed a new peace on the city. The terms included a levy of six hundred talents, an enormous sum that indicates the growing wealth of the Arevaci. His successor, L. Licinius Lucullus, found Numantia again subdued.[16]

Problems arose for Lucullus even before he got to Spain. Heavy casualties and limited rewards meant that enthusiasm for service on the Celtiberian frontier was rapidly declining. The consuls had to push hard to raise the necessary levy of troops. The tribunes responded by jailing them. The crisis was partly resolved when the young P. Cornelius Scipio Aemilianus volunteered to join the force of Lucullus.[17] The presence of the younger Scipio ensured that the war would be among the best recorded of the period.[18] The actions of Lucullus and the hostility of his political enemies at Rome and in the field meant that the accounts would be mostly negative. This hostile tradition makes it difficult to judge the motives behind his actions and the results.[19]

The mandate of Lucullus had been to crush the Arevaci. When he reached Citerior he found Numantia pacified. He could have either spent his time in actions of consolidation and local pacification or started new campaigns. He chose the latter and moved west. *Vaccaeos et Cantabros et alias incognitas adhuc in Hispania gentes subegit* is how Livy summarizes his actions.[20] The centers that figure prominently in his campaign allow us to locate more precisely his objectives. These were Cauca on the Eresma River, a tributary that flows northwest into the upper Duero; Intercatia on the Araduey, another tributary of the Duero; and Pallantia, the modern Palencia on the Carrión.

All of these communities apparently belonged to the tribe of the Vaccaei, a group that controlled a rich territory located at a pivotal point in the Iberian peninsula.[21] They had aided the Numantines to

---

[15] Polyb. 35.3.1–9; App. *Hisp.* 49; A. Astin (1976) p. 38–41; H. Scullard (1973) pp. 233–34.

[16] Strabo 3.4.13; App. *Hisp.* 50; H. Simon (1962) pp. 44–45; A. Astin (1967b) pp. 41–42.

[17] Polyb. 35.4.1–14; Livy *Per.* 48; E. Astin (1967b) pp. 42–46; W. V. Harris (1979) pp. 36–37.

[18] Polyb. 35.5.1; Val. Max. 3.2.6; Livy *Per.* 48; Pliny HN 37.9; Florus 1.33.11–12; Oros. 4.21.1–2.

[19] App. *Hisp.* 51; A. Schulten (1914) pp. 143–44; H. Simon (1962) pp. 46–56; W. V. Harris (1979) pp. 76–77.

[20] Livy *Per.* 48.

[21] A. Molinero Pérez (1951); F. Wattenberg (1959) pp. 20–24.

their east and were raiding into Carpetania to the southeast.[22] They also controlled access to the upper Duero from the west and the northwest. Their combined agricultural and pastoral way of life gave them a good resource base. No Roman commander could hope for peace on the frontier without that tribe subdued. This was especially true if they threatened to join the expanding Arevacian alliance system.

These strategic considerations are often overlooked in discussions of the campaigns of Lucullus. His actions were not particularly honorable, but they made strategic sense. He first moved against Cauca, whose inhabitants had been accused of attacking Roman-held territory in Carpetania. A surrender was negotiated, but then Lucullus turned against the suppliants and massacred many of them. Some escaped and were later restored to their home community by Scipio Aemilianus.[23] Lucullus' action, which happened at almost the same time as the massacre of a group of Lusitanians by Ser. Sulpicius Galba in Ulterior, shows a growing brutality on the part of Roman commanders, no doubt an outgrowth of the grim frontier wars in which they were engaged. From Cauca Lucullus turned northwest to Intercatia. That community surrendered and granted hostages.[24] An attack on Pallantia failed. On the whole, Lucullus, despite the furor that attended some of his actions, can be said to have succeeded. The Vaccaei had been taught to respect Roman power, and the growth of the Arevacian alliance system had been quelled. The Ebro frontier was to remain at peace for seven years.

New frontier problems were developing in Hispania Ulterior, beginning in 155 B.C. with the Lusitanian attacks.[25] In the following year the army of the governor L. Calpurnius Piso was defeated and suffered heavy losses. The Roman defenses collapsed, while Lusitanian raiders, joined by elements of the Vettones from the upper Tagus area, swept down to the coast. Especially hard hit was a coastal group called the Blastophoenicians, who had been brought over from North Africa by Hannibal.[26]

As with other Lusitanian raids, these attacks were apparently more complicated than a simple tribal looting expedition. The man held responsible was a certain Punicus.[27] He was killed early in the fighting

[22] App. *Hisp.* 51.

[23] App. *Hisp.* 51–52; A. Schulten (1914) pp. 342–50; A. E. Astin (1967) pp. 46–47; R. C. Knapp (1977a) p. 39.

[24] Livy *Per.* 48; App. *Hisp.* 53–55. The tribute imposed on the tribe included ten thousand cloaks and suggests the considerable wool-producing capacity of the group.

[25] App. *Hisp.* 56.

[26] Livy *Per.* 47; App. *Hisp.* 56.

[27] App. *Hisp.* 56; A. García Bellido (1945) pp. 47–59; S. L. Dyson (1975) pp. 148–49.

and little is known about him, but the name is suggestive. He appears to have been a native who was partly acculturated to the Punic-influenced groups of the coast. Although his political role is uncertain, he had elements of a charismatic leader who may have been part bandit and part tribal leader. His appearance and that of subsequent figures like Caesarus and Viriathus show that there were important social and political changes taking place in the frontier. These will be considered in greater detail during the discussion of Viriathus.

Punicus was succeeded by Caesarus, and the attacks continued. Captured Roman standards were paraded through Celtiberia, which helped to stimulate other revolts.[28] Lusitanians from beyond the Tagus raided the rich coastal tribe of the Cunei, capturing their important center at Conistorgis. They even crossed over to Africa and seized a son of Massinissa.[29] Finally the Roman governor, L. Mummius, caught up with the raiders and defeated them. Mummius returned to Rome for a triumph, but the wars still continued.[30]

It proved impossible to ensure stability in Lusitania with indirect means of border control. Punitive raids and even conquest were the only solutions. The next governor, M. Atilius Serranus, attacked the Vettones and captured the oppidum of Oxthracae.[31] This did not stem the raids, however. The successor of Serranus, Servius Sulpicius Galba, had to repulse a Lusitanian invasion on the middle Baetis. In the pursuit of the invaders, his army as ambushed.[32] The failures of frontier control evoked a certain restlessness among groups that had long been loyal. During this period a revolt of the Turduli had to be suppressed.[33]

Geography favored the Lusitanians. Their own terrain was rugged, and they could attack outward from a variety of directions along a long, exposed frontier. A combined operation was organized for 150 B.C. L. Licinius Lucullus of Citerior, who had wintered on the Baetis frontier, attacked Lusitania from above Corduba. Galba moved up the valley of the Guadiana into the heartland of Lusitania.[34] Threatened from two fronts, the Lusitanians asked Galba for terms.

The Lusitanians involved had surrendered to Serranus the previous

[28] Diod. 31.42; App. *Hisp.* 56–57; *CIL* 1. 546; J. M. Ramos y Loscertales (1942) pp. 319–20, 323 for name Caisaros.
[29] App. *Hisp.* 57; A. Tovar (1976) pp. 193–94, 209.
[30] App. *Hisp.* 57; A. Degrassi (1947) p. 557. After his capture of Corinth, Mummius sent some of the spoils of the city to Italica: *CIL* 2. 1119.
[31] App. *Hisp.* 58; A. Tovar (1976) p. 272.
[32] Livy *Per.* 48; App. *Hisp.* 58; Oros. 4.21.3.
[33] Florus 1.33.11.
[34] App. *Hisp.* 59.

year, but they claimed that their inherent poverty had forced them to resume raiding. From the perspective of their poor and overpopulated mountains, the rich settlements of the plain appeared as too tempting a target. Galba promised to resettle the natives, using an approach employed successfully in Liguria. The Lusitanians agreed, assembled, and were disarmed. Then the Romans attacked. Those who were not massacred were sold into slavery. One of the few who escaped was a young man named Viriathus, and the experience was to drive him to wars of revenge that would enflame the frontier for many years.[35]

The actions of Galba recalled the massacre of the Cauci perpetrated by Lucullus shortly before, and revived memories of the atrocities of Popillius Laenas in Liguria. It is true that the Lusitanians had violated their previous agreements with the Romans. Unlike the Statielli of Liguria, they were not completely innocent victims. Nevertheless, they had placed themselves in the *fides* of the Roman people. Politicians at Rome took up their cause. The tribune L. Scribonius Libo demanded the freedom of the Lusitanians and the condemnation of Galba. More important figures became involved. The aged Cato lent his *auctoritas* to the prosecution of Galba.[36] He was joined by L. Cornelius Cethegus and presumably others. The only known defender of Galba was Q. Fulvius Nobilior.[37] The division is interesting. Cato represented the old order of Roman imperial policy and a previous generation of Spanish experience. The Cornelii had a wide range of interests in the peninsula. Nobilior was a recent veteran of the Iberian frontier.

Since Galba was a famous speaker, the trial assumed an important place in the history of Roman rhetoric.[38] Unfortunately, only two points of his defense are preserved. One was his emotional appeal to the court that was regarded as a turning point in the decorum with which Roman trials were conducted. The other was a specific defense argument. Galba claimed that the Lusitanians had performed rituals, including the sacrifice of a man and a horse, that indicated they were about to take to the warpath. He had therefore been forced to undertake a preemptive attack.[39] Whatever his motives may have been, Galba appears to have made a correct ethnographic observation. It shows the sensitive use of intelligence concerning native activities by Roman

[35] Suet. *Galba* 3.2; App. *Hisp.* 60; Oros. 4.21.10.

[36] Cic. *Brut.* 89; Livy 39.40.12, *Per.* 49; Val. Max. 9.6.2; Gell. *NA* 13.25.15; App. *Hisp.* 60; N. Scivoletto (1961); E. S. Gruen (1968) pp. 12–16; F. della Corte (1969) pp. 119–21; A. E. Astin (1978) pp. 111–13.

[37] A. E. Astin (1978) p. 112.

[38] Cic. *De Or.* 1.227–29, 2.263, *Brut.* 80, 89-94; Val. Max. 8.1.2, 9.6.2.

[39] Livy *Per.* 49.

commanders.[40] Galba was acquitted and went on to become consul in
144 B.C.[41]

The deeds of Galba have been generally condemned, and the ac-
quittal has been regarded as a milestone in the moral decline of the
Republican government.[42] Viriathus appears almost as a *deus ex ma-
china* punishing the Romans for their atrocities and revealing the futil-
ity of an immoral frontier policy. Galba, however, had been placed in
a dilemma. The Lusitanian raids were having a disastrous effect on
his province. These natives had violated their *fides* shortly before, and
they would quite possibly do it again. Poverty and overpopulation
would continuously drive them to new attacks. Resettlement might
work, but suitable land had to be found in an apparently densely
populated area. Release of the enslaved natives as proposed by the
tribune Libo would only make matters worse. The Lusitanians, em-
bittered, still landless, and now more familiar with the ways of Rome,
would swell the bands of potential brigands on the frontier. In perspective, Galba may be seen as a shrewd if immoral practitioner of
frontier warfare. He knew the storm his actions would raise, but his
bloody solution may have appeared to many as the best available in
the bloody *Realpolitik* of the Lusitanian Wars.

One consequence of the actions of Galba was the appearance of the
vengeful bandit leader, Viriathus, on the Lusitanian frontier. Viriathus has assumed many guises in ancient and modern literature from
protonationalistic leader to romantic bandit figure.[43] More is known
now about the social and economic roots of banditry, and it is possible
to place Viriathus in a more realistic context.[44] First, it is necessary to
reconstruct as much as possible of the milieu in which he developed
and operated. The scattered ancient evidence makes this no easy task.
The fragments can be pieced together, however, to provide at least a
general outline.

Diodorus Siculus, writing in the first century B.C., gives the following description of the customs of the Lusitanians:

ἴδιον δέ τι παρὰ τοῖς Ἴβηρσι καὶ μάλιστα παρὰ τοῖς Λυ-
σιτανοῖς ἐπιτηδεύεται· τῶν γὰρ ἀκμαζόντων ταῖς ἡλικίαις
οἱ μάλιστα ἀπορώτατοι ταῖς οὐσίαις, ῥώμῃ δὲ σώματος καὶ
θράσει διαφέροντες, ἐφοδιάσαντες αὐτοὺς ἀλκῇ καὶ τοῖς
ὅπλοις εἰς τὰς ὀρεινὰς δυσχωρίας ἀθροίζονται,

[40] Strabo 3.3.6.
[41] Val. Max. 6.4.2; A. E. Astin (1967b) pp. 104–5.
[42] E. S. Gruen (1968) pp. 12–15.
[43] A. Schulten (1917); H. G. Gundel (1970) pp. 122–23; *R. E.* 2 R 176, 203–30.
[44] S. L. Dyson (1975) pp. 148–50.

συστήματα δὲ ποιήσαντες ἀξιόλογα κατατρέχουσι τὴν Ἰβηρίαν καὶ ληστεύοντες πλούτους ἀθροίζουσι.[45]

One special custom is followed among the Iberians and especially among the Lusitanians: among those who are at the prime of life, those poorest in property, but outstanding in strength and courage, furnish themselves with weapons and resources, gather in the harsh mountain regions, and forming quite significant bands they overrun Iberia and collect wealth by plundering.

This poverty of the land was a theme stressed often by the ancients in describing Lusitania. The area had its fertile parts, however. Polybius says of these parts

αὐτόθι διὰ τὴν τοῦ ἀέρος εὐκρασίαν καὶ τὰ ζῷα πολύγονα καὶ οἱ ἄνθρωποι, καὶ οἱ ἐν τῇ χώρᾳ καρποὶ οὐδέποτε φθείρονται.[46]

Because of the mild climate, both beasts and men are prolific, and the fruits in the field never spoil.

These fertile areas could only prosper if their safety was assured. Strabo describes the problem well:

οἱ δὲ ἀμυνόμενοι τούτους ἄκυροι τῶν ἰδίων ἔργων καθίσταντο ἐξ ἀνάγκης, ὥστ᾽ ἀντὶ τοῦ γεωργεῖν ἐπολέμουν καὶ οὗτοι, καὶ συνέβαινε τὴν χώραν ἀμελουμένην στεῖραν οὖσαν τῶν ἐμφύτων ἀγαθῶν οἰκεῖσθαι ὑπὸ ληστῶν.[47]

They, in turn, defending themselves against them, were of necessity without control over their own activities, so that instead of farming they too engage in warfare, and the untended region, barren of its native resources, came to be inhabited by bandits.

The result was the banditry that long plagued the Lusitanian frontier.

Compounding the problem was the widespread distribution of a pastoral economy.[48] Flocks moved between contiguous upland and lowland zones. The herdsmen were often tough and rootless men who knew both plain and mountain but had no real attachment to either. Viriathus began as a herdsman. His easy transition *ex pastore venator, ex venatore latro* must have been duplicated many times on the Lusitanian frontier.[49]

---

[45] Diod. 5.34.6–7; A. García y Bellido (1945) pp. 18–19, 25–27.
[46] Polyb. 34.8.4
[47] Strabo 3.3.5
[48] J. Caro Baroja (1970).
[49] Livy *Per.* 52; A. García y Bellido (1945) p. 12.

Other men wanted to seek freedom beyond the reach of Roman control. Mining operators had brought large numbers of slaves into the mountains and worked them under brutal conditions.[50] Escape into banditry must have been possible for some of them. The large estates required labor for both crops and herds. Slaves and poor free workers were employed, and they too would form a fertile recruiting ground for the bandit groups.[51]

The sources are too scanty to provide any real insight into the social origins of the men who fought with Viriathus. Viriathus himself came from Oxthracae and was presumably a regular, tribalized Lusitanian until the massacre of Galba destroyed most of his community. At that point, he became a rootless bandit operating in the no man's land of the Baetis frontier. Sources convey the impression that his followers were an equally alienated lot drawn from diverse areas of Lusitania and Celtiberia, and held together by common dangers and the charisma of Viriathus.

Viriathus in many respects fits the classic pattern of the bandit. The English social historian E. J. Hobsbawn describes the preconditions for what he calls "social banditry":

> It is universally found wherever societies are based on agriculture (including pastoral economies) and consist largely of peasants and landless laborers ruled, oppressed and exploited by someone else— lords, governments, lawyers and even banks.[52]

Many of these preconditions fit nicely into the world of second-century B.C. Lusitania. Other elements in Hobsbawn's paradigm also suit Viriathus. Bandits normally come from the mobile margins of society and appear in times of crisis and change.[53] They are men of action and not ideology.[54] Most begin their careers after some affair of honor or injustice, and treachery usually plays a part in their death.[55] They survive partly by blending into the local society and partly by working out compromises with the local authorities and power brokers who are willing to deal with them in order to keep banditry at an acceptable level.[56]

Hobsbawn, as a Marxist, is interested in the social role of the bandit

[50] Strabo 3.2.10 notes that Polybius estimated that forty thousand men were working the mines of Carthago Nova alone.

[51] For a similar situation in colonial Mexico see P. Powell (1952) p. 62.

[52] E. J. Hobsbawm (1969) p. 15.

[53] E. J. Hobsbawm (1969) pp. 17, 25–30.

[54] E. J. Hobsbawm (1969) pp. 19–20.

[55] E. J. Hobsbawm (1969) pp. 36, 42.

[56] E. J. Hobsbawm (1969) pp. 79–83.

within traditional European society. He argues that the social bandit as he appeared in places like nineteenth-century Italy was closely linked with the peasants. "It would be unthinkable for a social bandit to snatch the peasant's (though not the lord's) harvest in his own territory or perhaps even elsewhere."[57] In other areas, however, such as among the Haduks of the Balkans, the bandit groups became more autonomous, tending to separate themselves from the peasantry.[58]

The evidence suggests that the Lusitanian bandits, and especially the followers of Viriathus, were closer to the more autonomous type. Viriathus' sense of fairness as an individual and a leader was proverbial. This was necessary if he was to remain a successful bandit captain. There is no evidence that he showed any sympathy for the average Iberian tribesman who lived in the Roman sector. He extorted money from the farmers along the frontier with the threat of destroying their crops, and he rustled cattle from places like Segobriga.[59] His main compromises were with the rich and the powerful, and he even linked himself by marriage to one of the wealthy Roman clients of the frontier. One feels that to the unfortunate small farmers and herdsmen caught between the brigands of Viriathus and the soldiers of Rome, the idea of social banditry would have seemed as strange as that of benevolent imperialism.

Several years elapsed before Viriathus appeared as a full-fledged threat to Rome. Then in 147 B.C. he organized the ambush of the praetor C. Vetilius, which launched his career as bandit leader.[60] His main center of activity was Carpetania and the districts of the upper Baetis. Here his bands found rich spoils, more native cooperation, and escape routes into the mountains. By raiding over the borders of both provinces, he could exploit jurisdictional differences between the two governors. Faced with this clever bandit, the Roman commanders proved singularly ineffective. In 146 B.C. C. Plautius, the governor of Ulterior, pursued him into the interior but was ambushed and defeated near the Tagus. His colleague, Claudius Unimanus from Hispania Citerior, fared no better.[61]

The attention of Rome in 146 B.C. was focused on the campaigns that culminated in the destruction of Carthage and Corinth. With those tasks completed, the senate could turn to the deteriorating situation in Iberia. The statement *tantumque terroris is hostis intulit ut adversus eum*

---

[57] E. J. Hobsbawm (1969) p. 14.

[58] E. J. Hobsbawm (1969) pp. 61–71.

[59] Frontin. *Str.* 3.10.6.

[60] App. *Hisp.* 61–63; Oros. 5.4.1.

[61] Florus 1.33.15–17; App. *Hisp.* 64; Oros. 5.4.2; E. S. Gruen (1968) p. 29; H. G. Gundel (1970) p. 127.

consulari opus esset et duce et exercitu sums up the concern at Rome.[62]
Q. Fabius Maximus Aemilianus, son of the Spanish veteran Aemilius
Paullus and brother of Scipio Aemilianus (the conqueror of Carthage),
was elected consul and sent to Ulterior.[63] Although he inherited his
father's network of connections in the peninsula, he had not held command in the area and in fact had no known frontier experience. Moreover, the regular army in Spain had been decimated and demoralized,
and Aemilianus was forced to bring with him fresh forces.

Viriathus was undaunted by the unseasoned commander. He crossed
the Baetis and moved into the hills east of the river. Near Osuna he
defeated the army of Aemilianus with its commander absent.[64] Aemilianus managed to score limited victories over the raiders of Viriathus during the next year, but his tenure could hardly be considered
a raging success.[65]

Meanwhile, ominous developments were emerging on the Ulterior
frontier that threatened to weaken permanently the Roman position.
During his first years, Viriathus had conducted hit-and-run raids. Now
he seems to have begun establishing permanent bases in the upper
Baetis region. For the first time, the sources mention cities (*poleis*) controlled by Viriathus. At least one Roman frontier magnate, Astolpas,
made his arrangements with Viriathus and married off his daughter
to the bandit.[66] Military deserters were evidently entering the bandit
bands in substantial numbers. They must have been joined by agri-
culturalists who could not till their fields in security, and by slaves
escaped from the mines. The retreat of the settled frontier so vividly
described by Strabo was under way.[67] Other bandit groups appear,
and their leaders bear names like Curius and Apuleius, which suggest
they were acculturated natives who had fled the Roman zone.[68]

The senate continued to send commanders who were unequal to the
task. The propraetor Q. Pompeius, who came in 143 B.C., was defeated by Viriathus and took refuge within Corduba. While he cow-
ered in the city, the bandits drove out the Roman garrison from Itucci
and ravaged the lands of the still pro-Roman elements among the Bastetani.[69] The only bright spot for the romans was the success of a

---

[62] Livy *Per.* 52.

[63] Vell. Pat. 2.5.3; Florus 1.33.17; App. *Hisp.* 65; A. E. Astin (1967b) pp. 99–103.

[64] App. *Hisp.* 65.

[65] App. *Hisp.* 65; A. E. Astin (1967b) pp. 106,142.

[66] Diod. 33.7.4; App. *Hisp.* 65. Not all the border natives deserted Rome. The warriors of Segovia did not waver in their pro-Roman loyalty even when Viriathus threatened to execute their wives and children: Frontin. *Str.* 4.5.22.

[67] Val. Max. 2.7.11; Frontin. *Str.* 4.1.42.

[68] App. *Hisp.* 68.

[69] App. *Hisp.* 66–67.

provincial force organized by C. Marcius of Italica, who used a knowledge of the area to inflict some setbacks on Viriathus.[70]

In 142 B.C. the consul Q. Fabius Maximus Servilianus was sent to Ulterior, and with his arrival the war against Viriathus took a decisive turn.[71] Strong measures were taken to restore morale to the army. These included cutting off the hands of deserters who were recaptured.[72] With confidence revived, Servilianus turned to his first task of stopping the development of a bandit zone in the hill country on the near side of the Baetis. More communities had gone over to Viriathus, and the process had to be reversed.[73] The Romans succeeded in retaking Itucci, but their advance was stopped nearby.[74] The ferocity of the fighting near Itucci shows the impressive forces that Viriathus commanded. His momentum, however, was checked, and he temporarily retreated into Lusitania.

Servilianus now began the pacification of other bandit strongholds in the area. Several centers were recaptured, and Servilianus felt secure enough to turn his attention to other frontier problems. Lusitanian groups had been raiding down the Guadiana and threatening the Cunei. These included the bandit armies of Apuleius, Curius, and Connoba. Servilianus turned against them in a series of bloody encounters and gradually pushed them back. References to mass executions, mutilations, and enslavements indicate the brutal thoroughness with which Servilianus waged war against these disruptive forces.[75]

Viriathus, however, had not lost his sense of tactical imagination, and in the end he succeeded in trapping the army of Servilianus in the rugged interior. The Roman general was forced to negotiate, and Viriathus, seeing the tide of fortune running against him, compromised.[76] He was declared an *amicus populi Romani*, and his followers received grants of land. At least some of the Viriathans were settled around the old Iberian center at Orso (modern Osuna) in the hill country of Andalusia, southeast of the Baetis.[77] The granting of land and a fixed place of settlement reflected lessons learned on other frontiers such as Liguria. The resettlement relieved population pressure in the

---

[70] App. *Hisp.* 66; A. Schulten (1917) p. 222. A.J.N. Wilson (1966) p. 25. n.3 suggests that Marcius was very likely a Roman veteran. This has a certain resemblance to the use of colonial troops from Placentia in the northeastern frontier of Italy.

[71] T.R.S. Broughton (1951) p. 474; A. E. Astin (1964).

[72] Diod. 33.1.4; Vell. Pat. 2.5.3; Val. Max. 2.7.11; Frontin. *Str.* 4.1.42; Florus 1.33.17.

[73] App. *Hisp.* 68.

[74] App. *Hisp.* 67–68.

[75] Livy *Per.* 53; App. *Hisp.* 68; Oros. 5.4.12.

[76] App. *Hisp.* 69.

[77] App. *Hisp.* 70. A. Tovar (1976) pp. 128–29.

Lusitanian mountains and placed the former bandits within the Roman domain, where their acculturation could be accelerated.

The agreement, though useful, was hardly consonant with Roman dignity. The senate did not openly reject it immediately, because they were facing serious recruiting problems for the Iberian wars. The friends and supporters of Servilianus were powerful enough to prevent the political humiliation given to other commanders who had worked with the enemy.[78] Fabius, however, received no official recognition for his accomplishments, even though his command represented a turning point in the Viriathan War. When he arrived in Spain the tide of frontier loyalties had been flowing against Rome; during his tenure the principal brigand bands had been destroyed and the bandit enclave in Andalusia eliminated. Viriathus had accepted the hegemony of Rome and settled on land with his followers within the Roman sphere.

The compromise agreement had hurt the *dignitas* of the *gens Serviliana*, as well as that of the senate, and it was not allowed to last. Q. Servilius Caepio, the brother of Servilianus and consul in 140 B.C., succeeded him in Hispania Ulterior. He gradually moved the senate in the direction of abrogating the agreement with Viriathus.[79] The Viriathan center at Orso was attacked, and Viriathus was forced to abandon Andalusia for the frontier of Carpetania. There he was harried by Caepio, who was joined by the consul of 139 B.C. M. Popillius Laenas. Viriathus was unable to raise sufficient forces and decided to negotiate with Laenas.[80]

At this point, three associates of Viriathus proposed to solve Rome's long-range frontier problems by offering to assassinate the bandit leader. Named Audax, Ditalco, and Minurus (or Nicorontes), they were described as close kinsmen and friends of Viriathus and inhabitants of Orso.[81] It can be presumed that few kinsmen of Viriathus had survived the massacre of Oxthracae. These men were possibly resettled relatives from Viriathus' marriage to the daughter of Astolpas, and represented old Roman frontier clients.

The proposal was enthusiastically received. Caepio and Laenas realized that true frontier peace would not be established as long as the legendary bandit and native charismatic leader was alive. Viriathus was murdered. It was not a noble moment in Roman history. But, like the kidnapping of the Gallic leader Bituitus a few years later, the

[78] Livy *Per.* 54; A. E. Astin (1967b) pp. 142–46.

[79] App. *Hisp.* 70.

[80] Livy *Per.* 54; App. *Hisp.* 70; T.R.S. Broughton (1951) p. 481; C. Cichorius (1908) p. 32.

[81] Diod. 33.21; Livy *Per.* 54; Val. Max. 9.6.4; App. *Hisp.* 74.

Roman commanders could have justified it on the grounds of military and political necessity.[82]

The bandit problem did not immediately disappear with the murder of Viriathus. A certain Tantalus was chosen his successor. After a spectacular raid toward Saguntum, he and his band were run to ground and forced to surrender. Caepio disarmed them and gave them land "so that they would not be driven to robbery by want."[83] Once again, military action was combined with social engineering. Caepio's successor, Decimus Junius Brutus, continued this process. Livy states that he *agros et oppidum dedit*.[84] More than one oppidum may have been involved. A center called Brutobriga is known from the Baetis area, and Brutus would seem to be its logical founder.[85] More important may have been his role in the foundation of Valentia.[86]

Livy clearly identified Brutus with the establishment of a Valentia. There are three Valencias in modern Spain, however, and the historian must decide which is to be associated with Brutus. One of these, Valencia de Minho, is post-classical and easily eliminated.[87] The second, Valencia de Alcántara, was located on the upper Guadiana. This would seem an inappropriate place for a settlement of recently reformed bandits in 138 B.C.[88] The land was not desirable and the Lusitanians would be close to their old homeland. They could easily revert to their old raiding habits if conditions became difficult.

Valencia del Cid on the southeastern coast of Spain seems a more likely location for the new community.[89] The center was surrounded by a rich coastal plain. The Lusitanians would be settled well within the frontier in the midst of Romanized natives. Parallels to the movement of Ligurians to southern Italy are obvious. Moreover, a small cluster of inscriptions with the Junian nomen have been found around Valencia del Cid while none have come to light near Valencia de Alcántara.[90]

An argument against identifying the Valentia in Livy with Valencia del Cid is that the archaeological investigations there have produced a

[82] According to Livy *Per.* 55, *P. Scipione D. Iunio coss interfectores Viriathi urbe pulsi sunt praemium negatum.* A. Schulten (1917) p. 227.

[83] App. *Hisp.* 75.

[84] Livy *Per.* 55; Diod. 33.1.3.

[85] Steph. Byz. p. 131 no. 2; H. Galsterer (1971) p. 15; R. C. Knapp (1977a) p. 19.

[86] Livy *Per.* 55; C. Torres (1951).

[87] C. Torres (1951) pp. 115–16.

[88] C. Torres (1951) pp. 114–15.

[89] C. Torres (1951) pp. 117–21. H. Galsterer (1971) p. 12 discusses the archaeological evidence for a second-century B.C. Roman settlement. O. Gil Farres (1966) pp. 128–29 notes that coin types of Valentia imitated those of Brutus.

[90] S. Dyson (1980–81) pp. 276–80.

predominantly Roman second-century B.C. occupation level. This use
of the archaeological evidence poses several problems. One is that only
small sections of the modern city have been investigated, and so a
native settlement could easily have been missed. More important, we
do not really know what the archaeological remains of the Viriathans
would be like. The literary evidence indicates that they were individuals who had been long removed from their tribal roots and that at
least some were partly Romanized. Because of the popularity of items
like black-glaze pottery with native people throughout the western
Mediterranean, it would not be surprising to see such items used by
the Viriathans too. By the same token, we might have expected the
Viriathans to have abandoned many of the elements in their native
culture that would survive in the archaeological record.

Until a great deal more is known about the archaeology of Valencia
and more sophisticated models are developed for associating material
culture and ethnic identity, negative archaeological evidence should be
used with caution. It is, of course, possible that Livy was mistaken.
It is more likely that some form of settlement existed at Valencia before the Viriathans arrived and that Brutus added the Viriathans to
it, perhaps in some form of informal *attributio*.

With these settlements, Brutus had completed the arrangements
necessary to end the Viriathan Wars. He now turned to larger frontier
problems in Lusitania. Before dealing with his advance to the northwest, however, we should return to Hispania Citerior, where the success of Viriathus and growing internal problems launched another series of frontier wars. There the problem was not an external bandit
leader, but the continued power and prestige of hill forts around Numantia and the Arevaci.

When the provincial commands were decided for 143 B.C., the senate was so concerned about the developing crisis in Hispania Citerior
that it assigned the area to the consul Q. Caecilius Metellus. He was
an experienced frontier fighter with a proven record. As a praetor in
Macedonia, he had arranged the surrender of the Macedonian leader
Andriscus and had carried on delicate negotiations with the Thracian
prince Byzes.[91] Similar tasks awaited him in Spain. By the time he
reached Citerior, the revolt was already widespread. The Numantines
were in arms and they had been joined by the people of Termantia.
Contrebia was soon to follow. The disturbed area now extended from
the upper Duero to the river Jiloca. The whole southern flank of the
Ebro was threatened, as were communications with Ulterior.[92]

[91] App. *Hisp.* 76; T.R.S. Broughton (1951) p. 461.
[92] App. *Hisp.* 76.

Metellus met the challenge with military decisiveness and diplomatic skill.[93] His quickly organized attack caught the Arevaci before
they could harvest their crops and prepare for a long siege in their
oppidum. They were forced to come to terms with the Romans. After
providing hostages, surrendering weapons, and providing a tribute that
included cloaks, hides, and horses, the Arevaci were restored to the
position of friend and ally of Rome.[94] Other centers proved more obdurate, and both Contrebia and Centobrica had to be stormed.[95]

Metellus could at the right moment soften his military bluntness
with skillful gestures of reconciliation. During the siege of Centobrica,
the defenders used the children of a chieftain named Rhoetogenes as
a barrier against the Roman siege machines. Rhoetogenes was a friend
of Rome, and Metellus immediately ordered the assault stopped. The
impact of this action is well described by Valerius Maximus.

> Quo quidem tam clementi facto, etsi non unius civitatis moenia,
> omnium tamen Celtiberarum urbium animos cepit effectique ut
> ad redigendas eas in dicionem populi Romani non multis sibi ob-
> sidionibus opus esset.[96]

> Indeed by so merciful a deed, even if he did not capture the walls
> of one town, nevertheless he won over the loyalty of all the Ibe-
> rian cities so that there was no need for many sieges to bring them
> back under the control of the Roman people.

This sense of chivalry also extended to the staff of Metellus. One
officer named Q. Occius engaged the Celtiberian Pyrresius in single
combat. When the Roman proved victorious, he refused to strip the
weapons from his defeated opponent, since, as Valerius Maximus notes:

> ille vero etiam petiit ut hospitii iure inter se iuncti essent quando
> inter Romanos et Celtiberos pax foret restituta.[97]

> He in fact even sought that they be joined by an oath of hospi-
> tality between themselves when peace should be restored between
> the Romans and the Celtiberians.

When Metellus left the province some progress had been made, but
much remained to be done. The Numantines balked when required
to surrender arms. Bandits were still active in the mountains around

[93] H. Simon (1962) pp. 101–8.
[94] Diod. 33.16; App. *Hisp.* 76.
[95] Vell. Pat. 2.5; Val. Max. 5.1.5; Florus 1.33.10.
[96] Val. Max. 5.1.5.
[97] Val. Max. 3.2.21. Livy *Per.* 54 notes that a Q. Occius fell fighting bravely in an
ambush set by the Lusitanians.

the Ebro. Metellus' successor, Q. Pompeius, faced these ongoing problems with considerably less support at home. He was an ambitious *novus homo* who had succeeded despite the opposition of such important families as the Metelli and a break with his former supporter, Scipio Aemilianus.[98] He has received bad press in the ancient sources, but his accomplishments would suggest that he deserves a better image.

Pompeius faced up to the twin tasks of controlling banditry and isolating Numantia. In the mountains south of the Ebro, his forces defeated the bandit chieftan Tanginus and captured many of his followers.[99] Equally productive were his attempts to reduce the support for Numantia. Termantia was apparently captured, while Laghi and Malia, towns held in part by Numantines, were recovered. Some of the captured Numantines were released and sent back to their oppidum, no doubt to encourage pro-Roman sentiment among their fellow citizens.[100]

Pompeius now made the difficult decision to winter before Numantia. Despite the hardships it would impose, the action made sense.[101] The Numantines apparently had extensive herds and needed the freedom to move their animals to different seasonal pastures; they also needed to plant and cultivate crops. The continuous presence of the Romans could hinder these efforts. Gradually the Celtiberians edged toward peace encouraged by the conciliatory attitude of Pompeius. An agreement was reached by which the Numantines were to surrender any prisoners and deserters held by them, and to provide hostages. The Celtiberians also had to present a large indemnity of silver.[102]

The ultimate failure of Pompeius proved to be political, rather than military. His rise to power as a *novus homo* had left a trail of enemies. His agreement was denounced as a disgrace. Finally, in a craven effort to save his political fortunes, he deserted the cause of the Celtiberians.[103] The agreement was voided, and Pompeius was placed on trial for illegal acts done during his governorship. Despite a battery of impressive accusers, however, he was acquitted.[104]

War on the Numantine frontier continued with the oppidum yet to

[98] Diod. 33.16; A. Schulten (1911) pp. 600–2; T.R.S. Broughton (1951) pp. 477, 480, 482; A. E. Astin (1967b) pp. 121–22.

[99] App. *Hisp.* 77.

[100] Diod. 33.17.1; Livy *Per.* 54; App. *Hisp.* 77; H. Simon (1962) pp.111–16.

[101] App. *Hisp.* 78; Oros. 5.4.13.

[102] App. *Hisp.* 79.

[103] App. *Hisp.* 79; A. E. Astin (1967b) pp. 148–50.

[104] Cic. *Font.* 23; Val. Max. 8.5.1; App. *Hisp.* 83; A. E. Astin (1967b) pp. 129, 178; E. S. Gruen (1968) pp. 34–37.

be subdued and the Romans facing the increasing danger of war spreading to other areas. M. Popillius Laenas had only limited success in stopping this process.[105] By the time the consul of 137 B.C., C. Hostilius Mancinus, reached Citerior, rumors were spreading that the Vaccaei and Cantabrians planned to join the war.

C. Hostilius Mancinus stands as a ridiculous, slightly pathetic figure in the history of the Celtiberian Wars.[106] Little is known about him or his family, but there is no indication in the record that he had frontier experience. This lack of background quickly proved fatal. His army was ambushed and trapped. The Romans were saved only when Mancinus subordinate, Ti. Sempronius Gracchus, used his influence as the son of the great Iberian frontier pacifier and negotiated a humiliating peace. The agreement was quickly abrogated by the senate, and the decision was made to turn Mancinus over to the enemy to expiate any divine retribution that might come with breaking the treaty.[107] Naturally, the Arevaci refused to receive him. The slightly farcical scene of Mancinus standing naked before the walls of Numantia represents the nadir of Rome's efforts against the Celtiberians.

The successors of Mancinus avoided disaster but could do little more than continue the efforts at containing the revolt.[108] Clearly a more impressive leader was needed, and in 134 the Romans turned to P. Cornelius Scipio Africanus Aemilianus, the destroyer of Carthage. Elected consul, he was sent out to reduce Numantia.[109] The career of this man has always been shrouded in controversy. He was a skilled propagandist, however, and the surviving accounts of the Numantine Wars owe much to writers such as Rutilius Rufus and Polybius who were part of his circle. Amid the pithy sayings and conventional accounts of discipline restored to a lax army, it is difficult to obtain a balanced picture of Scipio and his actions.[110]

Scipio basically continued the ongoing frontier policy but with the increased resources, prestige, and experience that a man of his standing could bring.[111] He had served in the area before, and he knew the

[105] Livy *Per.* 55; Frontin. *Str.* 3.17.9; App. *Hisp.* 79.

[106] T.R.S. Broughton (1951) p. 484; A. E. Astin (1967b) pp. 130–33.

[107] Livy *Per.* 55; Vell. Pat. 2.1.5; Florus 1.34.4–7; Plut. *Vit. Ti. Gracch.* 5–7; H. Simon (1962) pp. 149–59; A. E. Astin (1967b) pp. 150–52; A. Bernstein (1978) pp. 61–70.

[108] App. *Hisp.* 80–83; Oros. 5.5.13–14; H. Simon (1962) pp. 164–171; E. S. Gruen (1968) pp. 39–40.

[109] App. *Hisp.* 84.

[110] Cic. *Rep.* 1.17; Livy *Per.* 57; Val. Max. 2.7.1; Frontin. *Str.* 4.1.1; Plut. *Apoth. Scipio* 16; App. *Hisp.* 85; A. Balil (1955) p. 48; F. Wattenberg (1959) p. 35; H. Simon (1962) p. 175.

[111] A. E. Astin (1967b) pp. 136, 153–60.

terrain and people and could rely on extensive familial connections that were so important in Iberian frontier war. The scorched-earth policy begun by his predecessors was resumed. The land of active Numantine supporters was ravaged. At the same time, reconciliation was attempted. The refugees from Cauca who had escaped from Lucullus were restored to their homes.[112]

With groups like the Vaccaei under control, Scipio could turn to Numantia itself. Spanish allies were summoned to swell his already impressive army. This allowed a full siege, but also demonstrated basic Iberian loyalty to Rome in the face of a common enemy.[113] Other Arevacian centers that attempted to support Numantia were harshly treated. When the young men of Lutia (modern Lantalucia) plotted to join the Numantines, the elders of the community warned Scipio. The youths had their hands cut off by the Romans as a warning to others.[114] The results of the siege became a foregone conclusion. Numantia was finally captured and destroyed. The historical judgment on the heroism of the Numantines remains clear, although that on the character and motives of Scipio has been more clouded.[115]

The long war on the Ebro was over, and the greatest hill fort of the Celtiberians lay in ruins. A senatorial commission was dispatched to rearrange the affairs of the province.[116] Unfortunately we know neither the members of this commission nor its specific accomplishments. Political adjustments had to be made after the defeat of the Arevaci. The tribe's power was reduced while that of its smaller neighbors was probably increased. By the time of Pliny, a people known as the Pelendones controlled Numantia.[117] Numantia itself was resettled relatively soon after its capture and became a successful Romanized town.[118]

The Romans regularized the collection of tribute. The spread of native coinages in Hispania Citerior, especially in the areas drained by the middle Ebro, may be partly related to the increased need for cash. Native coinage had existed before, but the period from 133 to 82 B.C. saw a marked increase in its use. Some of these coins were issued in silver, but the great majority were in bronze.[119] From the

[112] App. *Hisp.* 87–89; A. Schulten (1914) pp. 143–44.

[113] App. *Hisp.* 92; A. Balil (1955) p. 41. H. Simon (1962) p. 179 estimates that possibly one half of Scipio's army was Spanish auxiliaries. On the siege of Numantia itself see H. J. Hildebrandt (1979).

[114] App. *Hisp.* 94.

[115] Diod. 32.4.5; Livy *Per.* 59; Florus 1.34.8–17; App. *Hisp.* 95–98; J. Caro Baroja (1968) pp. 22–28; A. E. Astin (1967b) pp. 155–60.

[116] App. *Hisp.* 99; R. Bernhardt (1975) pp. 423–24.

[117] Pliny *HN* 3.26. Ptol. 2.6.56, however, has it controlled by the Arevaci.

[118] *CIL* 2 pp. 388–90; O. Gil Farres (1966) p. 114.

[119] O. Gil Farres (1966) pp. 114–16.

Iberian language inscriptions on the coins, numismatists have been able to identify at least fifty distinct issuing groups.[120]

Coins of the earliest phase were based on the uncial standard and should therefore be placed earlier than 100 B.C. These are made of bronze, and most are found in the upper Baetis area of Hispania Ulterior, with a scattering along the coast and in the lower Ebro valley. The silver is virtually limited to the Ebro and its tributaries.[121] Semi-uncial bronzes are found almost exclusively in the Ebro drainage. Imitations are found in the middle Ebro and along the headwaters of some of the rivers that flow out of the Meseta.[122]

The purpose of these coins is uncertain.[123] Although some were silver and thus suitable for the payment of wages and tribute, most were made of bronze. This is a development similar to the spread of local coinages in Languedoc in the early stages of Roman administration. It may be related to the Roman effort at stressing the ethnic identity of small centers at the expense of larger federations. It may also reflect the growing sophistication of local markets as Iberia became integrated into the Mediterranean economic system.

The regularization of the road network was crucial to both the internal development of the province and the security of the frontier. As in other areas, the network here was based in part on preexisting routes.[124] It also reflected the military needs of the Republican province. The first milestone we have is that of Q. Fabius Labeo, probably dating to 110 B.C.[125] It marked the road from Tarraco to Ilerda (Lérida) that linked the coastal port with the Egre River valley and Pyrenees frontier. This road continued across the flank of the Pyrenees into Osca, which was to become an important center by the time of the Sertorian Wars.[126] The two roads that linked Contrebia with the coast were probably also developed during this period.[127] Other interior routes that reflect Republican strategic needs are thse from Sermone to Saltus, Bilbilis to Toledo, and the Ebro to Palentia.[128] Palentia became the end point of a road that ran from Segovia through Cauca and

[120] L. Villaronga (1977) pp. 12–13.

[121] O. Gil Farres (1966) pp. 115, 164–65.

[122] O. Gil Farres (1966) pp. 171, 177.

[123] R. C. Knapp (1977).

[124] C. Sanchez Albornoz (1949) p. 15 n. 50.

[125] *CIL* 1.2 823, 824; T.R.S. Broughton (1951) pp. 543–44, (1952) p. 464; A. Balil (1955) pp. 49–50.

[126] K. Miller (1916) cols. 157–58.

[127] K. Miller (1916) cols. 174–76.

[128] K. Miller (1916) cols. 151, 163 K. 45, 168–70 K. 47–48, 174–75; A. Balil (1955) pp. 48–49.

Intercatia, places that had figured prominently in the annals of the Celtiberian Wars.[129]

The progress of Romanization among the natives during these years can be only dimly surmised. The literary record is poor, and we have just begun to tap the potential that the archeological record has for contributing to our understanding. More thorough excavation of oppida should yield material on cultural change similar to that recovered in recent years in France. Evidence of importation into interior sites of items like black-glaze pottery, which is already known from Numantia, will be especially important.[130] The evolution of the coinage in the Saguntum area is an indication of the cultural changes taking place. The earliest coins have a combined Iberian-Latin Arse-Saguntum legend, with the names of both native and Roman magistrates. The types gradually change, until the latest have only Roman names and the designation Saguntum. This does not mean that the natives had disappeared. It is more likely that their ruling elites had been absorbed into the local Roman social and political structure.[131]

The frontier peace opened the province to Italian emigrants seeking economic opportunity. The extent of the movement is difficult to gauge.[132] Although there were mercantile opportunities similar to those in Gaul, the agricultural land was limited and the native population relatively dense. It is known that in 122 B.C. Q. Caecilius Metellus drew three thousand Romans from Spain for his Balearic colony.[133] We do not know exactly who these people were. Some may have been pensioned soldiers who had found less opportunity in Iberia than they had hoped. Others may have been Romanized natives or the progeny of mixed marriages. It suggests that the Spanish provinces were not in a position to absorb new settlements. The future course of the area was to be determined largely by the Romans and natives who lived there.

Relative peace settled on the Citerior frontier. Some unrest was reported in the next few decades, but apparently no wars developed until Sertorius enflamed the whole area.[134] In the meantime, in Ulterior the stage was being set for the last big advance of the Republican era, one that would carry the Roman armies into Lusitania. The decision was certainly a legacy of the Viriathan Wars. The Romans had seen how easy it was for raiders to move through the mountain passes

---

[129] K. Miller (1916) col. 173.

[130] A. Balil (1955) p. 50.

[131] O. Gil Farres (1966) pp. 126–27.

[132] A.J.N. Wilson (1966) pp. 22–27.

[133] Strabo 3.5.1; Florus 1.43; Oros. 5.13.1; M. G. Morgan (1969) esp. pp. 229–31.

[134] T.R.S. Broughton (1951) pp. 575, 573n.5, (1952) pp. 4, 7, 10–11, 13, 15; A. Degrassi (1947) p. 562.

and river valleys and attack friendly tribes. The frontier was too close to the coast, and the natives beyond were too uncertain. Control of the river valleys of the west coast, such as the Tagus and the Duero, was needed before a secure balance could be attained.

There were additional factors that urged a Roman advance into Lusitania. Since the Bronze Age, a sophisticated native culture had been developing along the Atlantic coast of the Iberian peninsula.[135] The dense concentration of *castros* (fortified camps), especially in the region between the Duero and the Minho, testifies to the prosperity of this area during the Iron Age.[136] Strabo comments on the agricultural richness of coastal Lusitania and laments that the potential was not fully realized because of the continuing problem of mountain raids.[137] At the same time, these raids hindered the development of Roman mining interests in an area known to be rich in metallic resources.[138] Strategic factors also favored the Roman conquest of Lusitania. In Hispania Citerior the Roman armies had pushed up the Ebro as far as Pallantia. A frontier line in Ulterior based on the Tagus or Duero would shorten lines of communication and leave only a small mountainous part of the peninsula outside Roman control.

Brutus did not intend a total conquest of Lusitania. Instead he wanted control of the western coastal plain, the main river valleys, and the immediately adjacent mountain areas. During his first year of campaigning, he seems to have followed the now familiar route up the Guadiana to the Tagus. He then moved down the Tagus to the coast. Olisipo (Lisbon) was fortified, providing the Romans with a strong point at the mouth of the Tagus and a center that could serve as the focus of Romanization on the coastal plain.[139] The native centers that cooperated with the Romans and that had strategic importance were treated leniently. The *castro* at Coimbra, located at the juncture of plain and mountain on the Rio Mondego, continued to be occupied and developed into a prosperous Romanized community.[140] Talabriga (Aveiro), located between the Duero and Tagus, escaped destruction despite the several rebellions of its inhabitants.[141] The settlement at Conimbriga (Cundeixa-a-Velha) developed into a Romanized center under the Empire.[142]

---

[135] H. N. Savory (1968) pp. 85–165.
[136] J. Maluguer de Motes (1963) pp. 42–45, 56, 71.
[137] Strabo 3.3.4.
[138] C. Domerque and R. Freire d'Andrade (1971).
[139] Strabo 3.3.1; A. Tovar (1976) pp. 266–68.
[140] Pliny *HN* 4.113; A. Tovar (1976) pp. 260–62.
[141] Pliny *HN* 4.113; App. *Hisp.* 73; A. Tovar (1976) p. 257.
[142] J. Alarcáo, R. Etienne, A.Moutinho-Alcarcáo, and S. da Ponte (1979) pp. 247–74.

With the coast secure, Brutus moved up the Tagus valley again. He established a base at Moron (Almeiron), about ninety kilometers up the river.[143] From there he could advance up the Zezere valley and begin pacifying the mountainous region between the Tagus and the Duero. The remains of the Roman camp discovered by Adolph Schulten at Viseu may well be a relic of this campaign.[144]

The Romans did not stop at the Duero. The territory between the Duero and the Minho was thickly settled, and the native culture was a continuation of that to the south. The *castro* at Braga, which along with its neighboring *castros* controlled access to mountain and plain, was a key to control of the area.[145] Braga was evidently stormed by the Romans. Communities that cooperated with the conqueror, however, had a different fate. At nearby Briteiros occupation continued, and the settlement shows evidence of gradual Romanization.[146]

A detailed understanding of the methods used by Brutus to gain control of this area can only come from rigorous archaeological investigation like that taking place in the south of France. Appian describes the systematic seizure of *castros* as part of the strategy for the reduction of banditry.[147] Strabo notes that most "cities" (probably large *castros* or oppida) were reduced to mere villages. Livy uses the expression *expugnationibus urbium usque ad Oceanum*.[148] As we have seen, these destructions were selective. Appian himself states that Brutus gave pardon to those who asked for it.[149] The still limited archaeological evidence indicates that Briteiros was not an isolated case of a community where occupation continued. It appears that the Romans concentrated their attacks on these centers that refused to cooperate, while those that had a future place in the Romanization process or in frontier defense were spared.

As in other frontier areas, the Romans encouraged the development of new Roman-oriented communities as well as a loyal native aristocracy. The ancient itineraries mention centers named Forum Bibiloriarum, Forum Limicorum, Forum Narbasorum, and Forum Gigurniorum, all in the area east of Braga.[150] No precise evidence of their foundation date exists. Their location would fit a pre-Augustan fron-

---

[143] Strabo 3.3.1; A. Schulten (1933) p. 533; A. Tovar (1976) p. 265.
[144] A. Schulten (1933) p. 534; A. Tovar (1976) p. 256.
[145] App. *Hisp.* 71–72.
[146] J. Maluquer de Motes (1963) pp. 44–45.
[147] App. *Hisp.* 71.
[148] Livy *Per.* 55; Strabo 3.3.5.
[149] App. *Hisp.* 71.
[150] Ptol. 1.2.5; K. Miller (1916) col. 167. J. Caro Baroja (1970) pp. 46–47 relates these to the development of tribal markets.

tier in which Roman control of the mountains was tenuous and administrators wanted to encourage the Romanization of the hill tribes through the development of market contacts. A similar approach was used on the Ligurian frontier. Also mentioned in the itineraries are two praesidia, one at Juan de Camba on the southern bank of the Minho near Caldelas and the other east of Braga near modern Basto.[151] Again, their location is best suited to serve the needs of the Republican frontier. The effort at developing personal loyalties in the area is shown by the relatively wide distribution of individuals bearing the Junian name.[152]

Brutus completed his campaign in the northwest by marching up the Duero to join his colleague Lepidus in the attack on Pallantia. The coordinated attack, though not completely successful, showed the advantage of shortening lines of communication and providing control of strategic river valleys that linked the two provinces. Brutus returned home to a well-deserved triumph.[153] An indicator of his success is that no other major wars are reported in Hispania Ulterior until 114 B.C.

Peace must always have been tenuous on the frontier. The mountain districts were still poor and overpopulated. Banditry remained endemic. Diodorus Siculus, drawing on Poseidonius who visited the area around 100 B.C., provides the following description:

διὸ καὶ Ῥωμαῖοι πολλάκις ἐπ' αὐτοὺς στρατεύσαντες τῆς μὲν πολλῆς καταφρονήσεως ἀπέστησαν αὐτούς, εἰς τέλος δὲ τὰ ληστήρια καταλῦσαι πολλάκις φιλοτιμηθέντες οὐκ ἠδυνήθησαν.[154]

Therefore the Romans, often having made war against them, stripped them of their great disdain, but despite frequent attempts they were unable to break up the bands of robbers.

The experience of Marius when he went to Ulterior as governor in 114 B.C is typical.[155] Complaints were increasing about unfair taxation on the one hand and growing banditry on the other. The two were probably not unconnected. Oppressive taxation would drive natives into the hills to join the bandits. Their raids would reduce the ability of others to pay the taxes, in turn encouraging more flow into the mountains. Marius apparently met both challenges. His requisitions

[151] K. Miller (1916) cols. 166–67.
[152] S. L. Dyson (1980–81) pp. 276–80.
[153] Val. Max. 8.14.2; A. Degrassi (1947) p. 558; H. Simon (1962) pp. 163–71.
[154] Diod. 5.34.7.
[155] Plut. Vit. Mar. 6.1.

of grain were considered fair, and he was successful in reducing the bandit menace.

By the last years of the second century, the threat of frontier warfare in Ulterior was growing. The praetor of 112 B.C., L. Calpurnius Piso Frugi, was killed in action on the frontier.[156] His successors were able to stabilize the situation, but little more.[157] The problem spurred the senate to send out Q. Servilius Caepio in 109 B.C. He was the third generation of his family to govern Ulterior and could draw on a solid network of personal connections.[158] His two years of campaigning in Lusitania were sufficiently successful to win him a triumph.[159]

Unfortunately the scanty sources do not allow a precise reconstruction of the campaign. It seems to have been concentrated in the west. A place called Caepiana was located in the territory of the Celtici in western Lusitania between Pax Julia and the sea.[160] Also along the western coast have been found two of the relatively few inscriptions in Iberia that bear the Servilian name.[161] Again, peace was transitory. In 105 B.C. a Roman army was mauled by the Lusitanians,[162] in 102 B.C. M. Marius attacked the Lusitanians,[163] and in 98 B.C. L. Cornelius Dolabella was awarded a triumph *ex Hispania ulteriore de Lusitaneis*.[164]

The senate saw the need for a new effort in Lusitania, and in 97 B.C. it assigned the consul P. Licinius Crassus to Hispania Ulterior. He remained there until 93 B.C., when he returned to celebrate a triumph.[165] The sources are again inadequate, and any reconstruction must be hypothetical. Place names provide some help. Ancient itineraries mention a Licinia located near Norba Caesarina and a Leuciana. There is also a Castra Liciniana near Norba at the pass that connects Montánchez and Guadalupe.[166] These suggest a combination of military camps and settlements of natives friendly to Rome that were intended to help secure the rugged country between the Guadiana and the Tagus. A place called Katraleukos by Ptolemy may well be an-

[156] Cic. *Verr.* 2.4.56; App. *Hisp.* 99; T.R.S. Broughton (1951) p. 538.
[157] App. *Hisp.* 99.
[158] Val. Max. 6.9.13; Eutropius 4.27.5.
[159] A. Degrassi (1947) p. 561.
[160] Ptol. 2.5.5.
[161] *CIL* 2. 195, 359.
[162] Julius Obseq. 42 (105 B.C.).
[163] App. *Hisp.* 100; T.R.S. Broughton (1951) p. 568.
[164] A. Degrassi (1947) p. 562.
[165] A. Degrassi (1947) p. 563; T.R.S. Broughton (1952) pp. 6, 10, 12–13, 15.
[166] K. Miller (1916) col. 150; A. Tovar (1976) p. 233–34. R. C. Knapp (1977a) p. 26 supports an earlier foundation.

other Castra Licinia. It was located near Evora in Portugal and could serve to protect the settlements in the plain from mountain raiders.[167]

Crassus also built a client network among the local notables in Lusitania. Inscriptions with the Licinian nomen are common in Olisipo (Lisbon) and reasonably abundant in the Emerta area. Others have been found between the Baetis and the Tagus. During the Marian persecutions in Italy the son of Crassus fled to Spain, where he found refuge with a certain Vibius Paciacus who was a rich landowner. The young Crassus then proceeded to raise a large body of supporters from his father's clients in the province.[168]

The campaign of Crassus advanced beyond the Tagus into territory already traversed by Brutus.[169] The Cassiterides are mentioned in connection with the advance, suggesting that the army penetrated well into northern Portugal. An episode in Plutarch that is probably connected with this campaign provides interesting insight into the ethnological sensitivity of a Roman commander. The tribe of the Eletonesii, who lived near Salamanca, had been accused of practicing human sacrifice, and their leaders had been summoned to explain these actions that were clearly repugnant to the Romans. When they claimed that the rituals merely followed local custom, they were let off with the admonition that they not do it again. Crassus, as consul, had prohibited human sacrifices at Rome, and the Lusitanian episode fits in well with the context of his campaign.[170] The sensitive handling of the issue by the Roman commander shows skill in reconciling Roman revulsion at a barbarous local custom with the need to maintain the loyalty of an important frontier group.

Crassus returned to Rome with the principal problems of the frontier solved. The pacification was not complete, however. His successor, P. Cornelius Scipio Nasica, faced a rebellion of native groups. The *principes* of the offending tribes were punished and their centers destroyed.[171] With this victory a calm settled on the Ulterior frontier that would only be broken by the struggles of the Civil Wars.

In the meantime, the frontier areas of Hispania Citerior were beginning to show restlessness after a long period of relative peace. The coins of C. Coelius Caldus in 99 B.C. have the wild boar of Clunia impressed upon them, suggesting that he was involved in frontier pac-

---

[167] Ptol. 2.5.5; A. Tovar (1976) p. 214.

[168] Plut. *Vit. Crass.* 4–6; A.J.N. Wilson (1966) pp. 30–31; S. L. Dyson (1980–81) pp. 280–83.

[169] Strabo 3.5.11.

[170] Strabo 3.3.6; Pliny *HN* 30.12; Plut. *Quaest. Rom.* 83. On Iberian human sacrifice see J. M. Blazquez Martinez (1955) pp. 116–17.

[171] Julius Obseq. 51 (94 B.C.).

ification.[172] In 98 B.C. the senate sent a consular governor to Citerior. He was T. Didius, who was a veteran of the Macedonian frontier, where he had defeated the Scordisci and had earned a triumph.[173]

The fragmentary sources suggest three areas of discord. First, the Arevaci were again in revolt. The reasons are not stated, but they probably included overpopulation, dissatisfaction with Roman administration, and the replenishment of the warrior class after two generations of peace. The uprising was evidently serious, since twenty thousand Celtiberians were supposedly slain.[174] The military camp recently excavated at Almazán, which was dated to the late second or early first century B.C., is possibly related to this campaign.[175]

The Vaccaei were also restless. One center of resistance was Termantia. Located on a ridge south of the Duero, it controlled access to the river valley from the east. Didius followed the standard Roman policy in such situations. The native inhabitants were forced to come down from their hilltop fort and live in the plain in an unfortified settlement. Less fortunate were the inhabitants of Colenda. After resisting the Romans, their oppidum was stormed and the native population sold into slavery.[176]

Near Colenda the governor of Ulterior, M. Marius, had settled some Celtiberians who had served with him. Their mission was most likely to defend the Duero valley from raiders coming down from the nearby hills. The idea had not worked. The land made available to the settlers had proved insufficient, and the Celtiberians themselves became brigands. Didius now made the decision to destroy them. Using the old frontier ruse of promising land grants, he lured the natives to their end.[177]

The third area of frontier unrest took the troops of Didius far south to Castulo on the Ulterior frontier. The Castulans, provoked by the excesses of Roman garrison troops in the area and aided by their neighbors, the Oretani, had revolted. Didius dispatched a tribune serving under him named Q. Sertorius. The revolt was quickly suppressed and Sertorius had his first success on the Spanish frontier.[178]

In 93 B.C. the senate dispatched the consul C. Valerius Flaccus to Hispania Citerior. As always, the use of a consular governor implies

[172] T.R.S. Broughton (1952) p. 3 n. 2; M. H. Crawford (1974) pp. 457–59.
[173] A. Degrassi (1947) p. 562; T.R.S. Broughton (1951) p. 571, (1952) pp. 4, 7, 10–11, 13, 15.
[174] Livy Per. 70; Front. Str. 2.10.1; App. Hisp. 99.
[175] G. Gamer and J. Ortego y Frías (1969) pp. 180–84.
[176] App. Hisp. 99; A. Schulten (1914) pp. 132–33.
[177] App. Hisp. 100; R. C. Knapp (1977a) pp. 51–52.
[178] Plut. Vit. Sert. 3.3–5; A. Schulten (1926) pp. 30–31.

serious problems. The only place specifically mentioned in the sources is a center called Belgida.[179] The scene is a familiar one. The people of the town were eager for revolt, but the elders hesitated. In frustration and anger, the rebels burned down the senate house around the heads of the community elders. Flaccus advanced on the town and punished the ringleaders of the uprising.[180] This was apparently not the only trouble spot, since Flaccus was to celebrate a full Celtiberian triumph.[181]

Frontier development in the Iberian peninsula was now at a point of transition. The main advances that were to be made under the Republic had taken place. Much of the area was under nominal Roman control, and Romanization was under way. Frontier magnates who cooperated with Rome could prosper. This is well illustrated by the treasure hoards that have been found in such areas as the upper Baetis.[182] These hoards, with their rich drinking vessels, jewelry, and money, depict a march aristocracy whose customs and material possessions reflect a combination of Roman and native ways.

The same situation is evident in one of the most important epigraphical documents of the period, the inscription of the Turma Salluitana, found in Italy in 1908.[183] This records the grant of citizenship made in 90 B.C. to a unit of Spanish cavalry that had served under Cn. Pompeius Strabo. Nearly thirty soldiers are listed from a variety of northern Iberian tribes. The inscription gives the names of fathers, as well as sons, and provides insight into the slow but steady pace of Romanization. Some of the figures, such as Sanibelser, son of Adingibas, are still purely native. One group from near Lerida, however, shows generational change. The fathers had indigenous names like Nesille and Enasagin, while the sons were called Otacilius and Cn. Cornelius. Until the decree of Pompeius Strabo they were not citizens, but the use of Roman nomenclature reflects an unofficial process of acculturation. This must have been widespread in both provinces by the first century B.C.[184]

At this point, the Iberian frontier became involved in the internal political struggles of the Roman state. The various factions rapidly discovered that the peninsula made an ideal place of refuge where family friends could be found and forces reordered for a resumption of war in Italy. Furthermore, the existence of a frontier with large

[179] T.R.S. Broughton (1952) pp. 14, 18.
[180] App. *Hisp.* 100.
[181] A. Degrassi (1947) p. 563.
[182] K. Raddatz (1969) pp. 18–19, 31–41, 45–60, 170.
[183] *ILS* 8888; N. Criniti (1970) pp. 189–204.
[184] N. Criniti (1970) pp. 189–91; S. L. Dyson (1980–81) pp. 294–99.

areas that were semipacified or even outside Roman control provided
resources and opportunities for commanders skilled in guerrilla warfare. For the natives the wars provided an opportunity to use their
warrior skill and to obtain a greater degree of independence by exploiting divisions among the Roman factions.

The exiles began arriving in Iberia very early. By 87 B.C. M. Junius
Brutus and other refugees were ready to leave Spain to join Marius
on his return to Italy.[185] Brutus had presumably fled to the protection
of a family client in Hispania Ulterior. The Sullan M. Licinius Crassus followed the same course and engaged in partisan fighting in Spain
before returning to Italy.[186] The natives probably accepted these bewildering political events better than the Romans. Loyalty for the
natives always had a strong personal and familial quality, while the
Roman state was a somewhat obscure abstraction.

The early involvement of Sertorius in Iberia probably followed this
pattern. Not surprisingly, this prominent Marian sought refuge in Citerior. He had served there before and developed contacts with both
the natives and the Italic immigrants. Bred in the rough country around
Nursia in Italy, he must have felt at home on the Iberian frontier.[187]
The recent Italian emigrants would have included many strong Mar-
ians. Sertorius had a sense of provincial attitudes, the sources of local
discontent, and the ways of winning loyalties. Through personal diplomacy he won over the principal figures in the province. Corrective
administrative actions bolstered support among the common people.
Taxes were reduced, and a well-publicized effort was made to avoid
billeting his troops on the local population.[188] His efforts were in vain,
however. Before Sertorius could complete his preparations, the Sullan
General C. Annius Luscus gained control of the Pyrenean passes. Sertorius was forced to flee.[189]

Sertorius was in North Africa when a delegation of Lusitanians
invited him to be their leader.[190] The question immediately arises about
the identity of these Lusitanians. They were probably not from one
of the unconquered groups of the interior. Those natives did not have
access to the sea and probably lacked the sophistication necessary to
carry out such a mission. They were more likely Romanized coastal
Lusitanians. They were depicted as anti-Roman rebels, but this
impression may be deceiving. Factional fighting was already develop-

---

E. Badian (1958) p. 266.
[186] E. Badian (1958) p. 266.
[187] A. Schulten (1926) p. 19.
[188] Plut. *Vit. Sert.* 6.3–5.
[189] Plut. *Vit. Sert.* 7.
[190] Plut. *Vit. Sert.* 10.

ing, and they seem more likely to have been envoys representing rest-less Marian clients in southwestern Lusitania than tribesmen from the hills.

The confused accounts of the early actions of Sertorius in Spain make it difficult to reconstruct his intentions and strategy. He landed near the Strait of Gibraltar and fled into the mountains behind Carteia and Gades.[191] This was far from the Lusitanians who had originally called him to Iberia. Perhaps Sullan forces blocked him or he found the support in the southwest to be less than he had expected. He decided to rely on the interior natives in the west. This is different from his strategy elsewhere in the peninsula, where he used a com-bination of exiles, Roman settlers, and highly acculturated natives. Sertorius was resourceful in adjusting to a given situation, however and had the ability to use native forces.

Sertorius did not abandon his hope of gaining control of the Lusi-tanian coast. His capture of the oppidum at Lagobrigae (Lagos) on the Algarve coast was a key part of this plan.[192] Lagobrigae commanded a rich, Romanized area and had relatively easy access to the uplands and the mountains. After being taken by Sertorius, it was besieged by the new Sullan Commander Q. Caecilius Metellus Pius, and then rescued by Sertorius. He had overextended his resources, however, and the success was brief. The war shifted permanently to the inte-rior.

Metellus was a complex figure whose abilities have often been un-derrated. His father had long served in North Africa, and he knew from this experience in a similar situation the problems and possibili-ties of frontier warfare. He realized the weaknesses in the position of Sertorius, and developd a strategy that would first contain and then drive back the Marian.[193] The aim of this strategy was to cut off Sertorius from the coast and create an internal frontier of scorched earth, garrisons, and natives loyal to the Sullan or Metellan cause. In the words of Sallust.

illo profectus vicos castellaque incendere et fuga cultorum deserta igni vastare neque late aut securus nimis, metu gentis ad furta belli peridoneae.[194]

Having set out thither, he burned the villages and the forts and laid waste by for those areas abandoned by the flight of the farm-

[191] Sall. *H*. 1.105.

[192] Plut. *Vit. Sert*. 13.4–6.

[193] A. Schulten (1921) p. 66. See D. Gillis (1969) pp. 714–15 on Sallust's denigration of Metellus.

[194] Sall. *H*. 1.112.

ers nor was he overly confident because of his fear of a people experienced in the tricks of war.

Once again, place names allow us to fill in the gaps in the literary sources and reconstruct some elements of the campaigns of Metellus. Sallust mentions that Dipo, a *validam urbem*, was captured by Metellus. Located northeast of modern Evora, the center would allow the Metellans to prevent Sertorians from going down to the coastal plain.[195] In the upper Tagus-Guadiana river area were several places with Metellan associations. The first was Metellinum, the modern Medillín on the upper Guadiana near Merida.[196] The name suggests a Metellan foundation. Its position was ideal for controlling access to the Guadiana valley. Although later overshadowed by Augusta Emerita (Merida), the road system indicates its early importance. Roads linked Metellinum with the important Republican staging center at Corduba, with the northern frontier of Hispania Ulterior through Mirobriga, and with the western coast by way of a route that passed through Dipo and Ebora.[197]

A Roman road connected the Guadiana with the Tagus. Along this was a place named Castra Caecilia. Excavations undertaken there by Adolph Schulten revealed an important camp that he dated to the Metellan period.[198] The camp seems to have been designed for long-term occupation, and there was evidence, including Iberian coins, of a native presence. Schulten found traces of a violent destruction and associated it with the supposed failure of the Metellan campaign.[199] This conclusion must be treated with caution, though, especially since the name persisted, implying some ongoing settlement.

A third locality associated with Caecilius Metellus is a Vicus Caecilius on a branch of the Rio Alagón, north of the Tagus.[200] The term *vicus* suggests a local settlement whose inhabitants remembered their association with Metellus. Its placement helped it control access to the Tagus. In later times, a road passed through the *vicus* on its way to Salamanca. The final community to be associated with Metellus is a

[195] Sall. *H*. 1.113.
[196] K. Miller (1916) cols. 158–59; A. Tovar (1976) p. 231.
[197] K. Miller (1916) col. 159; K. 44.
[198] K. Miller. (1916) col. 155; A. Schulten and P. Paulsen (1928), (1930), (1932).
[199] A. Schulten and P. Paulsen (1928) pp. 11–14; A. Tovar (1976) pp. 237–38. The coins included thirty-three Iberian as well as twenty-five Roman issues: A. Schulten and P. Paulsen (1932) p. 349. C. Callejo Serrino (1968) p. 148–49 thinks a native *vicus* survived until the foundation of nearby Norba in 35–34 B.C. R. C. Knapp (1977a) pp. 81–82.
[200] K. Miller (1916) col. 155; H. Berve (1929) p. 214; A. Tovar (1976) p. 216.

Caeciliana located on the coast south of Lisbon.[201] It was probably designed to encourage Romanization and to form a point of resistance to any Sertorian raids on the coastal plain.

I would argue that we have in these settlements and camps of Metellus a type of protolimes system that was designed to control the river valley and ultimately access to the coast. Some of the places were initially military camps. Later they were linked by roads. The persistence of the names, however, implies a continuity of settlement. The distribution of inscriptions with the Caecilian nomen many of which have been found around Lisbon, supports this.[202] There could have been people who drifted down the Tagus valley from the interior settlements, or natives who lived at such places as Caeciliana on the coastal plain. A small concentration is to be found around Ebora and a scattering along the line linking Metellinum with Vicus Caecilius. Literary evidence for the existence of such a Caecilian client network is provided by Caesar, who mentions a certain Caecilius Niger *hominem barbarum . . . qui bene magnam manum Lusitaniorum haberet.*[203]

The central question is whether Metellus succeeded. The view presented by the ancient writers was not flattering. Aged and fat, he was the ideal counterfoil to the dashing Sertorius. This may not be fair. Metellus appears to have attained his objectives and sealed off Sertorius from the area. No more attacks on coastal Lusitania are recorded.

This was not, however, the end of the Sertorian War on the Ulterior frontier. Hirtuleius, one of the lieutenants of Sertorius, besieged Consabra (Consuegra) southeast of Toledo.[204] Interestingly enough, the local natives refused to join the Sertorian cause. Sertorius himself raided as far west as the territory of the Characitani west of Complutum.[205] In 77–76 B.C. Metellus wintered at Corduba and was lavishly feted by the natives.[206] The honors may have been exaggerated, but they reflected the appreciation felt for his efforts at keeping the province relatively safe and preventing the reappearance of the conditions found under Viriathus. With the defeat of a Sertorian force at Italica in 76 B.C. and the defeat and death of Hirtuleius at Segovia in 75 B.C., the Sertorian threat to Hispania Ulterior finally ended.[207]

In the meantime, Sertorius had centered his effort in Citerior. There the Sullan position had declined rapidly, and Sertorius could consider

[201] K. Miller (1916) col. 183; A. Tovar (1976) p. 216.
[202] S. L. Dyson (1980–81) pp. 284–87.
[203] Caes. *BHisp.* 35.3–4.
[204] Frontin. *Str.* 4.5.19.
[205] Plut. *Vit. Sert.* 17.
[206] Cic. *Arch.* 26.
[207] Livy 91 fr. 18 (Loeb); Frontin. *Str.* 2.3.5; Florus 2.10.7; Oros. 5.23.10.

extending his power south of the Ebro.[208] In that region he met considerable Celtiberian resistance. The Sertorian army had to assault the oppidum at Contrebia, which was an important center on the route between the middle Ebro and coastal Saguntum.[209] Celtiberians around Contrebia constantly harassed the Romans during the siege. Clearly, Sertorius had been more successful in winning the support of the Romanized natives of the Ebro than the warriors of the Meseta.[210] This is reflected in the actions that Sertorius took immediately after the capture of Contrebia. The natives were disarmed, and all deserters were turned over to the Romans. The Contrebians were then ordered to slay all the runaway slaves in their town.[211] These demands show Sertorius neither as a social bandit nor as a defender of the free Celtiberians. Instead he appears as a leader with his main support based in the upper classes of Roman and Romano-Iberian society, whose privileges of class and property he had to defend. This same attitude lay behind his founding the school at Osca where the sons of Celtiberian leaders would receive a Roman education.[212]

Cn. Pompeius Magnus was dispatched to Spain in 77 B.C. With his arrival, four years of confused and often bitter fighting began.[213] It was very much a frontier war, with natives and Romans both involved. Among the local populace, traditions of loyalty to individuals and families remained strong. They must have in fact felt bewildered by the way the Romans divided among themselves. Livy's account of the early fighting on the Ebro provides some sense of this confusion.[214] The community of Gracchuris was loyal to the Sullans, while nearby Calagurris was a Sertorian stronghold. The Arevaci supported Sertorius, while the Berones were Sullans. It took vigorous campaigning on the part of Sertorius to ensure the temporary loyalty of the area.

The Ebro valley and its communities remained a continuing battleground. There is no evidence that Sertorius ever controlled the lower part of the valley. Lerida marks the southeastern border of his attacks, and Osca the most easterly of his strong points. The center of conflict was farther up the valley, and involved areas and communities that had been important in the Numantine Wars.

[208] Sall. *H.* 1.85, 122; Oros. 5.23.30.

[209] Livy 91 fr. 18 (Loeb).

[210] E. Gabba (1973) pp. 303–6, 333.

[211] Livy 91 fr. 18 (Loeb).

[212] Plut. *Vit. Sert.* 14; A. Schulten (1926) pp. 82–83. A parallel can be found here with the mission schools for young Indians where they were part hostages and part students: J. Axtell (1981) pp. 253–54.

[213] Livy *Per.* 94; Frontin. *Str.* 2.11.2; Plut. *Vit. Pomp.* 17–19.

[214] Livy 91 fr. 18 (Loeb); Oros. 5.23.11.

Pompey moved up the river in 75 B.C. He captured Clunia and may even have wintered among the Vaccaei.[215] In the following year he captured Cauca, but failed to seize Pallantia. Even as Sertorian resistance crumbled in 73–72, oppida like Auxum, Termantia, and Calagurris remained Sertorian strongholds. The death of Sertorius did not end their resistance. More bitter fighting was necessary before the frontier system on the Ebro was restored.[216]

Much of the rest of the Sertorian-Pompeian struggle cannot be regarded as strictly frontier warfare. Sertorius revived some of the strategies of the Scipios in the third century by seizing the eastern Meseta and using the mountain passes to sweep down on the coastal communities.[217] Many other border areas saw fighting, but it was more the conflict of rival Roman armies and thus outside our concern.

A final word should be said about Sertorius, since he is often compared with Viriathus as a person who used native forces to oppose the advance of the Romans. He was a soldier who understood the indigenous people wherever he went, who could learn their language and even play on their local customs and superstitions. The sacred white stag that accompanied Sertorius is an excellent example of this.[218] He was not a social bandit or a friend of the unconquered indigenous population. He used those forces only when it suited his needs. His true interests lay with the Romano-Iberian establishment and the recently arrived Roman refugee population. Like the Civil War of the next generation, the Sertorian War was basically a struggle between Romans and their clients.

One result of the prolonged Sertorian War was confusion and disorder both within the province and on the frontier. Towns and countryside had suffered, and the losses were heavy for rich and poor alike.[219] The delicate, carefully built network of provincial and frontier relationships that had allowed the Romans to control the Iberian peninsula with a limited military investment had been disrupted. This is especially evident on the Pyrenees frontier, where fighting had been fierce. Many people had fled into the mountain fastnesses. Some, like the Sertorian Aufidius, were content to live out their lives in obscurity in some mountain village.[220] Others would use the mountains as a staging area for bandit raids against the Roman settlements. The Ser-

[215] Sall. *H.* 2.94; Livy *Per.* 92; Plut. *Vit. Sert.* 21.
[216] Diod. 37.225; Livy *Per.* 96; Plut. *Vit. Pomp.* 20, *Vit. Sert.* 26–27; App. *BCiv.* 1.114–15.
[217] *Frontin. Str.* 2.5.31; Plut. *Vit. Sert.* 18; Oros. 5.23.6.
[218] Val. Max. 1.2.4; Frontin. *Str.* 1.11.13; Plut. *Vit. Sert.* 11, 20; Gell. *NA* 15.22.
[219] Pliny *HN* 3.18.
[220] Plut. *Vit. Sert.* 27.4.

torian Wars had also sharpened the military skills of such mountain folk as the Aquitanians. They, too, were ready to join in attacking lowland settlements.[221]

Pompey appears at his best in the dispositions that he made after his victory over Sertorius.[222] He understood the needs of the Pyrenees natives who had to be controlled but whose partly pastoral life required movement between lowland and highland zone. The foundation of Lugdunum Convenarum and Pompaelo, located on opposite sides of the mountains, was a key element in his frontier arrangements. Isidore of Seville describes the aims of these foundations:

> idem et Vascones . . . quos Cnaeus Pompeius edomita Hispania et ad triumphum venire festinans de Pyrenaei iugis deposuit et in unum oppidum congregavit. Unde et Convenarum urbs nomen accepit.[223]

> And likewise the Vascones whom Cnaeus Pompey when Spain had been conquered while hastening to return for his triumph brought down from the ridges of the Pyrenees and collected into one town. And from that action the city received its name of the Convenae or the Refugees.

References to both Vettones and Arevaci living at Convenarum show that the settlement comprised natives drawn from a variety of tribes who were moved to an area well removed from their homeland.[224]

The early development of Lugdunum Convenarum has already been discussed. The community of Pompaelo (modern Pampelona) played a similar role for the peoples on the southwestern slope of the Pyrenees. Located on the upper Arga river, it controlled the routes that led down from the western Pyrenees toward the Ebro and such communities as Calagurris and Grachurris.[225] By the time of the Empire it had become a road junction.[226]

The actions of Pompey and his colleagues returned the Iberian frontier zones to something of their former condition. In the period between Sertorius and the Civil Wars, Roman strategy and native reaction changed little. Some military action was necessary. In 69 B.C. M. Pupius Piso Frugi Calpurnianuas was granted a triumph for his actions in Spain.[227] In 56–55 B.C. Q. Caecilius Metellus Nepos had to

---

[221] Caes. *BGall*, 3.23.5–6.
[222] Caes. *BCiv*. 1.61.3, 2.18.7; Plut. *Vit. Pomp*. 21.1; E. Gabba (1970) pp. 147–48.
[223] Isid. *Etym*. 9.2.107.
[224] R. Gavelle (1960).
[225] Athen 14.657F; Strabo 3.4.10.
[226] K. Miller (1916) cols. 170–71, 174.
[227] A. Degrassi (1947) p. 565; T.R.S. Broughton (1952) pp. 124, 129.

suppress a revolt of the Vaccaei. Clunia was again the center of the action.[228]

It is the governorship of C. Julius Caesar about which we have the most information for this period, and the deeds of Caesar form a fitting finale to this study of the Republican frontier in Iberia. As with most other aspects of his career, the actions of Caesar as governor of Hispania Ulterior are surrounded with controversy.[229] Social and economic problems continued to plague the area, probably in part as a result of the strains imposed by Romanization. Caesar mediated disputes between creditors and debtors, thus alleviating a situation that must have contributed to the endemic banditry.[230]

Caesar undertook a series of actions against native centers in his frontier zone. He claimed that the campaigns were necessary to suppress banditry, while his political enemies argued that he had provoked war to win military prestige. The conflicts started in the mountainous area between the Duero and the Tagus. The natives refused Caesar's demands to come down from the mountains and settle in the plain, instead fleeing toward the north.[231] This provided Caesar with an excuse to follow in the footsteps of Decimus Brutus Callaicus and attack the northwestern part of the peninsula. The actions were evidently successful, since Caesar was entitled to a triumph.[232] The permanent impact should not be exaggerated, however. Livy claimed that *Lusitanos subegit*. Other sources pictured Caesar as conquering the whole of the northwest and Augustus only redoing what Caesar had basically accomplished.[233] The hard fighting of the Cantabrian campaigns of Augustus refutes this notion.

With the wars of Caesar, the problems of the frontier in Iberia began to blend with those of the Civil Wars and the actions of Augustus. The Civil Wars even more than those of Sertorius were affairs among Romans.[234] The internal disturbances could not but help to encourage restless native elements. References to banditry continued, and frontier protection was still necessary. Caesar noted that *hic etiam propter barbarorum crebras excursiones omnia loca quae sunt ab oppidis remota turribus et munitionibus retinentur*.[235] Other references exist to these frontier towers.[236]

[228] Dio Cass. 39.54.1–2; F. Wattenberg (1963) pp. 28–29.
[229] Cic. *Balb.* 43; Livy *Per.* 103; Vell. Pat. 2.43.4; Suet *Caes.* 18; App. *Hisp.* 102; M. Gelzer (1968) pp. 61–63.
[230] Cic. *Balb.* 43, 63; Plut. *Vit. Caes.* 12.1–2.
[231] Plut. *Vit. Caes.* 12.1; Dio Cass. 37.52.3–37.53.4.
[232] Plut. *Vit. Caes.* 12.2–13.1.
[233] Livy *Per.* 103; Dio Cass. 37.53.
[234] J. Harmond (1970); E. Gabba (1970).
[235] Caes. *BHisp.* 8.3
[236] Caes. *BHisp.* 8.3–6; Pliny *HN* 3.5.169; A. García y Bellido (1945) pp. 55–63.

Banditry remained widespread. Varro comments that bandits prevented full use of the rich farmland of Lusitania.[237] He probably knew
this from personal experience, since he had served in Hispania Ulterior during the 40s. Cicero mentions bandits around Castulo, and in
48 B.C. Cassius Longinus had to drive back frontier raiders.[238] Important brigands such as Corocotta could still operate in the Iberian
peninsula during the reign of Augustus.[239] No real end of the problem
could come until Augustus could complete the conquest of the peninsula and establish a firm administration over the whole area. An inscription of 2 B.C. from Hispania Ulterior claimed that by the actions
of Augustus *provincia pacata est*.[240] Nevertheless, many soldiers remained in the area during the early Empire. Even after two centuries
of warfare, Iberia, like Sardinia, remained one of the unfinished frontier legacies of the Republic.

[237] Varro *Rust*. 1.16.2.
[238] Cic. *Fam*. 10.31.1.
[239] Dio Cass. 56.43.3.
[240] *CIL* 6. 31267; A García Bellido (1945) pp. 66–68.

CHAPTER 7

THE ROMAN FRONTIER IN
SARDINIA AND CORSICA

The frontiers of northern Italy and Liguria were vital to the heartland of Rome. Failure of border management there would allow hostile tribes to attack the core Roman territory in Italy and even threaten Rome itself. Stable border areas in the north were essential for the survival and development of Roman Italy. The great expenditure of time, money, and blood by the state demonstrates their importance during the third and second centuries B.C.

With the expansion of Rome into the Mediterranean, frontier control became more complicated. Rome had to think not only of the defense of Italy but also of its increasing role as the protector of frontiers inherited from the peoples that had been conquered or brought into the alliance system. Each of these frontiers required strategic planning and political considerations, as well as basic decisions about the degree Rome wanted to commit its national interest and finite resources. Each frontier zone had its own involved history going back long before the period of Roman expansion. And each contributed in different ways to the cumulative experience that was the Republican frontier.

Of these frontier systems, none posed more difficult problems for Roman decision-makers than Sardinia and Corsica. First of all, their very geographical position made them unique. Like Sicily, they were not part of continental Italy but were so close and accessible to the peninsula that their development was inextricably bound up with the mainland. Control of the islands by a hostile power would pose a threat to Italy itself and to developing Roman interests in the north-western and western Mediterranean.

The two islands differed greatly in their backgrounds. In Sardinia, at the time of the first Phoenician contacts in the ninth century B.C. the native groups were at widely varying levels of social and political development. The nearly six centuries of Phoenician and Carthaginian occupation that followed resulted not only in widespread Punic settlement and Punic influence but also in the formation of a mixed Punic-Sardinian social group that was to have an impact on the early stages of Romanization. In Corsica, meanwhile, geography had limited more severely the degree of colonial penetration. The frontier there proved

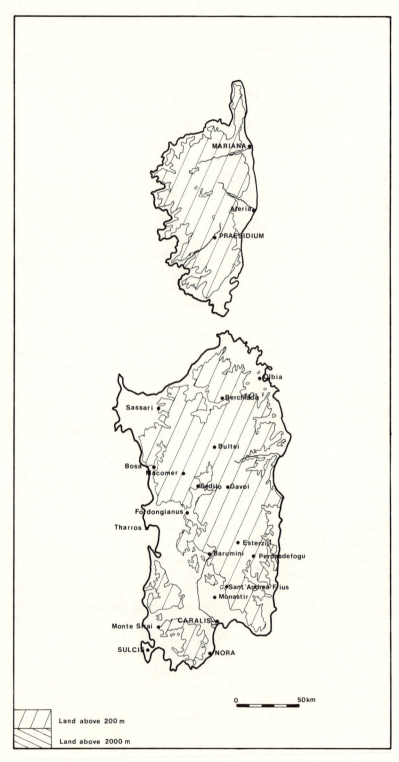

4. *Sardinia and Corsica*

less problematic for Rome in its social and economic implications. For this reason the frontier experience in each island will be considered individually, with greater emphasis given to the more important and better documented Sardinian frontier.

SARDINIA

Sardinia is only 230 kilometers from Italy, but the face turned toward the Italian shore is rough and inhospitable, with only one good harbor at Olbia on the northeastern coast. The better harbors, the main access routes to the interior, and the more fertile land lie in the west and southwest. A large plain surrounds modern Cagliari (ancient Caralis). Branches of this extend into the river valleys of the Cixerri, Samassi, and Mannu and link Cagliari with the northeast. In the west-central part of the island is the level expanse of the Campidano. Another flat area can be found between Alghero and Porto Torres in the northwestern part. This limited distribution of good land meant that most settlement would concentrate in the western half of the island in the plains and in the transition zones between the mountains and plains.[1] The western and southwestern focus also made the island attractive to Phoenician and Carthaginian settlers who had interests in Sicily, North Africa, and Spain. At the same time, Sardinia was far from Roman and Punic centers of power. The island's relative isolation, along with its rugged terrain, gave rise to strongly independent cultural developments.

A total recapitulation of the prehistory of Sardinia is not necessary for an understanding of Punic and Roman frontier development there.[2] The events of the later Bronze Age and the Iron Age are important, though, since they engendered traditions that were still alive when the Romans arrived. The first Phoenicians coming as early as the ninth century B.C. found an old and relatively sophisticated culture whose main physical expression was the nuraghi, or stone towers.[3] The nuragic culture was the culmination of a long indigenous development whose outlines are only now beginning to be understood.

The tradition stretches back at least to the era when metals came into common use in the Mediterranean. Trade contacts had already placed Sardinia in a larger Mediterranean context.[4] In fact, the origin

[1] Sil. *Pun.* 12.372 notes the inhospitable face of Sardinia that points toward Italy. Sil. *Pun.* 12.372; R. King (1975) pp. 23–24, 82–85; G. Lilliu (1962) p. 6; M. Guido (1964) pp. 23–29; G. Lilliu (1967) pp. 1–7.
[2] M. Guido (1964); G. Lilliu (1962).
[3] G. Lilliu (1962); M. Guido (1964) pp. 106–86.
[4] W. Bray (1963) pp. 155–90; M. Guido (1964) pp. 44–67.

of these contacts probably predates metallurgy, since Sardinia pos-
sesses obsidian.[5] This would have drawn outsiders to the western coast
of the island, establishing a pattern of trade and island development
that continued as groups in the Mediterranean switched from the use
of stone to the use of copper as their basic material for tools and
weapons.

One result of these interactions during the second millenium B.C.
was the appearance of the so-called nuragic culture.[6] The name is
derived from the stone towers found in abundance on the island. Although reliable construction dates for these are still few, the mid-
second millenium B.C. seems to be the period when most began to be
built. The heaviest concentration of the towers is in the upland between the two hundred and seven hundred meter levels in the west-
central and northwestern part of Sardinia. They presently are less
common in the lowlands. Continuous occupation and agricultural activity since the Phoenician period has resulted in the dismantling of
many nuraghi in the more fertile areas.[7]

It is obvious that not all of the nuraghi were built at the same time,
although only more carefully controlled excavations will provide a clear
picture of the evolution of this cultural form.[8] The builders of many
of the earliest ones must have been the Sardinian clans who positioned
their towers to protect a certain territory and control the transhumance routes so important in developing a semipastoral society.[9]

By the late Bronze Age the Sardinians had expanding horizons.
Archaeological finds show that they were involved in trading metals
with the powers of the eastern Mediterranean.[10] They may have taken
to piracy and mercenary service as the world of the late Bronze Age
collapsed.[11] The nuragic culture survived this collapse. By the tenth
century B.C. it developed new contacts with the eastern Mediterranean
and entered its most important phase. This is reflected in the appearance of fortified nuragic systems such as Barumini and Nuraghi Or-
rubiu.[12] At Barumini an elaborate nuragic complex is surrounded by
a large village, suggesting a feudal system with a warrior elite deriving
its support from a dependent peasantry.[13] The importance of warfare

[5] M. Guido (1964) p. 44; G. Lilliu (1967) p. 21.
[6] M. Guido (1964) pp. 106–13; G. Lilliu (1962) pp. 158–207.
[7] M. Guido (1964) pp. 106–9; R. King (1975) pp. 37–41.
[8] M. Guido (1964) pp. 110–27; G. Lilliu (1962) pp. 15, 208–309.
[9] G. Lilliu (1962) p. 249.
[10] M. Guido (1964) pp. 110–11.
[11] M. Guido (1964) pp. 187–91.
[12] G. Lilliu (1959); M. Guido (1964) pp. 113–17, 121–27.
[13] M. Guido (1964) pp. 139–44; G. Lilliu (1962) pp. 352–56.

during this period is shown by the many finds of weapons like swords, daggers, and axes in hoards scattered around Sardinia.[14]

Our most vivid insight into the world of the nuragic warriors and their dependents comes from the bronze figurines that have been found on Sardinian sites.[15] Their usefulness in reconstructing the Sardinian society of the period makes them the equivalent of the great situlae and embossed plaques from the Este culture of Italy. We have warrior-leaders with cloak, dagger, and staff, and fighting men with shield, bow, and sword.[16] Animals, both wild and domestic, are prominent, reflecting the importance of hunting and herding for the Sardinians.[17] Other figures of strange and unexplained form presumably have religious associations.[18]

One factor in the development of the nuraghic society was the appearance of the first Phoenician traders and settlers. The first trade contacts have left few traces, but by the eighth century permanent Punic settlements began to be founded.[19] As with most Phoenician foundations, these were cautious coastal centers. The three earliest were Nora on the southeastern coast, Sulcis in the southwest, and Tharros on the west-central shore. The two other main Phoenician settlements that followed slightly later were Caralis (Cagliari), at the northern end of the Mannu River, and Bithia.[20] The centers were all placed to allow traders easy access to the pastoral products and mineral resources of the island. An indication of their small size is that relatively few objects of the eighth or even the seventh century B.C. have been found at the sites.[21] Centers like Bithia and Sulcis, however, underwent considerable expansion in the seventh and sixth centuries B.C. By the sixth and early fifth centuries, Sulcis began to develop its own back country by building such fortified outposts as Monte Sirai.[22] These Phoenician communities influenced the inhabitants of the nu-

---

[14] M. Guido (1964) pp. 156–72.

[15] M. Guido (1964) pp. 172–78; G. Lilliu (1962) pp. 328–35.

[16] M. Guido (1964) pls. 46–53.

[17] M. Guido (1964) pls. 54–55.

[18] M. Guido (1964) p. 176 pl. 61; G. Lilliu (1962) pp. 343–47.

[19] Paus. 10.17.9; M. Guido (1964) pp. 192–94; S. Moscati (1966) pp. 226–34, (1968) pp. 33–35; F. Barreca (1971).

[20] M. Guido (1964) pp. 194–96; S. Moscati (1968) pp. 38–43; S. M. Cecchini (1969) pp. 60–68, 93–98, 102–8, 126–31, 133–38; F. Barreca (1971) p. 16.

[21] Paus. 10.17.9 has Caralis as a Carthaginian foundation. A large Punic cemetery has been found there: V. Bertoldi (1947) p. 7. The name Karalis is non-Punic, as is that of Nora: V. Bertoldi (1947) pp. 10–16; S. Moscati (1968) pp. 43–50.

[22] F. Barreca (1961); S. Moscati (1968) pp. 55–62. F. Barreca (1971) pp. 19–20 notes the limits of Phoenician power trying to expand in the face of militant natives. Good evidence of this is the destruction levels at Monte Sinai.

raghi but hardly posed a threat or even altered very greatly the indigenous cultural development.[23]

By the late sixth century B.C. the situation had changed. In Phoenicia the advance of the Babylonians and the capture of Tyre reduced the power and independence of the coastal cities. The western Mediterranean now became the sphere of the Punic colonial foundation at Carthage.[24] Colonial rivalries among Carthaginians, Etruscans, and Greeks intensified, culminating in the battle of Alalia off Corsica in 535 B.C. After this, Greek and Etruscan contacts with Sardinia remained limited. The Carthaginians decided to turn the Punic position on the island from separated trading enclaves to extensive territorial control.[25]

These expanded ambitions brought the Carthaginians into direct conflict with the warriors of the nuraghi. One reaction among the natives appears to have been to build nuraghi that could withstand the sophisticated siege techniques of the Carthaginians. Archaeological destruction levels at nuragic sites reflect this increased Carthaginian offensive.[26] The campaigns of Hasdrubal and Hamilcar seem to have broken the back of organized Sardinian resistance by 509 B.C.[27]

The military actions were accompanied by social, demographic, and economic changes. The goal of the Carthaginians was to control the fertile lowlands in the west of the island, as well as the main harbors.[28] Full conquest of the mountains, especially to the east, was beyond their resources and was probably considered unnecessary. The Sardinians still needed trade goods and lowland pastures for their herds. Interchange between the Punic and native areas continued, as finds of Punic coins in the interior attest.[29] To ensure a modicum of control and protection for the lowlands, a series of forts was established in southwestern Sardinia at such places as Monte Sirai, Monte Crabu, and Pani Loriga, and in coastal Sardinia at sites such as San Simeone, Sedilio, and Fordongianus. Each of these commanded access to a val-

[23] G. Lilliu (1948); S. Moscati (1968) pp. 62–64.

[24] D. Harden (1971) pp. 49–50.

[25] Diod. 4.29.6, 5.15.4–5; Just. *Epit.* 18.7, 19.1; Paus. 4.23; Oros. 4.6.7–9; M. Guido (1964) pp. 200–2; S. Moscati (1966) pp. 220, 222–23, (1968) pp. 21–26, 71. Just. *Epit.* 18.7.1–2 has the first expedition of Malco end in defeat.

[26] S. Moscati (1968) p. 28.

[27] Just. *Epit.* 19.1.1–7; S. Moscati (1966) p. 223, (1968) pp. 24–26.

[28] M. Guido (1964) pp. 202–9; S. Moscati (1966) p. 241.

[29] Diod. 4.30.5–6, 5.15.5 mentions pastoralism in Sardinia under the Carthaginians. S. Moscati (1968) pp. 72–78. S. Moscati (1966) pp. 246–47 and G. Lilliu (1948) p. 341 see a relation between these money concentrations and trade in animals.

ley leading out of the mountains and was in an excellent position to monitor movements between the nuragic upland and Punic lowland.[30]

In the lowlands, the Carthaginians encouraged agricultural development. Farms and orchards played an increasing role in the economy of Sardinia. The conditions that were to make Sardinia an early granary for Rome were largely created by the Carthaginians who relied heavily on Sardinian grain.[31] The people who did this were both Carthaginians and native Sardinians. The Carthaginian conquest meant an increasing flow of Punic settlers into the island. This is best expressed in the archaeological record, where the remains from the Carthaginian period are much more abundant than those for the Phoenician one.[32] The North African cities never had a large surplus population, however, and were never in the position to ship many of their own people to Sardinia.

We can assume that the Carthaginians followed their normal practice and incorporated willing natives into their colonial system. Although many Sardinians were killed or driven as refugees into the mountains, many more presumably threw in their lot with Carthage and reaped the benefit of the relative peace and prosperity that the Carthaginian control brought.[33] One such man was Hampsicora, a Sardinian with a Punic name, who led the early native resistance against Rome. Significantly, he came from Cornus in the west-central part of the island, an area with a particularly high concentration of nuraghi.[34] Notables like Hampsicora maintained regular contact with the people in the hills.

The Carthaginians had military as well as economic reasons for encouraging these contacts. Mercenaries were the backbone of the Carthaginian army, and the Punic leaders regarded Sardinia as a good place to recruit tough mountain warriors for their forces.[35] For the warriors of the interior, whose opportunities to raid the lowlands were being increasingly restricted, mercenary service must have seemed a tempting outlet. Such recruitment would curb the bellicose population and establish networks of relationship in the interior.[36]

One probable indication of this activity is the abundance of Cartha-

[30] S. Moscati (1975).

[31] Diod. 11.20.4–5, 21.16.1; G. Lilliu (1948) p. 349; S. Moscati (1968) pp. 81–82, 109.

[32] Cic. Scauro. 42; G. Lilliu (1948) pp. 345–49; S. Moscati (1968) pp. 81–82.

[33] V. Bertoldi (1947). For parallel developments in North Africa, especially related to the spread of agriculture, see J. A. Ilevbare (1973) pp. 28–30.

[34] E. Bouchier (1917) pp. 66–68.

[35] Paus. 10.17.5; A. García y Bellido (1952) p. 651.

[36] Diod. 14.95.1.

ginian coins found in the interior mountains at such sites as Bultei, Gavoi, and Perdasdefogu.[37] Some of the money may have been acquired through raiding or from the sale of pastoral products, but accumulations of several hundred to several thousand coins most likely came from the paychests of returning Sardinian mercenaries. If these warriors represented the old nuragic ruling class, this influx of wealth would have fortified old status relationships. If they were new warriors now enriched and made more sophisticated by contact with the outside, the result would have been social conflict with the old order. In either case, these returning mercenaries would have spread the taste for Mediterranean goods and would thus have drawn the mountain folk increasingly into the Carthaginian cultural and economic order. At the same time, they acquainted their fellow Sardinians with Carthaginian tactics and skills, as well as weaknesses in their political, social, and military organization. This in turn increased the effectiveness of the raids from the mountains into the plains.

Another factor complicated the border situation. Most of the garrisons on Sardinia must have been largely manned by troops drawn from other dependencies of Carthage. For some, the free mountains beyond their forts must have served as a tempting escape from the dissatisfactions of military life. We can presume that as a steady flow of deserters went into the backcountry, they were joined by escaped slaves and displaced peasants from the low country, all contributing to the banditry problem.

These trends led to the creation of an intermediate zone between the settled inhabitants of the plain and the internal mountaineers. Living in this zone were legitimate pastoralists with their seasonal migrations, bandits living just beyond the areas of Carthaginian control, and restless returned mercenaries. (It was similar to the situation that developed in Lusitania.) It probably had a certain resemblance to what Owen Lattimore, in his research on the Chinese border, called the "inner frontier."[38] Many individuals had Punic military training and cultural ties with the Carthaginian society. At the same time, their status as outlaws and marginal people forced them to look to the people of the mountains for support. Under the best circumstances they could serve as intermediaries between the two groups. At worst they could, with their superior military and organizational skills, heighten the effectiveness of the raids coming down from the mountains.

The Roman decision to move into Sardinia was directly related to

[37] S. Moscati (1966) pp. 245ff. notes that experts think this money was coined in Sardinia.
[38] O. Lattimore (1951).

her need to neutralize the island during the long Carthaginian conflict.[39] During the First Punic War, Roman generals raided the island.[40] The end of that war brought changes in Rome's role in the western Mediterranean. Rome was now the dominant naval power in the area and had acquired its first overseas possession in the island of Sicily. The control of Sardinia and Corsica was becoming important. The growing weakness of Carthage had allowed the island to slide into chaos, a condition that kindled new anxiety at Rome. The stage was set for dramatic intervention.

The spark was the outbreak of the great mercenary revolt in North Africa in 240 B.C.[41] Knowledge of the uprising spread throughout the Carthaginian world and in Sardinia stimulated the mercenary garrisons on the island to rebel.[42] A relief force, also composed of mercenaries, was sent to suppress the uprising, but it too joined the revolt. The soldiers then turned on the Carthaginian residents in the island and massacred them in large numbers. Polybius claimed that the Carthaginians had been exterminated, but this is certainly an exaggeration.[43]

The anger of the mercenaries was directed at the Carthaginian officials and new arrivals from North Africa. A large Punic-oriented element probably survived on the island. The mercenaries managed to hold the towns until they quarreled with the "natives" and were forced to flee to Italy.[44] These natives could not have been unsubdued inhabitants of the mountains, for they would not have been in a position to dislodge the professional soldiers from well-defended towns. Instead they must have been the Punicized natives and old Punic settlers. They might initially have welcomed the relief from Carthaginian taxation and administrative harassment, but they quickly became disenchanted with the bands of unruly mercenaries living in their midst.

Rome could not help but be concerned with the events in Sardinia. They bore an uncomfortable resemblance to developments in Sicily in the years immediately before the outbreak of the First Punic War. The Senate refused an initial request of the mercenaries that Rome assume control of the island. A year later, however, when the plea

---

[39] Diod. 15.27.4 refers to a planned Roman colony of 378 B.C. I. Didu (1972) doubts evidence for early colonial attempts by Rome. The reference probably results from confusion with a fourth-century mainland colony.

[40] Polyb. 3.24.11; Zonaras 8.10; A. Degrassi (1947) p. 548; S. Moscati (1968) pp. 83–84.

[41] B. H. Warmington (1964) pp. 200–4.

[42] S. Moscati (1968) p. 84.

[43] Polyb. 1.79.1–7.

[44] Polyb. 1.79.5–6.

was repeated, the Romans changed their position and began their formal occupation of the island.[45] This hesitancy shows that the Roman leadership did not take the action lightly. Nevertheless, the move has been roundly condemned in the historical sources, both ancient and modern. Polybius makes the obvious comparison with the Mamertines and harshly denounces Rome for its Sardinian decision.[46] Commentators have generally regarded this as a piece of post-Punic War Roman arrogance, whose hubris helped bring on the nemesis of the Second Punic War.[47]

The decision has a certain justification when considered in terms of Roman interests and responsibilities in the area. Sardinia was sliding into chaos, and there was no guarantee that the Carthaginians could regain control and restore order. The increasing power of the lowland natives and the removal of the Carthaginian garrisons would lead not only to internal disaster but also to a revival of piracy. Rome had assumed responsibility for the safety of the sea lanes near Italy in the wake of her maritime victory of the First Punic War. Rome always had a great fear of any disordered elements within her sphere of influence, and this sphere now included Sardinia.

The consul for 238 B.C., Tiberius Sempronius Gracchus, seized the island. The nature and extent of his accomplishments is unclear. The sources are limited, and there is some confusion about the campaigns of the elder Gracchus and those of his grandson in 177 B.C.[48] Florus provides the clearest account:

> Sardiniam Gracchus arripuit. Sed nihil illi gentium feritas Insanorumque—nam sic vocantur—immanitas montium profuere. Saevitum in urbes urbemque urbium Caralim ut gens contumax vilisque mortis saltem desiderio patrii soli domaretur.[49]

> Gracchus captured Sardinia. But the ferocity of the peoples and the frightfulness of the Mad Mountains—for so they are called— provided no advantage for him. There were savage attacks on the cities and on the foremost of the cities Caralis, so that a people rebellious and without concern for death might at least be controlled by their desire for their native land.

The emphasis was on gaining control of the towns, and especially of Caralis. That center would provide the Romans with a harbor con-

---

[45] Polyb. 1.83.11, 1.88.8–12.
[46] Polyb. 3.28; F. Walbank (1957) p. 356.
[47] P. Meloni (1975) pp. 35–37; W. V. Harris (1979) pp. 191–93.
[48] T.R.S. Broughton (1951) p. 221.
[49] Florus 1.22.35.

venient for communication with Italy, and ready access to the fertile, thickly settled southwestern section of the island. The campaign of Gracchus did not involve extensive military effort, and he was not awarded a triumph.[50]

The Romans faced many problems as they began their occupation of Sardinia. They inherited all the difficulties that the Carthaginians had encountered in controlling the mountainous interior of the island. In addition, they had to deal with the initial hostility of the lowland Punic-Sardinians, who had participated in the expulsion of both the Carthaginians and the mercenaries and would not look with enthusiasm on the arrival of a new conquering power. As an entirely alien force, Rome faced the dangerous possibility that her presence would bring mountaineer and lowlander together in resistance. Moreover, there was the danger of Carthaginian interference, since a mutual cultural identity had built up over centuries of contact. Carthage would find in Sardinia many sympathetic elements if it wished to foment trouble against Rome.

These factors combined to incite a revolt in 236 B.C. Gracchus had probably gained control of the cities, but had done little to extend Roman power into the countryside and the mountains. Carthaginian agents were actively fomenting rebellion, presumably among the lowland groups, both urban and rural, that hardly found Roman domination to their liking.[51] The senate responded vigorously, however. Carthaginian ships were ordered to stay away from the ports of Sardinia that were natural centers of strong pro-Punic sympathy, and the consul of 235 B.C., T. Manlius Torquatus, was sent to the island.

It is clear, even from the limited source material, that Torquatus was the person responsible for establishing a firm Roman control in Sardinia. In the words of Velleius:

Sardinia inter primum et secundum bellum Punicum ductu T. Manlii consulis certum recepit imperi iugum.[52]

Sardinia between the First and Second Punic War by the leadership of T. Manlius the consul received the firm yoke of Empire.

Relatively little is known about Torquatus, but because he was awarded a triumph, he apparently undertook successful military campaigns. His task was evidently not complicated, for he had only one year in office.[53] His most important accomplishment was probably the crea-

[50] P. Meloni (1949) pp. 122–24, (1975) pp. 35–37; G. DeSanctis (1967) pp. 272–73.
[51] P. Meloni (1949) p. 127, (1975) p. 40.
[52] Vell. Pat. 2.38.2.
[53] Livy Per. 20; Eutropius 3.3; Oros. 4.12.2; A. Degrassi (1947) p. 549.

tion of a client network like that which formed the basis of Roman control in any newly acquired territory. Torquatus' connection with powerful people in the island was probably the reason for his being sent back there in 215 B.C., when the uprising of Hampsicora again threatened Roman control.[54]

The Romans apparently thought that Torquatus had completely suppressed resistance in the old Punic zone, and that the island was ready for regular administration. In 234 B.C. a praetor, P. Cornelius, was dispatched.[55] As was often the case, however, the Romans had overestimated the degree of their control. Cornelius was soon faced by a revolt that must have been in part provoked by his own organizing and tax-collecting activities. The problems for Rome compounded. Trouble in Sardinia was matched by unrest in Corsica and Liguria. The army in Sardinia was decimated by disease, a problem that was to haunt generations of Romans fighting on the island.[56] Among the victims was the praetor himself. After restoring relative order in Corsica, the consul Sp. Carvilius Maximus moved to Sardinia, assumed the duties of praetor, and temporarily suppressed the uprising. The fighting was fierce, and the results were transitory. Maximus was granted a triumph, but almost immediately the Sardinians rebelled.[57]

Another consul, M' Pomponius Matho, was assigned to Sardinia in 233 B.C. The details of his activities are scarce, but the general outline seems clear. Resistance was still centered in the southwestern part of the island, with the Carthaginians as the *agents provocateurs*. So seriously did they menace the Roman position that the senate dispatched an embassy to Carthage with threats of war if Punic interference in Sardinia continued. The reply was truculent, but neither side pressed the issue to the point of combat. More bitter campaigning lay ahead for the Romans. Matho was awarded a triumph, but the strife continued.[58]

In 232 B.C. both consuls, M. Aemilius Lepidus and M. Publicius Malleolus, were sent to Sardinia.[59] They appear to have conducted a two-stage campaign. The first stage was conducted in the southwest and central part of the island, and the Romans emerged victorious. When they turned against a tribe called the Corsi, however, they were

[54] P. Meloni (1975) pp. 41–42.
[55] P. Meloni (1949) p. 130; T.R.S. Broughton (1951) p. 224.
[56] Zonaras 8.18. On the disease-ridden climate of Sardinia see Paus. 10.17.6; Livy 23.34.11; Suet. *Tib.* 36.2; Tac. *Ann.* 2.85.3; Strabo 5.2.7; Cic. *Fam.* 7.24.1, *Quint.* 2.3.7.
[57] Zonaras 8.18; A. Degrassi (1947) p. 549; P. Meloni (1949) pp. 131–32.
[58] Zonaras 8.18; A. Degrassi (1947) p. 549; P. Meloni (1949) pp. 132–33.
[59] T.R.S. Broughton (1951) p. 225; P. Meloni (1975) pp. 45–46.

defeated and lost much of the spoils taken in the earlier actions. The identity and location of these Corsi has been the subject of considerable scholarly dispute.[60] The name suggests that they were natives of Corsica. Some have argued that the Roman commanders, after suppressing the revolt in Sardinia, crossed to the other island, but a tribal group called Corsi also inhabited the Gallura region of northern Sardinia.[61]

The reference to loot lends support to the argument for a campaign based in Sardinia.[62] It appears improbable that the Roman commanders would transport booty from Sardinia to Corsica, only to lose it while fighting on the Corsican frontier. A continuing campaign in the northeast of Sardinia makes considerable sense for other reasons. The wars of the previous years restored Roman control in the old Punic-Sardinian areas. The growing Roman involvement increased the value of the port of Olbia on the northeastern coast of the island. It was the closest harbor to the Italian coast and allowed rapid communication, especially with the northern frontier on the island. The position of Olbia was similar to that of Genoa on the Ligurian coast. The Carthaginians had begun developing the area relatively late, although the concentration of nuraghi around Olbia suggests that trade may have been going on for a long time before the foundation of a formal Punic settlement.[63] Like Genoa, Olbia had a small hinterland. A secure communication route had to be established through mountainous territory, and a key factor in securing this route was the pacification of the Corsi. It was most likely in the course of this action that the baggage train of the Roman army was ambushed.[64]

In 231 B.C. this series of pacification campaigns came to an end.[65] Both consuls were dispatched to Sardinia. M. Pomponius Matho, probably the brother of the Matho who was awarded a triumph in 233, was apparently assigned the task of securing a frontier in the southwest.[66] There the network of contacts developed by his kinsman would have served both him and Rome well. The back of the Punic-Sardinian resistance in the lowlands had evidently been broken. Now

[60] P. Meloni (1949) pp. 134–37 and n. 38.

[61] Pliny *HN* 3.7.85; Paus. 10.17.5; Ptol. 3.3.6. The Gallura area of Sardinia was a logical entry point for Corsicans who have historically contributed a great deal to the repopulation of the area: R. King (1975) p. 69.

[62] Zonaras 8.18; P. Meloni (1949) pp. 136–37.

[63] *Not. Scav.* (1911) p. 241; A. Taramelli (1936) p. 45; S. Moscati (1966) pp. 242–43. On the remains at Olbia see D. Levi (1950) pp. 5–120; G. Maetzke (1961) pp. 51–52; F. Barreca (1967) pp. 103–26.

[64] P. Meloni (1949) pp. 136–37.

[65] P. Meloni (1975) pp. 46–49.

[66] A. Degrassi (1947) p. 549; T.R.S. Broughton (1951) pp. 224–26.

the problem was to control the intermediate zone between mountain
and lowland. This was the area of the transhumants whose mobile life
and knowledge of both plain and mountains made them difficult to
control. The complexities of fighting in this transitional zone is shown
by a passage in Zonaras:

καὶ Μάρκος μὲν Πομπώνιος Σαρδόνας ἔφερε, καὶ μαθὼν τοὺς
πλείονας αὐτῶν ἐς σπήλαια ὑλώδη καὶ δυσεξεύρετα κατα-
δύντας, μὴ δυνάμενός τε αὐτοὺς εὑρεῖν, κύνας ἐκ τῆς
Ἰταλίας μετεπέμψατο εὑρίνας, καὶ δι' ἐκείνων τὴν στίβον
καὶ τῶν ἀνθρώπων καὶ τῶν βοσκημάτων εὑρὼν πολλὰ ἀπετέ-
μετο.[67]

Marcus Pomponius was besieging the Sardinians, and he knew
that many of them were hiding in caverns that were concealed by
woods and were difficult to uncover. When he could not find
them, he sent for keen-scented dogs from Italy, and with their
help he found the trail of both the men and their herds, and he
killed many of them.

Such actions inspired among the hill people a fear of the new colonial
power. Nevertheless, it represented only the beginning of a long campaign to dominate the backcountry of Sardinia.

Less successful were the efforts of Matho's colleague, C. Papirius
Maso.[68] Olbia seems to have been his base of operations, and his assignment was to advance the Roman frontier behind the seaport. The
Corsi were driven back from the plains of Olbia. When the Roman
forces attempted to pursue the Corsi into the mountains, though, they
were repeatedly ambushed.[69] Only with the greatest difficulty did Maso
achieve limited success and establish the rudiments of a frontier system. The ambiguity with which his accomplishments were viewed at
Rome is reflected in his triumph. Denied a full triumph by the senate,
he celebrated one at his own initiative on the Alban Mount.[70]

With the campaign of 231 B.C., the first stage of pacification on
Sardinia ended. A viable frontier had been established. Principal opponents were vanquished, and a system of faithful clients was established. Tribal groups bordering the lowlands either were defeated or
had reconciled to Roman rule. By 227 the Romans felt the situation
secure enough to return the island to praetorian administration.[71] The

[67] Zonaras 8.18; P. Meloni (1949) pp. 139–40.
[68] Zonaras 8.18; P. Meloni (1949) pp. 137–38.
[69] Cic. Nat. D. 3.20.52; Festus Epit. pp. 131–32.
[70] Val. Max. 3.6.5; A. Degrassi (1947) p. 549.
[71] T.R.S. Broughton (1951) p. 229.

sixteen years after 231 B.C. passed in relative peace. We can presume that there was some trouble, but apparently nothing beyond the limit that Rome was prepared to tolerate. Resentment over the imposition of taxes and the inefficiency and abuses of Roman administration probably continued. The problems rose in times of crisis, when Rome stepped up its demands on the developing agricultural resources.' The first report of new unrest came in 225 B.C., when the Romans were preparing for a war against the Gauls. The danger was sufficiently great for one of the consuls, C. Atilius Regulus, to be dispatched to Sardinia. His actions restored peace.[72]

Ten years passed before another outbreak. In the meantime, the international political and strategic situation had changed dramatically. Rome was now reeling from the defeats at the hand of Hannibal in 217–216 B.C. Carthage was thinking about restoring its former position in the western Mediterranean; and Sardinia, where a large, conservative, Punic-oriented population still existed, would have been a prime objective. Already in 217 B.C. a Carthaginian fleet had appeared off the island, and the Romans had taken additional hostages from the native population.[73]

Carthaginian agents must have found considerable discontent on the islands. The desperate conditions at Rome had forced the senate to adopt harsh and rapacious fiscal and administrative measures. The general tribute and grain exactions had become heavy.[74] These demands fell especially on the Punic-Sardinian landowners of the lowlands, where the lingering ethnic, cultural, and sentimental ties to Carthage were most strong. Additional factors favored the Carthaginians. The Roman garrison on the island was small, and it probably had been seriously depleted by the demands of wars in Italy and the ravages of disease affecting most units that served for long periods in Sardinia. Roman interests had been maintained largely by the skills and experience of the praetor Aulus Cornelius Mammula.[75] He had served for several years and was described as *provinciae peritum*. He was most likely a kinsman of the first praetor to serve on the island, and drew upon traditional familial ties to help maintain order and Roman influence. He was replaced by a man inexperienced in Sardinian affairs, however, and this information was conveyed to Carthage by a secret Sardinian embassy.[76]

[72] Polyb. 2.23.6–7; T.R.S. Broughton (1951) p. 230; P. Meloni (1975) pp. 49–50.
[73] Polyb. 3.96.7–12; Livy 22.31.1; Zonaras 8.26; P. Meloni (1975) pp. 50–52.
[74] Livy 23.32.8–9; Val. Max. 7.6.1; P. Meloni (1975) pp. 52–53.
[75] T.R.S. Broughton (1951) pp. 244, 250.
[76] Livy 23.21.2–6, 23.32.8–11.

This was a classic native revolt situation.[77] In the history of modern colonization, native revolts have tended to occur at moments when the position of the imperial power is seriously weakened by other domestic or external problems and when the general level of native discontent is suddenly increased by new, harsher administrative measures. The leaders in the native society who usually spark the revolt are from the semiacculturated groups who understand the problems of the dominant power and have some sense of the strengths and weaknesses of its masters, but who are not totally disassociated from their preconquest past. From this group emerges a new part-native, part-colonial leadership capable of welding these elements into effective revolt. The preconditions had developed in Sardinia, and the island awaited the appearance of a charismatic leader.

The man who assumed this leadership role was named Hampsicora, and he came from Cornus on the west-central coast of the island. The area around Cornus (modern Santa Caterina Pittinuri) has an especially high density of nuraghi, indicating its importance in the late Bronze and Iron Ages. Punic finds from its cemeteries show acculturation and identification with the Carthaginian overlords of the island.[78] Hampsicora is described by Livy as *tam auctoritate atque opibus longe primus* among the Sardinians. Members of his class had prospered as the Carthaginians encouraged large-estate agriculture and pastoralism on Sardinia. His name suggests identification with the Punic rulers.[79]

Hampsicora, a shrewd and practical native leader, had made his peace with Rome. If he had not, his fortunes would not have survived unimpaired in the early years of the new administration. A possible expression of this new loyalty was the Roman-sounding name of his son Hostus. Punic nomenclature in Sardinia was extremely conservative, with Semetic-sounding names persisting well into the imperial age.[80] The name Hostus is clearly not a direct adaptation from the dominant Roman aristocracy, which is often found with natives in other frontier areas. It would seem to be instead a gesture toward Romanization by a native trying to merge three diverse cultural worlds.

The power base of Hampsicora can be partly reconstructed from the ancient sources. It grew out of native Sardinian practices, Carthaginian developments, and Roman impositions. Control of Cornus was, of course, essential. Allied to that center were several local tribes (*civi-*

[77] S. L. Dyson (1971), (1975).

[78] M. Guido (1964) p. 108 fig. 29; S. Moscati (1968) pp. 172–73, 181.

[79] Livy 23.32.10–11. A. Taramelli (1936) pp. 43–44 considers Hampsicora to be a Carthaginian. V. Bertoldi (1947) p. 8 n. 1; P. Meloni (1975) pp. 55–56.

[80] Cic. *Scaur.* 42; *CIL* 10. 7513, 7856; V. Bertoldi (1947) pp. 7–9.

tates). The alliance system was certainly traditional, but the Carthaginians and Romans had found it expedient to leave it intact.[81] It provided Hampsicora with strong support in the lowlands. He also had connections with groups called the *pelliti Sardi* in the mountains.[82] This grew out of the symbiotic relationship that existed between highland and lowland in Sardinia, and the way that the great magnates exploited it. Not only did farmers and herders meet to exchange goods; the *principes* played a role in developing the transhumant economy of the island, which brought them into contact with the "skin clad" people of the interior.

Carthaginian agents certainly played some background role in the revolt, but the Sardinians rose before Carthaginian forces could arrive and assist them. No doubt they saw their opportunity when the Roman position was further weakened by the debilitating illness of the new governor, Q. Mucius Scaevola.[83] The revolt leader, Hampsicora, was able to rouse the native groups around Cornus. The Sardinians, and presumably many Punic-Sardinians, who were closer to the Roman center at Caralis and bound to Rome by ties of self-interest and personal loyalty remained faithful. To strengthen the Roman position and bring to the scene a man experienced in Sardinian affairs, the senate dispatched as governor T. Manlius Torquatus, who had begun the pacification of Sardinia twenty years earlier. The choice was a shrewd one.[84]

Torquatus arrived with his own fresh troops and reorganized the Roman army on the island. Having secured the loyalty of the southwest, he advanced toward Cornus. Hampsicora, who saw that a sustained rebellion required the support of warriors from the interior, had gone to recruit the *pelliti Sardi*. His son Hostus, who had been left in charge of the rebel forces, rashly entered into battle with the Roman army and was disastrously defeated.[85]

The defeat would have ended the revolt if the Carthaginians had not landed an expeditionary force and bolstered the flagging native resistance. Torquatus was forced to retreat in the direction of Caralis. The Punic-Sardinian army advanced, ravaging the land of those Sardinians who still remained loyal to Rome. The Romans turned and defeated the opposing army. The back of the rebellion was broken. Hostus and Hampsicora were dead, and the principal Carthaginian figures were taken prisoner. Cornus was captured, and the tribes who

[81] Livy 23.40.5–6.
[82] Livy 23.40.3–4.
[83] Livy 23.34.10–15.
[84] Livy 23.34, 23.40.15–16; T.R.S. Broughton (1951) p. 256.
[85] Livy 23.40.1–7; P. Meloni (1975) p. 58.

supported the rebellion were forced to give hostages and pay additional tribute. The foundations of Roman rule in Sardinia were restored.[86]

Although the island remained restless in the aftermath of the revolt, the governor, Q. Mucius, had recovered his health and had built his own network of personal connections. In the interest of administrative continuity, he was retained there for three more years. At a time when Roman manpower resources were strained to the limit the garrison was maintained at two legions, which indicates the potential for trouble the Romans recognized in Sardinia.[87] After Q. Mucius the senate sent L. Cornelius Lentulus, the third of that family to serve in Sardinia during the short history of Roman administration.[88]

The best indication of the secure Roman hold on the island was the change in Carthaginian tactics. They did not attempt to establish a second front or even a fifth column, but limited themselves instead to coastal raiding aimed at such centers as Olbia and Caralis. Even in last desperate days of the war, when the Carthaginians stimulated and led effective partisan movements in Liguria and Cisalpine Gaul, they did not seem to regard Sardinia as a fruitful area for this kind of action.[89] The Romans had wisely left the social, economic, and even political structure of the island intact, and the native leaders saw more reason for staying with Rome than throwing in their lot with the uncertain future of Carthage. Rome's own greater sense of security is evident in the last years of the Punic War, when praetors were assigned to the island for single terms only and more attention was devoted to Sardinia's potential as a naval base.[90]

All was not peaceful on the island. The interior mountains were, of course, largely unpacified; but the Romans were willing there, as in other mountainous frontiers, to accept a low level of violence rather than attempt the arduous task of total conquest. More serious were the strains that Romanization brought to lowland Sardinian society. Sardinia was becoming an increasingly important granary for the Roman armies serving in North Africa. From 204 to 202 B.C., large quantities of grain left Sardinia for Africa. No doubt the Romans also demanded other items, especially wool for cloth from the large Sar-

[86] Livy 23.40–23.41.7; P. Meloni (1975) pp. 59–61.
[87] Livy 24.10.4, 24.11. 2–3, 24.44.5, 25.3.6.
[88] Livy 26.1.11–12; T.R.S. Broughton (1951) p. 273.
[89] This is surprising when it is considered that strong Punic elements were still to be found in places like Caralis: A. Taramelli (1913), (1936).
[90] Livy 27.22.6–7, 28.46.14, 30.2.4. Part of the reason for the Romans' success was their willingness to leave Punic institutions intact. An example is the inscription from Pauli Gerrei in the mountains of Barbagio, which is trilingual and mentions suphetes with Punic names: *CIL* 10. 7856; A. Taramelli (1936) pp. 45–46.

dinian herds.[91] The increased exactions would have created serious problems for the large landowners who had just recovered from the aftermath of the revolt of Hampsicora. Moreover, we know from other examples later in the history of the Empire that the cost of Romanization in the form of a changed way of life was often high. The economy was strained, and cash was in short supply.[92] References to debt and the increased activity of money-lenders indicate the extent of the problem. As tensions increased, the Romans weakened their military position by drawing off five thousand allied soldiers to serve against Philip V of Macedon.[93]

Fortunately, the senate had learned from experience and chose to apply administrative correctives before military intervention was necessary. M. Porcius Cato, a rising senator with an already established reputation for probity and administrative skill, was appointed praetor in Sardinia for the year 198 B.C.[94] He attacked two sources of local discontent: the expensive way of life of Roman administrators that had to be supported by the locals, and the growing problem of debt. Official expenses of the praetor and his staff were cut to the bone, and a systematic campaign was waged against the money-lenders. The actions proved effective. Even though Cato continued the tribute in grain and clothing, unrest among the lowland Punic-Sardinians subsided, and for nearly two decades little is heard of trouble in Sardinia.

New problems emerged by the end of the 180's, centering on the internal frontiers of Sardinia. A passage in Livy sums up the situation:

Ilienses adjunctis Balarorum auxiliis pacatam provinciam invaserant nec eis invalido exercitu et magna parte pestilentia absumpto resisti poterat. Eadem et Sardorum legati nuntiabant orantes ut urbibus saltem—iam enim agros deploratos esse—opem senatus ferret.[95]

The Ilienses with the support of the Balari had invaded the pacified part of the province nor could resistance be mounted with the army weakened and to a great degree weakened by disease. Also the ambassadors of the Sardinians announced these same things, begging that the senate provide help for the cities now that the fields themselves had been devastated.

The location of one of these groups, the Balari, has recently been clarified by the discovery of an inscription at Berchidda, near Castro

[91] Livy 29.36.1–2, 30.24.5, 30.36.2–4.
[92] M. F. Gyles (1964).
[93] Livy 31.8.10–11.
[94] Livy 32.27.3; Nepos Cato 1.4; A. E. Astin (1978) pp. 20–21.
[95] Livy 41.6.6–7. The delegation actually arrived in Rome in 178 B.C., but the problems can be traced back to 181 B.C.

Oschiri, that mentions them.[96] The Ilienses were apparently located
nearby, probably in the mountain chain of Oceane and the mountains
of Ala.[97] The attacks of the tribesmen threatened the plain of Olbia
and its communications with the rest of the island, and endangered
settled native supporters of Rome. This was to fuel instability and
banditry similar to that which took place in Spain in the later second
century B.C.

A delegation from Sardinia appeared in Rome in 178 B.C., but the
problems were already well known to the senate. In 181 B.C. the praetor M. Pinarius Rusca, after defeating the natives in Corsica, crossed
over to Sardinia and defeated the Ilienses.[98] A very unstable frontier
peace was evidently established. The embassy from the island in 178
B.C. impressed on the senate the gravity of the situation. In 177 B.C.
the island was made into a consular province, and one of the newly
elected consuls, Ti. Sempronius Gracchus, was made governor. He
was the son of the man who in 238 had occupied the island. As praetor
and proconsul, he had just completed a successful tour in Hispania
Citerior, where his combination of military and political abilities had
brought a stable peace to that turbulent frontier.[99] Two legions, auxiliaries, and naval forces were assigned to him. Not since the days of
the Hannibalic Wars had the island seen such a large force. In addition, the praetor of 178 B.C., T. Aebutius, was retained in Sardinia.
The wars in Sardinia, with their encircling movements and coordinated actions, required the service of two experienced commanders.

Gracchus certainly applied in Sardinia what he had learned in Spain.
He also used the approach recently developed in Liguria, where the
emphasis had been on reducing the force of population in the mountains. The fighting was spread over two years. Details are sparse, but
the sources emphasize the heavy casualties that Gracchus inflicted on
the native population. Twelve thousand natives were supposedly slain,
and some eighty thousand were rounded up as prisoners and sold into
slavery. This massive influx of captives deflated the price of slaves,
and in fact the expression *Sardi venales* became a colloquialism for a
cheap item.[100]

Even if the numbers are somewhat exaggerated, the casualty figures
are striking. First of all, the capture of so many natives in the moun-

[96] P. Meloni (1971) pp. 242–43, (1975) pp. 70–71.
[97] P. Meloni (1975) p. 71.
[98] Livy 40.34.13.
[99] P. Meloni (1975) pp. 71–75.
[100] Livy 41.6.5–7, 41.8.3–5, 41.9.1–2, 41.12.4–7, 41.15.6–7; P. Meloni (1975) pp. 73–
74. Cf. A. J. Toynbee (1965) vol. 2 pp. 170–73 on the relative intensity of slaving in
Sardinia compared with Molossia.

tain strongholds of Sardinia was an impressive military feat. In addition, the figures suggest severe overpopulation in the mountain zones.[101] The Ligurian approach had been partly applied, but here the Romans saw little potential for resettlement and acculturation, and little danger of new migrations onto the island. The use of modified Ligurian tactics by a Spanish-trained commander operating in Sardinia demonstrates the pooling of frontier experience in the second-century B.C. Western Roman Empire.

In the wake of his military victories, Gracchus made several administrative changes. Along with such normal steps as demanding hostages, he doubled the tribute in grain.[102] This may at first seem strange. The inhabitants of the agricultural districts had suffered considerable losses from the raids of the mountaineers and the subsequent wars, and harsh new levies would seem to exacerbate an already tense situation. But Gracchus had acquired in Spain a reputation as a sensitive frontier organizer. A man whose treaties in Citerior became the watchword for fairness would hardly have lost his sense of judgment when he arrived in Sardinia. The Spanish treaties had also stressed grain tribute, and there is reason to suppose that the Romans saw the grain exaction as a means of encouraging settled agriculture. Moreover, the resources of Sardinia had apparently not been surveyed for a number of years. The Pax Romana must have resulted in an expansion of agricultural resources and the ability of the province to pay. Perhaps the best testimony to the wisdom of Gracchus' policy is that the triumph he celebrated on 23 February 175 B.C. was the last to be celebrated for victories over Sardinia until 122 B.C.[103]

Our information on Sardinia during much of the second century is scarce. There is no reason to assume that the mountain frontier had been pacified, but ongoing violence was apparently kept at an acceptable level. At least twice during this period the praetor assigned to Sardinia was given other administrative tasks.[104] Serious disturbances may have developed by 163 B.C., since in that year Ti. Sempronius Gracchus was sent back to the island.[105] Further unrest developed in 126 B.C. and required the presence of the consul L. Aurelius Orestes. He evidently remained as proconsul until 122 B.C., when he returned to celebrate the first Sardinian triumph in half a century.[106] C. Grac-

[101] See P. Meloni (1975) pp. 100–1 for population estimates.
[102] P. Meloni (1975) pp. 97–98.
[103] Livy 41.28.8–9; A. Degrassi (1947) p. 555.
[104] Livy 45.12.13, 45.16.4.
[105] T.R.S. Broughton (1951) pp. 440–42; P. Meloni (1975) pp. 75–76.
[106] Livy Per. 60; A. Degrassi (1947) p. 560; T.R.S. Broughton (1951) pp. 508, 511–12, 514, 518; P. Meloni (1975) p. 76; R. Rowland (1976) p. 88.

chus, the future reformer and son of the pacifier of the Ilienses, served
as quaestor under Orestes. He represented the third generation of
Sempronii to serve on the island, and he demonstrated the effectiveness of his contacts by raising ample supplies from the cities of Sardinia.[107] The location of these wars is not stated, but presumably they
centered on the interior mountain frontiers.

The last Republican triumph recorded for Sardinia was that awarded
to M. Caecilius Metellus. Again the campaign was apparently prolonged. Metellus was consul in 115 B.C. but did not celebrate his triumph
until 111 B.C. Unfortunately, the ancient writers were mainly interested in two Metelli celebrating a triumph at the same time and provide little information on what they had done to deserve the triumphs.[108]
We do possess one telling piece of evidence on Metellus' activities,
though, and it may be possible to link this with other information to
form a picture of frontier development on one part of Sardinia at the
end of the second century B.C.

In A.D. 69 the Roman officials in Sardinia were forced to adjudicate
boundary disputes between two groups called the Galilenses and the
Patulcenses Campani.[109] The Galilenses had been occupying *per vim*
land belonging to the Patulcenses. The problem was not a new one.
Helvius Agrippa in A.D. 69 was the third imperial official to have
rendered judgment in the matter. The Galilenses had persisted in what
seems to have been a pattern of infiltration and squatting, and the
patience of Agrippa was decidedly wearing thin. The history of the
litigation went back to a decree of M. Metellus, undoubtedly the governor and triumphator of the 115–111 B.C. period. This also allows us
to locate at least some of the campaigns of Metellus. The inscription
was found near Esterzili, located on the upper reaches of the Flumen-
dosa River on the southern slopes of Monti dei Gennargentu, in the
east-central part of the island. Evidently, the Romans were using that
important river valley to penetrate into one of the principal mountain
masses of Sardinia.

Even more information can be extracted from the inscription. It
obviously reflects the ongoing tension between upland and lowland
peoples on the Sardinian frontier. The Galilenses were a local group.
The Patulcenses Campani, however, bear a name that is not Sardinian. The nomen Patulcius belongs to the Italian mainland. It occurs
most frequently around Puteoli in Campania. An ultimately Etruscan

[107] Plut. *Vit. C. Gracch.* 1.4–2.5; Gell. *N.A* 15.12; *De Vir. Ill.* 65.1; P. Meloni (1975)
pp. 98–99.
[108] Vell. Pat. 2.8.2; Eutropius 4.25; A. Degrassi (1947) p. 561; T.R.S. Broughton
(1951) pp. 531, 541; P. Meloni (1975) pp. 76–77; R. J. Rowland (1976) p. 89.
[109] *CIL.* 10. 7852, *ILS* 5947; R. J. Rowland (1976) p. 92.

origin has been suggested.[110] The name represents a non-Sardinian element living by the late second century B.C. in one of the frontier valleys. The nature of the group is uncertain. One thinks first of some officially sponsored settlement on the model of the Liguri Cornelii et Baebiani in Samnium. But the name Patulcius does not suggest a second-century B.C. Roman magistrate. Similar designations were used in the case of large estates where the inhabitants were named after the owner or founder. Such estates are attested in Republican Sardinia, although the owners have what appear to be Punic or Punic-Sardinian names.[111] The tradition of Sardinian-landed magnates with estates on the plain-mountain frontier can be traced back to such figures as Hampsicora. They were to be found on other frontiers such as Hispania Ulterior and Gaul. The Romans of the second century B.C. had every reason to encourage these institutions.[112]

The triumph of Metellus was the last one granted for victories on the Sardinian frontier. T. Albucius did achieve some successes in Sardinia in 105–104 B.C., but they were not of the magnitude to deserve a triumph. In fact, Albucius was tried and sent into exile on his return.[113] The Romans seem to have accepted that there would always be some turbulence in Sardinia and that minor actions of frontier pacification hardly deserved triumphal honors.

In Sardinia, as in the northwestern part of the Iberian peninsula, many frontier problems remained unresolved. In both places the goals set by the Republic administrators had not been accomplished. The frontiers of Liguria and cisapadane Gaul had been pacified; in transpadane and transalpine Gaul effective frontier control had been achieved and was only disrupted by Caesar's conquest. The Sardinian unrest, however, continued into the early Empire. In Spain Augustus launched a massive military offensive that resulted in near pacification of the Cantabrian mountains, but in Sardinia he continued to tolerate the basic Republican approach.[114] Study of the imperial references can provide us with insight into conditions on the Sardinian frontier during the last century of the Republic.

[110] A. Taramelli (1918) pp. 291–92; G. Serra (1952) p. 414; W. Schulze (1933) p. 142.

[111] E. Pais (1923) pp. 332–33; P. Meloni (1975) pp. 122–25. A. Taramelli (1918) pp. 291–92 stresses the "cordon" effect these people had in the frontier areas.

[112] P. Meloni (1975) pp. 119–20.

[113] Cic. Prov. Cons. 15, Div. Caec. 65; T.R.S. Broughton (1951) pp. 556, 560; P. Meloni (1975) pp. 77–78, 110.

[114] On the basically "unconquered" nature of Barbagia through much of Sardinian history see R. King (1975) pp. 137–53. But several instances of nuraghi incorporated into later Roman structures and tombs with both pre-Roman and Roman occupants suggest ongoing continuity of occupation and gradual Romanization: R. Rowland (1977) pp. 465–68.

The problems of Sardinia are vividly described by Strabo. He was writing in the first century A.D., but undoubtedly was using earlier material. His account deserves extensive quotation:

τῇ δ' ἀρετῇ τῶν τόπων ἀντιτάττεταί τις καὶ μοχθηρία· νο-
σερὰ γὰρ ἡ νῆσος τοῦ θέρους, καὶ μάλιστα ἐν τοῖς εὐκαρ-
ποῦσι χωρίοις· τὰ δ' αὐτὰ ταῦτα καὶ πορθεῖται συνεχῶς
ὑπὸ τῶν ὀρείων οἱ καλοῦνται Διαγησβεῖς.
τέτταρα δ' ἐστὶ τῶν ὀρείων ἔθνη, Πάρατοι, Σοσσινάτοι,
Βάλαροι, Ἀκώνιτες, ἐν σπηλαίοις οἰκοῦντες, εἰ δέ τινα
ἔχουσι γῆν σπόριμον, οὐδὲ ταύτην ἐπιμελῶς σπείροντες,
ἀλλὰ τὰς² τῶν ἐργαζομένων καθαρπάζοντες, τοῦτο μὲν τῶν
αὐτόθι, τοῦτο δ' ἐπιπλέοντες τοῖς ἐν τῇ περαίᾳ, Πισά-
ταις μάλιστα. οἱ δὲ πεμπόμενοι στρατηγοὶ τὰ μὲν ἀντέ-
χουσι, πρὸς ἃ δ' ἀπαυδῶσιν, ἐπειδὰν μὴ λυσιτελῆ τρέφειν
συνεχῶς ἐν τόποις νοσεροῖς στρατόπεδον, λείπεται δὴ
στρατηγεῖν τέχνας τινάς· καὶ δὴ τηρήσαντες ἔθος τι τῶν
βαρβάρων (πανηγυρίζουσι γὰρ ἐπὶ πλείους ἡμέρας ἀπὸ τῆς
λεηλασίας), ἐπιτίθενται τότε καὶ χειροῦνται πολλούς.¹¹⁵

Against the virtue of the place there is ranged also a certain negative aspect: for the island is plague-ridden in summer, and above all the fertile regions, which are also continually laid waste by the mountain people called Diagesbeis.

There are four mountain tribes, the Paratoi, Sossinatoi, Balaroi, and Akonites, who dwell in caves, and if they possess any sowable land, they do not sow it conscientiously, but rather plunder the lands of those who do cultivate, whether in their own neighborhood, or by sailing against those in the harbor, above all the Pisatae. The generals who are sent are sufficient for some of them, but inadequate against others, and since it does not pay to maintain an army continually in plague-ridden regions, the only recourse is to plan certain stratagems. And so, keeping close watch over some one of the barbarian tribes (for they hold festivals for several days after a raid), they attack them at that time and capture many.

Diodorus Siculus writing in the mid-first century B.C. provides a similar description of the Sardinian mountaineers.¹¹⁶ His near contemporary, Varro, writes:

¹¹⁵ Strabo 5.2.7.
¹¹⁶ Diod. 5.15.4–6.

Multos enim agros egregios colere non expedit propter latrocinia vicinorum ut in Sardinia quosdam qui sunt prope Oeliem.[117]

Indeed it is not worthwhile to cultivate many fertile fields on account of the banditry caused by people dwelling nearby as is the case in Sardinia with certain ones near Oelies.

Livy also noted that the Ilienses were not yet under control in his own time.[118] Finally, Dio states that in A.D. 6 Augustus had to take over the governing of Sardinia, since the island was overrun with *leistei*, a term meaning either brigands or pirates.[119]

Brigandage and frontier raiding were not easily ended. Legionaries as well as auxiliaries had to be dispatched to the island. Insecurity persisted into the reign of Tiberius. In A.D. 19 the emperor sent to Sardinia four thousand men who were suspected of having participated in Jewish and Egyptian rites.[120] The avowed purpose of this action was *coercendis illic latrociniis et, si ob gravitatem caeli interissent, vile damnum*.

Tacitus does not state how these exiles were to be used in fighting banditry. They do not appear to have organized in a military unit. It is equally difficult to imagine them as reduced to the state of semiconvicts. If that had been the case, they would have guarded the frontier with little skill and enthusiasm, and would in fact have tended to escape across the frontier, swelling the number of brigands. The most reasonable solution would be to see them as forced settlers on the exposed farms and villages of the frontier zone. In that situation they would have had some stake in the effective defense of the agricultural zone and would have lessened the burden on the Roman military. Their role was quite possibly similar to that of the Patulcenses Campani of the second century B.C.

A military diploma discovered in the area of Anela, at the head of a valley northeast of Macomer in central Sardinia, provides evidence of continued need for settlers to defend frontier regions even in the first century A.D.[121] The soldiers were legionaries retired from the First Adiutrix. The inscription dates from the reign of Galba. Almost all of

---

[117] Varro *Rust*. 1.16.2.

[118] Livy 40.34.13.

[119] Dio Cass. 53.12, 55.28; Josep. *AJ* 18.35; *CIL* 14. 2954. A. Taramelli (1928) discusses an inscription with dedications to Augustus by *civitates Barbariae* found at Fordongionus. As late as A.D. 13–14 a legate of Augustus was road building on the island: *Not. Scav.* (1883) p. 428.

[120] Tac. *Ann.* 2.85.

[121] *CIL* 10. 7891. On Sardinians in Roman military service in general see R. J. Rowland (1974) pp. 223–27; F. Porra and I. Didu (1978–79).

the men were from Caralis. They were presumably settled in this northern frontier zone to prevent the mountaineers from coming down the river valleys to raid the settlements below. Evidence of frontier insecurity and the need for garrisons continues into the second century A.D.[122] Suggestive is a grave found at S. Andrea Frius on the edge of the mountains northeast of Monastir.[123] In a tomb that can be dated to the late second century A.D. a man was buried with his weapons. It seems that even during the height of the Pax Romana frontiersmen in Sardinia lived, died, and were buried with their weapons at their sides.

In Sardinia, as elsewhere, the creation of a frontier during the Republic was not just a matter of military pacification and tribal decimation. It involved building roads, establishing settlements, and, most important, cultivating a Mediterranean high-culture life that would provide the basic support for Roman rule. Of the purely mechanical aspects of Sardinian frontier development under the Republic, we have relatively little evidence. The Romans certainly inherited a communications network started by the Carthaginians and continued its expansion. This probably centered on the southwestern and west-coast roads that linked older communities like Caralis, Nora, Sulci, Tharros, Cornus, and Bosa.[124] More important under the Empire were the two roads that left Caralis and passed north through the central part of the island, one heading for Turris Libisonis on the northwestern coast and the other for Olbia on the northeastern coast. The military importance of the second route, which flanked and penetrated mountain areas and linked Caralis with the Italian-oriented port of Olbia, is obvious. The date of its construction is uncertain. All known milestones are very late. One clue is the location of the town of Valentia along it. That center dates to the second century B.C.[125] Another central island road, one that must have increased in importance during the Republic, connected some of the most fertile areas of the island and provided a route through the mountains to Olbia. Milestones show that it had been completed by the Augustan period, although many portions were older.[126] The eastern coastal road that ultimately linked

[122] R. J. Rowland (1976) p. 93 notes the increase in coin hoards; *CIL* 14. 2954 mentions a *praefectus* in Sardinia. *CIL* 10. 7833, 7890 mention cohorts in area of Nuoro under Domitian and Nerva composed of Sardinians and Ligurians.

[123] A. Taramelli (1923).

[124] K. Miller (1916) col. 408; E. Pais (1923) pp. 303–4, 320; P. Meloni (1975) pp. 279–85.

[125] K. Miller (1916) col. 409; P. Meloni (1975) pp. 276–79.

[126] K. Miller (1916) cols. 409–10; P. Meloni (1975) pp. 269–76.

Olbia and Caralis had a particularly early origin. Punic remains, including what seems to be a milestone, have been found along it.[127]

The roads in Sardinia, as in other provinces, formed but one element in a system designed to provide security. Also necessary were border client groups, settlements, and some garrisons. Building a client network proved difficult. The Romans did not find in Sardinia the stable, independent tribes like those that helped hold the frontier in Narbonese Gaul. Cicero notes that *quae est enim praeter Sardiniam provincia, quae nullam habeat amicam populo Romano ac liberam civitatem.*[128]

The Roman use of settlers on large frontier estates as a means of border defense has already been discussed. Apparently lacking in Republican Sardinia were widespread *ad viritim* settlements and formal colonies. The impressive row of foundations that were to be found along the Via Aemilia facing the Ligurian mountains did not have their parallels in Sardinia. The combination of a dense local population and the bad reputation of the climate probably discouraged migration. Only one place name suggests Republican origins. This is Valentia, situated in central Sardinia at modern Nuragus, slightly to the west of Esterzili. Located at the junction of ecological zones, the community was well placed to serve as an instrument of Romanization. Several references have already been made to the importance of places bearing augurial names like Valentia in the development of the Republican frontier in the west. Finds at the site show that it was a center for trade in Punic goods as early as the seventh century B.C. It also had a garrison under the Empire.[129]

In the areas behind the tense frontier, the adjustment of a basically Mediterranean population to Roman administration continued. Cicero notes that Pompey made significant grants of citizenship to the Sardinians; and the name of one Sardinian he mentioned, Cn. Domitius Sincaius, suggests that other Roman officials did the same thing.[130] But these changes and the equally slow process of Romanization in the interior are beyond the scope of this study.[131] It is now time to turn to the partner island of Sardinia.

---

[127] K. Miller (1916) cols. 408–9; P. Meloni (1975) pp. 285–89.

[128] Cic. *Scaur.* 44–45.

[129] Pliny *HN* 3.85; E. Pais (1923) pp. 134–35; P. Meloni (1975) pp. 256–58. Livy 32.1.6 mentions land given to soldiers who fought in Sardinia, but does not say where they were settled. Ennius, who fought in the revolt of 216 and returned to Rome with Cato, may have been one of those settlers: A. E. Astin (1978) pp. 16–18.

[130] Cic. *Scaur.* 43.

[131] The detailed study of this Romanization process is still in the early stages. For potential methods and materials see such works as R. J. Rowland (1977). A. Sanna (1957) suggests that the Latin language spread into the interior at a very late date.

CORSICA

The history of frontier development in Corsica does not seem to have the complexities of development in Sardinia. In part, this may be because of the paucity of the evidence. The Romans were not particularly interested in Corsica, and the literary references and inscriptions reflect that.[132] The island does not possess abundant and impressive remains of the indigenous culture like those found on Sardinia. In recent years, however, Corsican studies have become more active, and we have an increasingly full picture of a social evolution in which Rome played a considerable role.[133]

Corsica is even more rugged than Sardinia and does not have large areas of fertile plain comparable to those found on Sardinia. The shaping features are the mountains and the rivers. The water courses flow both east and west, dividing the island into natural sections that formed the basis of tribal units. The ethnic divisions described by Ptolemy correspond closely to those natural areas created by the river valleys.[134] Only on the eastern coast are there reasonably sized plains, which were in Roman times controlled by the centers of Aleria and Mariana. The river valleys also expedited transhumance and the linking of coast and mountains. Sheep and cattle, as well as honey, wax, and timber, are mentioned as important products of Corsica.[135] Cattle were branded by individual owners, suggesting that they were indicators of wealth. This supports the notion of a developing aristocracy hinging on the control of herds based in the fortified centers on the island.[136] Already by the late Bronze Age, there was developing, especially in the southwest, a culture represented by megalithic construction, the presence of stone towers, and large, though somewhat stylized, stone sculpture. This also suggests growing wealth, considerable tribal strife, and the appearance of a ruling chieftain group.[137]

Corsica's geographical position gave it a special place in the larger Mediterranean world. The island is naturally well located for those wishing to connect with Italy, the south of France, and the Iberian peninsula, especially in a period when long sea voyages were greatly feared. Prevailing winds and currents enhanced its position.[138] Pho-

---

[132] J. and L. Jehasse (1973) p. 23.

[133] R. Grosjean (1966); C. V. Pergola (1980).

[134] J. Jehasse (1976b) pp. 851–53.

[135] Theophr. *Hist. Pl.* 5.8.1; Diod. 5.13.4–5; Livy 40.34.13, 42.7.2; Vegetius 5.7; J. and L. Jehasse (1979) pp. 316–20.

[136] Diod. 5.14.1.

[137] R. Grosjean (1966); J. and L. Jehasse (1973) pp. 12–16; R. Grosjean (1976) pp. 101–14.

[138] J. and L. Jehasse (1973) pp. 12–16, (1979).

caean Greeks settled at Aleria about 565 B.C., and the colony was reinforced twenty years later. The Greek penetration of the area aroused the fears of Carthage and the Etruscans. After a bloody victory at the battle of Alalia in 535 B.C., the Phocaeans thought it more prudent to withdraw northward to develop their interests on the southern coast of France.[139]

These outside contacts and struggles for hegemony set in motion a series of cultural developments on the island that gave rise to a mixed native, Etruscan, and Greek society and stimulated interaction between the settlers on the shore and the Iron Age groups of the interior. The most vivid indication of these developments are the finds made in the cemeteries around Aleria. During the fifth century B.C. these burials received an impressive range of imported goods from Greece, Etruria, and the Punic world. Graffiti of the fifth to the mid-fourth century show the presence of Greek, Etruscan, and even Roman elements. The graves have also yielded material of obviously native origin, suggesting that natives mingled with the foreign groups.[140] In the century before the Roman conquest Etruscan goods dominate, although cultural material from other groups in central Italy including Rome is represented.[141]

These influences spread toward the interior. Pastoralists linked the two zones, and the coastal traders wanted the forest products and beeswax of the natives. A traffic in human flesh developed early. As Corsican slaves came to be prized, slave raiding became commonplace.[142] Moreover, by the 470s Corsican mercenaries were active in foreign wars. The slaves never returned, but mercenaries probably did, contributing to the Mediterranization of the interior.[143]

Rome's interest in Corsica developed out of an involvement in the Etruscan sphere of influence. Latin graffiti of the fourth century B.C. have been found on the island. The fourth-century B.C. Greek scholar Theophrastus claimed that the Romans planned to establish a colony there. The finds at Aleria and our growing realization of Rome's early outreach into the western Mediterranean make this claim less absurd than some have assumed.[144] As Etruscan and western Greek power weakened and the threat from Carthage increased, the Romans cast an increasingly wary eye toward Corsica. During the early stages of the

---

[139] Herod. 1.166; Strabo 6.1.1; F. Benoit (1961); J. and L. Jehasse (1973) pp. 18–19.

[140] J. and L. Jehasse (1973) pp. 37–80, (1979) pp. 334–42.

[141] J. and L. Jehasse (1979) pp. 342–47.

[142] Strabo 5.2.7.

[143] Herod. 7.165.

[144] Theophr. *Hist. Pl.* 5.8.2; Plut. *Parall. Min.* 13B mentions a Valerius Torquatus exiled in Corsica. J. and L. Jehasse (1973) pp. 20, 90–91, 100.

First Punic War, L. Cornelius Scipio seized Aleria and raided the island, actions that brought him a triumph.[145]

The Romans in Corsica, as in Sardinia, asserted their control gradually. Formal annexation seems to have come in 238 B.C., but it is with 236 B.C. that we clearly see the process of pacification at work. Zonaras' passage reveals the problems of frontier control:

Οὖαρος δὲ ἐπὶ Κύρνον ὁρμήσας, καὶ μὴ δυνηθεὶς ἀπορίᾳ πλοίων περαιωθῆναι, Κλαύδιόν τινα Κλινέαν σὺν δυνάμει προέπεμψε. κἀκεῖνος τοὺς Κυρνίους καταπλήξας ἐς λόγους ἦλθε, καὶ ὡς αὐτοκράτωρ τυγχάνων ἐσπείσατο. Οὖαρος δὲ τῶν συνθηκῶν μὴ φροντίσας ἐπολέμησε τοῖς Κυρνίοις, ἕως αὐτοὺς ἐχειρώσατο. οἱ δὲ Ῥωμαῖοι, τὸ παρασπόνδημα ἀποπροσποιούμενοι, ἔπεμψαν αὐτοῖς ἐκδιδόντες τὸν Κλαύδιον· ὡς δ᾽ οὐκ ἐδέχθη, ἐξήλασαν αὐτόν.[146]

Varus, having set out for Corsica, but unable to make the crossing for want of ships, sent a certain Claudius Clineas ahead with some forces. Now he, having intimidated the Corsicans, entered into negotiations, and made a treaty as the one who happened to have the power. Varus, however, took no account of the agreement and waged war against the Corsicans, until he defeated them. The Romans, alleging a violation of the treaty, expelled Claudius and sent him to the Corsicans; when he was not received, they drove him out.

The dilemmas of the situation are clear. Clíneas had opted for a rapid solution that combined a quick military strike with gestures of reconciliation and a negotiated peace. No doubt as an ambitious Roman he was attempting to steal an advantage over his commander. He certainly exceeded his authority. Moreover, it can be questioned whether this approach, which might have been used by a senior commander like Ti. Sempronius Gracchus after a long war had decimated the enemy, could be applied in a province that had hardly felt the weight of Roman arms. Varus, fresh from fighting the Boii, must have been aware that frontier peace did not come quickly or easily.

References to the progress of Roman subjugation of Corsica in the late third and second centuries B.C. are few. The lack of a large, sophisticated Punic-Corsican population meant that Corsica did not experience the tensions felt in Sardinia during the Second Punic War. One small revolt is mentioned for 234 B.C. In general, the Romans seem to have been content to dominate Aleria and exercise the mini-

---

[145] Florus 1.18.15–16; A. Degrassi (1947) p. 548.
[146] Zonaras 8.18.

mal control necessary over the interior. This insured frontier peace, the continuation of trade networks, and the collection of some tribute. The remains from the Alerian cemetery suggest that the prosperity of that community declined during the first years of Roman occupation.[147]

Three campaigns of some magnitude are mentioned during the first half of the second century B.C. In 181 B.C. the praetor M. Pinarius quickly suppressed a tribal outbreak and imposed a tribute of 100,000 pounds of wax.[148] A more serious war started in 174 B.C. and continued into the following year, when it was brought to a successful conclusion by C. Cicereius. Few details, aside from that the wax tribute was doubled, are provided. The senate did not think the accomplishments worthy of a triumph, and Cicereius had to celebrate one on his own initiative.[149] The senate did vote a *supplicatio* for the successes of the consul M' Juventius Thalna in Corsica in 163 B.C. The presence of a consul implies serious trouble, but unfortunately no details on the war have survived.[150]

Evidence for other frontier consolidation is equally sparse. Even in imperial times, the island had only one substantial section of road that ran along the eastern coast. A spur ran inland to a place called Praesidio (modern Zicavo) on the upper Taravo River. The name suggests a garrison, but we have no information on its origin.[151] The only attested new Republican settlement was at Mariana on the northeastern coast near the mouth of the Golo River. Aleria did receive Sullan colonists.[152]

Strabo and Diodorus, using material dating to the period of the late Republic, convey the impression that Corsica was a primitive place. Strabo is especially harsh:

οἰκεῖται δὲ φαύλως, τραχεῖά τε οὖσα καὶ τοῖς πλείστοις μέρεσι δύσβατος τελέως, ὥστε τοὺς κατέχοντας τὰ ὄρη καὶ ἀπὸ ληστηρίων ζῶντας ἀγριωτέρους εἶναι θηρίων. ὁπόταν γοῦν ὁρμήσωσιν οἱ τῶν Ῥωμαίων στρατηγοί, καὶ προσπεσόντες τοῖς ἐρύμασι πολὺ πλῆθος ἕλωσι τῶν ἀνδραπόδων, ὁρᾶν

[147] Zonaras 8.18; J. and L. Jehasse (1973) pp. 113–18, (1979) p. 347.

[148] Livy 40.19.6–8, 40.34.12–13.

[149] Livy 41.21.1–2, 42.1.3–4, 42.7.1–2; A. Degrassi (1947) p. 556.

[150] Val. Max. 9.12.3; Pliny *HN* 7.182; T.R.S. Broughton (1951) p. 440.

[151] K. Miller (1916) cols. 411–12; E. Pais (1923) pp. 304–6. Throughout the Roman period the sea lanes remained an important means of connection between Corsican centers: C. V. Pergola (1980) p. 312.

[152] Pliny *HN* 3.80; K. Miller (1916) cols. 411–12; E. T. Salmon (1970) pp. 129–30, 192–93 nn. 246, 248.

ἔστιν ἐν τῇ Ῥώμῃ καὶ θαυμάζειν ὅσον ἐμφαίνεται τὸ θη-
ριῶδες καὶ τὸ βοσκηματῶδες ἐν αὐτοῖς.[153]

It [Corsica] is ill-inhabited, since it is rough land and in most parts
quite impassable, so that those who dwell in the mountains and
live off brigandage are wilder than animals. And so, whenever
Roman generals land there, attack their strongholds and capture
a large number of slaves, one may see them at Rome and wonder
at the extent to which they manifest the qualities of wild beasts
and cattle.

Diodorus is rather more romantic in his description:

Οἱ δ᾽ ἐγχώριοι τροφαῖς μὲν χρῶνται γάλακτι καὶ μέλιτι
καὶ κρέασι, δαψιλῶς πάντα ταῦτα παρεχομένης τῆς χώρας,
τὰ πρὸς ἀλλήλους βιοῦσιν ἐπιεικῶς καὶ δικαίως παρὰ πάν-
τας σχεδὸν τοὺς ἄλλους βαρβάρους.[154]

For food the inhabitants use milk and honey and meat, which the
land provides in abundance, and toward one another they act
fairly and justly, more so than almost all other barbarians.

The choice provided is between the noble savage and those whose
primitive life is ugly, brutish, and short; but the sense of savagery is
clear. Under the Empire mention is made of the many political sub-
divisions of the natives, with Pliny citing thirty-two *civitates* and Ptolemy thirty-one.[155]

Despite the ethnic division and manifest underdevelopment, the Romans evidently maintained the level of control that they wanted without great problems. The links between coast and interior that had
developed over the centuries aided the process. Roman diplomacy built
on these contacts and encouraged a minimal stability. One of the few
inscriptions from the island provides some insight into this process. It
concerns a boundary dispute between the Mariani, settlers of the old
Marian colony on the northeastern coast, and the tribe of the Vanacini. It was found at Erbalunga, which places the Vanacini in the Cap
Corse region at the extreme northern point of Corsica.[156] Such litigation between lowland and upland groups is already familiar from Sardinia. The inscription is addressed to the tribal *magistratibus et senato-
ribus*, the magnates whom the Romans cultivated in order to insure
peace and order. It dates to the reign of Vespasian, although the Va-

[153] Strabo 5.2.7.
[154] Diod. 5.14.1.
[155] Pliny *HN* 3.80; Ptol. 3.2; J. Jehasse (1976b) pp. 851–52 chart 2.
[156] *CIL* 10. 8038.

nacini already had a long-term friendly relationship with Rome. Mention is made of *beneficia* as early as 27 B.C. They had evidently been long-standing clients of Rome whose support was necessary to ensure the peace of the farmers of Mariana.

The admittedly exiguous evidence from Corsica suggests that here we are dealing with a frontier where Rome set for itself limited, realistic objectives and maintained them skillfully with limited means. Full conquest of the island would have been difficult and was probably considered unnecessary. The Romans did not plan to colonize the area and did not have a large, settled native population to protect. The centuries of contact with the larger Mediterranean context had encouraged a degree of symbiosis and mutual dependency that the Romans had only to maintain. As long as traders were not molested, the few farmers on the island could work in relative peace, and the tribute of war flowed in, Rome was happy. If the natives could move freely with their herds, hunt in the interior, and trade with the coast, they too were content. A certain level of brigandage was tolerated. When diplomacy failed, occasional raids by the Roman forces might be necessary to remind the natives of the power of Rome. What is striking again is Rome's realism and restraint in its approach to the problems of a frontier.

CONCLUSION

Virtually every catch phrase applied to frontier experiences, from the "escape valve" and the "inner frontier" to "regeneration through violence," has a certain relevance for the Roman Republican frontier. No one phrase alone, however, can explain what took place in this long-lasting and immensely varied process. The fact of this complexity is in itself worthy of reflection. It is the relation of the history of the Republican frontier in the west to general frontier patterns that will be the main focus of these concluding remarks.

An important aspect of the Roman frontier in the west was the nature of imperialism as it developed in that part of the Empire. It is easy to stress the aggressive qualities that were built into the Roman political and ideological system and reinforced as the stakes of wealth, power, and prestige increased during the course of the late third, second, and first centuries B.C.[1] Wars in northern Italy, Gaul, and Spain yielded impressive triumphs and brought wealth to the conquerors and the state. In a more minor key, Ligurian and Alpine triumphs could flatter the ego of less prestigious officials and could be used to the point where they became a political joke. Few of the principal wars, however, when carefully investigated without preconceived notions about innate Roman aggression, can be demonstrated to owe their origin to unrestrained triumph-hunting or naked exploitation. Significantly, the archetypical example of such behavior during the Republic, Caesar's conquest of Gaul, came at the end of the period and changed a policy of restraint and a subtle system of border control that had evolved in the area in the late second and early first centuries B.C. Lucrative victories were more generally to be sought in the eastern part of the Roman Empire. The tendency of highly ambitious Roman commanders to prefer eastern over western assignments is a testimony to this.

Most changes in the western frontiers were either a Roman response to alterations in inherited arrangements or the logical extension of an initially modest commitment. Such a claim obviously relates the western Roman experience to the school of modern imperialism that stresses the often indirect, even haphazard nature of the empire-building process.[2] This can clearly be seen in the long history of the Gallic conflict, which gradually drew the Romans from the southern *ager Gallicus* to

[1] E. Badian (1967); P. A. Brunt (1978); W. V. Harris (1979).
[2] D. J. Robinson, J. Gallagher, and A. Denny (1961); J. Galbraith (1963).

the border of the Alps. In the northwestern Mediterranean, connections with Saguntum and Massilia created intersecting obligations for Rome that ultimately led to the control of southern Gaul and much of the peninsula.

This particular evolution was the result of several distinctive features of the Roman frontier in the west. Some of the features can be found in other border situations, but this combination was in many ways unique. The advancing frontiers of the Republic did not cross any ecologically distinctive divide or encounter peoples of radically different military organization or way of life. Such frontiers of contrast existed in northwestern China, Byzantine-Seljuk central Turkey, eastern Russia, and even the Great Plains of the United States and the pampas of Argentina. In these areas an advancing line of agricultural settlements encroached on the territory of horseback nomads, and the conspicuous difference between the two cultures posed massive problems.[3] The Republican generals faced the problem of raiding in many areas where topography and social organization gave considerable advantage to the enemy, but these groups were still agricultural-pastoralists of a kind familiar to Rome. They did not have to deal with efficient cavalry forces like those of the Indians of Argentina or North America or of some of the raiders of the late Empire.[4]

Social organization and way of life on both sides of the frontier were similar because the ecology was similar. The Republican frontier in the west developed within the Mediterranean zone. Inhabitants of the Italian peninsula found a familiar world in Sardinia, southern Gaul, or Spain, where climate, terrain, soil, and vegetation were all basically the same. It was only with Caesar that Rome made her leap to the north and attempted to unite the European and Mediterranean worlds.[5]

There was little pressure from outside forces during the time of Republican frontier development, which lent a certain stability to the process. Although raiding was a problem, continuous migration was not. This distinguished the Republican frontiers from those of the late Empire. The invasions of the Cimbri and the Teutones represented a unique experience for this period. The Gallic folk movement into northern Italy seems to have been largely spent by the time the Romans entered the area. This meant that the Romans dealt with a relatively stable situation across the frontier, or at least one that changed

---

[3] On the Chinese and Russian frontiers see O. Lattimore (1951), (1962); M. Mikesell (1968) pp. 155–56; J. Eadie (1977). Also comparable is the nomad-farmer frontier in later Byzantine Anatolia: S. Vryonis (1975).

[4] R. C. Padden (1953); M. Mikesell (1968) pp. 163–64; D. Wishart (1976) pp. 314–16.

[5] W. P. Webb (1931); D. A. Hess (1979); S. Thompson (1973).

gradually enough for them to grasp the nature of the change and make appropriate adjustments. In Liguria, northern Italy, and Iberia, groups in the mountains and plains had long traditions of interaction on which the Romans could build their policy. Even in areas like Narbonese Gaul where internal and external factors were changing the native societies, the pace of change was sufficiently gradual to allow the Romans to adjust.

Equally fortunate for the Roman administrators was the relative lack of pressure from settlers to extend the sphere of Roman control ever outward. I have argued that, except for the *ager Gallicus*, the frontier areas in the west experienced relatively little settlement of emigrants from the Italian core areas. Here the contrast with the United States frontier is striking. Throughout history, those in charge of border areas have looked on the frontier settler with mixed emotions. Although settlement can accelerate the process of acculturation, it also strains relations with the natives.[6]

The reasons for these differences are several. Most of the areas in the Roman Empire were well populated by groups that the Romans wanted to befriend rather than eliminate. In places like Liguria where the Romans did practice removals, the land was marginal and held little for Italian settlers. After the period of the consolidation of the *ager Gallicus*, the Roman colonial impulse was largely spent, and colonies beyond the borders of Italy never became popular. Most likely, few Romans were willing to pull up stakes and move great distances to new lands. Unlike the United States frontier, this one was no escape valve for urban poor; and the decimations of the Second Punic War had relieved any pressures of overpopulation in the Italian countryside.[7] The main groups that went to the provinces were the traders who tended to settle in the emerging centers and the exploiters of specific resources.[8]

The important exception was, of course, the area of Aemilia. There the Gallic population was dramatically reduced, and a number of settlements and individual farmsteads were founded. This bears the closest relation to the Turnerian United States frontier experience, and it is not surprising that it has been used by historians seeking parallels in the two cultures.[9] Often forgotten is that the *ager Gallicus* was the

---

[6] W. Jacobs (1950); J. Galbraith (1963) pp. 7–8; J. M. Sosin (1967) pp. 15–19, 82–84; A. Scham (1970) pp. 92–93; J. Eadie (1977) p. 233.

[7] F. J. Turner (1920) pp. 1–38; F. Shannon (1945). See R. K. Edmonds (1978) on the escape valve as a factor in Chinese and Japanese frontier settlement.

[8] P. Powell (1952); J. Axtell (1975).

[9] P. L. MacKendrick (1957).

exception and not the rule for Roman Republican expansion in the west.

In most frontier areas the largest group of rural settlers was probably the retired or discharged soldiers. This was especially true for the Iberian provinces, where the armies experienced the most prolonged campaigns and probably had the most extensive garrison duty. These discharged veterans were less of an irritant, however, than the settlers fresh from the home country or the second- or third-generation pioneers who brought with them preconceptions of natives and how to deal with them. The veterans knew the area, the natives, and the problems of life along the border. Many of them chose to remain because they had put down roots in the local community, established familial ties with the natives, and found life in the area appealing. Of course, some of these ex-soldiers must have antagonized frontier peace as they smuggled, engaged in unscrupulous trade with the natives, or displayed military bravado. Nevertheless, with their native wives and half-Roman children and their ties to native soldiers with whom they had served, these veterans must have formed an important bridge between native and Roman society.

Every frontier also has had the individual whose way of life placed him between the two cultures, or who actually deserted his own culture to follow native ways. He is Leatherstocking, the *coureur des bois*, or the white Indian of the American frontier.[10] This phenomenon is documented along the Republican frontier, especially in Iberia. Escaped slaves and military deserters must have been familiar figures in the oppida just beyond the area of Roman control.

The intermingling and intermarriage of Roman and native, of conqueror and conquered, points to another advantage that Rome had in creating a new society in the western Mediterranean. This was a lack of a strong sense of racial difference or of an unbridgeable cultural superiority. The Romans did not have to engage in prolonged debates like the famous Los Casos-Sepulveda controversy to prove to themselves the basic human equality of the people they conquered and wished to incorporate into their system.[11] The wars with the Gauls in Italy came closest to genocide, and certainly in specific situations the feelings of animosity ran too deep to be bridged. Still, the Romans generally felt that the natives, once conquered, could be made part of the Roman system. In fact, one cannot help but feel that the Romans

[10] J. Axtell (1975); R. Cook (1981) p. 186; H. Giliomee (1981) pp. 77–78.

[11] On racism in Roman society see T. J. Haarhoff (1948) pp. 217–20; D. B. Saddington (1961); A. Sherwin-White (1967) pp. 2–12. For similar questions in other frontier societies see C. J. Jaenon (1976) pp. 155, 161–65; J. Muldoon (1975). On the Los Casos-Sepulveda debates see L. Hanke (1959).

looked on the wars in the west much as the British looked on the combats along the northwestern frontier of India. In both cases, brave men from two warrior cultures faced each other in honest combat. Although frontier combat had not become the area of escape found in the *Agricola* of Tacitus, it was still the situation in which *virtus* could best be displayed. Moreover, the warrior aristocrats, once either defeated or reconciled, could become clients who would provide models of Romanization for the rest of society. Service in the border areas must have seemed a relief to many Romans after dealing with thieving Greeks, mendacious Syrians, and decadent Egyptians.

Economic processes as well as social ones complicated the frontier for the Romans. Mining and trading created special problems. Frontier historians have identified the mining or resource frontier as a distinctive type.[12] It involves the advance into new territory with the aim of controlling the sources of valuable raw materials. The mining frontier may represent a salient in a general frontier advance. In most cases, the exploitation of mineral resources is an activity that is dependent on cheap labor. Either the native population is pressed into service in the mines, which happened in Spanish Central and South America, or slaves or other sources of inexpensive labor are imported. The combination of brutal labor conditions and uncontrolled territory nearby led to the flight of fugitives across the border, the formation of bandit groups, and the proliferation of raiding.

Again it is Iberia, and especially Hispania Ulterior, that provides the best Roman example of this. Mining was a central activity there, slaves were employed in large numbers, and banditry became a serious problem. In two other mining areas among the Alpine Salassi and the tribes of Noricum, the Romans were not able to obtain a permanent hold over the mineral resources, and the exploitation was left largely in the hands of the natives. This resulted in a symbiotic relationship in which natives and Romans exchanged raw materials for finished products.

Transfrontier trade was more common. In almost all areas, the Romans inherited preexisting trade networks. Etruscans and Greeks traded with the natives in northern Italy, Greeks with Gauls in France, Veneti with the tribes of Slovenia, and Carthaginians with groups in Sardinia and the Iberian peninsula. This trade ranged from the simple exchange of trinkets for local produce to extended commercial networks that linked the southern and northern extremes of the European continent.

Local trade networks shifted and spread as the Romans expanded

[12] P. Powell (1952); M. Lombardi (1975).

their sphere of influence and consolidated their hold on areas. The Romans appreciated the role that trade played in the acculturation process.[13] Markets were encouraged, and the possibilities for interchange multiplied. More intensive archaeological investigation, combined with better models to explain the relationship between material exchange and culture change, will in the next few years present a clearer picture of this local trade and the way it shaped the frontier.

Long-distance trade posed somewhat different problems. The two most extended and complicated examples of this kind of network were to be found in the Rhône corridor of Gaul and in the routes that extended over the Alps into Noricum. The distances involved, the value of the materials exchanged, and the number of individuals and groups included made these very different from the local-exchange networks.[14] Their existence created the possibility for considerable economic and social change, and even disruption. This was especially true when goods of great value were involved or when the processes of procurement and exchange modified the behavior or social fabric of a group. The trade in wine and slaves in transalpine Gaul certainly had such effects.

The flow of Mediterranean luxury goods into the native societies produced more gradual but equally significant social and economic changes. The position of some individuals and families improved as they gained control over access to this trade and the rewards that it brought. Warfare over control of the trade routes assumed ever more dangerous proportions as the stakes increased. New concentration of power in the hands of wealthy families or charismatic leaders made the Romans nervous and prompted intervention. This happened in the case of the Arverni under Bituitus. On the other hand, the Romans also appreciated the role that more centralized leadership could have in encouraging frontier stability. The lack of this was painfully obvious in a place like Liguria. Loyal leaders among groups like the Aedui and the tribes of Noricum could not only foster trade but also provide an additional buffer to the frontier system.

Such buffers were necessary, since the Romans had only limited, formal means at their disposal to ensure frontier peace. The extent of the Roman garrison force in the west during the Republic is uncertain,

[13] On trade used as a means of control on other frontiers see J. Eadie (1977). This prolonged development of trade also meant that the frontier areas were not isolated from Mediterranean diseases and that the spread of diseases did not have the impact on the frontier that it did in North America: L. Thompson and H. Lamar (1981) pp. 26–27.

[14] Comparable might be the fur-trading networks on the American frontier: D. Wishart (1976); R. Cook (1981) pp. 182–88.

but it is clear that nothing like the imperial *limes* organization existed. Garrisons are occasionally mentioned, but such references are rare. Even some of those must have been formed from little more than local militia. During times of trouble, the governors could call in large military units. In the longer intervals of relative peace, they were forced to act with the support of limited professional military resources.

The lack of a professional civil service inhibited Roman control in the field. The administrator had a small staff that was generally composed of young men with relatively little experience. Staff continuity from one administration to the next was minimal. He was in an even worse position than British administrators of the nineteenth and twentieth centuries who also depended on tiny administrative and military support groups to control large areas of alien territory.[15]

This weakness of military and administrative position fostered certain actions on the part of the Roman frontier administrator. He had to rely heavily on important figures in the local society. Considerable emphasis has been placed in provincial studies on the close relationship between the governor and such intrusive elements as traders and absentee landowners. In part, this is because much of our information comes from Rome, where those groups had a big impact. Traders and overseas owners of latifundia actually contributed little to stabilizing the frontier line. Governors had to establish relationships with the rising native families of the towns and with rural magnates and border chieftains. These patron-client alliances became hereditary and played an important role in ensuring frontier stability. The system had its limitations, though. There was always the danger that the Roman official, like his British successor many centuries later, might be placed "in a cloudy and unreal atmosphere in which complaisant chiefs and delusive interpreters stand between him and the tribal masses who watch silently, unwilling or unable to voice their true needs or grievances."[16] The recurring native revolts testify that such breakdowns in communications did occur. But the Roman administrator had few alternatives to a semiofficial and semipersonal system of management.

One factor that made Republican border management precarious and at the same time workable was that the frontier was often an arbitrary political line and relationships already existed between individuals and groups on the two sides. The Romans had every reason to cultivate these contacts as long as they encouraged peace. This often

[15] For similar problems in modern imperialism see L. H. Gann and P. Duignan (1967) pp. 212–13; M. Perham (1960) chap. 3; R. Heussler (1963).
[16] M. Perham (1960) p. 263; R. Sullivan (1979).

involved direct diplomatic action by Republican officials. Our sources provide only fleeting glimpses of this border diplomacy, but its complexity, sophistication, and importance should not be underestimated. The experience of the Republic provided the Romans with skills in ethnic diplomacy that served later imperial and Byzantine administrators extremely well. The result was the creation of a frontier system that included Aedui and Alpine tribes as well as Allobroges and Veneti. The Republican frontier was similar in many ways to that of dynastic China, where again a set of relationships united groups on both sides of a political boundary.

The system reconstructed in this study has stressed restraint over hasty action. Although brutality and rapacity were always present on the frontier, other subtle qualities were probably more often in evidence. Moreover, it was not a world that allowed simple, absolute solutions. The occasional raiding, burning, and beheading had to be tolerated, because the Romans were unable to respond to every provocation. The Roman commander worked mainly to keep frontier violence within acceptable limits and to prevent the development of situations in which he might lose control and have to call for outside assistance.

Implicit in this practice of restraint and exercise of diplomacy is some degree of policy planning directed by the senate. Discussion of such long-term policy planning may appear strange to historians used to thinking about the senate mainly in terms of factional strife and clan advancement. It would be anachronistic to speak of think tanks and formal strategic studies, but we should credit the Romans with sufficient sophistication to develop a long-range strategy and the institutions to execute it.[17] A starting point was provided by the Roman aristocratic family that accumulated a web of provincial contacts and a valuable treasury of experience in dealing with frontier situations. It is certainly true that these families had selfish interests to protect, but they were balanced by considerations of prestige, honor, and even concern for the higher interests of the state.

This individual and familial experience was pooled in the Roman senate, where decisions affecting Roman policy were hammered out. No frontier area was the preserve of a single family. Diverse and often conflicting interests forced debate and the careful monitoring of the activities of administrators in the field. Moreover, the senate was the repository of tradition for a people conscious of the lessons of the past. By the end of the Republic, the Romans had an exceptionally rich experience in the tribal management appropriate to the western fron-

<hr>

[17] E. Luttwak (1976).

tier. It is not surprising that those aristocrats who were always aware
of the need to combine tradition with innovation should have developed the subtle policy described in the preceding chapters. Significantly, it was Julius Caesar, the man who overthrew the Republic,
who most radically and brutally altered Republican frontier policy.

Finally, some comment needs to be made about ethical judgments
of Roman imperialism in the western Mediterranean during the Republic. We should by now have learned some modesty and toleration
in judging the imperial actions of past societies. In frontier situations
morality always has a relative quality. One must remember the burning farmhouse outside the walls of Placentia, as well as the skeletons
of the slain in a hill fort in Liguria or Spain: and the native chieftain
willing to sell into slavery his fellow tribesmen, as well as the Mediterranean trader who buys them. The concept of noble savage is as
limiting as that of noble administrator taking up the white man's burden.

The Romans certainly practiced all the terror and violence familiar
to the frontier, constrained only by their relatively primitive technol-
ogy of destruction. The stark lists of slaves and the statistics of slaugh-
ter bear this out. Ambitious commanders perpetrated deeds considered unjust even within the Roman set of values, and their superiors
at Rome proved unwilling or unable to stop them. But our own experience in the west, and in Vietnam, has taught us the difficulty of
preventing such atrocities in the brutal conditions of imperial and frontier
wars.

More striking than the images of Roman atrocities are the instances
when the Romans sought to censure those who committed them, and
to right the wrongs done in their name. An aged Cato defending the
rights of some distant Lusitanians or a tribune seeking the freedom of
obscure, enslaved Ligurians should be remembered as well as the ruth-
less Sulpicius Galba and the arrogant Popillius Laenas. Moreover, the
reflections in the Roman literary tradition about the ambiguous morality of imperialism should not be dismissed as lightly as often hap-
pens. From our own experience we should know how difficult it is to
attain the level of social self-criticism seen in a Sallust or a Tacitus.[18]

Perhaps the most positive result of the Roman frontier experience
in the west is the stable and prosperous provincial society that it made
possible. Archaeology still has a long way to go in illuminating the
Republican substratum that underlies the more visible world of the

[18] For examples of Roman self-criticism cf. Sall. *Hist.* 4.69.5; *Jug.* 81.1; Livy 3.66.4;
Vell. Pat. 2.27.1; Just. *Epit.* 38.4.2; J. Palm (1959); D. Earl (1967) pp. 40–41; D. Timpe
(1965).

Empire. The relative stability that the frontier system provided, however, allowed the growth of this society in the last centuries of the Republic. Only with natives largely satisfied with Roman rule and protected from outside forces could the Roman west that underlies European civilization be created. This was the legacy made possible by the creation of the Roman frontier.

BIBLIOGRAPHY

Agostinetti, P. 1972. *Documenti per la protostoria della Val d'Ossola*. Milano.

Alarcáo, J., and R. Etienne. 1979. "Conimbriga, ville de Lusitanie." *Latomus* 38:877–90.

Alarcáo, J., R. Etienne, A. Moutinho Alarcão, and S. da Ponte. 1979. *Fouilles de Conimbriga*. Vol. 7, *Trouvailles Diverses—Conclusions Générales*. Paris.

Albenque, A. 1948. *Les Rutènes*. Paris.

Alfieri, N., and P. E. Arias. 1958. *Spina*. München.

Alföldi, A. 1963. *Early Rome and the Latins*. Ann Arbor.

Alföldy, G. 1974. *Noricum*. London.

Aliger, M. 1967. "Nages (Gard): Des origines à la fin de l'ère antique." *Celticum* 16:1–63.

Allen, D. F. 1969. "Monnaies à la croix." *Numismatic Chronicle*, 7th ser., 9:33–78.

Almagro, M. 1943. *Ampurias*. Barcelona.

———. 1961. *Merida*. Merida.

Almagro-Basch, M. 1969. *Excavaciones en la Palaíopolis de Ampurias*. Madrid.

———. 1977. "L'origine de l'art ibérique à la lumière des récentes découvertes." *Revue archéologique*, 275–82.

Ambrosi, A. 1972. *Corpus delle statue stele lunigianes: Collana storica della Liguria orientale*, no. 6. Bordighera.

Amilibia, A. M. 1968. "Sobre el comercio cartaginés en España." *Pyrenae* 4:129–40.

Andrén, A. 1940. *Architectural Terracottas from Etrusco-Italic Temples*. Lund.

Andreotti, R. 1969. "Gli studi storici su Veleia negli ultimi quindici anni." *Atti del III Congresso di Studi Veleiati*, 1–16. Milano.

Arbos, P. 1922. *La vie pastorale dans les Alpes Françaises*. Paris.

———. 1923. "The Geography of Pastoral Life." *Geographical Review* 13:559–75.

Arcelin, P. 1976. "Les civilisations de l'Age du Fer en Provence." *La Préhistoire Française*, vol. 2, ed. J. Guilaine, 657–75. Paris.

Arcelin, P., and L. Chabot. 1980. "Les céramiques à vernis noir du village préromain de la Cloche." *Mélanges de l'Ecole Française de Rome: Antiquité* 92:681–72.

Arias, P. E. 1948. "I Galli nella regione emiliana." *Emilia preromana* 1:33–41.

Arias, P. E. 1953. "Casola Valsenio (Ravenna)—Scoperta di una necropoli, S. Martino in Gattara (Brisighella)—Materiali archeolo-
gici." *Notizie degli Scavi*, 218–27.
———. 1962. "Due situle bronze paleovenete a Spina." *Hommages à
Albert Grenier*, ed. M. Renard, 141–44. Bruxelles.
Arribas, A. 1964. *The Iberians*. New York.
———. 1967. "La necropolis bastitana del Mirador de Rolando (Gra-
nada)." *Pyrenae* 3:67–105.
———. 1967. "Nuevos hallazgos fenicios en la costa andaluza medi-
terránea." *Zephyrus* 18:121–27.
Arrighi, P. 1971. *Histoire de la Corse*. Toulouse.
Arslan, E. A. 1971. "Ritrovamenti preromani a Garlasco." *Oblatio:
Raccolta de Studi di Antichità ed Arte in Onore de Aristide Calderini*,
59–79. Como.
———. 1975–76. "Paesaggio rurale nella zona pedemontana tra Veneto e Lombardia tra il." *Atti Ce S.D.I.R.* 7:39–61.
———. 1978. "I Celti in Transpadana." *I Galli e l'Italia*, 81–84. Roma.
Astin, A. E. 1964. "The Roman Commander in Hispania Ulterior in
142 B.C." *Historia* 13:245–54.
———. 1967a. "Saguntum and the Origins of the Second Punic War."
Latomus 26:577–96.
———. 1967b. *Scipio Aemilianus*. Oxford.
———. 1978. *Cato the Censor*. Oxford.
Aurigemma, S. 1940. *Velleia*. Roma.
Axtell, J. 1972. "The Scholastic Philosophy of the Wilderness." *William and Mary Quarterly* 29:335–66.
———. 1975. "The White Indians of Colonial America." *William and
Mary Quarterly* 32:55–88.
———. 1981. "The Invasion Within: The Contest of Cultures in
Colonial North America." *The Frontier in History*, ed. H. Lamar
and L. Thompson, 237–69. New Haven.
Badian, E. 1954. "The Prefect at Gades." *Classical Philology* 49:250–
52.
———. 1958. *Foreign Clientelae (264–70 B.C.)*. Oxford.
———. 1964. *Studies in Greek and Roman History*. Oxford.
———. 1966. "Notes on *Provincia Gallia* in the Late Republic." *Mélanges d'archéologie et d'histoire offerts à André Piganiol*, 901–18. Paris.
———. 1967. *Roman Imperialism in the Late Republic*. Pretoria.
Baldacci, P. 1967–68. "Alcuni aspetti dei commerci nei territori cisalpini." *Atti Ce S.D.I.R.* 1:5–50.
———. 1972. "Importazioni cisalpine e produzione apula." *Recherches
sur les amphores romaines*. Collection de l'Ecole Française de Rome,
vol. 10, 8–20. Roma.

———. 1977. "Una bilingue latino-galllica di Vercelli." *Atti dell'Accademia Nazionale dei Lincei* 32:335–47.

Balil, A. 1955. "Algunos aspectos del proceso de la romanización de Cataluña." *Ampurias* 17:39–58.

———. 1956. "Un factor difusor de la romanización: Las tropas hispánicas al servicio de Roma (siglos III-I a. de J.C.)." *Emerita* 24:108–34.

Bane, R. 1976. "The Development of Roman Imperial Attitudes and the Iberian Wars." *Emerita* 44:409–20.

Banti, L. 1931. "L'ager Lunensis e l'espansione etrusca a nord dell'Arno." *Studi Etruschi* 5:163–83.

———. 1937. *Luni.* Firenze.

———. 1973. *Etruscan Cities and Their Culture.* Berkeley.

Barfield, L. 1972. *Northern Italy before Rome.* New York.

Barnett, H. G. 1956. *Anthropology in Administration.* Evanston.

Barreca, F. 1961. "La città punica in Sardegna." *Bollettino del Centro di Studi per la Storia dell'Architettura* 17:27–43.

———. 1971. "Sardegna." *L'espansione fenicia nel Mediterraneo*, ed. S. Moscati, 7–27. Roma.

Barruol, G. 1961. "Oppida préromains et romains en Haute-Provence." *Cahier Rhodaniens* 8:64–94.

———. 1969. *Les peuples préromains du sud-est de la Gaule—Etude de géographie historique. Revue archéologique de Narbonnaise*, suppl. 1.

———. 1972. "Les Elisyques et leur capitale, Naro/Narbo." *Congrès de la Fédération Historique du Languedoc Méditerranéen et du Roussillon* 45:49–63.

———. 1976. "Les civilisations de l'Age du Fer en Languedoc." *La Préhistoire Française*, vol. 2, ed. J. Guilaine, 676–86. Paris.

Barruol, G., U. Gilbert, and G. Rancoule. 1961. "Le défunt héroïsé de Bouriège (Aude)." *Rivista di Studi Liguri* 27:45–60.

Barruol, G., and G. Sauzade. 1969. "Une tombe de guerrier à Saint-Laurent-des-Arbres (Gard)." *Rivista di Studi Liguri* 35:14–89.

Battaglia, R. 1957. "Del paleolitico alla civiltà atestina." *Storia di Venezia*, vol. 1, 77–177. Venezia.

Baumgartel, E. 1937. "The Gaulish Necropolis of Filottrano in the Ancona Museum." *Journal of the Royal Anthropological Association* 67:231–86.

Bayet, J. 1962. "L'étrange omen de Sentinum et le celtisme en Italie." *Hommages à Albert Grenier*, ed. M. Renard, 244–56. Bruxelles.

———. 1964. *Tite-Live, Histoire Romaine*, tome 5. Paris.

Beeler, M. S. 1956. "Venetic and Italic." *Hommages à Max Niedermann*, 38–48. Bruxelles.

Beltrán Lloris, M. 1973–74. "Nueva elementa para el conocimento de las escrituras antiquas del SW peninsular: la estela de Siruela (Badajoz)." *Caesaraugusta* 37–38:125–39.

Beltrán Martínez, A. 1964. "Algunos datos para el estudio del lugar de la muerte de Amílcar Barca." *Caesaraugusta* 23–24:87–94.

———. 1977. "Novedades de Arqueología Zaragozana." *Caesaraugusta* 41–42:151–202.

Benedict, C. 1942. "The Romans in Southern Gaul." *AJPhil.* 63:39–48.

Benoit, F. 1947. "Les fouilles d'Entremont en 1946." *Gallia* 5:81–122.

———. 1949a. "La légende d'Héraclès et la colonisation grècque dans la delta du Rhône." *Lettres d'humanité* 8:104–40.

———. 1949b. "L'aire méditerranéenne de la 'tête-coupée.' " *Rivista di Studi Liguri* 15:243–55.

———. 1954. "Les fouilles d'Entremont en 1953–54." *Gallia* 12:285–94.

———. 1956. "Epaves de la côte de Provence, typologie des amphores." *Gallia* 14:23–34.

———. 1957. *Entremont, capitale celto-ligure.* Aix-en-Provence.

———. 1961. "Les fouilles d'Aléria et l'expansion hellénique en Occident." *Comptes Rendus de l'Académie des Inscriptions et Belles-Lettres*, 159–73.

———. 1962. "La 'barbarie' Ligure." *Rivista di Studi Liguri* 28:117–24.

———. 1963. "Les itinéraires commerciaux en Provence dans l'antiquité." *Actes du VIIe Congrès de l'Ass. G. Budé*, 362–86. Aix-en-Provence.

———. 1965. *Recherches sur l'hellénisation du midi de la Gaule.* Aix-en-Provence.

———. 1966. "La romanisation de la Narbonnaise à la fin de l'époque républicaine." *Rivista di Studi Liguri* 32:287–303.

———. 1968. "Résultats historiques des fouilles d'Entremont (1946–1967)." *Gallia* 26:1–31.

Benson, L. 1969. "The Historian as Mythmaker: Turner and the Closed Frontier." *The Frontier in American Development*, ed. D. M. Ellis, 3–19. Ithaca.

Beretta, I. 1954. *La romanizzazione della valle d'Aosta.* Milano.

Berkhofer, R. 1981. "The North American Frontier as Process and Context." *The Frontier in History*, ed. H. Lamar and L. Thompson, 43–75. New Haven.

Bermond Montanari, G. 1969a. "S. Martino in Gattara-Scavi, 1963." *Notizie degli Scavi*, 5–37.

———. 1969b, "La necropoli protostorica di San Martino in Gattara (Ravenna)." *Studi Etruschi* 37:213–28.

Bernabo Brea, L., and G. Chiappella. 1951. "Nuove scoperte nella necropoli preromana di Genova." *Rivista di Studi Liguri* 17:163–200.

Bernhardt, R. 1975. "Die Entwicklung römischer amici et socii zu civitates liberae in Spanien." *Historia* 24:411–24.

Bernstein, A. 1978. *Tiberius Sempronius Gracchus: Tradition and Apostasy.* Ithaca.

Bertacchi, A. 1965. "Aquileia: le più antiche fase urbanistiche." *Notizie degli Scavi*, suppl. 1–11.

———. 1972. "Topografia di Aquileia." *Antichità Altoadriatiche*, vol. 1, 43–58. Udine.

Bertoldi, V. 1947. "Sardo-Punica." *Parola del Passato* 2:5–38.

Berve, H. 1929. "Sertorius." *Hermes* 64:199–227.

Bienkowski, P. R. von. 1908. *Die Darstellungen der Gallier in der hellenistische Kunst.* Wien.

Billington, R. A. 1966. *America's Frontier Heritage.* New York.

———. 1981. *Land of Savagery, Land of Promise.* New York.

Blanc, A. 1953. "Les traces de centuriation romaine et les origines de la cité de Valence." *Rivista di Studi Liguri* 19:35–42.

———. 1953. *Valence romaine: Cahier Valentinois I.* Valence.

———. 1975. *Ardèche: Carte archéologique de la Gaule romaine—fasc. 15.* Paris.

Blanco, Freijeiro A., and G. de LaChica. 1960. "De situ Iliturgis." *Archivo Español de Arqueología* 33:193–96.

Blanco, Freijeiro A., and J. M. Luzón. 1969. "Pre-Roman Silver Miners at Riotinto." *Antiquity* 43:124–31.

Blazquez-Martinez, J. M. 1955. "La interpretación de la pátera de Tivisa." *Ampurias* 17:111–30.

———. 1958. "Sacrificios humanos y representaciones de cabezas en la peninsula ibérica." *Latomus* 17:27–48.

———. 1961. "Las relaciones entre Hispania y el Norte de Africa durante el gobierno bárquida y la conquista romana (237–19 a.J.C.)." *Saitabi* 11:21–43.

———. 1962. "La expansión celtíbera en Carpetania, Bética, Levante y sus causas." *Celticum* 3:409–28.

———. 1963. "El impacto de la conquista de Hispania en Roma (154–83 a.C.)." *Klio* 41:168–86.

———. 1964. "Causas de la romanización de España." *Hispana* 24:5–26, 165–85, 325–48, 485–509.

———. 1965. "Cástulo en las fuentes histórico-literarias anteriores al Imperio." *Oretania* 21:123–28.

———. 1967. "Las alianzas en la Península Ibérica y su repercusión en la progresiva conquista romana." *Revue Internationale des Droits de l'Antiquité*, 3d ser., 14:209–43.

Blazquez-Martinez, J. M. 1969. "Fuentes griegas y romanas referentes
    a Tartessos." *Tartessos y sus Problemas: V. Symposium de Prehistoria
    Peninsular*, 91–110. Barcelona.
———. 1975. *Tartessos y los orígenes de la colonización fenicia en occidente*.
    Salamanca.
Bloch, G. 1913. "L'aurum Tolosanum." *Revue des études anciennes* 15:278–
    80.
Bloch, G., and J. Carcopino. 1952. *Histoire romaine II: La République
    romaine des Grecques à Sulla*. Paris.
Bloch, R. 1966. "Traditions celtiques dans l'histoire des premiers siè-
    cles de Rome." *Mélanges d'archéologie, d'épigraphie et d'histoire offerts
    à Jérôme Carcopino*, 125–37. Paris.
Bonfante, L. 1979. "I popoli delle situle: una civiltà protourbana."
    Dialoghi di Archeologia, n.s., 1:73–94.
Bonuzzi, V. 1971. "L'agricultura nel territorio veronese in età ro-
    mana." *Il territorio veronese in età romana*, 97–106. Verona.
Bosch-Gimpera, P. 1940. "Two Celtic Waves in Spain." *Proceedings of
    the British Academy* 26:25–148.
———. 1966. "Les soldats ibériques agents d'hellénisation et de ro-
    manisation." *Mélanges Carcopino*, 141–48. Paris.
Bosch-Gimpera, P., and P. Aguado Bleye. 1962. *Historia de España
    II—España Romana*. Madrid.
Boucher, S. 1970. "Importations étrusques en Gaule à la fin du VIIe
    siècle, Av.J.C." *Gallia* 28:193–206.
Bouchier E. 1917. *Sardinia in Ancient Times*. Oxford.
Boyer, R., and P. A. Février. 1959. "Stations routières romaines de
    Provence." *Rivista di Studi Liguri* 25:162–85.
Braccesi, L. 1971. *Grecità adriatica*. Bologna.
Braudel, F. 1976. *The Mediterranean and the Mediterranean World in the
    Age of Philip II*. New York.
Bray, W. 1963. "The Ozieri Culture of Sardinia." *Rivista de Scienze
    Preistoriche* 18:155–90.
Brizio, E. 1899. "Il sepolcreto gallico di Montefortino." *Monumenti
    Antichi* 9:616–792.
Brizio, L. B. 1967–68. "Bergamo romana: Ricerche storico-epigra-
    fiche." *Atti Ce S.D.I.R.* 1:51–105.
Broughton, T.R.S. 1951. *The Magistrates of the Roman Republic*, vol. 1.
    Cleveland.
———. 1952. *The Magistrates of the Roman Republic*. vol. 2. Cleveland.
———. 1959. "The Romanization of Spain: The Problem and the
    Evidence." *Proceedings of the American Philosophical Society* 103, no.
    5:645–51.
Brown, F. E. 1980. *Cosa: The Making of a Roman Town*. Ann Arbor.

Brunel, J. 1945. "Etienne de Byzance et le domaine marseillais." *Revue des études anciennes* 47:122–33.

Brunt, P. A. 1971. *Italian Manpower (225 B.C.–A.D. 14)*. Oxford.

———. 1978. "Laus Imperii." *Imperialism in the Ancient World*, ed. P.D.A. Garnsey and C. R. Whittaker, 159–91. Cambridge.

Bryce, J. 1914. *The Ancient Roman Empire and the British Empire in India*. Oxford.

Burckhardt, C. J. 1967. *Richelieu and His Age*, vol. 1. New York.

Burnand, Y. 1975. *Domitii Aquenses: Une famille de chevaliers romains de la région d'Aix-en-Provence, mausolée et domaine*. Paris.

Burns, T. S. 1977. "The Alpine Frontiers and Early Medieval Italy to the Middle of the Seventh Century." Paper presented at the third Oklahoma Symposium in Comparative Frontiers. Abstract in *Comparative Frontier Studies* 5 (Winter):1.

Burstein, S. M. 1979. "Heraclea Pontica: The City and Its Subjects." *The Ancient World* 2:25–28.

Calderini, A. 1930. *Aquileia Romana*. Milano.

———. 1938. "Storia e leggenda intorno alle origini di Milano." *Lombardia Romana*, 13–35. Milano.

———. 1942. "Galli e Romani davanti alla storia." *Rivista di Studi Liguri* 8:5–19.

Callegari, A. 1938. "Este-Scoperta dei resti di una stipe votiva a Caldevigo sul Colle del Principe. Cronistoria delle scoperte fatte in Caldevigo." *Notizie degli Scavi*, 227–56.

Callejo Serrino, C. 1968. "La Arqueología de Norba Cesarina." *Archivo Español de Arqueología* 41:121–49.

Campardou, J. 1957. "L'oppidum préromain de Pech Maho à Sigean (Aude)." *Etudes Roussillonaises* 6:35–65.

Carcopino, J. 1957. *Promenades historiques aux pays de la Dame de Vix*. Paris.

Caro Baroja, J. 1968. *Interpretaciones de la guerra de Numancia*. Madrid.

———. 1970. "Organización social de los pueblos del Norte de la Península ibérica en la antigüedad." *Legio VII Gemina*, 13–62.

Cary, M. 1949. *The Geographic Background of Greek and Roman History*. Oxford.

Casal, L. A. 1979. "Consideraciones en torno a Tartessos y el origen de la cultura ibérica." *Archivo Español de Arqueología* 52:175–94.

Cassola, F. 1972a. "Storia di Aquileia in età romana." *Antichità Altoadriatiche*, vol. 1, 23–42. Udine.

———. 1972b. "La politica romana nell'alto Adriatico." *Antichità Altoadriatiche*, vol. 2, 43–64. Udine.

Castagnoli, F. 1952. "La centuriazione di Lucca." *Studi Etruschi* 20:285–90.

Castagnoli, F. 1974. "Topografia ed urbanistica di Roma nel IV secolo a.c." *Studi Romani* 22:425–43.

Castelin, K. 1961. "Oro celtico in Italia settentrionale." *Congresso internazionale di Numismatica* 2:185–94.

Cecchini, S. M. 1969. *I ritrovamenti fenici e punici in Sardegna.* Roma.

Cervi, M. C. 1969. "Il castelliere ligure dei Cerri e il sisteme difensivo dei Liguri Veleiati." *Atti del III Congresso di Studi Veleiati*, 179–84. Milano.

Cessi, R. 1957. "Da Roma a Bisanzio." *Storia di Venezia*, vol. 1. Venezia.

Chabot, L. 1968. "Les castellas de Rognac et l'étang de Berre à l'époque préromaine." *Rivista di Studi Liguri* 34:151–215.

Chapotat, G. 1970. *Vienne gauloise: le matériel de La Tène III trouvé sur la colline de Sainte-Blandine.* Lyon.

Charmasson, J. 1967. "La pénétration de l'hellénisme par les vallées de la Tave et de la Cèze (Gard)." *Ogam* 19:145–68.

———. 1972. "Grecs et celtes dans la basse vallée du Rhône." *Omaggio a Fernando Benoit*, vol. 2, 106–26. Bordighera.

Chevallier, R. 1959. "Rome et l'Italie du nord." *Revue des études latines* 37:132–50.

———. 1962. "Note sur trois centuriations romaines: Bononia, Ammaedara, Vienne." *Hommages à Albert Grenier*, ed. M. Renerd, 403–18. Bruxelles.

———. 1970. "Possibilités d'inventoire et de typologie de l'habitat préromaine en Gaule: problèmes méthodologiques." *Studi sulla città antica: Actes du Congrès de Bologne*, 19–35.

———. 1975. "Gallia Narbonensis. Bilan de 25 ans de recherches historiques et archéologiques." *Aufstieg und Niedergang der römischen Welt*, vol. 2.3, ed. H. Temporini and W. Hasse, 686–828. Berlin.

———. 1976. *Roman Roads.* Berkeley.

———. 1980. *La romanisation de la Celtique du Pô.* Paris.

Chilver, G.E.F. 1941. *Cisalpine Gaul.* Oxford.

Cichorius, C. 1908. *Untersuchen zu Lucilius.* Berlin.

Clavel M. 1970. *Béziers et son territoire dans l'Antiquité.* Paris.

Clavel-Leveque, M. 1973–74. "Structures urbaines et groupes hétérogènes." *Atti Ce S.D.I.R.* 5:7–39.

Clemente, G. 1974. *I Romani nella Gallia meridionale (II–I sec. a.C.).* Bologna.

Clerc, M. 1916. *Aquae Sextiae.* Aix-en-Provence.

Coarelli, F. 1978. "Elmo bronzeo da Pizzighettone." *I Galli e l'Italia*, 108. Roma.

Colbert de Beaulieu, J. B. 1958. "Une suite de statères d'or attribués aux Arvernes." *Revue Belge de numismatique* 104:63–72.

———. 1966. "Umlauf und Chronologie der gallo-keltischen Münzen." *Jahrbuch für Numismatik und Geldgeschichte*, 45–62.

———. 1973. *Traité de numismatique celtique I, méthodologie des ensembles.* Paris.

Collis, J. 1975. *Defended Sites of the Late La Tène in Central and Western Europe.* British Archaeological Reports, suppl. ser. 2. Oxford.

Colonna, G. 1974a. "Ricerche sugli Etruschi e sugli Umbri a nord degli Apennini." *Studi Etruschi* 42:3–24.

———. 1974b. "I Greci di Adria." *Rivista storica dell'antichità* 4:2–21.

———. 1979. "Scavi e scoperti." *Studi Etruschi* 47:462–535.

Contreras de la Paz, R. 1962. "La conquista de Cástulo por Publio Cornelio Escipión." *Oretania* 4:125–37.

Conway, R. S. 1916. "Some Votive Offerings to the Venetian Goddess Rehtia." *Journal of Royal Anthropological Institute* 48:227–35.

Cook, R. 1981. "The Social and Economic Factor in North America." *The Frontier in History*, ed. H. Lamar and L. Thompson, 175–208. New Haven.

Cooter, W. S. 1976. "Roman Frontier Regions in Temperate Europe." *Comparative Frontier Studies* 3 (Summer):1–3.

———. 1977. "Medieval Frontiers and the Medieval Slave Trade." *Comparative Frontier Studies* 7 (Summer):1–2.

Corbett, J. H. 1971. "Rome and the Gauls, 285–280." *Historia* 20:656–64.

Corradi, G. 1939. *Le strade romane dell'Italia occidentale.* Torino.

Corte, F. della. 1969. *Catone Censore.* Firenze.

Coupry, J. 1968. "Olbia de Ligurie." *Rivista di Studi Liguri* 34:237–46.

Crawford, M. H. 1969a. "The Financial Organization of Republican Spain." *Numismatic Chronicle*, 7th ser., 9:79–84.

———. 1969b. *Roman Republican Coin Hoards.* London.

———. 1974. *Roman Republican Coinage.* Cambridge.

———. 1977. "Republican Denarii in Romania: The Suppression of Piracy and the Slave Trade." *JRS* 67:117–24.

Criniti, N. 1970. *L'epigraphe di Asculum di Gn. Pompeo Strabone.* Milano.

Crumley, C. 1974. *Celtic Social Structure: The Generation of Archaeologically Testable Hypotheses from Literary Evidence.* Anthropological Papers, no. 54. Museum of Anthropology, University of Michigan, Ann Arbor.

———. 1976. *Spatial Aspects of Continuity and Change in Protohistoric and Historic Gaul.* NSF Research Proposal and Annual Report.

Culican, W. 1970. "Almuñécar, Assur and Phoenician Penetration of the Western Mediterranean." *Levant* 2:28–36.

Cunliffe, B., and T. Rowley, eds. 1976. *Oppida and the Beginnings of Urbanisation in Barbarian Europe*. British Archaeological Reports, suppl. ser. 11. Oxford.

Dardaine, S. 1969–70. "Veleia-prosopographie et société." *Atti Ce S.D.I.R.* 2:217–34.

Dauggs, J. P., and F. Malacher. 1976. "Les civilisations de l'Age du Fer dans le Massif-Central." *La Préhistoire Française*, vol. 2, ed. J. Guilaine, 734–52. Paris.

Davidson, I. 1980. "Transhumance, Spain and Ethno-Archaeology." *Antiquity* 54:144–47.

De Caro, S. B. 1978. "Aes grave italico con testa di Gallo-Ariminum, III secolo a.c." *I Galli e l'Italia*, 259–60. Roma.

Déchelette, J. 1902. "Montefortino et Ornavasso; étude sur la civilisation des Gaulois cisalpins." *Revue archéologique* 40:244–83.

———. 1903. *L'oppidum de Bibracte*. Paris.

———. 1904. *Les Fouilles du Mont Beuvray de 1897 à 1901*. Paris.

Degrassi, A., 1939. "Frammenti de elogi e di una dedica a Romolo del foro di Augusto." *Bollettino della Commissione Archeologica del Governatorato di Roma* 67:5–10.

———. 1947. *Inscriptiones Italiae*, vol. 13, fasc. 1. Roma.

———. 1954. *Il confine nord-orientale dell'Italia-romana*. Bern.

———. 1962. "Nuovi miliari arcaici." *Hommages à Albert Grenier*, ed. M. Renard, 499-513. Bruxelles.

———. 1963. "Popaius Senator." *Memorie Accad. Naz. Lincei*, 8th ser., 11:143–47.

Degrassi, N. 1945. "Una tomba del I secolo a.C. a Misano Gera d'Adda (Bergamo)." *Rivista di Studi Liguri* 11:47–56.

De Marinis, R. 1978. "Carzaghetto, Misano di Gera d'Adda." *I Galli e l'Italia*, 91–100. Roma.

De la Ville de Mirmont, H. 1904. "Cicéron et les Gaulois." *Revue celtique* 25:163–80.

DePachtere, F. G. 1912. "Les Campi Macri et le sénatus-consulte Hosidien." *Mélanges Cagnat*, 169–86. Paris.

———. 1920. *Le table hypothécaire de Veleia*. Paris.

DeSanctis, G. 1967. *Storia dei Romani*, 2d. ed., vol. 3, pt. 1. Firenze.

DeSimone, C. 1978. "I Galli in Italia: testimonianze linguistiche." *I Galli e l'Italia*, 261–69. Roma.

DeWever, J. 1966. "La Χώρα massaliote d'après les fouilles récentes." *L'Antiquité classique* 35:71–117.

DeWitt, N. 1940. "Massilia and Rome." *TAPA* 71:605–15.

———. 1941. "Rome and the 'Road of Hercules.' " *TAPA* 72:59–69.

Dobesch, G. 1976. "Zum Hospitium Publicum zwischen Rom und dem Regnum Noricum." *Römisches Osterreich* 4:17–37.

Domerque, C., and R. Freire d'Andrade. 1971. "Sondages 1967 et 1969 à Aljustrel (Portugal): Note préliminaire." *Conimbriga* 10:99–116.

Donati, A. 1975. "Scritture, società e cultura: Le iscrizioni romane." *Storia della Emilia Romagna*, vol. 1, ed. A. Berselli, 213–33. Bologna.

Donnadieu, A. 1954. "La campagne de Marius dans la Gaule Narbonnaise (104–102 av. J.C.)." *Revue des études anciennes* 56:281–96.

DoPaco, A., and J. B. Leal. 1966. "Castelo da Lousa, Mourao (Portugal). Una fortificación romana de la Margen Izquierda del Guadiana." *Archivo Español de Arqueología* 39:167–83.

D'Ors, A. 1971. "El progresso de la epigrafía Romana de Hispania (1963–1967)." *Acta of the Fifth International Congress of Greek and Latin Epigraphy, Cambridge 1967*, 253–64.

Dreizehnter, A. 1975. "Pompeius als Städtegründer." *Chiron* 5:213–46.

Ducati, P. 1910. "Le pietre funerarie felsinee." *Mon. Ant.* 20:357–727.

Dugand, J. E. 1970. *De l'Aegitna de Polybe au trophée de la Braque*. Paris.

Duncan-Jones, R. P. 1976. "Some Configurations of Landholding in the Roman Empire." *Studies in Roman Property*, ed. M. I. Finley, 7–34. Cambridge.

Dupre, W. 1973. "La place de la vallée de l'Ebre dans l'Espagne romaine." *Mélanges de la Casa de Velázquez* 9:133–75.

Duval, P. M. 1949. "A propos de milliaire de Cn. Domitius Ahenobarbus trouvé dans l'Aude en 1949." *Gallia* 7:207–31.

———. 1958. "Les inscriptions gallo-grecques trouvées en France." *Actes du Colloque sur les influences helléniques en Gaule (Dijon)*, 63–69.

———. 1968. "Le milliaire de Domitius et l'organisation de la Narbonnaise." *Revue archéologique de Narbonnaise* 1:3–6.

Dyson, S. L. 1968. "Caesar and the Natives." *Classical Journal* 63:341–46.

———. 1970. "Caepio, Tacitus, and Lucan's Sacred Grove." *Classical Philology* 65:36–38.

———. 1971. "Native Revolts in the Roman Empire." *Historia* 20:239–74.

———. 1975. "Native Revolt Patterns in the Roman Empire." *Aufstieg und Niedergang der römischen Welt*, vol. 2.3, ed. H. Temporini and W. Hasse, 38–175. Berlin.

———. 1980–81. "The Distribution of Roman Republican Family Names in the Iberian Peninsula." *Ancient Society* 11–12:257–99.

Eadie, J. 1977. "Peripheral Vision in Roman History." *Ancient and Modern Essays in Honor of Gerald F. Else*, ed. J. D'Arms and J. Eadie, 215–34. Ann Arbor.

Earl, D. C. 1967. *The Moral and Political Tradition of Rome*. Ithaca.

Ebel, C. 1975. "Pompey's Organization of Transalpina." *Phoenix* 29:358–73.

———. 1976. *Transalpine Gaul: The Emergence of a Roman Province*. Leiden.

Edmonds, R. K. 1978. "Chinese and Japanese Frontiers in Northeast Asia." *Comparative Frontier Studies* 12 (Fall):1–3.

Elkins, S., and E. McKitrick. 1954. "A Meaning for Turner's Frontier." *Political Science Quarterly* 69:321–53, 567–602.

Ercolani, E. 1975. "Aspetti e problemi della circulazione monetaria: dai mezzi di scambio premonetali alla zecca di Ravenna." *Storia della Emilia Romagna*, vol. 1, ed. A. Berselli, 199–211. Bologna.

Errington, R. M. 1970. "Rome and Spain before the Second Punic War." *Latomus* 29:25–57.

Etienne, R. 1953. "Les passages transpyrénéens dans l'Antiquité." *Annales du Midi* 67:295–311.

———. 1962. *Bordeaux antique*. Bordeaux.

Etienne, R., and J. Fontaine. 1979. "Histoire et archéologie de la péninsule ibérique antique, chronique II, 1973–1977." *Revue des études anciennes* 81:105–99.

Euzennat, M. 1980. "Ancient Marseille in the Light of Recent Excavations," *AJArch.* 84:133–40.

Ewins, U. 1952. "The Early Colonization of Cisalpine Gaul." *PBSR* 20:54–71.

———. 1955. "The Enfranchisement of Cisalpine Gaul." *PBSR* 23:73–98.

Fabre, G. 1952. *Les civilisations protohistoriques de l'Aquitaine*. Paris.

Facchini, F. 1968. "I resti scheletrici del sepolcreto gallico di S. Martino in Gattara (Ravenna)." *Studi Etruschi* 36:73–90.

Fallers, L. A. 1966. "A Note on the 'Trickle Effect.'" *Class, Status and Power*, ed. R. Bendix and S. M. Lipset, 402–5. New York.

Faust, M. 1975. "Die Kelten auf der iberischen Halbinsel: Sprachliche Zeugnisse." *Madrid Mitteilungen* 16:195–207.

Fernández, R. R. 1975. *La ciudad romana de Illici*. Alicante.

Fernández-Chicarro y de Diós, C. 1969. "El habitat humano en el bajo Guadalquivir a través de algunas fotos aéreas." *Tartessos y sus Problemas: V. Symposium de Prehistoria Peninsular*, 7–13. Barcelona.

Fernández-Miranda, M. 1979. "Horizonte cultural tartéssico y hallazgos griegos en el sur de la Peninsula." *Archivo Español de Arqueología* 52:49–66.

Ferron, J. 1970. "A propos de la civilisation phénicienne d'Occident." *Latomus* 29:1026–37.

Ferrua, A. 1948. *Itineria Italica, v. 9 fasc. 1: Augusta Bagiennorum et Pollentia*. Roma.

Février, P. A. 1973. "The Origin and Growth of the Cities of Southern Gaul to the Third Century A.D.: An Assessment of the Most Recent Archaeological Discoveries." *JRS* 63:1–28.

Fiorentini, G. 1963. "Primi osservazioni sulla ceramica campana nella valle del Po." *Rivista di Studi Liguri* 29:7–52.

Fleming, A. 1971. "Territorial Patterns in Bronze Age Wessex." *Proceedings of the Prehistoric Society* 37:138–66.

Fletcher, D. 1954. *La edad del hierro en el Levante Español*. Madrid.

Flexner, J. T. 1979. *Lord of the Mohawks*. Boston.

Fogolari, G. 1940. "Scavo di una necropoli preromana e romana presso Adria." *Studi Etruschi* 14:431–42.

———. 1956. "Dischi bronzei figurati de Treviso." *Bollettino d'Arte* 41:1–10.

Fogolari, G., and G. B. Pellegrini. 1958. "Iscrizioni etrusche e venetiche di Adria." *Studi Etruschi* 26:103–54.

Formentini, U. 1949. "Ligures Celeberrimi nella riviera di Levante e nel suo retroterra." *Rivista di Studi Liguri* 15:209–22.

Forni, G. 1953. "Manio Curio Dentato, uomo democratico." *Athenaeum* 31:170–240.

Forteleoni, L. 1961. *Le emissioni monetale della Sardegna Punica*. Sassari.

Fraccaro, P. 1919. "Lex Flaminia de agro Gallico et Piceno viritim dividundo." *Athenaeum* 7:73–93.

———. 1956a. "La colonia romana di Eporedia (Ivrea) e la sua centuriazione." *Opuscula* 1:93–121.

———. 1956b. "Intorno ai confini ed alla centuriazione degli agri di Patavium e di Acelum." *Opuscula* 1:71–92.

Frank, T. 1922. *Vergil, A Biography*. New York.

Frankenstein, S., and M. J. Rowlands. 1978. *The Internal Structure and Regional Context of Early Iron Age Society in Southwestern Germany*. Bulletin of the Institute of Archaeology, University of London.

Frey, O. H. 1966. "Der Ostalpenraum und die antike Welt in der frühen Eisenzeit." *Germania* 44:48–66.

Frova, A. 1968. "Una tomba gallo-ligure nel territorio della Spezia." *Rivista di Studi Liguri* 34:289–300.

Furman, N. 1976. *Walter Prescott Webb: His Life and Impact*. Albuquerque.

Furr, L. R. 1929–30. "The Nationality of Vergil." *Classical Journal* 25:340–46.

Gabba, E. 1970. "Aspetti della lotta in Spagna di Sesto Pompeo." *Legio VII Gemina*, 133–55. Leon.

———. 1973. *Esercito e società nella tarda Repubblica romana*. Firenze.

Gagé, J. 1954. "La balance de Kairos et l'épée de Brennus." *Revue archéologique*, 43:141–76.

———. 1962. "Les 'busta Gallica', Camille et l'expulsion de Februarius." *Hommages à Albert Grenier*, ed. M. Renard, 707–20. Bruxelles.

———. 1975. "Les Gaulois à Clusium." *Revue historique* 513:5–33.

Gagnière, S., J. Granier, and R. Perrot. 1962. "Un oppidum de la basse vallée du Rhône: Le Rocher des Doms à Avignon." *Cahiers ligures de préhistoire* 11:48–77.

Galbraith, J. 1963. *Reluctant Empire*. Berkeley.

Gallet de Santerre, H. 1962. "Ensérune, An Oppidum in Southern France." *Archaeology* 15:163–71.

———. 1968. "Fouilles dans le quartier ouest d'Ensérune (Insula N.X.)." *Revue archéologique de Narbonnaise* 1:39–83.

Galsterer, H. 1971. *Untersuchungen zum römischen Städtewesen auf der iberischen Halbinsel*. Berlin.

Gamer, G., and J. Ortego y Frías. 1969. "Neue Beobachtungen am römischen Lager bei Almazán (prov. Soria)." *Madrid Mitteilungen* 10:172–84.

Gann, L. H., and P. Duignan. 1967. *Burden of Empire*. Stanford.

García y Bellido, A. 1945. *Bandas y guerrillas en las luchas con Roma*. Madrid.

———. 1952. *Histoire de l' Espagne—Espagne Protohistorica*. Madrid.

———. 1960. *Colonia Aelia Augusta Italica*. Madrid.

———. 1963. "Los auxiliares hispanos en los ejércitos romanos de ocupación (200 al 30 antes de J.C.)." *Emerita* 31:213–26.

———. 1966. "Los 'mercatores,' 'negotiatores' y 'publicani' como vehículos de romanización en la España romana preimperial." *Hispania* 104:497–512.

———. 1970. "Los hallazgos cerámicos del área del templo romano de Córdoba." *Archivo Español de Arqueología* 43:8–58.

García y Bellido, A., H. Schubart, and H. G. Niemayer. 1971. "Espagne." *L'espansione fenica nel Mediterraneo*, ed. S. Moscati, 145–60. Roma.

García Moreno, L. A. 1979. "Justino 44,4 y la historia interna de Tartessos." *Archivo Español de Arqueología* 52:111–30.

Garrod, H. W. 1912. "Vergil." *English Literature and the Classics*, ed. G. S. Gordon. Oxford.

Gavelle, R. 1960. "Lugdunum Convenarum et l'Espagne." *Revue de Comminges* 73:127–45.

Gayraud, M. 1970. "L'inscription de Bram (Aude) et les toponymes Eburomagus, Hebromagus, Cobiomagus en Gaule méridionale." *Revue archéologique de Narbonnaise* 3:103–14.

———. 1972. "La population de Narbonne gallo-romaine: Remarques sur les sources d'une étude." *Congrès de la Fédération Historique du Languedoc Méditerranéen et du Roussillon*, 45:195–203.

Gelzer, M. 1933. "Römische Politik bei Fabius Pictor." *Hermes* 68:129–66.

———. 1968. *Caesar, Politician and Statesmen*. Cambridge, Mass.

Gerin-Richard, H. de. 1929. *Le sanctuaire préromain de Roquepertuse*. Marseille.

———. 1934. "L'habitat retranché des Baou-de-Sainte-Marcel." *Provincia* 14:58–83.

Ghirandini, G. 1901. "Padova-di un singolare bronzo paleoveneto scoperto presso la basilica de S. Antonio." *Notizie degli Scavi*, 314–21.

Gil Farres, O. 1966. *La moneda hispánica en la edad antigua*. Madrid.

Giliomee, H. 1981. "Processes in Development of the Southern African Frontier." *The Frontier in History*, ed. H. Lamar and L. Thompson, 76–122. New Haven.

Gillis, D. 1969. "Quintus Sertorius." *Rendiconti Litt. Istituto Lombardo* 103:711–27.

Gordon, M. 1934. "The Family of Vergil." *JRS* 24:1–12.

Gorini, G. 1971. "La circulazione del denario repubblicano nell'agro veronese." *Il territorio veronese in età romana*, 502–16. Verona.

Gosse, G. 1942. "Las minas y el arte minero de España en la Antiqüidad." *Ampurias* 4:43–68.

Götzfried, K. 1907. *Annalen der Römischen Provinzen beider Spanien, 218–154 B.C.* Erlangen.

Gourvest, J. 1956. "L'oppidum de Constantine." *Notes de archéologie celtique et gallo-romaine* 5:51–62.

Govi, C. M. 1978. "Rocca San Casciano." *I Galli e l'Italia*, 133–37. Roma.

Gras, M. 1973–74. "Céramique d'importation étrusque à Bithia (Sardaigne)." *Studi Sardi* 73:131–39.

Grazzi, L. 1972. *Parma Romana*. Parma.

Grenier, A. 1912. *Bologne villanovienne et étrusque, VIIIe–IVe siècles avant notre ère*. Paris.

———. 1958. "La centuriation romaine de la colonie de Valence." *Gallia* 16:281–84.

———. 1959. *Carte archéologique de la Gaule romaine—fasc. XII: Département de l'Aude*. Paris.

Griffith, G. T. 1935. *The Mercenaries of the Hellenistic World*. Cambridge.

Grosjean, R. 1966. "Recent Work in Corsica." *Antiquity* 40:190–98.

Grosjean, R. 1971. "Diorama de la civilisation torréene corse." *Mélanges d'études corses offerts à Paul Arrighi*, 166–94. Aix-en-Provence.

Gruen, E. S. 1968. *Roman Politics and the Criminal Courts, 149–78 B.C.* Cambridge, Mass.

Guerrero, M. 1969. " 'Asta Regia' Una Ciudad Tartesica." *Tartessos y sus Problemas: V. Symposium de Prehistoria Peninsular*, 111–18. Barcelona.

Guido, M. 1964. *Sardinia.* New York.

Gundel, H. G. 1970. "Probleme der römischen Kampfführung gegen Viriathus." *Legio VII Gemina*, 111–30. León.

Guy, M. 1955. "Vues aériennes monstrant la centuriation de la colonie de Narbonne." *Gallia* 13:103–118.

Gyles, M. F. 1964. "Effects of Roman Capital Investment in Britain under Nero." *Laudatores Temporis Acti*, ed. M. F. Gyles and E. W. Davis, 99–109. Chapel Hill.

Haarhoff, T. J. 1948. *The Stranger at the Gate.* Oxford.

Hanke, L. 1959. *Aristotle and the American Indians.* Chicago.

Harden, D. 1971. *The Phoenicians.* Harmondsworth.

Harmond, J. 1970. "César et l'Espagne durant le second bellum civile." *Legio VII Gemina*, 181–203. León.

Harris, W. V. 1971. *Rome in Etruria and Umbria.* Oxford.

———. 1979. *War and Imperialism in Republican Rome, 327–70 B.C.* Oxford.

Hatt, J. J. 1959. *Histoire de la Gaule romaine.* Paris.

———. 1970. *Celts and Gallo-Romans.* London.

Hess, D. A. 1979. "Pioneering as Ecological Process: A Model and Test Case of Frontier Adaptation." *The Frontier, Comparative Studies*, vol. 2, ed. W. W. Savage and S. I. Thompson. Norman, Okla.

Heuberger, R. 1938. "Die Gaesaten." *Klio* 31:60–80.

Heurgon, J. 1952. "La date des gobelets de Vicarello." *Revue des études anciennes* 54:39–50.

———. 1974. "Caton et la Gaule cisalpine." *Hommages à W. Seston*, 231–47. Paris.

Heussler, R. 1963. *Yesterday's Rulers.* Syracuse.

Hildebrandt, H. J. 1979. "Die Römerlager von Numantia." *Madrid Mitteilungen* 20:238–71.

Hirschfeld, O. 1913a. "Gallische Studien I." *Kleine Schriften*, 47–96. Berlin.

———. 1913b. "Aquitanien in der Römerzeit." *Kleine Schriften*, 209–38. Berlin.

———. 1913c. "Die Haeduer und Arverner unter Römischer Herrschaft." *Kleine Schriften*, 186–208. Berlin.

Hirth, K. 1978. "Interregional Trade and the Formation of Prehistoric Gateway Communities." *American Antiquity* 43:35–45.

Hobsbawm, E. 1969. *Bandits.* London.

Hoffman, W. 1952. "Zur Vorgeschichte von Caesars Eingreifen in Gallien." *Der altsprachliche Unterricht* 4:1–22.

Holland, L. 1961. *Janus and the Bridge.* American Academy in Rome Papers and Monographs, no. 21. Roma.

Holleaux, M. 1957. "Lampsaque et les Galates en 197–196 B.C." *Etudes d'épigraphie et d'histoire grecque*, vol. 5. 141–55. Paris.

Homeyer, H. 1960. "Zum Keltenexkurs im Livius 5 Buch (33.4–35.3)." *Historia* 9:345–61.

Horowitz, D. 1978. *The First Frontier: The Indian Wars and America's Origins, 1607–1776.* New York.

Hübner, E. 1869. "Ein Decret des L. Aemilius Paulus." *Hermes* 3:243–60.

Hummler, M., et al. 1983. *Bagnolo San Vito (Forcello).* Birmingham University Field Archaeology Unit Report no. 5 (1981–82), 14–16.

Ilevbare, J. A. 1973. "Some Aspects of Social Change in North Africa in Punic and Roman Times." *Museum Africum* 2:24–44.

Inglieri, R. 1953. "Postilla all'iscrizione del console Manio Acilio Glabrione scoperta a Luni." *Rivista di Studi Liguri* 19:115–20.

Jacobs, W. 1950. *Wilderness Politics and Indian Gifts: The Northern Colonial Frontier, 1748–1763.* Lincoln, Nebr.

———. 1971. "The Fatal Confrontation: Early Native–White Relations on Frontiers of Australia, New Guinea and America: A Comparative Study." *Pacific Historical Review* 40:283–309.

———. 1972. *Dispossessing the American Indian: Indians and Whites and the Colonial Frontier.* New York.

———. 1973. "The Indian and the Frontier in American History—A Need for Revisions." *Western Historical Quarterly* 4:43–56.

Jaenon, C. J. 1976. *Friend and Foe.* Columbia.

Jannoray, J. 1955. *Ensérune, Contribution à l'étude des civilisations préromaines de la Gaule méridionale.* Paris.

Jehasse, J. 1976a. "Informations Archéologiques—Circonscription de la Corse." *Gallia* 34:503–9.

———. 1976b. "Les civilisations de l'Age du Fer en Corse." *La Préhistoire Française*, vol. 2, ed. J. Guilaine, 847–55. Paris.

Jehasse, J., and L. Jehasse. 1966. "La Grande-Grèce et la Corse aux IVᵉ et IIIᵉ siècles avant J.-C." *Mélanges d'archéologie, d'épigraphie et d'histoire offerts à Jérôme Carcopino*, 529–54. Paris.

———. 1973. *La nécropole préromaine d'Aléria (1960–1968). Gallia*, suppl. 25. Paris.

Jehasse, J., and L. Jehasse. 1979. "The Etruscans and Corsica." *Italy Before the Romans*, ed. D. Ridgeway and F. Ridgeway, 313–52. London.

Jehasse, L. 1973. "La céramique étrusque d'Aléria." *Etudes Corses* 1:7–34.

Joffroy, R. 1960. *L'oppidum de Vix et la civilisation hallstattienne finale dans l'Est de la France*. Paris.

Jolivet, V. 1980. "Exportations étrusques tardives (IVe–IIIe siècles) en Méditerranée occidentale." *Mélanges de l'Ecole Française de Rome: Antiquité* 92:681–724.

Jullian, C. 1908. *Histoire de la Gaule*, vol. 1. Paris.

———. 1914. *Vercingetorix*. Paris.

———. 1920. *Histoire de la Gaule*, 2d ed. vol. 3. Paris.

———. 1975. "Koiné commerciale et culturelle phénico-punique et ibérolanguedocienne en Méditerranée Occidentale à l'Age du Fer." *Archivo Español de Arqueología* 48:22–90.

Jully, J. J. 1976. "Graffites sur vases attiques en Languedoc méditerranéen Roussillon et Catalogne." *Dialogues d'Histoire Ancienne* 2:53–70.

Kastelic, J. 1965. *Situla Art*. New York.

Kimmig, W. 1958. "Kulturbeziehungen zwischen der nordwestalpinen Hallstattkultur und der mediterranen Welt." *Actes du Colloque sur les influences helléniques en Gaul*, 75–87. Dijon.

King, R. 1975. *Sardinia*. Harrisburg, Pa.

Kleiner, F.G.S. 1973. "Gallia Graeca, Gallia Romana and the Introduction of Classical Sculpture in Gaul." *AJArch.* 77:379–90.

Knapp, R. C. 1977a. *Aspects of the Roman Experience in Iberia, 206–100 B.C. Anejos de Hispania Antigua*, 9. Valladolid.

———. 1977b. "The Date and Purpose of the Iberian Denarii." *Numismatic Chronicle*, 7th ser., 17:1–18.

———. 1978. "The Origins of Provincial Prosopography in the West." *Ancient Society* 9:187–222.

———. 1980. "Cato in Spain, 195/194 B.C.: Chronology and Geography." *Studies in Latin Literature and Roman History II*, ed. C. Deroux. Collection Latomus, no. 168:21–56. Bruxelles.

———. 1983. *Roman Córdoba*. Berkeley.

König, I. 1970. *Die Meilensteine der Gallia Narbonensis*. Bern.

Kramer, F. R. 1948. "Massilian Diplomacy Before the Second Punic War." *AJPhil.* 69:1–26.

Kriss, H. 1965. *Mostra dell'Arte delle situle del Po al Danubio*. Firenze.

Kruta, V. 1978. "Celtes de cispadane et transalpins aux IVe et IIIe siècles avant notre ère: Données archéologiques." *Studi Etruschi* 46:149–74.

Kruta Poppi, L. 1975. "Les celtes à Marzabotto." *Etudes celtiques* 14:345–76.

Labrousse, M. 1968. *Toulouse antique*. Paris.

Laffi, U. 1966. *Adtributio e Contributio*. Pisa.

Laffranque, M. 1964. *Poseidonios d'Apamée*. Paris.

Laistner, M.L.W. 1947. *The Greater Roman Historians*. Berkeley.

Lamboglia, N. 1932. *La prima fase delle guerre romano-liguri 238–230 C.* Collana storica archaeologica della Liguria occidentale, vol. 1, no. 6. Imperia.

———. 1933. *Le guerre romane—ingaune e la romanizzazione della Liguria di Ponente*. Collana storica archeologica della Liguria occidentale, vol. 2, no. 1.

———. 1936. "I limiti dell'espansione etrusca nel territorio dei Liguri." *Studi Etruschi* 10:137–52.

———. 1937. "La via Aemilii Scauri." *Athenaeum* 15:57–68.

———. 1939. *Liguria Romana*, vol. 1. Alassio.

———. 1947. "La Cohors Ligurum e la romanizzazione de Cemenelum." *Rivista di Studi Liguri* 13:21–28.

———. 1959. "Prata Liguriae." *Rivista di Studi Liguri* 25:5–22.

———. 1960a. "Bibliografia critica." *Rivista di Studi Liguri* 26:305–29.

———. 1960b. "Le necropoli ligure di Chiavari." *Rivista di Studi Liguri* 26:91–220.

———. 1972a. "Le Regnum des Ligures Elisyci." *Congrès de la Fédération Historique du Languedoc Méditerranéen et du Roussillon* 45:65–69.

———. 1972b. "La quarta campagna nelle necropoli ligure di Chiaveri." *Rivista di Studi Liguri* 38:103–36.

Lambrechts, P. 1954. *L'exaltation de la tête dans la pensée et dans l'art des Celtes*. Brugge.

Latte, K. 1960. *Römische Religionsgeschichte*. München.

Lattimore, O. 1951. *Inner Asian Frontiers of China*, 2d ed. New York.

———. 1962. *Studies in Frontier History, Collected Papers 1928–1958*. London.

———. 1963. "Chingis Khan and the Mongol Conquests." *Scientific American*, Aug., 55–68.

Leglay, M. 1964. "Les fouilles d'Alba Augusta Helviorum (Ardèche)." *CRAcad. Inscr.*, 401–15.

Lejeune, M. 1954. "Notes de linguistique italique: XII les dédicaces du sanctuaire de Lagole." *Rev. Et. Lat.* 32:120–38.

———. 1956. "L'inscription gauloise de Briona." *Festschrift Niederman*. Bruxelles.

———. 1968–70. "La préture en Narbonnaise et l'inscription gauloise de Vitrolles. *Etudes classiques* 3:133–39.

————. 1971. *Lepontica*. Paris.

LeJeune, M. 1978. *Ateste à l'heure de la romanisation (étude anthroponymique)*. Firenze.

Le Lannou, M. 1941. *Pâtres et paysans de la Sardaigne*. Tours.

Lepore, E. 1970. "Strutture della collonizzazione focea in Occidente." *Parola del Passato* 25:19–54.

LeRoux, P. 1972. "Structures agraires antiques dans la région de Séville: Essai de problématique." *Mélanges de la Casa de Velázquez* 8:593–640.

Le Roy Ladurie, E. 1978. *Montaillou: The Promised Land of Error*. New York.

Levi, A. 1952. *Barbarians on Roman Imperial Coins and Sculpture*. Numismatic Notes and Monographs, no. 123. New York.

Levi, D. 1950. "Le necropoli puniche di Olbia." *Studi Sardi* 9:5–120.

Lilliu, G. 1948. "Rapporti fra la civiltà nuragica e la civiltà fenicio—punica in Sardegna." *Studi Etruschi* 18:323–372.

————. 1959. "The Proto-Castles of Sardinia." *Scientific American*, 62–69.

————. 1962. *La civiltà dei Sardi*. Turino.

Liou, B. 1973. "Direction des recherches archéologiques sous-marines." *Gallia* 31:571–608.

Livadie, C. A. 1967. "L'épave étrusque du Cap d'Antibes." *Rivista di Studi Liguri* 33:300–26.

Lizop, R. 1931. *Histoire de deux cités gallo-romaines; les Convenae et les Consoranni*. Toulouse and Paris.

Lombardi, M. 1975. "The Frontier in Brazilian History: A Historiographical Essay." *Pacific Historical Review* 44:437–57.

Lopez Monteagudo, G. 1977. "Panorama actual de la colonización griega en la península ibérica." *Archivo Español de Arqueología* 50:3–14.

Lo Porto, G. F. 1952. "Una necropoli di età repubblicana nell'Alessandrino." *Rivista di Studi Liguri* 18:46–66.

Luttwak, E. 1976. *The Grand Strategy of the Roman Empire*. Baltimore.

MacDonald, A. H. 1974. "The Roman Conquest of Cisalpine Gaul (201–191 B.C.)." *Antichthon* 8:44–53.

MacKendrick, P. L. 1957. "Roman Colonization and the Frontier Hypothesis." *The Frontier in Perspective*, ed. W. D. Wyman and C. B. Kroeber, 5–20. Madison.

Mackensen, M. 1975. "The State of Research on the 'Norican' Silver Coinage." *World Archaeology* 6:249–75.

MacLeod, W. 1967. "Celt and Indian: Britain's Old World Frontier in Relation to the New." *Beyond the Frontier*, ed. P. Bohannan and F. Plog, 25–42. Garden City, N.Y.

Maetzke, G. 1961. "Architettura romana in Sardegna." *Bollettino del Centro di Studi per la Storia dell'Architettura* 17:49–61.

Maluquer de Motes y Nicolau, J., et al. 1963. *Historia de España*, vol. 1.3. Madrid.

———. 1969. "Los Fenicos in Cataluña." *Tartessos y sus problemas: V. Symposium de Prehistoria Peninsular*, 24–250. Barcelona.

Mandelbaum, D. G. 1965. "Alcohol and Culture." *Current Anthropology* 6:281–93.

Mansuelli, G. A. 1961. *Catulle Veronese*. Verona.

———. 1962. "Problemi storici della civiltà gallica in Italia." *Hommages à Albert Grenier*, ed. M. Renard, 1067–93. Bruxelles.

———. 1963. *I Cisalpini*. Firenze.

———. 1964. *Arte e civiltà romana nell'Italia settentrionale*. Bologna.

———. 1965. "Formazione delle civiltà storiche nella pianura padana orientale." *Studi Etruschi* 33:3–47.

———. 1967. "L'arte della situle fra Mediterraneo ed Europa." *Atti del primo simposio internazionale di protostoria italiana*, 105–7. Roma.

———. 1971. *Urbanistica ed architettura della Cisalpina romana fino al III sec. e.n.* Collection Latomus, no. 111. Bruxelles.

———. 1972. "Problemi urbanistici dell'abitato e del territorio di Forum Livi." *Studi Romagnoli* 33:3–12.

———. 1978. "Le fonti storiche sui Celti cisalpini." *I Galli e l'Italia*, 71–75. Roma.

Mansuelli, G. A., and R. Scarini. 1961. *L'Emilia prima dei Romani*. Milano.

Marchesetti, C. 1903. *I castellieri preistorici di Trieste e della regione guilia*. Trieste.

Martin-Granel, H. 1944. "Les fouilles de l'oppidum du Cayla à Mailhac (Aude)." *Gallia* 2:1–24.

Martin Vells, R. 1960. *La circulacion monetaria ibérica*. Valladolid.

Mattingly, H. B. 1962. "The Foundation of Narbo Martius." *Hommages à Albert Grenier*, ed. M. Renard, 1159–71. Bruxelles.

Mazzarino, S. 1966. *Il pensiero storico classico*. Bari.

McKay, A. 1971. *Vergil's Italy*. Bath.

Megaw, J.V.S. 1966. "The Vix Burial." *Antiquity* 40:38–44.

Meloni, P. 1949. "Sei anni di lotte di Sardi e Corsi contro i Romani (236–231 av. Cr.)." *Studi Sardi* 9:121–41.

———. 1971. "Stato attuale dell'epigrafia latina in Sardegna e nuove acquisizioni." *Acta of the Fifth Epigraphic Congress*, 241–45. Oxford.

———. 1975. *La Sardegna romana*. Sassari.

Mercando, L. 1978. "Problemi della civiltà gallica nelle marche." *I Galli e l'Italia*, 163–67. Roma.

Mikesell, M. 1968. "Comparative Studies in Frontier History." *Turner and the Sociology of the Frontier*, ed. R. Hofstadter and M. Lipset, 152–71. New York.

Milisauskas, S. 1978. *European Prehistory.* New York.

Miller, K. 1916. *Itineraria Romana.* Stuttgart.

Milner, Clyde A., II. 1981. "Indulgent Friends and Important Allies: Political Process on the Cis-Mississippi Frontier and Its Aftermath." *The Frontier in History*, ed. H. Lamar and L. Thompson, 123–48. New Haven.

Mohen, J. P. 1976. "Les civilisations de l'Age du Fer en Aquitaine." *La Préhistoire Française*, vol. 2, ed. J. Guilaine, 761–69. Paris.

Molinero Pérez, A. 1951. "Una necrópolis del Hierro Céltico en Cuellar (Segovia)." *2 Congreso nacional de Argueología*, 337–54. Madrid.

Moretti, G. 1914. "Serravalle Scrivia—Scavi nell'area della città di Libarna." *Notizie degli Scavi*, 113–34.

Morgan, M. G. 1969. "The Roman Conquest of the Balearic Isles." *California Studies in Classical Antiquity* 2:217–31.

———. 1971. "Lucius Cotta and Metellus: Roman Campaigns in Illyria during the Late Second Century B.C." *Athenaeum* 49:271–301.

Moscati, S. 1966. "La penetrazione fenica e punica in Sardegna." *Memoria dell'Accademia dei Lincei*, 8th ser., 12:215–20.

———. 1968. *Fenici e Cartaginesi in Sardegna.* Milano.

———. 1975. "A Carthaginian Fortress in Sardinia." *Scientific American*, 80–86.

Mostra dell'Etruria Padana e della città di Sprine. 1961. Bologna.

Muldoon, J. 1975. "The Indian as Irishman." *Essex Institute Historical Collections* 111:267–89.

Münzer, F. 1905. "Atticus als Geschichtschreiber." *Hermes* 40:50–100.

Nash, D. 1975. "The Chronology of Celtic Coinage in Gaul: The Arvernian 'Hegemony' Reconsidered." *Numismatic Chronicle*, 7th ser., 15:204–18.

———. 1976. "The Growth of Urban Society in France." *Oppida and the Beginnings of Urbanisation in Barbarian Europe*, ed. B. Cunliffe and T. Rowley. British Archaeological Reports, suppl. ser. 11, 95–134. Oxford.

———. 1978. "Territory and State Formation in Central Gaul." *Social Organisation and Settlement*, ed. D. Green, C. Haselgrove, and M. Spriggs. British Archaeological Reports, intern. ser. 47, 455–76. Oxford.

Nash, E. 1961. *Pictorial Dictionary of Ancient Rome.* New York.

Negroni Catacchio, N. 1975–76. "La frequentazione dei passi alpini del San Bernardino e dello Spluga in rapporto al divenire della Civiltá di Golasecca." *Atti Ce S.D.I.R.* 7:447–72.

Nenci, G. 1958. "Le relazioni con Marsiglia nella politica estera romana." *Rivista di Studi Liguri* 24:24–97.

Nickels, A. 1976. "Contribution des fouilles de l'arrière-pays d'Agde
à l'étude du problème des rapports entre Grecs et indigènes en
Languedoc (VIᵉ–Vᵉ siècles)." *Mélanges de l'Ecole Française de Rome:
Antiquité*, 88:141–57.

Nicolini, G. 1974. *The Ancient Spaniards*. Farnsborough.

Niemayer, H. G., M. Pellicer, and H. Schubart. 1964. "Eine altpu-
nische Kolonie an der Mündung der río Vélez." *Arch. Anz.* 3:477–
92.

Nierhaus, R. 1966. "Die wirtschaftlichen Voraussetzungen der Vil-
lenstadt von Italica." *Madrid Mitteilungen* 7:189–205.

Noè, E. 1974. "La produzione tessile nella Gallia cisalpina in età romana." *Rendiconti Litt. Istituto Lombardo*, 108:918–32.

Ogilvie, R. 1965. *A Commentary on Livy*, bks. 1–5. Oxford.

———. 1976. *Early Rome and the Etruscans*. Glasgow.

Osborne, B. S., and C. M. Roberson. 1978. "Conceptualizing the
Frontier Settlement Process: Development or Dependency."
Comparative Frontier Studies 11(Summer):1–3.

Padden, R. C. 1957. "Cultural Change and Military Resistance in
Araucanian Chile, 1550–1730." *Southwestern Journal of Anthropology* 13:103–21.

Padova preromana. 1976. Padova.

Pairault-Massa, F. H. 1978. "Talamone." *I Galli e l'Italia*, 207–19.
Roma.

Pais, E. 1918. *Dalle guerre puniche a Cesare Augusto*, vol. 2. Roma.

———. 1923. *Storia della Sardegna e della Corsica durante il dominio romana*. Roma.

Pallottino, M. 1962. "Gli Etruschi nell'Italia del Nord, nuovi dati e
nuove idee." *Hommages à Albert Grenier*, ed. M. Renerd, 1207–16.
Bruxelles.

———. 1978. *The Etruscans*. Harmondsworth.

Palm, J. 1959. *Rom, Römertum und Imperium in der griechischen Literatur
der Kaiserzeit*. Acta Soc. Hum. Litt. Lundensis LVII. Lund.

Panciera, S. 1957. *Vita economica de Aquileia in età romana*. Venezia.

———. 1972. "Porti e commerci nell'alto Adriatico." *Antichità Altoadriatiche*, vol. 2, 79–112. Udine.

Pascal, C. B. 1964. *The Cults of Cisalpine Gaul*. Collection Latomus,
no. 75. Bruxelles.

Pascucci, G. 1956. "Cimbri e Teutoni in Cesare." *Studi italiani di filologia*, 361–73.

Pauli, L. 1971. *Studien zur Golasecca Kultur*. Heidelberg.

Pautasso, A. 1960. *Le monete preromane dell'Italia settentrionale*. Varese.

Pautasso, A. 1962–63. "Le monete preromane dell'Italia settentrionale." *Sibrium*, vol. 7.

———. 1975–76. "Le monetazioni preromane con leggende in alfabeto leponzio emesse da popoli delle regioni alpine." *Atti Ce S.D.I.R.* 7:473–500.

Pearce, R. H. 1965. *The Savages of America*. Baltimore.

Peckham, H., and C. Gibson, eds. 1969. *Attitudes of Colonial Powers toward the American Indian*. Salt Lake City.

Pellegrini, G. B., and G. Fogolari. 1957–58. "Iscrizioni etrusche e venetiche di Adria." *Studi Etruschi* 26:103–54.

Pelletier, A. 1966. "De la Vienne gauloise à la Vienne romaine: Essai d'étude stratigraphique." *Cahiers Rhodaniennes* 13:144–54.

Pellicer, M. 1962. "La cerámica ibérica del Valle del Ebro." *Caesaraugusta* 19–20:37–78.

Pergola, C. V. 1980. "Prima miscellanea sulla Corsica Romana." *Mélanges de l'Ecole Française de Rome: Antiquité* 92:303–28.

Perham, M. 1960. *Lugard*, vol. 2. London.

Pericot Garcia, L. 1952. *L'Espagne avant la conquête romaine*. Paris.

Perrin, M., and R. Perichon. 1974. "Un site de La Tène dans la Vallée de la Saône, Champ-Semard, près de Tournus (Saône-et-Loire)." *Gallia* 32:225–42.

Peyre, C. 1969. "Problèmes actuels de la recherche sur la civilisation celtique dans la Cispadane." *Revue archéologique*, 165–77.

———. 1979. *La Cisalpine Gauloise du IIIe au Ier siècle avant J.-C.* Paris.

Piana Agostinetti, P. 1972. *Documenti per la protostoria della Val d'Ossola*. Milano.

Piccottini, G. 1977. "Die Stadt auf dem Magdalensberg." *Aufstieg und Niedergang der römischen Welt* vol. 2.6, ed. H. Temporini and W. Hasse, 263–301. Berlin.

Piggott, S. 1965. *Ancient Europe*. Edinburgh.

Polanyi, K. 1966. *Dahomey and the Slave Trade*. Seattle.

Polanyi, K., C. Arensberg, and H. Pearson. 1957. *Trade and Market in the Early Empire*. Glencoe, Ill.

Polledri, H. C. 1967. "Via Aemilia Scauri." *Studi classici ed orientali* 16:256–72.

Pomponi, F. 1965. "Rome et les Volques." *Congrès de la Fédération Historique de Languedoc Méditerranéen et du Roussillon*, 38:109–15.

Pontiroli, G. 1967–68. "Cremona e il suo territorio in età romana." *Atti Ce S.D.I.R.* 1:165–211.

Popoli e civiltà dell'Italia antica, vol. 4. 1980.

Porra', F., and I. Didu. 1978–79. "Due nuove iscrizioni di ausiliari in Sardegna." *Atti Ce R.D.A.* 10:140–53.

Potter, T. W. 1979. *The Changing Landscape of South Etruria*. New York.

Powell, P. 1952. *Soldiers, Indians and Silver*. Berkeley.

Preynat, J. P. 1962. "Un site de La Tène en Forez, l'oppidum d'Essalois." *Ogam* 14:287–314.

Prieur, J. 1968. *La Province romaine des Alpes cottiennes*. Villeurbanne.

Prosdocimi, A. L. 1967. "L'iscrizione di Prestino." *Studi Etruschi* 35:199–222.

Py, M. 1968. "Les fouilles en Vaunage et les influences grècques en Gaule méridionale." *Rivista di Studi Liguri* 34:57–106.

Raddatz, K. 1969. *Die Schatzfunde der Iberischen Halbinsel vom Ende des dritten bis zur Mitte des ersten Jahrhunderts vor Chr. Geb*. Madrid Forschungen, no. B-5. Berlin.

Radke, G. 1964. "Römische Strassen in der Gallia Cisalpina und der Narbonensis." *Klio* 42:299–318.

———. 1969. "Die territoriale Politik des C. Flaminius." *Festschrift für F. Altheim*, ed. R. Stiehl and H. E. Stier, 366–86. Berlin.

———. 1955. "Veleia." *Pauly-Wissowa* 8.A.1:621–23.

Radmilli, A. 1962. *Piccola guida della preistoria italiana*. Firenze.

———. 1963. *La preistoria d'Italia alla luce delle ultime scoperte*. Firenze.

———. 1972. "La cultura dei castellieri." *Antichità Altoadriatiche*, vol. 2, 7–16. Udine.

Rambaud, M. 1953. *L'art de la déformation historique dans les commentaires de César*. Paris.

Ramos y Loscertales, José M. 1942. "Hospicio y clientela en la España Céltica." *Emerita* 10:308–37.

Rancoule, G., and O. Taffanel. 1972. "Narbonne préromaine et ses relations avec l'arrière-pays." *Congrès de la Fédération Historique du Languedoc Méditerranéen et du Roussillon* 45:127–33.

Rancoule, S. 1970. "Ateliers de potiers et céramique indigène au Ier s. av. J.-C." *Revue archéologique de Narbonnaise* 3:33–70.

Randall-MacIver, D. 1927. *The Iron Age in Italy*. Oxford.

Ranger, T. O. 1967. *Revolt in Southern Rhodesia, 1896–97*. Evanston.

Ratti, E. 1967–68. "Alcuni gentilizi nelle epigrafi romane del Nord-Italia e la loro distribuzione." *Atti Ce S.D.I.R.* 1:219–49.

Ray, A. J. 1974. *Indians in the Fur Trade*. Toronto.

Renaud, J. 1962. "Notes sur l'Oppidum d'Essalois (Loire)." *Ogam* 14:57–67.

Renfrew, C. 1976. *Before Civilization*. Harmondsworth.

Reynolds, J., M. Beard, R. Duncan-Jones, and C. Roueche. 1981. "Roman Inscriptions, 1976–1980." *JRS* 71:121–43.

Riccioni, G. 1962. "Un monumento di arte venetica." *Hommages à Albert Grenier*, ed. M. Renard, 1315–21. Bruxelles.

———. 1968. "Antefatti della colonizzazione di Ariminum alla luce delle nuove scoperte." *Atti del convegno di studi sulla città etrusca e italica preromana*, 263–73. Bologna.

Richard, J.C.M. 1972. "Les monnayages indigènes de Narbonne et sa région." *Congrès de la Fédération Historique du Languedoc Méditerranéen et du Roussillon* 45:135–49.

———. 1973. *La région montpellieraine à l'époque pré-romaine*. Collection Latomus, no. 130. Bruxelles.

Ridgeway, F. R. 1979. "The Este and Golasecca Cultures: A Chronological Guide." *Italy Before the Romans*, ed. D. Ridgeway and F. R. Ridgeway, 419–87. New York.

Righini, V. 1970. *Lineamenti di storia economica della Gallia Cisalpina: La produttività fittile in età repubblicana*. Bruxelles.

———. 1975. "Profilo di storia economica." *Storia della Emilia Romagna*, vol. 1, ed. A. Berselli, 173–98. Bologna.

Rittatore Vonwiller, F. 1962. *Como preromana e le sue necropoli*. Como.

———. 1966. *La necropoli preromana della Ca' Morta: Scavi 1955–1965*. Como.

———. 1975–76. "Un nuovo complesso di incisioni di età protostorica nelle prealpi." *Atti Ce S.D.I.R.* 7:547–52.

Robert, A. 1965a. "Urbanisme préhistorique, les oppida préromains du Gard." *La Vie Urbaine* 1:1–11.

———. 1965b. "Les oppida du Gard." *Celticum* 12:207–24.

Roberti, M. M. 1973–74. "Due piani regolatori nella Milano Romana." *Atti Ce S.D.I.R.* 5:305–25.

Robinson, D., J. Gallagher, and A. Denny. 1961. *Africa and the Victorians*. New York.

Robinson, E. G.S 1956. "Punic Coins of Spain and Their Bearing in the Roman Republic Series." *Essays in Roman Coinage Presented to Harold Mattingly*, ed. R.A.G. Carson and C.H.V. Sutherland, 34–53. Oxford.

Robson, D. O. 1934. "The Samnites in the Po Valley." *Classical Journal* 29:599–608.

———. 1938. "The Nationality of the Poet Caecilius Statius." *AJPhil.* 59:301–8.

Rodríguez Adrados, F. 1946. "La 'fides' ibérica." *Emerita* 14:129–208.

———. 1950. "Las rivalidades de las tribus del nordeste español y la conquista romana." *Estudios dedicados a Menéndez Pidal*, 563–88. Madrid.

Rolland, H. 1936. "Fouilles d'un habitat preromane à Saint-Rémy-de-Provence." *Provincia* 16:193–243.

———. 1949. "L'expansion du monnayage de Marseille dan le pays celtoligure." *Rivista di Studi Liguri* 15:139–48.

————. 1958. "L'influence de la Grèce sur l'architecture dans la basse vallée du Rhône." *Colloque sur les influences helléniques en Gaul*, 113–22. University of Dijon 16.

————. 1960. *Glanum*. Paris.

————. 1961. "Monnaies gallo-grècques." *Congresso Internazionale di Numismatica*, 111–19. Roma.

————. 1962. "Le sanctuaire des Glaniques." *Hommages à Albert Grenier*, ed. M. Renard, 1339–46. Bruxelles.

————. 1963. "La stratigraphie de Saint-Blaise." *Comptes Rendus de l'Acádemie des Inscriptions et Belles-Lettres*, 81–89.

————. 1968. "Nouvelles fouilles du Sanctuaire des Glaniques." *Rivista di Studi Liguri* 34:7–39.

Rossi, R. F. 1972. "La Romanizzazione dell'Istria." *Antichità Alto-adriatiche*, vol. 2, 65–78. Udine.

Rostaing, C. 1973. *Essai sur la toponymie de la Provence*. Marseille.

Rowland, R. J. 1974. "Sardinians in the Roman Empire." *Ancient Society* 5:223–29.

————. 1976. "Numismatics and the Military History of Sardinia." *Akten des XI Internationalen Limeskongresses*, 87–112. Budapest.

————. 1977. "Aspetti de continuità culturale nella Sardegna romana." *Latomus* 36:460–70.

————. 1978. "Two Sardinian Notes." *Zeitschrift für Papyrologie und Epigraphie* 30:166–72.

Rowlands, M. 1973. "Modes of exchange and the incentives for trade with reference to later European prehistory." *The Explanation of Culture Change*, ed. C. Renfrew, 589–600. London.

Rubio, L. 1949. "Los Balbos y el imperio romano." *Anales de Historia Antigua y Medieval*, 67–119. Buenos Aires.

Russell, P. 1978. "Redcoats in the Wilderness." *William and Mary Quarterly* 35:605–28.

Sabattini, A. 1972. "I Campi Macri." *Rivista storica dell' antichità* 2:257–60.

Saddington, D. B. 1961. "Roman Attitudes to the *Externae Gentes* of the North." *Acta Classica* 4:90–102.

Sagnes, J. 1970. "Agde antique." *Congrès de la Fédération Historique du Languedoc Méditerranéen et du Roussillon* 43:51-62.

Sahlins, M. D. 1962–63. "Poor Man, Rich Man, Big-Man, Chief: Political Types in Melanesia and Polynesia." *Comparative Studies in Society and History* 5:285–303.

Salmon, E. T. 1933. "The Last Latin Colony." *Classical Quarterly* 27:30–35.

————. 1935. "Rome's Battles with Etruscans and Gauls in 284-2 B.C." *Classical Philology* 30:23–32.

Salmon, E. T. 1970. *Roman Colonization Under the Republic*. Ithaca.

Sánchez Albornoz, C. 1949. "El proceso de romanización de España desde los Escipiones hasta Augusto." *Anales de Historia Antiqua y Medieval*, 5–36. Buenos Aires.

Sanmartí-Greco, E. 1973. "El taller de las pequeñas estampillas en la Península Ibérica." *Ampurias* 35:135–73.

Sanna, A. 1957. "La romanizzazione del centro montano in Sardegna." *Filologia Romanza* 4:30–48.

Santoro, P. 1978. "Le migrazioni dei Celti." *I Galli e l'Italia*, 25–29. Roma.

Sartori, F. 1960. "Galli transalpini trangressi in Venetiam." *Aquileia Nostra* 31, col. 1–40.

Sassatelli, G., and D. Vitali. 1978. "Bologna." *I Galli e l'Italia*, 117–25. Roma.

Saumagne, C. 1962. "Une colonie latine d'affranchi Carteia." *Revue historique* 40:135–52.

Saunders, C. 1981. "Political Processes in the Southern African Frontier Zones." *The Frontier in History*, ed. H. Lamar and L. Thompson, 149–74. New Haven.

Savory, H. N. 1968. *Spain and Portugal*. New York.

Scagliarini, D. C. 1975. "Il territorio e le città in epora romana." *Storia della Emilia Romagna*, vol. 1, ed. A. Berselli, 147–71. Bologna.

Scarani, R. 1970. "Emilia-Rinvenimenti in località varie." *Notizie degli Scavi*, 35–68.

Scham, A. 1970. *Lyautey in Morocco*. Berkeley.

Scheers, S. 1968. "Le premier monnayage des Ambiarii." *Revue Belge de Numismatique*, 114:45–73.

———. 1969. *Les monnaies de la Gaule inspirées de celles de la République romaine*. Leuven.

Schubart, H. 1964. "Grabungen auf dem bronzezeitlichen, Graberfeld von Atalaia in Sud Portugal." *Madrid Mitteilungan*. 5:11–54.

Schubart, H., and H. G. Niemeyer. 1969. "La factoria paleopúnica de Toscanos." *Tartessos y sus Problemas: V. Symposium de Prehistoria Peninsular*, 203–219. Barcelona.

Schule, G. W. 1960. "Probleme der Eisenzeit auf der iberischen Halbinsel." *Jahrbuch des Römisch-Germanischen Zentralmuseums* 7:55–125. Mainz.

———. 1969. "Tartessos y el Hinterland," *Tartessos y sus Problemas: V. Symposium de Prehistoria Peninsular*, 15–32. Barcelona.

Schulten, A. 1911. "Polybius und Poseidonios über Iberien und die iberischen Kriege." *Hermes* 46:569–607.

———. 1914. *Numantia I, Die Keltiberer und ihre Kriege mit Rom*. Munich.

———. 1917. "Viriathus." *Neue Jahrbuch* 39:209–37.

———. 1926. *Sertorius.* Leipzig.

———. 1928. "Iliturgi." *Hermes* 63:288–301.

———. 1929. *Numantia IV: Die Lager bei Renieblas.* Munich.

———. 1933. "Forschungen in Spanien, 1928–1933." *Arch. Anz.*, 513–66.

Schulten, A., and P. Paulsen. 1928. "Castra Caecilia." *Arch. Anz.*, 1–29.

———. 1930. "Castra Caecilia." *Arch. Anz.*, 37–87.

———. 1932. "Castra Caecilia." *Arch. Anz.*, 47:334–87.

———. 1974. *Iberische Landeskunde.* Baden-Baden.

Schulze, W. 1933. *Zur Geschichte lateinischer Eigennamen.* Berlin.

Schutz, H. 1983. *The Prehistory of Germanic Europe.* New Haven.

Scivoletto, N. 1961. "L'oratio contra Galbam e le *Origines* di Catone." *Giornale italiana filologica*, 63–68.

Scullard, H. H. 1930. *Scipio Africanus in the Second Punic War.* Cambridge.

———. 1967. *The Etruscan Cities and Rome.* Ithaca.

———. 1970. *Scipio Africanus: Soldier and Politician.* Ithaca.

———. 1973. *Roman Politics, 220–150 B.C.* Oxford.

Sereni, E. 1957. "Différenciation et évolution vers l'Etat des communautés ligures." *Etat et Classes dans l'Antiquité esclavagiste, Recherches internationales à la lumière du marxisme* 2:53–100.

———. 1971. *Comunità rurali nell'Italia antica.* Roma.

Serra, G. 1952. "Etrusci e Latini in Sardegna." *Mélanges de Philologie Romaine offerts à M. Karl-Michaelsson*, 407–50. Goteborg.

Shannon, F. 1945. "A Post-Mortem on the Labor Safety-Valve Theory." *Agricultural History* 19:31–37.

Sharp, W. F. 1976. *Slavery on the Spanish Frontier: The Columbian Choco, 1680–1816.* Norman, Okla.

Shaw, B. D. 1979. "Rural Periodic Markets in Roman North Africa as Mechanism of Social Integration and Control." *Research in Economic Anthropology* 2:91–117.

Shaw, D.J.B. 1977. "Urbanism and Economic Development in a Preindustrial Context: The Case of Southern Russia." *Journal of Historical Geography* 3:107–22.

Sheehan, B. W. 1969. "Indian-White Relations in Early America: A Review Essay." *William and Mary Quarterly* 26:267–86.

———. 1973. *Seeds of Extinction.* Chapel Hill.

Sherwin-White, A. 1966. *The Letters of Pliny.* Oxford.

———. 1967. *Racial Prejudice in Imperial Rome.* Cambridge.

Simon, H. 1962. *Roms Kriege in Spanien, 154–133 v. Chr.* Frankfurt am Main.

Skydsgaard, J. E. 1974. "Transhumance in Ancient Italy." *Analecta Romana Instituti Danici* 7:7–36.

Sobreques, S. 1970. *España Geográfica*. Barcelona.

Solier, Y. 1964–65. "Postes frontière Elysiques des Corbières: Recherches 1964." *Bulletin de la Commission Archéologique de Narbonne* 28:7–35.

———. 1968a. "Une tombe de chef à l'oppidum de Pech-Maho." *Revue archéologique de Narbonnaise* 1:7–37.

———. 1968b. "Céramique puniques et ibéro-puniques sur le littoral du Languedoc du VIème siècle au début du IIème siècle avant J. C." *Rivista di Studi Liguri* 34:127–49.

Solier, Y., and J. Giry. 1972. "Les recherches archéologiques à Montlaurés: Etat des questions." *Congrès de la Fédération Historique du Languedoc Méditerranéen et du Roussillon* 45:77–111.

Sommella, P. 1973–74. "Urbanistica di Lucca Romana." *Atti Ce S.D.I.R.* 5:281–86.

Sordi, M. 1960. *I rapporti romano-ceriti e l'origine della* civitas sine suffragio. Roma.

Sosin, J. M. 1967. *The Revolutionary Frontier, 1763–1783*. Albuquerque.

Soutou, A. 1969. "Répartition géographique des plus anciennes monnaies gauloises à la Croix." *Ogam* 21:155–69.

Soyer, J. 1973. "Les centuriations de Provence (I)." *Revue archéologique de Narbonnaise* 6:197–232.

Stevenson, C. H. 1919. "Cn. Pompeius Strabo and the Franchise Question." *JRS* 9:95–101.

Sumner, G. V. 1967. "Roman Policy in Spain before the Hannibalic War." *Harvard Studies in Classical Philology* 72:205–46.

———. 1970. "Proconsuls and Provinciae in Spain, 218/7–196/5 B.C." *Arethusa* 3:85–102.

———. 1972. "Roman Spain and the Outbreak of the Second Punic War: Some Clarifications." *Latomus* 31:469–80.

Susini, G. C. 1965. "Aspects de la romanisation de la Gaule Cispadane: Chute et Survivance des Celtes." *Comptes Rendus de l'Académie des Inscriptions et Belles-Lettres*, 143–63.

———. 1969. "I Veleiati de Plinio e l'origine di Regium Lepidi. Dalla tribù alle città." *Atti del III Convegno di Studi Veleiati*, 173–78. Milano.

———. 1975. "La cispadana romana." *Storia della Emilia Romagna*, vol. 1, ed. A. Berselli, 103–46. Bologna.

———. 1977. "L'altare de Baggiovara e considerazioni sui Campi Macri." *Athenaeum* 55:141–49.

———. 1978. "Popaeus Senator." *Scritti storico-epigrafici in memoria di Marcello Zambelli*, 343–53. Roma.

Sutherland, C.H.V. 1939. *The Romans in Spain, 217 B.C.–A.D. 117*. London.

Taffenal, O., and J. Taffenal. 1956. "Les civilisations préromaines dans la région de Mailhac (Aude)." *Etudes Roussillonaises* 5:7–29, 103–30.

———. 1960. "Deux tombes de chefs à Mailhac." *Gallia* 8:1–37.

Tamaro, B. 1925. Duino-Timavo-Scoperta di iscrizioni romane." *Notizie degli Scavi* 1:3–20.

———. 1965. "Il restauro della porta detta dei leoni-Verona." *Notizie degli Scavi* 20:12–34.

Tamassia, A. M. 1967. "Note di Protostoria mantovana: Rivalta e la Valle del Mincio." *Studi Etrusci* 35:361–79.

———. 1970. "Mantova-Scavi in piazza Paradiso." *Notizie degli Scavi* 24:5–34.

Tamborini, F. 1950. *L'origine della civiltà gallo-italica secondo più recenti studi*. Varese.

Taracenea, B. 1943. "Cabajas-trofeo en la España céltica." *Archivo Español de Arqueología* 18:57ff.

———. 1946. "La necropolis romana de Palencia." *Archivo Español de Arqueologia* 21:144–46.

Taramelli, A. 1913. "Cagliari-Nuova-Iscrizione nel giardino Birocchi, in località SS Annunziata." *Notizie degli Scavi*, 87–89.

———. 1918. "Cuglieri-Ricerche ed esplorazioni nell'antica Cornus." *Notizie degli Scavi*, 285–331.

———. 1923. "S. Andrea Frius—Tomba di età romana scoperta nell'abitato." *Notizie degli Scavi*, 290–92.

———. 1928. "Un omaggio della 'civitates barbariae' di Sardegna ad Augusto." *Atti del Primo Congresso Nazionale di Studi Romani*, 269–74.

———. 1936. "Relazioni di Roma con l'elemente punico nella Sardegna." *Roma* 14:43–48.

Tarradell, M. 1968. "Grafito greco-ibérico de la comarca de Alcoy sobre campaniense A." *Rivista di Studi Liguri* 34:355–62.

Taylor, L. R. 1960. *The Voting Districts of the Roman Republic*. Papers and Monographs of the American Academy at Rome, no. 20. Roma.

Tchernia, A. 1969. "Directions des recherches archéologiques sous-marines." *Gallia* 27:465–99.

Thenot, A. 1978. "I caratteri dell'Arte Celtica." *Galli e l'Italia*, 34–67. Roma.

Thevenot, E. 1969. *Les voies romaines de la Cité des Eduens*. Bruxelles.

Thompson, L., and H. Lamar. 1981. "The North American and Southern African Frontiers." *The Frontier in History*, ed. H. Lamar and L. Thompson, 14–42. New Haven.

Thompson, S. 1973. *Pioneer Colonization: A Cross-Cultural View*. Reading, Mass.

Thouret, G. 1880. "Über den gallischen Brand." *Jahrb. f. cl. Phil.*, suppl. 11:104.

Thouvenot, R. 1940. *Essai sur la province romaine de Bétique*. Paris.

Tibiletti Bruno, M. G. 1966. "L'iscrizione di Prestino." *Rendiconti Litt. Istituto Lombardo* 100:279–319.

———. 1969. "Il mondo culturale di Como." *Memorie dell'Istituto lombardo*, 30 no. 3:170–171, 238–49.

———. 1970. "Frammenti epicorici da Mantova." *Notizie degli Scavi*, 29–34.

Tierney, J. J. 1960. "The Celtic Ethnography of Posidonius." *Proceedings, Royal Irish Academy* 60, sect. C:189–275.

Timpe, D. 1965. "Caesars gallischer Krieg und das Problem desrömische Imperialismus." *Historia* 14:189–214.

Torelli, M. 1978. "I Galli a Roma." *I Galli e l'Italia*, 226–28. Roma.

Torres Rodríquez, C. 1951. "La fundación de Valencia." *Ampurias* 6:113–21.

Tovar, A. 1974. *Iberische Landeskunde Band 1: Baetica*. Baden-Baden.

———. 1976. *Iberische Landeskunde, Band 2: Lusitania*. Baden-Baden.

Toynbee, A. J. 1965. *Hannibal's Legacy*. Oxford.

Tozzi, P. 1971. "Iscrizioni latine sull' arte lanaria bresciana e Virgilio Georgiche IV.277.8." *Athenaeum* 49:152–57.

———. 1972. *Storia Padana Antica*. Milano.

———. 1974. *Saggi de Topografia Storica*. Firenze.

———. 1975. "Indicazioni sul primitivo stanziamento della colonia di Modena." *Rivista storica dell'anticità* 5:47–52.

———. 1976. "Per la identificazione di tratti di vie romane." *Athenaeum* 54:296–99.

Treves, P. 1932. "Sertorio." *Athenaeum* 10:127–47.

Truscelli, M. 1934. "I 'Keltika' di Posidonio e loro influenza sulla posteriore ethografia." *Rend. Linc.*, n.s. 9:609–730.

Turner, F. J. 1920. *The Frontier in American History*. New York.

Ucelli, P. G. 1967–68. "Iscrizioni sepolcrali di Milano dal I al IV Secolo d.c. ed il problema della loro datazione." *Atti Ce S.D.I.R.* 1:109–28.

Uggeri G. 1975. *Le romanizzazione dell'antico delta padano*. Ferrara.

———. 1977. "Nuovi testi epigrafici dell'antico delta padano." *Atene e Roma*, n.s., 22:126–37.

Ulrich Bansa, O. 1957. "Monete rinvenute nelle necropoli di Orna-vasso." *Rivista italiana di numismatica*, 5th ser., 59:6–69.

Vallette, P. 1944. "Isidore de Séville et la fondation de Milan." *Mélanges d'histoire et de littérature offerts à Monsieur Charles Gilliard*, 93–102. Lausanne.

Vatin, C. 1968–70. "Maisons d'Ensérune." *Etudes classiques* 3:123–30.

Vaughan, A. 1965. *New England Frontier, Puritans and Indians, 1620–1675*. Boston.

Verzar, M, and F. H. Pairault-Massa. (1978). "Civitalba." *I Galli e l'Italia*, 196–203. Roma.

Villard, F. 1960. *La céramique grècque de Marseille*. Paris.

Villaronga, L. 1973. *Las monedas hispano-cartaginesas*. Barcelona.

———. 1977. *The Aes Coinage of Emporion*. British Archaeological Reports, suppl. ser. 23. Oxford.

Vitali, D. 1978. "Il territorio bolognese in epoca gallica." *I Galli e l'Italia*, 126–28. Roma.

Vryonis, S. 1975. "Nomadization and Islamization in Asia Minor." *Dumbarton Oaks Papers* 29:43–71.

Walbank, F. 1957. *A Historical Commentary on Polybius*. Oxford.

———. 1965. "Political Morality and the Friends of Scipio Aemilianus." *JRS* 55:1–16.

Walker, M. J. 1983. "Laying a mega-myth: Dolmens and drovers in prehistoric Spain." *World Archaeology* 15:37–50.

Ward-Perkins, J. B. 1962. "Etruscan Towns, Roman Roads and Medieval Villages—The Historical Geography of Southern Etruria." *Geographical Journal* 128:389–405.

Warmington, B. H. 1964. *Carthage*. Harmondsworth.

Wattenberg, F. 1959. *La región vaccea*. Madrid.

———. 1960. "Los problemas de la cultura celtibérica." *Primer symposium de prehistoria de la peninsula ibérica*, 151–77. Pamplona.

———. 1963. *Las cerámicas indígenas de Numancia*. Madrid.

Webb, W. P. 1931. *The Great Plains*. New York.

Wells, C. M. 1974. "The Ethnography of the Celts and the Algonkian-Iroquoian Tribes: A Comparison of Two Historical Traditions." *Polis & Imperium, Studies in Honor of Edward Togo Salmon*, ed. J.A.S. Evans, 265–78. Toronto.

Wells, P. S. 1977. "Late Hallstatt Interactions with the Mediterranean." *Ancient Europe and the Mediterranean*, ed. V. Markotic, 189–96. Warminster.

———. 1980a. "Contact and Change: An Example on the Fringes of the Classical World." *World Archaeology* 12:1–7.

———. 1980b. *Culture Contact and Culture Change*. Cambridge.

Wells, P. S., and L. Bonfante. 1979. "West Central Europe and the Mediterranean." *Expedition* 21:18–24.

Whatmough, J. 1933. *The Prae-Italic Dialects of Italy.* Cambridge, Mass.

Whittaker, C. R. 1978. "Carthaginian Imperialism in the Fifth and Fourth Centuries." *Imperialism in the Ancient World*, ed. P. D. Garnsey and C. R. Whittaker, 59–90. Cambridge.

Wiegels, R. 1974. "Livy per 55 und die Gründung von Valentia." *Chiron*, 4:153–76.

———. 1982. "Iliturgi und der 'deductor' Ti. Sempronius Gracchus." *Madrid Mitteilungen* 23:152–221.

Wightman, E. 1976. "Il y avait en Gaule deux sortes de Gaulois." *Assimilation et Résistance à la Culture Gréco-Romaine dans le Monde Ancien*, ed. D. M. Pippidi, 407–19. Paris.

Will, E. L. 1979. "The Sestius Amphoras: A Reappraisal." *Journal of Field Archaeology* 6:339–50.

Wilson, A.J.N. 1966. *Emigration from Italy in the Republican Age of Rome.* Manchester.

Wiseman, T. P. 1970. "Roman Republican Road-Building." *PBSR* 38:122–52.

———. 1971. *New Men in the Roman Senate, 139 B.C.–A.D. 14.* Oxford.

Wishart, D. 1976. "Cultures in Co-operation and Conflict: Indians in the Fur Trade in the Northern Great Plains, 1807–1840." *Journal of Historical Geography* 2:311–28.

Wolf, H. J. 1968. "Zum Typus Valentia Pollentia-Potentia." *Beiträge zur Namenforschung*, n.s., 3:190–98.

Wolski, J. 1956. "La prise de Rome par les Celtes et la formation de l'annalistique Romaine." *Historia* 5:24–52.

Woodruff, P. 1954. *The Men Who Ruled India.* New York.

Yavetz, Z. 1962. "The Policy of C. Flaminius and the Plebiscitum Claudianum." *Athenaeum* 40:325–44.

Zaninovic, M. 1975–76. "Alcuni esempi della continuità di insediamenti nella regione delmata delle Alpi dinariche." *Atti Ce S.D.I.R.* 7:625–34.

Zucchi, P. 1967. "Per la cronologia delle necropoli di Chiavari: i rasoi lunati e le fibule in bronzo." *Rivista di Studi Liguri* 33:185–203.

Zuffa, M. 1956. "I frontoni e il fregio de Civitalba nel museo civico di Bologna." *Studi in onore di Aristide Calderoni e R. Paribeni*, 269–88. Milano.

———. 1978. "I Galli sull'Adriatico." *I Galli e l'Italia*, 138–53. Roma.

INDEX

Library of Congress Cataloging in Publication Data

Dyson, Stephen L.
The creation of the Roman frontier.

Bibliography: p.
Includes index.
1. Rome—Provinces—History. 2. Rome—Colonies—
History. 3. Rome—Boundaries—History. 4. Rome—
Frontier troubles. I. Title.
DG59.A2D97 1985   937   84-42881
ISBN 0-691-03577-6